European Studies in Asia

As countries across Asia continue to rise and become more assertive global powers, the role that Higher Education has played, and continues to play, in this process is an issue of growing pertinence. Furthermore, understanding the relationship between Europe and Asia fostered by historical and contemporary knowledge transfer, including Higher Education, is crucial to analysing and encouraging the progress of both regional integration and inter-regional cooperation.

With a specific focus on international Higher Education, *European Studies in Asia* investigates knowledge transfer and channels of learning between Europe and Asia from historical, contemporary and teaching perspectives. The book examines a selection of significant historical precedents of intellectual dialogue between the two regions and, in turn, explores contemporary cross-regional discourses both inside and outside of the official frameworks of the European Union (EU) and the Asia–Europe Meetings (ASEM). Drawing on extensive case studies based on many of his own teaching experiences, Georg Wiessala addresses key questions, such as the nature and construction of the European Studies in Asia curriculum; aspects of 'values', co-constructed learning and adult pedagogy in the discipline of European Studies in Asia; the politics of Asian host cultures, the 'internationalization' of Asian Higher Education and the experiences and expectations of tertiary sector students of this subject in Asia, Australia and New Zealand. In doing so, the author articulates a range of outcomes for the further development of Higher Education cooperation agendas between Asia and Europe, in the discipline of European Studies, and in related fields such as International Relations.

This case study-led book makes an original and novel contribution to our understanding of European Studies in Asia. As such, it will be of great interest to students and scholars of Asian Education, Comparative Education, European Studies and International Relations.

Georg Wiessala is Deputy Director and Professor of International Relations at the Institute of Educational Leadership, University of Malaya, Malaysia.

Routledge contemporary Asia series

1 **Taiwan and Post-Communist Europe**
Shopping for allies
Czeslaw Tubilewicz

2 **The Asia–Europe Meeting**
The theory and practice of interregionalism
Alfredo C. Robles, Jr

3 **Islamic Legitimacy in a Plural Asia**
Edited by Anthony Reid and Michael Gilsenan

4 **Asian–European Relations**
Building blocks for global governance?
Edited by Jürgen Rüland, Gunter Schubert, Günter Schucher and Cornelia Storz

5 **Taiwan's Environmental Struggle**
Toward a green silicon island
Jack F. Williams and Ch'ang-yi David Chang

6 **Taiwan's Relations with Mainland China**
A tail wagging two dogs
Su Chi

7 **The Politics of Civic Space in Asia**
Building urban communities
Edited by Amrita Daniere and Mike Douglass

8 **Trade and Contemporary Society Along the Silk Road**
An ethno-history of Ladakh
Jacqueline Fewkes

9 **Lessons from the Asian Financial Crisis**
Edited by Richard Carney

10 **Kim Jong Il's Leadership of North Korea**
Jae-Cheon Lim

11 **Education as a Political Tool in Asia**
Edited by Marie Lall and Edward Vickers

12 **Human Genetic Biobanks in Asia**
Politics of trust and scientific advancement
Edited by Margaret Sleeboom-Faulkner

13 **East Asian Regionalism from a Legal Perspective**
Current features and a vision for the future
Edited by Tamio Nakamura

14 **Dissent and Cultural Resistance in Asia's Cities**
Edited by Melissa Butcher and Selvaraj Velayutham

15 **Preventing Corruption in Asia**
Institutional design and policy capacity
Edited by Ting Gong and Stephen Ma

16 **Expansion of Trade and FDI in Asia**
Strategic and policy challenges
Edited by Julien Chaisse and Philippe Gugler

17 **Business Innovation in Asia**
Knowledge and technology networks from Japan
Dennis McNamara

18 **Regional Minorities and Development in Asia**
Edited by Huhua Cao and Elizabeth Morrell

19 **Regionalism in China–Vietnam Relations**
Institution-building in the Greater Mekong subregion
Oliver Hensengerth

20 **From Orientalism to Postcolonialism**
Asia-Europe and the lineages of difference
Edited by Sucheta Mazumdar, Kaiwar Vasant and Thierry Labica

21 **Politics and Change in Singapore and Hong Kong**
Containing contention
Stephan Ortmann

22 **Inter-Ethnic Dynamics in Asia**
Considering the other through ethnonyms, territories and rituals
Edited by Christian Culas and François Robinne

23 **Asia and Latin America**
Political, economic and multilateral relations
Edited by Jörn Dosch and Olaf Jacob

24 **Japan and Africa**
Globalization and foreign aid in the 21st century
Edited by Howard P. Lehman

25 **De-Westernizing Communication Research**
Altering questions and changing frameworks
Edited by Georgette Wang

26 **Asian Cities, Migrant Labor and Contested Spaces**
Edited by Tai-Chee Wong and Jonathan Rigg

27 **Diaspora Literature and Visual Culture**
Asia in flight
Sheng-mei Ma

28 **Alterities in Asia**
Reflections on identity and regionalism
Edited by Leong Yew

29 **Soft Power in Japan–China Relations**
State, sub-state and non-state relations
Utpal Vyas

30 **Enhancing Asia–Europe Co-operation through Educational Exchange**
Georg Wiessala

31 **History Textbooks and the Wars in Asia**
Divided memories
Edited by Gi-Wook Shin and Daniel C. Sneider

32 **The Politics of Religion in South and Southeast Asia**
Edited by Ishtiaq Ahmed

33 **The Chinese/Vietnamese Diaspora**
Revisiting the boatpeople
Edited by Yuk Wah Chan

34 **The Dynamics of Social Capital and Civic Engagement in Asia**
Vibrant societies
Edited by Amrita Daniere and Hy Van Luong

35 **Eurasia's Ascent in Energy and Geopolitics**
Rivalry or partnership for China, Russia and Central Asia?
Edited by Robert E. Bedeski and Niklas Swanström

36 **Asian Popular Culture in Transition**
Edited by John A. Lent and Lorna Fitzsimmons

37 **Sexual Diversity in Asia, c.600–1950**
Edited by Raquel Reyes and William G. Clarence Smith

38 **Asia's Role in Governing Global Health**
Edited by Kelley Lee, Tikki Pang and Yeling Tan

39 **Asian Heritage Management**
Contexts, concerns, and prospects
Edited by Kapila D. Silva and Neel Kamal Chapagain

40 **Genocide and Mass Atrocities in Asia**
Legacies and prevention
Edited by Deborah Mayerson and Annie Pohlman

41 **Child Security in Asia**
The impact of armed conflict in Cambodia and Myanmar
Cecilia Jacob

42 **Vietnamese–Chinese Relationships at the Borderlands**
Trade, tourism and cultural politics
Yuk Wah Chan

43 **Asianism and the Politics of Regional Consciousness in Singapore**
Leong Yew

44 **Agency in Asia Pacific Disaster Relief**
Connectivity, conflict and community resilience
Edited by Minako Sakai, Edwin Jurriëns, Jian Zhang and Alec Thornton

45 **Human Trafficking in Asia**
Forcing issues
Edited by Sallie Yea

46 **Democracy or Alternative Political Systems in Asia**
After the strongmen
Edited by Michael Hsin-Huang Hsiao

47 **European Studies in Asia**
Contours of a discipline
Georg Wiessala

European Studies in Asia
Contours of a discipline

Georg Wiessala

LONDON AND NEW YORK

First published 2014
by Routledge
2 Park Square, Milton Park, Abingdon, Oxon OX14 4RN
711 Third Avenue, New York, NY 10017, USA

Routledge is an imprint of the Taylor & Francis Group, an informa business

First issued in paperback 2017

Copyright © 2014 Georg Wiessala

The right of Georg Wiessala to be identified as author of this work has been asserted by him in accordance with sections 77 and 78 of the Copyright, Designs and Patents Act 1988.

All rights reserved. No part of this book may be reprinted or reproduced or utilised in any form or by any electronic, mechanical, or other means, now known or hereafter invented, including photocopying and recording, or in any information storage or retrieval system, without permission in writing from the publishers.

Notice:
Product or corporate names may be trademarks or registered trademarks, and are used only for identification and explanation without intent to infringe.

British Library Cataloguing in Publication Data
A catalogue record for this book is available from the British Library

Library of Congress Cataloging in Publication Data
Wiessala, Georg
  European studies in Asia: contours of a discipline / Georg Wiessala.
  pages cm. – (Routledge contemporary Asia series)
  Includes bibliographical references and index.
  1. Europe–Study and teaching (Higher)–Asia. 2. Education and globalization–Asia. 3. Education (Higher)–Asia. 4. Asia–Relations–Europe. 5. Europe–Relations–Asia. I. Title.
  LA1058.7.W54 2014
  940.07115–dc23
                                                         2013036775

ISBN: 978-0-415-64219-4 (hbk)
ISBN: 978-1-138-06930-5 (pbk)

Typeset in Times New Roman
by Wearset Ltd, Boldon, Tyne and Wear

This book is dedicated in loving memory of my parents,
Georg Wiessala and Margret Wiessala, née Müller

Contents

Foreword xiv
Acknowledgements xvi
List of abbreviations xviii

1 **The globalization of knowledge and the subject of European Studies in Asia: themes and theoretical frameworks** 1
   Introduction: a strange manga album 1
   Inter-civilizational dialogue, past and present 2
   Structure of this book and the case studies on teaching experience 3
   Aspects of knowledge-based Asia–Europe cooperation: diplomacy and faith 5
   Mirrors of the world and of the soul: books, documents, papers and printing presses 6
   Pedagogy, personality and pictorial learning spaces 9
   Orientalized constructivism: theoretical frameworks and international relations theories from Asia 11
   Chapter conclusions and scene-setting 13

PART I
Theoretical aspects and historical predecessors 15

2 **An ocean of emptiness – and a steppe in time: Central Eurasia and the geography of knowledge along the Silk Roads** 17
   Introduction: beyond von Richthofen – broadening the scope of Silk Road research 17
   The geopolitical enabling conditions of the Silk Road in an Asia–Europe perspective 19
   Nomads in search of the East and the West 23

x *Contents*

Europeans on the Silk Roads 25
East meets West: learning and syncretism in art and culture 27
Religions and seats of learning as catalysts for Asia–Europe knowledge transfer 31
Overcoming the suffering of ignorance: Nālandā University and its modern legacies 33
Chapter conclusions 37

3 **Hearts and souls – silver and spice – missionaries and Mandarins: Portuguese knowledge management and Jesuit missionary enterprise in Asia**   40
Introduction: mission and diplomacy in the age of 'empires' 40
The Portuguese Empire as a channel of East–West knowledge transfer 42
God's soldiers: empire, the Jesuit missionary enterprise and its educational context 43
The Jesuit letter-books: word-pictures for Europe and the Republic of Letters 45
The power of knowledge: Lusitanian information control and censorship 49
'Barbarians for the love of God' – Jesuit accommodation and religious salesmanship 50
The Jesuits in India 53
Constantinian conversions and canonical controversies: the Jesuits in China 55
The 'pastoral of the intellect': the Jesuit mission to Japan 62
Black legends and hagiographies: resistance to the Jesuits' approach 64
Chapter conclusions 66

4 **Finding Europe in Nagasaki and Ayutthaya: the Japanese Leonardo and the Siamese falcon**   69
Introduction: a word-picture and a journey to Tokugawa Japan 69
Tokugawa intellectual life and the 'red-haired Gaijin' on Deshima 71
Under the spell of the West: Shiba Kōkan (1747–1818) and the Rangaku Movement 74
Peripatetic painters and Europeans on progress: the idea of the 'journey' in the meeting of Japan and Europe 77
Japanese diplomats, Siamese falcons and white elephants in the Venice of the East 80

Irregular rhythms of involvement: early European–Asian encounters in Siam 81
European sources and the 'burden of Higher Education' 83
A microcosm and a Siamese game of thrones: law, science and diplomacy 84
Legacies, historiography and the power of personalities in the 'Wild West of Asia' 87
Chapter conclusions 91

PART II
Contemporary representations and actors   95

5 Travels of the mind: exhibitions, websites and public events connecting with European Studies in Asia   97
Introduction: the subject of exchange and learning in Asia–Europe relations through the prisms of public 'blockbuster' exhibitions, smaller events and museum displays 97
Four 'blockbuster' exhibitions with high relevance to European Studies in Asia (2000–2010) 98
Four smaller exhibitions with relevance for European Studies in Asia (2002–2013) 107
Smaller exhibitions, permanent displays, research projects and key publications 110
Chapter conclusions 118

6 Contemporary actors, networks and institutions in the European Studies in Asia discipline: co-constructed curriculum leadership and Higher Education regionalism   120
Introduction: European Studies in Asia – 'soft power' and product placement? 120
The Asia–Europe Foundation, Singapore 127
The Asia–Europe Meeting, ASEM Ministers of Education Meeting, ASEM Rectors' Conference and South East Asia–Europe: Higher Education and Research Forum 129
The ASEAN University Network and the South East Asian Ministers of Education Organization 133
The National Centre for Research on Europe and the 'perceptions' projects: a successful 'dual embedding' of the European Studies discipline 136
Chapter conclusions 139

PART III
Teaching Europe in Asia: case studies 145

7 Teaching comparative regionalism and the EU in South East Asia: 'sons of the soil', student politics and European Studies in Malaysia 147

Political tsunamis, sultans of sting and sodomy: politics in Malaysia in 2013/2014 147

Policy copying or policy learning? The state of Malaysian Higher Education in 2013/2014 149

Colonial baggage and the emergence of 'European' studies in Malaysia 153

The Asia–Europe Institute, University of Malaya, Kuala Lumpur (2011–2014) 154

'Something special to Asia': the 'glocal' perspective of the AEI management and staff 157

Teaching a regional integration module at the Asia–Europe Institute (AEI) (4–15 April 2011 and 9–19 April 2012) 162

Working at the AEI as Senior Visiting Research Fellow (visiting only) (March to June 2013) 165

Leaders, learner voices and career choices: student views of European Studies in Malaysia 168

Chapter conclusions 174

8 The art of good *Feng Shui* in Brussels: taking European Studies in Asia to the capital of Europe, 2002–2012 177

Background: the evolution of the EU Foreign Policy Seminar series and EIPA 177

An integrated programme content with a broad remit 180

A hint of adult pedagogy: assessing and meeting learner preferences 181

The geopolitical embedding of the training and the content of the 'Asia' section 183

Structure and content of the 'Asia session' 184

Interactive elements: 'images' and 'votes' 187

Mission impossible: the role of evaluation and the impact of feedback 190

Connections with my general work 192

Lessons learned and the theory–practice nexus 194

The future of the EIPA Seminars 195

Chapter conclusions 196

Contents xiii

9 **'Between Vladivostok and Africa': teaching and debating EU studies in New Zealand and Australia, 1999–2014**   199
Introduction: some background to European Studies in the Antipodes 199
The CERC in Melbourne and the School of Social and Political Sciences at the University of Melbourne (2000–2010) 202
A Jean Monnet public lecture at the University of Melbourne, 2010 203
The NCRE in Christchurch, New Zealand and my 2010 visit to the University of Canterbury 205
The NCRE in 2013 208
The student voice from New Zealand, 2013 210
A Malaysian student's outlook on the NCRE 212
The future of the NCRE: curriculum development in the face of change 216
Chapter conclusions 219

10 **Overall conclusions: priorities and pedagogies of the 'European Studies' discipline in Asia**   221

Appendices   226
Selected websites   250
Bibliography   260
Index   278

Foreword

This book makes an important and significant contribution to the field of European Studies in Asia by looking at knowledge transfer, including channels of knowledge, and focusing on the examination of key ideas and Higher Education from historical, contemporary and teaching perspectives. Combining the historical precedents of intellectual dialogue between the two regions and contemporary, interdisciplinary, cross-regional discourses with practical teaching experience and the impact of official forums such as ASEM and ASEF, Georg Wiessala proffers a range of outcomes for the development of Higher Education cooperation agendas between Asia and Europe in the discipline of European Studies and related fields.

The discipline of European Studies in Asia has been called a pedagogic 'laboratory' in all manner of contexts: a testing-ground for the transmission of European foreign policy and cultural diplomacy concepts in the East; an area of experimentation with new curriculum ideas, ranging from a traditional suite of source-subjects from law, politics and history, to a much broader portfolio, embracing the study of regions, identities and cultures. It is a subject that brings together, in the sense of a true 'people-to-people-dimension', students with vastly different learning styles and expectations towards the International Relations and European (Union) Studies Higher Education experience.

What unites many of these aspects is that in this, still relatively new, field of study, structures, syllabi and curricula are emanating from a much broader range of sources as is the case in other disciplines. The chapters of this book demonstrate how, on the basis of the channels of learning, opened up by historical predecessors, contemporary European Studies in Asia is becoming a 'co-constructed', and continually evolving, discipline. It bridges both geographical and mental distance by means of not just a consensus over what should be taught about Europe in Asia, but also a dialogue, between learners and lecturers, policy-makers, think-tanks, universities, regional associations and European Studies Centres, about how content can be made relevant, and become localized in Asia.

In this sense, European Studies in Asia is a subject area in the transmission of which the purposeful exercise of educational leadership is especially important. Where dynamic and distributed leadership in teaching and learning in Higher Education, student-centred learning and European Studies in Asia overlap, you will, more often than not, find the best and most innovative European Studies courses. What some writers now call Higher Education inter-regionalism provides the canvas for a more creative approach to this subject, involving a multitude of actors and methods, many of which are being introduced in this book.

It is my view that this book is an excellent contribution to an increasingly important field. At the Institute of Educational Leadership (IKP) at the University of Malaya, we see the potential not only to add to the number of players shaping the future European Studies in Asia discipline but also – in making available our pedagogic and leadership expertise – to provide an important hub for future development and innovation in this area.

Professor Alma Harris
Director
Institute of Educational Leadership (Institut Kepimpinan Pendidikan)
University of Malaya
Kuala Lumpur, August 2013

Acknowledgements

Being raised up by standing on the shoulders of others is really the only way to achieve anything. At no time in my academic career have I been more convinced of the truth of this, and of the interconnectedness of all beings. It is because others were there for me when it mattered, that I can sit here now and write these acknowledgements.

My gratitude goes, first and foremost, to my family. To my wife, Mim, who, for this book, more so than for my previous humble efforts, had to put up with my more prolonged absence, necessitated by my work in Asia. You are, indeed, the honey in my bee hive, Maureen. Many thanks also to my stepchildren, James and Rebecca, and their partners and children, for their love and support.

I would like to also acknowledge the help provided by the University of Malaya in Kuala Lumpur, Malaysia and by Tan Sri Professor Ghaut Jasmon, En. Yusoff Musa and all colleagues at Institut Asia–Eropah and Institut Kepimpinan Pendidikan at UM. A cordial thank you to my good friend HE Dato Professor Amir Jaffar, and to Professors Karim and Fumitaka, my AEI Fellow Musketeers (visiting only) for three months. *Terima kasih dan jumpa lagi.* Your kindness shines through these pages.

In regard to the Institut Kepimpinan Pendidikan (IKP) at Universiti Malaya, I am grateful to Professors Alma Harris, Michelle Suzette Jones and Esther Gnanamalar Sarojini Daniel, for taking me on in the first place, and for giving me the space, both physically and mentally, to write large parts of this book in *Wisma R & D* in Kuala Lumpur.

Thank you also to Dr Sathiamoorthy Kannan, Dr Sailesh Sharma, Dr Tee Meng Yew, Suhaila Nasir, (Princess) Diana Mohd. Jalaludin, NorAishah Abd. Latiff, Khairun Nisa Ismail, Noormei Azura Zakaria, Muhamad Redza Bin Roslan and the entire IKP crew, for the support provided and for listening to my occasional ravings. We will stay in touch, *insyallah*.

Moreover, my thanks are due to the team at the National Centre for Research on Europe (NCRE) at the University of Canterbury in Christchurch, New Zealand, especially Professors Natalia Chaban and Martin Holland, Drs Katharine Vadura and Selena Kelly, and Yvonne Grosch and Rebecca Morgan, for their help and advice.

In Europe, a heart-felt *dank u wel*, once again, goes to Professor Simon Duke and Danielle Jacobs, at the European Institute for Public Administration in Maastricht for their steady friendship and kind help, and for providing me with access to the kind of experience which has now informed parts of this book. Closest to home, many thanks to Abbie Thomasson and Stewart Ellis at Myerscough College, for their excellent PTLLS course, which has put me in a position to learn more about my teaching and to write anything that makes sense about adult pedagogy.

Georg Wiessala
Kuala Lumpur, August 2013

Abbreviations

ACA	Academic Cooperation Association
ACANSRS	Association for Central Asian Civilizations & Silk Road Studies
ADB	Asian Development Bank
AEI	Asia–Europe Institute (Institut Asia–Eropah), University of Malaya
AHM	Amsterdams Historisch Museum (AHM, now: Amsterdam Museum)
ANUCES	Australian National University Centre for European Studies
APAIE	Asia-Pacific Association of International Education
APEC	Asia-Pacific Economic Cooperation
APQN	Asia-Pacific Quality Network
APRU	Association of Pacific Rim Universities
ARF	ASEAN Regional Forum
ASAIHL	Association of Southeast Asian Institutions of Higher Learning
ASEAN	Association of Southeast Asian Nations
ASEAN HRMECH	Working Group for an ASEAN Human Rights Mechanism
ASEF	Asia–Europe Foundation
ASEM	Asia–Europe Meeting
ASEMME	ASEM Education Ministers Meeting
ASEM RC	ASEM Rectors' Conferences
ASEMUS	Asia–Europe Museum Network
AsiaNET	Finnish University Network for Asian Studies
AsiaRes	Baltic Research Centre for East Asian Studies
AUAP	Association of Universities of Asia and the Pacific
AUN	ASEAN University Network
BICCS	Brussels Institute for Contemporary China Studies
CAREN	Central Asia Research and Education Network
CEERC	Contemporary Europe Research Centre, University of Melbourne

CEIBS	China Europe International Business School
CEPS	Centre for European Policy Studies
CES	Chulalongkorn University, Bangkok, Centre for European Studies
CESAA	Contemporary European Studies Association of Australia
CESDF	Fudan University Centre for European Studies
CEUA	China–EU Association
CLEER	Centre for the Law of EU External Relations
CRI	China Radio International
CSIG	Centre for the Study of International Governance (Loughborough University, UK)
DSEU	Diplomatic System of the EU Network, Loughborough University, UK
EAEA	European Association for the Education of Adults
EAHEP	European Union Asia Higher Education Platform
EAIE	European Association for International Education
ECAN	European Union China Academic Network
ECCRD	Euro Chinese Centre for Research and Development
EHEA	European Higher Education Area
EIAS	European Institute for Asian Studies, Brussels
ENCARI	European Network for Contemporary Academic Research on India
EPC	European Policy Centre
ERASMUS	European Region Action Scheme for the Mobility of University Students
ESiA	European Studies in Asia (Asia–Europe Foundation)
ESRUC	Eurasian Silk Road Universities Consortium
EUA	European University Association
EUCAM	European Union Central Asia Monitoring Project
EUCN	European Union Centres Network (New Zealand)
EUI	European University Institute, Florence, Italy
EUIJ	European Union Institute in Japan, Kansai
EU-LDC	European Union Least Developed Countries Network
EURASHE	European Association of Institutions in Higher Education
EUROPALIA	International Arts Festival, Belgium
EuroSEAS	European Association for South East Asian Studies
EUSA	European Union Studies Association
EUSA-NZ	European Union Studies Association New Zealand
EUS-AP	European Union Studies Association Asia-Pacific
EUSI	European Union Studies Institute, Tokyo, Japan
FPRC	Foreign Policy Research Centre, New Delhi, India
GIARI	Global Institute for Asian Regional Integration, Waseda University, Japan
HRWF	Human Rights Without Frontiers

IAU	International Association of Universities
ICD	Institute for Cultural Diplomacy (Germany)
IEAA	International Education Association of Australia
IEEM	Institute of European Studies of Macau, China
IIAS	International Institute for Asian Studies, The Hague, The Netherlands
IIE	Institute of International Education
IISH	International Institute of Social History, Amsterdam, The Netherlands
IKP	Institute of Educational Leadership (*Institut Kepimpinan Pendidikan*), University of Malaya, Kuala Lumpur, Malaysia
ISCSP	Instituto do Oriente (Orient Institute), Lisbon, Portugal
ISEAS	Institute of Southeast Asian Studies, Singapore
JNI	Japan–Netherlands Institute
LEANES	Linking European and Asian Networks in the Field of Environmental Sciences
MEEUC	Monash University European and EU Centre
MOHE	Ministry of (Higher) Education, Malaysia
MSA	Muzium Seni Asia (Asian Arts Museum), University of Malaya, Kuala Lumpur, Malaysia
NCRE	National Centre for Research on Europe, University of Canterbury, Christchurch, New Zealand
NEAR	Network for Education and Academic Rights
NEHA	Nederlands Economisch-Historisch Archief
NESCA	Network of European Studies Centres in Asia
NIAS	Nordic Institute for Asian Studies
OCEANS	Organization for Cooperation, Exchange and Networking Among Students (European Commission)
REDI	Regional EU–ASEAN Dialogue Instrument
RMITEUC	RMIT University European Union Centre, Melbourne, Australia
SEAEU–HERF	Southeast Asia–Europe Higher Education and Research Forum (ASEM 8, 2010)
SEA–EU-Net	South East Asia–EU Education Network
SEAMEO	South East Asian Ministers of Education Organization
SEAMOLEC	SEAMEO Open Learning Centre
SEAMEO-RIHED	SEAMEO Regional Centre for Higher Education and Regional Development
SEASPF	South East Asian School Principals Forum
SIIA	Singapore Institute of International Affairs
SOAS	School of African and Oriental Studies, London, UK
TEIN	Trans-Eurasia Information Network
UACES	University Association for Contemporary European Studies, London, UK

UC	University of Canterbury, Christchurch, New Zealand
UMAP	University Mobility in Asia and the Pacific (Australia)
UNESCAP	United Nations Economic and Social Commission for Asia and the Pacific

1 The globalization of knowledge and the subject of European Studies in Asia

Themes and theoretical frameworks

Introduction: a strange manga album

Voilà, c'est étrange ça n'est ce-pas, Monsieur? The shop assistant passes over the counter what I have just bought. It is a strange image, indeed, and not a little shocking: the cover on a thin album of *bandes dessinées*, which I picked up in a small shop in the *Galleries du Roi* in Brussels – where else would one buy comic-strips? This one is Japanese manga style though. On its rather gruesome cover, a dead body on a slab is covered in blood and has no head. A strong, electric lamp illuminates the headless corpse and the three men surrounding it – two Japanese and one Dutchman. One of the Japanese wears two swords, the sturdy, red-haired Dutchman a blood-splattered apron. On the walls of the small, evidently Japanese, room are anatomical drawings and charts of the human body, evidently not Japanese. Books with more such drawings and pictures lie scattered around. A skeleton is seen in the foreground of the image, its lifeless jaws dropping, almost leaving the picture plane. The drawing is immaculate though; I cannot help but admire the striking realism.

This is obviously a dissection, or an autopsy of some kind, but where and when did it take place? A clue may be in the title of this graphic novel: *Rangaku – La Cité Sans Nuit*. The 'night-less city' was actually Edo (now Tokyo), the capital of the Japanese Tokugawa Shōgunate (1600–1868). The 2007 book is a French co-production by Luca Enoch, Maurizio Di Vincenzo and Jean-Jacques Rouger.[1] It recounts the story of the Dutch in Japan, of sword-bearing *samurai*, translators, surgeons and merchants, of their adventures with the Japanese, of political intrigues, conspiracies and the dangers of 'foreign' knowledge. Especially the kind of knowledge the Dutch brought: charts and books, many of them including illustrations. These would have been of particular interest to the group of Japanese scholars and intellectuals who were interested in 'Dutch Science', 'Western Science' or 'European Studies' (*rangaku*) at the time. Artists like Shíba Kōkan, for example, who influenced Hokusai, and whom we are going to meet again in Chapter 4.

Inter-civilizational dialogue, past and present

Once I have read the album, it occurs to me that here is a fictionalized account of real-life events, of the meeting of Asia and Europe, and, perhaps, the teaching of some kind of a prototype of 'European Studies' in Asia. As I get deeper into this particular exchange, which will eventually become a case study in this book (Chapter 4), I realize that there are many other early varieties of 'European Studies in Asia', and that I cannot write a book about this subject without giving some thought, and acknowledgement, to them. Many of these historical encounters are helpful in illustrating one of my main arguments in this book: that the dissemination of ideas and knowledge, religions, philosophies and documents has always helped societies in Asia and Europe to mutually constitute themselves, to choose the ways in which they learn from one another and to determine the purpose of these learning encounters.

Apart from the unique case of the Dutch in Japan, I could have chosen to put in the spotlight one of the, perhaps, better known stories of East–West intellectual encounter ever: the 'discovery' (or supposed discovery) of Eastern thought, Asian religions and philosophies such as Hinduism or Buddhism, by the European 'Orientalists' of the nineteenth and early twentieth centuries – many of them English, French and German. As I did, indeed, do this elsewhere (Wiessala, 2011), another possibility was to focus on the role of ancient and modern 'mythologies', 'foundation-narratives', fictions and romances – for example, the *Alexander-Romance* (Stoneman, 2008) – which have had such a powerful hold over the transmission of ideas from West to East in the history of Asia–Europe dialogue. Fascinating as this blend of real and imagined knowledge undoubtedly is, as a background to the modern discipline of 'European Studies' in Asia, I needed something more tangible.

Closer to the subject of inter- and cross-cultural encounters, I hit upon a comparison between 'Hellenization' – the influence of Greece on its colonies in the Western and Eastern Mediterranean – and the spread of Indian ideas throughout South East Asia ('Indianization'). This was tempting. There were two distinct periods – before and after the conquests of Alexander of Macedon ('the Great') in Asia. These offered different modes of civilizational influence and of the spread of 'Europe' eastwards: by the sword and through what we might term 'cultural diplomacy' in modern parlance. Acharya (2013) makes a masterful study of this subject, using concepts like 'localization', which are highly relevant to the theoretical foundations of teaching 'Europe' in 'Asia' in 2014 (see below). Overall however, the 'Hellenization-versus-Indianization' comparison has indirectly informed, rather than directly steered, the argument in this book; it appears in various places – for instance, in the chapter about the 'Silk Roads' and the fusion-art of Ghandara (Chapter 2).

Other than this, I toyed with a range of other, tantalizing, possibilities in respect of the precursors of European Studies in Asia: early relations between Holland and Indonesia, for instance, are of interest to those concerned with 'civilizational impacts' of civilizations, and 'contributions' of one to another

(Hobson, 2004; Ringmar, 2007), and those who are investigating influences between world cultures and global historiographies (Lach and Van Kley, 1994; Burke, 2000; Pagden, 2008; Mahbubani 2008; Acharya, 2013; University of Malaya Centre for Civilizational Dialogue (UMCCD), 2013: 1–20). With reference to Benedict Anderson's well-known, and prolific, work on Indonesia, Acharya judiciously observes (2013: 28) that 'the arrival of "Western" ideas, for example, in the wake of the advent of Dutch capitalism and technology and rational secularism in the late nineteenth century, generated reform movements in traditional Javanese Islam' (cf. Steenbrink and Jansen, 2006).

The relationship between Islam and the West, of course, including issues of mutual education, knowledge transfer and learning, could have given a wholly different angle to this book, had I chosen to enlarge on it. But this area, in particular, has been well-covered. Furthermore, I also considered including aspects of the earlier international histories of Asian countries, which today have a strong presence in the 'European Studies' discipline. The example of Christian missionaries in the Philippines, who caused the Christian Holy Week to become linked to *Tagalog* cultural and spiritual ideas, was a good example for a case of European influence 'amplifying', rather than destroying, indigenous learning practices. Lastly, the ceramic shards dropped from European ships passing through the strategically important Straits of Malacca, in modern Malaysia, have been shown to have a significant influence on Malay art, pottery and architectural forms. There are many other examples of ways in which Europeans and Asians have learned from one another (see also Wiessala, 2011).

Structure of this book and the case studies on teaching experience

The main reason I have chosen (in Chapters 2–4) to amplify pre-modern Siam, Japan, Central Asia and the Portuguese Maritime Empire (the *padroão* system and the *Estado da Índia*) is that these encounters, in particular, of an earlier period of globalization, had both a significant religious dimension and very real repercussions and echoes for our own time, with regard to learning and the general East–West intellectual dialogue and meeting in education. These specific historical examples and their modern equivalent paradigms of exchange and 'people-to-people' meetings in the new Europe–Asia global web of learning can bring to the surface many valuable patterns, lessons and models which can be referred to in the teaching of Politics, International Relations and European Studies in Asia in the twenty-first century.

Last but not least, the case studies of my own teaching experience – most of it in Asia and Australasia, and some in Europe – which I have chosen to include as Part III of this book (Chapters 7–9), point to the many ways in which the understanding of the teaching of (some of) the constituent disciplines of European Studies, such as history, law and culture, has been both constructed and enriched, for both lecturer and student, by the examination of such areas as 'culture', 'faith', 'values', 'identities' and 'human rights discourse'. A meaningful construction, or co-construction, of knowledge depends first of all on experience, skill and respect afforded to diversity inside the cultures of those who aspire to teach and those who wish to widen their intellectual horizons by learning. This is especially true for many Asian societies, in which Confucian, Buddhist and related ethics are continuing to place a very high value on life-long learning and self-improvement.

I am further claiming in this book that, in a subject such as 'European Studies', the way teachers and lecturers employ their pedagogic and interpersonal skills, as well as their enthusiasm and vision, makes all the difference to a successful inter-cultural learning experience. There is a very thin line, however, between culturally literate, and sensitive international pedagogy, and euro-centric proselytizing, especially in an international relations subject which is as prone to political interference, political propaganda and agenda-setting as is European Studies, and European Union Studies.

The recent geopolitical paradigm shifts in Asia and the Middle East, and the historical evolution of the discipline of 'European Studies', from its beginnings in 'Area Studies' in the late 1980s onwards, demonstrate some vital developments; aspects which, in my opinion, ought to be very much in the foreground of the contemporary ways in which this subject is being taught. There can, for example, be little doubt that the interdisciplinary method, combining 'traditional' source-subjects such as law, politics, economics and history, and recent, innovative additions such as inter-religious dialogue, terrorism studies and the study of inter-regionalism can be a meaningful, more 'holistic' way forward in teaching this subject, and that it requires constant attention, sensitive curriculum development and intelligent updating. I am very much inspired by the recent scholarship on 'open-source leadership', which translates into teaching European Studies as a method of instruction that 'bounces off' the learners and involves them in generating curricula and learning topics by creating integrated, interactive communities in which the lecturer and the learner are inspired to contribute on a more even footing. The work of Gadman and Cooper (2009), for example, translates very convincingly to the concerns of this book.

In this same context, the European (Union) Studies in Asia discipline will benefit from being framed around, conceptualized by and infused with the charisma of exceptional pedagogic leaders, Professors and learner-focused teachers with a true vision of how the subject will develop in the East. Too many former 'European Studies Centres' have gone to ground because this purposeful vision was lacking, and the subject has become subsumed – consumed one is perhaps tempted to say – in the 'also-ran' category, over-shadowed by some of its bigger 'parent-disciplines', such as Law, International History, Economics and the often diffuse category of 'Business Studies'. As later chapters aim to show, personality, collaboration and informed, open-source leadership, when skilfully combined, can work miracles for Asian students of European Studies; when lacking, the 'bounce' can very quickly disappear from the 'bungee' of the subject. There are many today teaching European Studies in Asia who run thriving hubs of study and possess the drive and force of personality needed. When reading through the next few chapters, the reader is encouraged to keep in mind a few wider questions, prefigured by the historical examples which form the core of the next few chapters. Among those enquiries, in my view, the following are the most significant for European Studies in Asia: how to 'move the goalposts' by keeping the discipline evolving in a dynamic, strategic and inspiring manner, based on the lessons learned from historical precedent? How much do the examples of 'historical personalities' mean today? Should European Studies, when taught in Asia, be a vehicle, and a channel, for other 'messages', agendas and contents, of a political, human rights, religious or value-connected nature? How dependent is the subject on the shifting policies of a 'host' culture, and how open to political interference and censorship? And how far should what Germans of my generation often call '*Multikulti*' go: an accommodation of values with that host culture which may be at odds with those perceived as congruent with a 'European', 'value-based' identity? Those questions, and many related ones, will also provide the intellectual bridge leading from the 'historical' to the 'contemporary', and finally the 'experience-based', chapters, which the reader is invited to explore in this book.

Aspects of knowledge-based Asia–Europe cooperation: diplomacy and faith

A number of further themes in the history of early European contacts with Asia in general can be usefully singled out at this stage. They will be enlarged and revisited through the investigations in later sections of this book. On the most fundamental level, perhaps, the historical examples can be interpreted as a microcosm of the many facets and levels of Asia–Europe cooperation, and of Asians and Europeans learning from one another. While motives of trade and empire were often uppermost in this process, there have always been other layers and players in this exchange (van der Cruysse, 2002a, 2002b). Religious zeal and (European) missionary activities, for instance, frequently followed the flag; at other times the relationship between mammon and soul-harvesting appears reversed.

At all times, however, there was a more or less indissoluble connection between the merchants' motives and the perceived *mission civilisatrice* of many Western visitors to Asia. This dynamic bundle of motives, by necessity, brought Europeans into contact – and frequently conflict – with Asian interlocutors and counterparts, and with a wide range of indigenous polities, rulers and societies. This, in turn, necessitated diplomatic manoeuvring, and what we would, perhaps, call 'inter-cultural' skills today. This was quickly picked up by many of the Asians whom the Europeans came into contact with: various groups of foreigners were, at times, played off against one another for political gain, recruited to a variety of domestic banners and used as mercenaries and military advisors, in Siam, Japan and elsewhere. The (Christian) *Shimabara* revolt in Japan in 1637–1638 is a case in point; Masanobu (1978: 27) points out that the Dutch 'Protestant captain did not object to firing on Catholic converts'. The travel literature of the time contains evidence of other reasons for a movement of Europeans

6 *The globalization of knowledge*

into Asia, ranging from *Wanderlust* and a sense of adventure, to the pursuit of astronomy, surveying, medicine, botany and a raft of other disciplines. The role of religion, as a channel for knowledge transfer, and the yoking of the cart of science to the ox of religion are topics we will encounter in some more depth in the subsequent chapters of this book, in China, Central Asia, Japan and other places.

If the early Indian monastic University *Nālandā Mahavihara* was, arguably, one of the predecessors of modern institutional Higher Education exchange between the East and the West, then its multi-layered legacy points to another contextual aspect at the heart of modern European Studies in Asia; a point which will pervade the remainder of this book. I am referring to the role of 'faith-based' exchange, religious enquiry and inter-faith cooperation as key drivers informing all manner of knowledge transfer, including, notably, cultural influence and artistic inter-penetration. In fact, in the global history of ideas, few themes can be as central to learning in an East–Westerly orientation as faith, religion and art as vehicles for conquest, both peaceful and aggressive, both practical and intellectual (Acharya, 2013). The key concept of using one epistemology, or system of knowledge (e.g. science), as a 'shop-window' and 'vehicle' for another one (e.g. faith) stands out as a *leitmotiv* in Asia–Europe learning.

The chapters which follow aim to show glimpses of what, in today's parlance by institutions, such as the Asia–Europe Foundation (ASEF), may be called 'global inter-religious discourse'. The twin contentions of this book are as follows: not only does the examination of religious exchange constitute a key inroad into the conceptualization of overall educational East–West dialogue and Higher Education exchange; it is also an invitation to expand existing analytical tools and frameworks, to incorporate into theories of international relations a range of more holistic and constructivist perspectives, which can help to expand horizons of understanding as to how knowledge is acquired, justified, imbued with purpose, disseminated and exported.

However, other trends also emerge from the historical example in Chapters 2–4: the deployment of techniques of diplomacy, for instance, the idea of trade-diplomacy and 'travelling embassies', the concepts of adaptation, cultural assimilation and integration; all of those existed in the past, and all of them are still easily recognizable in the Europe–Asia relations of our day. It seems that, in the history of ideas, very little is ever 'new'. In Asia–Europe exchange, in particular, there are many eloquent predecessors of today's agendas, learning styles and channels of knowledge.

Mirrors of the world and of the soul: books, documents, papers and printing presses

Documents such as the Thai (Burmese and Malay) *Annals* on the one hand and the multitude of European writings about Siam on the other hand, especially the plethora of reports by European visitors to Ayutthaya in the seventeenth century (see Chapter 4),[2] open many perceptual doors to the informed consideration of the significant impact of writing (and art) in the context of the wider European–Asian discourse. Books and printing presses are key pivots in the development of human knowledge, in the progress of Europe–Asia relations and in the evolution of any discipline which deserves the name of 'European Studies' and 'European Studies in Asia'. The written, and published, word as a catalyst of change, exchange, debate and learning underpins East–West dialogue, and East–West pedagogy, at all stages in their histories. The production of books, and the availability of printing presses in both Europe and Asia, from the fifteenth to the seventeenth centuries, constituted one of the most significant enabling conditions, for the 'global' exchange of knowledge, between East and West.

It was, to a large degree, the printed text and the image on a page, which led to what Brotton (2002: 18–19) terms 'Renaissances' – not only on the Iberian and Italian peninsulas in Europe, but also throughout the Islamic world, Africa, China and South East Asia. Brotton (2012: 4) also finds a fundamental dichotomy which printing introduced to Asia–Europe relations: next to an explosion of learning and creativity, the spread of new ideas in print also introduced anxiety and instability. European divisions, enshrined in printed books as core vehicles of the European Reformation, carried new perceptions and realities into the Asia known at the time, influencing, for example, domestic and foreign policies of countries like Japan (see Chapter 4). The transportation of a printing press there, following a Japanese embassy to Rome in 1586, is a case in point. However, in later centuries, European presses had 'checkered careers' in Asia East (Lach and Van Kley, 1998, Vol. III, Book 1: 304).

Print also led to a greater need for 'control', as evidenced in the 1563 creation, by the Council of Trent, of an *Index* of forbidden books, deemed 'heretical' (see Chapter 3). Most importantly perhaps, printing irrevocably changed perceptions of information and channels of knowledge with regard to both Asia and Europe. No work of art symbolizes this better than Holbein's famous painting of *The Ambassadors*. The impact on the speed and mobility of international knowledge transfer, of the printing presses, set up from the mid-sixteenth century, by Jesuits in Nagasaki, Goa, Macao and elsewhere, will be examined in some more detail in the chapters covering the Silk Roads, the Jesuit Order and Japan, respectively. The influence of mission-presses did not only lie in the larger issues of defining and disseminating scientific, artistic, religious and practical matter, although perhaps this is their most important legacy. I would argue that on a par with this has to be the simple, but crucial, fact that innumerable Asians in India, China and Japan were actually employed in these presses and came into direct contact with Europeans, their faiths and ideas, frequently through the medium of dictionaries and linguistic works.

In Europe, the history of the printed word and the lower price of books, rather than manuscripts, encouraged rising literacy, stimulated a thriving trade and produced a dynamic competition between printing centres like Venice, Paris, Mainz, Cologne, Antwerp, Lisbon, and, of course, the Vatican and Medici presses in Rome (*Typographia Vaticana, Typographia Medicea*). The latter specialized in the production of Christian materials in oriental languages (Lach and Van Kley,

1994, Vol. I, Book 1: Chapter IV; Vol. II, Book 3: 528). The centres of book production moved in and out of a Dutch predominance in consequence of wars and religious instabilities on the continent, but cities like Rome and Coímbra remained hubs for production, copying and intellectual power for long periods of time. As the numbers of the European reading public steadily grew, the literate eventually had available to them a snowballing number of books on Asia. A number of specific sources, such as the Indian and Japanese letter-books and epistolary communications of the Jesuit missionaries in Asia, will be investigated in some more breadth in Chapter 3.

Apart from religious output, European printers produced a wide range of written works and items of cartography, which enabled a much higher degree of East–West exchange. Among those printed were encyclopaedic works and the secular accounts of merchants and navigators, cartographers and scientists, crisscrossing Asia. Notably for the legacies of learning between Asia and Europe, many printers in Europe, if they were sufficiently 'business-savvy', attempted to produce both 'official' and 'unofficial' versions of works, with the latter often 'embellished', and thus of considerably more practical, and anecdotal, interest for contemporary research (Lach and Van Kley, 1994, Vol. 1, Book 1: 150–151). As the example of the Portuguese (Chapter 3) will show, many printing presses and their outputs were subject to extreme levels of information control, censorship and secrecy in places such as Rome, Lisbon and Venice.

Ringmar claims that the emergence of European printing culture facilitated both 'reality-readjustments', such as the Reformation, and a 'technology of reflection', which contributed to an early global commercial advantage of Europe over Asia. By contrast, it has been claimed that the Italian historian Paulus Jovius (1483–1552) was the first European writer to suggest that the art of printing had been transmitted – overland on the Silk Roads from China to Europe – long before Johann Gensfleisch zum Gutenberg made his discoveries in Germany in the mid-fifteenth century. Jovius made this claim in his 1550 book series *Historiarum Sui Temporis*. Álvaro Semedo (see Chapter 3) is reputed to have been one of the first Westerners to report on Chinese printing presses and the Chinese examination system, opening Europe's eyes to the sophistication of an alien culture, at least as advanced as their own. This was to have profound consequences for the transmission of learning in East and West.

The invention of block-printing in China from at least the early eighth century is further highlighted by Hobson (2004: 183–186), who seeks to dismantle the 'myth of Johann Gutenberg', showing how printing travelled West, facilitated by Mongol conquests. The *Diamond Sutra*, the earliest woodblock-printed book (868) was, after all, among the key European 'discoveries' on the Silk Roads (Chapter 2; Hansen, 2012: 24, 179, 236, 241; Morgan and Walters, 2012). In addition to this, Lach and Van Kley (1994, Vol. II, Book 1: 78) demonstrate how the availability of Chinese printed textiles, playing cards and art prints influenced European xylographic (block) printing, and (possibly) moveable-type printing too. The distribution, through the missionaries, of medical and botanical prints was another key inter-cultural stimulus, as seen in the writings of the

Portuguese apothecary Tomé Pires and in the case of Tokugawa Japan (Chapters 3 and 4).[3] Davies (1996: 445) is thus essentially correct in characterizing Gutenberg as 'successor to an ancient line of Chinese woodblocks'.

There is not a great conceptual distance between these observations and our own, more 'modern', discourses surrounding globalization and the internet. Thus Burke (2000) situates Asia–Europe educational regionalism in frameworks such as 'modernity' and 'localization'; in addition to this, many scholars, as well as the EU's strategy papers, are interpreting education and Higher Education (HE) as necessary avenues towards competitiveness, university reform and the construction of regional identities. As far as universities are concerned, these strands will be taken up again later in this book – for example, in Chapters 6 and 8.

Pedagogy, personality and pictorial learning spaces

Some further thoughts are offered here which may link our initial case study to the issues of the history and the contemporary mainstream of European Studies picked up throughout the middle sections of this book. People are, perhaps, the best embodiment of what many call 'soft' power in international relations today (James and Mok, 2005; De Prado, 2007: 97). 'European Studies in Asia', in particular, has always depended on the power of strong, charismatic personalities with skills and adaptability. It is not just since the invention of the 'people-to-people-dimension' during the Asia–Europe Meetings from 1996 (ASEM, see Chapter 6) that the role of visionary, enterprising, personalities in Asia–Europe relations has been recognized.

What applies to all educational processes and learning, especially 'higher' learning, is true in particular for a relatively young discipline such as European Studies in Asia. If European Studies is to be successful and efficient in the East, then it has to evolve by means of recognition of the constructive nature of learning, and by teaching interpreted as 'open-source leadership' (e.g. Gadman and Cooper, 2009). This involves intensive networking, openness and transparency, student-centred learning and much more. This will become clear in the third principal section of this book, in the context of my own teaching experiences in Asia and beyond. Where vision and educational leadership are missing, European Studies in Asia is, inevitably, failing; where they met and converge, the future is bright and lies in the East.

While many early, charismatic figures, such as Constantine Phaulkon and many of the Jesuits across Asia, ultimately suffered a rather 'destructive' fate (see Chapters 3 and 4), they nevertheless left significant legacies as teachers, advisors to kings and governments and independent scholars and academics. There were Europeans who went to great lengths to 'go native', in contrast to the Asians who became part of early 'embassies' to Europe or came to live in the West. Some from the West who went native were eccentric and went 'over the top', to become 'more Catholic than the Pope' – or more Asian than the Asians – but even these eccentrics, I would argue, can teach us a lot today. Figures such as Roberto de Nobili in India, Constantine Phaulkon in Siam, Adam Schall and the other Jesuits in China, India and Japan, deliberately or inadvertently, pushed the boundaries of what cultural adaptation meant and what was acceptable as a holistic learning experience (see Chapters 3 and 4). Their ultimate, sometimes tragic, failures notwithstanding, these personalities have laid the groundwork for the kind of global modernization that is claimed to have 'spared' some Asian countries the experience of 'full' colonization, and that has led others into the nineteenth and twentieth centuries and into the kind of 'European Studies in Asia' that we would recognize today in places such as *Universiti Malaya, Chulalongkorn University*, the *Singapore EU Centre* and many others.

Second, and to round off this initial *tour d'horizon* of the Asia–Europe pedagogic exchange, I would like to stress those sections in the 'historical' chapters which emphasize the pedagogic importance of (both secular and religious) art as part of the testimony and epistemology of intellectual Asia–Europe exchange. Almost all of the European sources, and many Asian ones (from Ayutthaya, for example, see Chapter 3 and Appendices), comment on such diverse, but related, matters as monastic schools and universities, the challenges facing the educational establishments and printing presses in Asian port cities, the legal status of foreigners in Asian host-societies, the preconceptions the Europeans brought to their host societies' legal and social systems, and the visible, visual, impact Europeans had on the progress of native styles of artistic expression. Next to Siam, this latter phenomenon is pronounced most clearly in the case of Tokugawa Japan (Chapter 4). There is thus an important legacy of history in this area: a reflection of the mutual perceptions among Asians and Europeans in terms of pictorial depiction and interpretation. Event today, by far the most powerful teaching tools a lecturer of European Studies in Asia can possibly use are paintings, caricatures, sketches and other visualizations of the East–West exchange (see Chapter 9). This is especially interesting where it is possible to use religious imagery, selectively and sensitively, in teaching.

As will be seen from the next few chapters, in all these areas of what may be seen as the journey of knowledge from West to East and vice versa, religious motivation has underpinned art at every turn, and in many different ways. The archaeological treasures and writings found along the Silk Roads (Chapter 2) bear eloquent testimony to many gods roaming in either direction; they also speak of religious syncretism and dialectic evolution. At times, what we might recognize as faith-based educational dialogue today motivated Europeans towards mission and travel in Asia, and – as in the case of the Jesuit method – contributed to the formation of entire educational syllabi and curricula, which had a lasting effect in both West and East (Chapter 3). However, 'religious art' was also created as a pedagogical teaching aid, a tactical means of access to an alien civilization and as a key channel for wider cultural and scientific exchange, aiding the formation of perceptions of the place of the 'East' and the 'West' in pre-modern international relations (see Chapters 2–4). In modern times, art and culture remain key drivers of a range of investigations into the intellectual, pedagogic and cultural relations between Asia and Europe. The 'revival' of 'culture' and 'localization' as explanatory modes of international relations, EU–Asia educational dialogue and EU 'agency' has received significant scholarly attention recently, from amongst a diverse range of analysts and observers (Quigley, 2005, 2006; Lawson, 2006; Acharya, 2013).

Most of these frameworks revolve around phenomena such as cultural exchange for the purposes of 'oiling the diplomatic wheels' between societies and communities, and of creating inter-culturally literate leaders (but see: Stokhof, 1999: 38; Apfelthaler *et al.*, 2006; Wiessala, 2011). Instead, I wish to approach the 'cultural' and 'learning' dimensions of EU–Asia relations from a slightly uncommon angle – through the prisms of thematic, 'blockbuster' exhibitions and contemporary policy initiatives resulting from processes like the Asia–Europe Meeting (see Chapter 5). The extensive 'on-line presence' of the subjects of East–West learning and of European (Union) Studies in Asia, through 'virtual' museums and collections, both invites and facilitates the construction of new theoretical frameworks of European Studies in Asia which revolve around the thematic clusters of 'object-studies', 'image' and 'perception'. Some of this work has been done in the 1980s and 1990s, through the analytical lens of the 'Asian Values' debates; some is now being channelled through the discussion of 'images' – both literally and metaphorically – in East and West in the context of projects such as *Europe in the Eyes of Asia* (see Chapters 5, 6 and 9) and others.

Orientalized constructivism: theoretical frameworks and international relations theories from Asia

In terms of the question of which political science theory may best account for the changing dynamics of an East–West cooperation around the transmission of ideas and knowledge, I have long been persuaded of the high value of social-constructivist analytical approaches to this sub-species of International Relations. There is little point in being exclusive, however, and I have argued elsewhere (Wiessala, 2011: 51–82) that many interpretations drawn from conceptualizations of 'globalization', 'values', 'culture', 'diplomacy', 'regionalism', 'adult pedagogy' and 'knowledge-management' can all contribute significantly to how intellectual, 'people-to-people' exchange between Europe and Asia can be configured. I remain convinced that those explanatory frameworks which leave behind materialist, structuralist and utilitarian modes of reference, to focus instead on the roles of culture, ideas and identities in shaping actors and constituting institutional agency, are best suited to shed light on a discipline such as European Studies in Asia.

In this way, and when thinking about how this area might meaningfully be informed by theory, Benedict Anderson's 'bridging' work both on the culture of South East Asian societies and on identities and 'imagined communities' (e.g. Anderson, 1990) is very pertinent in this context, as are the theoretical models suggested by Christiansen *et al.* (2001), on foreign policy, EU agency, 'principled actors' and 'structure' in the international exchange of ideas and the social construction of Europe. And the social-constructivist argument of Helene Sjursen (2003), in the area of what she terms 'communicatively competent' and 'communicatively rational' actors, can offer convincing background explanations of how a curriculum in an area like 'European Studies in Asia' might emerge from, and be shaped by, the structures and processes of political cooperation, cross-cultural dialogue and regional integration. The issue that many would raise, however, is that many of these approaches to international relations theory (IRT) are 'Western', and some not a little euro-centric. The question, from the point of view of this book, does, therefore have to be: is constructivism still the preferred explanatory framework for European Studies in Asia if one departs from 'Western IRT' and takes into account non-Western IRT – if such a thing does, in fact, exist, without being an offshoot of the intellectual hegemony of Western models?

Concern for the roles of societies, for 'epistemic communities', 'communication and education', 'Asian values and 'regional identities' have, indeed, led some writers to explore the modalities of what an 'Asian' or at least 'non-Western' mode of theorizing Asia–Europe relations, especially educational dialogue, might have to contribute. The work of Acharya and Buzan (2010) is arguably the most coherent survey so far in this area. It becomes relevant in attempting to shed light on IRT from an Eastern perspective. If one chooses to focus on just the two examples of Islamic IRT and IRT approaches from South East Asia, since they are congruent with some of the geographical scope of this book, then a range of perspectives appears which can inform a future, more 'holistic' approach to theorizing learning and exchange between Europe and Asia.

This is not the place to offer a comprehensive critique of non-Western IRT – and the overall question remains of whether, in spite of its existence, it does amount, in fact, to anything more than a 'reflection' of Western hegemonic, models: a Gramscian hegemony of Western models (Tadjbakhsh, 2010: 185). Leaving aside for a moment the issue of how societies can export knowledge abroad and, through this process, are 'augmenting' indigenous cultures ('localization', e.g. Acharya, 2013), two examples may suffice here to open up a few new conceptual-theoretical doors and vistas for the teaching of European Studies in Asia.

Tadjbakhsh (2010: 174) hypothesizes that, 'to understand behaviour among Islamic states, a constructivist approach is more appropriate than a mainstream realist and liberal' one. Interestingly, Tadjbakhsh contrasts the 'traditional', Islamic IR world view of the dichotomy of *Dar al Islam* (the abode of Islam) and *Dar al Harb* (the abode of war), with the equally traditional, post-Westphalian (Christian) world view, set in contra-distinction to the 'other' abode; at the time this was the Ottoman Empire. The legacies of the encounter between Islamic states such as Malaysia (Chapter 7) and European countries for knowledge-based international cooperation, and for European Studies in Asia, are unfolding not only in the Qur'an's well-known exhortations to Muslims, to 'pursue knowledge'; Islamic IRT also delivers theoretical strands concerning divergent epistemic approaches and interpretations of humanity, history and science (e.g. *jijad*, versus *itihad*), evident, for example, in the *Islamization of*

Knowledge project.[4] Tadjbakhsh is right in thus making the connections between 'normative theory', 'religion', 'culture' and 'identity'. No wonder then that his recommendation is for the pursuance of 'the constructivist road' in the Islamic version of organizing knowledge in international relations (2010: 187).

Similarly, Chong (2010), out of a desire to 'democratize' IRT and prevent theorists from ceasing to interrogate 'Asian' IRT alternatives as a result of a universalized 'Western', 'Gramscian' intellectual hegemony, is seeking to define alternatives to Western modernization. He too arrives on the constructivist road (Chong, 2010: 143):

> constructivists perform well in reclaiming power and interests from materialism, by showing how their content and meaning are constituted by ideas and culture. In this regard, non-western theorizing on, and from, South East Asia may serve the cause of democratizing the discipline of IR by calling attention to the roles of ideational forces, the possibility of South East Asian agency, and ultimately, community, among Asian states. It would not be surprising if scholars find similar echoes in the cases of China and India in their intellectual quest for another golden age in the next century.

For China, Yaqing Qin draws valuable inferences from the traditional Chinese Confucian *tianxia* world view and tributary system, which has had such an influence on the Silk Roads (Chapter 2), and from the ideas surrounding the *five relationships* of Confucianism and the question of political authority (Chapter 4). Here is an approach that combines morality and politics, a cultural system of IR which, for most of its history, did not, by contrast to 'Western' modernity, include notions such as 'sovereignty, 'nationalism' or 'internationalism' (Yaqing, 2010: 46). There are significant theoretical lessons to be learned here for those teaching European Studies in Asia, Law, Business and Human Rights.

Chapter conclusions and scene-setting

This chapter has begun to survey the many channels of learning which have linked Asia and Europe in the past – and from the past to the present. I have claimed that some of these linkages can be said to amount to an earlier version of 'European Studies in Asia', introducing and prefiguring the modalities of the exchange in later centuries. This has been found to be true, especially, for the cases of Europeans and Asians meeting on the 'Silk Roads', for the European presence in seventeenth-century Siam, for the work of the Jesuits in China, South East Asia and Japan from the sixteenth to seventeenth centuries, and in the case of the relations between the Dutch and the Japanese in Tokugawa Japan.

I have indicated in this first chapter that my main rationale for introducing the remainder of this book through these particular historical episodes has been the recognition of their 'pedagogical' content; this I understand as their lasting impact on how and why the subject of European Studies (or European Studies in Asia) is being taught today. The chapter has also surveyed the importance of

14 *The globalization of knowledge*

some key resources in the Asia–Europe relations of the past, mainly print, pictures and personalities, and has argued that there is no reason to abandon the richness of these resources in the European Studies lecture theatre in Asia today. The power of visionary and charismatic teachers is as important today as it has ever been in Asia–Europe relations. If those teachers, lecturers and Professors are also increasingly mindful of the history of the persuasive might of the image, and if they, furthermore, are leaning towards an open-source style of teaching – inviting learners to co-determine the European Studies in Asia content and syllabus with them – then, as I have argued here, we are making best use of the inspiring templates of the past.

Against the background of a burgeoning new area of non-Western international relations theory, and next to looking in some detail at this question of *what has the history of the meeting of Asia and Europe in education ever done for us*, I would like to invite readers on the journey that is this book, taking them in two further directions. The chapters on exhibitions and contemporary players (Chapters 5 and 6) will offer an exploration of the ways in which the subject of European Studies in Asia is currently being shaped, directed, used and disseminated in East and West. And the chapters covering my own teaching experience in the 'East' (and, in one case, in the 'West') (Chapters 7–9) aim to show how both historical precedent and contemporary curriculum building is working out in a variety of Asian classrooms and contexts. I am inviting the reader to accompany me on this intellectual journey now.

Notes

1 www.humano.com/assets/CatalogueArticle/35338/rangaku_1_original.jpg.
2 Witness the many investigations and translations available in, for example, the pages of the *Journal of the Siam Society*.
3 A very interesting analysis of the significant botanical and 'plant-hunting-related' aspects of the wider Asia–Europe exchange can be found in Lach and Van Kley (1994, Vol. II, Book 3: 427–445).
4 See, for instance, http://i-epistemology.net/islamization-of-kowledge/441-the-quest-for-an-islamic-methodology-the-islamization-of-knowledge-project-in-its-second-decade.html.

Part I
Theoretical aspects and historical predecessors

2 An ocean of emptiness – and a steppe in time

Central Eurasia and the geography of knowledge along the Silk Roads

Introduction: beyond von Richthofen – broadening the scope of Silk Road research

The Silk Road has enriched Europe's Renaissance and given the West *Yersina pestis*, the plague bacterium that caused the 'Black Death'. It has been a pathway for trades, migration and human DNA, religions and ideas, and a stage for conquest from both Asia and Europe. It has changed the dynamics of geopolitical ambition. To this day it continues to be a projection screen of romantic fantasies about a supposedly 'exotic' Asia. Tourism continues to thrive on this concept. In its subtitle, a recent publication on *Travelling the Silk Road* by the US Museum of Natural History (Norell *et al.*, 2011) refers to the Silk Road as an *ancient pathway to the modern world*.

Indeed, in 2013, the Silk Road,[1] in its modern incarnation in the Central Asian region, is again the subject of considerable strategic debate: international development planners, regional policy-makers and economic innovators speak of 'new' silk routes, inter-continental super-highways, knowledge corridors and new schemes for Asia's old Silk Road. Global commerce is re-routed by train from China to Europe, alongside the old oasis towns which determined what 'globalization' meant in an earlier age.

Next to giving rise to the planning of new (information) super-highways and 'corridors of learning', the Silk Road continues to inspire very significant amounts of a specialized research programme, which, as Elisseeff (2000: 17) has pointedly argued, continues to be 'clustered'. This means that, in spite of the diversity of research contributions, there is a certain degree of unity. In fact, the central theme suggests a predilection for subjects dealing with prospects, relations, transport, journeys, distances, neighbouring environments and speed of assimilation.

Recently, some scholars have sought to re-emphasize some of the basics though: the Silk Road was neither a road, nor was it all about silk; it was not just an East–West corridor between China and the West; it was about the dynamism of two basic human ways of life, pastoralist-agrarian and nomadic, not just about links between urbanized civilizations (Millward, 2013: 6–9). In the context of these changing research foci, this chapter proposes, above all, to investigate the

Asia–Europe dimension of the journey of people, trade and ideas along the Silk Road.

One way of doing this, I would argue, is to include art and music in the equation. As one good example of this, British Museum Director MacGregor (2010: 324) acknowledges cellist and composer Yo Yo Ma, who has an outstanding recorded reputation of unearthing and performing music from those regions which were once part of the Silk Roads. And Jordi Savall too, with the ensemble *Hesperion XXI* may surely be counted as one of the most innovative promoters of East–West learning, embodied in the music and cultures of the Silk Road.[2] Yo Yo Ma's phrase of finding 'elements of the world within the local' is, perhaps, one of the most powerful images of the mechanisms and motivations of bringing Europe to Asia, and of Europe–Asia intellectual exchange in general, beyond music and culture.

The term Silk Road (*Seidenstraße*), however, is not nearly as ancient as is often assumed. It has famously been attributed to the well-travelled German scholar and morpho-geologist Baron Ferdinand Freiherr (Count) von Richthofen (1833–1905). Von Richthofen had admitted to being quite over-awed at the prospect of surveying the enormous expanse of China; it seemed to him to be an endeavour bordering on hubris even to take on this gargantuan task.[3] Notwithstanding his emotions, he did proceed, coining the famous term in his book *Über die Centralasiatischen Seidenstrassen* [sic] ('On the Silk Roads of Central Asia'; Elisseeff, 2000: 2; Wood, 2003: 9). In regard to the term 'silk' itself, Donald Lach (Lach and Van Kley, 1994, Vol. II, Book 3: 490–491) derives its etymological origin as follows: 'from the first century AD [CE] to 1500 [CE], the most significant [European] import from Asia was silk. It is therefore not surprising that the Chinese *szŭ* should have become the Latin *sericum* and, eventually, the English "*silk*" '. Wood (2003: 29) remarks that the Romans knew of the '*Seres*', or 'Silk People', as a catch-all description of the inhabitants of East Asia.

Notwithstanding the comparative novelty of the terminology, it is often asserted (e.g. BWB, 2009: 11) that it was, in fact, the fourth-century Roman historian Ammianus Marcellinus (325/30–after 391) who was the first in the European classical tradition to reference the area which is today understood to be encompassed by the term 'Silk Road' (BWB, 2009: 47). More recently, some scholars have been more reticent to assert, as is frequently done, early trade connections between Rome and Han China (Farrington, 2002: 11–12). Hansen, for instance (2012: 20), finds that, 'the absence of archaeological or textual evidence suggests surprisingly little contract between ancient Rome and the Han dynasty', but accelerating relations by the time of the Tang dynasty (618–907 CE).

From a Chinese perspective, the origins of the road in the second century BCE lie in a consolidation and expansion of existing trade routes into China (Wood, 2003: 26). The key ones were the *Jade Road* from Tibet into modern Xinjiang and the *Fur Road* leading into China from Siberia. Sima Qian was China's most prominent historian of this time – some have, perhaps inappropriately, called him the 'Chinese Herodotus', or the 'Chinese Father of History'. He reported many other items commonly traded on this emerging 'proto-Silk Road'[4]: alcohol, foodstuffs, silks, hemp, cloth, dyes, maps, furs, lacquer ware, and copper and iron products (Smith, 2010: 71).[5]

Owing to the records of Sima Qian, the travels of Zhang Qian (Chang Ch'ien, see below) made the Chinese more keenly aware of the routes towards Afghanistan, and the Emperor Han Wudi (141–87 BCE) of the Han dynasty subsequently took a more active interest in foreign trade and issues of security and conquest.

The geopolitical enabling conditions of the Silk Road in an Asia–Europe perspective

Smith (2010: 77) posits that, with China connected to Central Asia in this way:

> interlocking routes now ran from one side of the Eurasian landmass to the other. By the early years of the first millennium CE, the sustained, systematic, large-scale movement of goods across a full, integrated land system, and a parallel sea system, had become a reality.

However, the traffic in high-value goods, faiths and ideas and people moving along this conglomerate of East–West channels collectively known as the Silk Roads (or the Silk Road) was always dependent on the shifting sands of power-play, wishful thinking and geopolitics. This, as Millward has argued (2013: 51), led to the two key processes by means of which knowledge could travel: convergence (similar phenomena occurring, in parallel, in different places) and diffusion (ideas or objects 'spreading' from one place to the next one).

In terms of the intellectual, religious and artistic dimensions of convergence and diffusion, there are, at least, four key geopolitical aspects that influenced the way Asia and Europe learned from one another, to varying degrees, over time, and across the very considerable geographical and mental distances involved. If, in the context of modern European Studies, analysts often mention the 'Four Freedoms' of the EU (those of the movement of 'goods', 'services', 'people' and 'money'), we can surely assume that the Silk Roads of old were more than a worthy predecessor and template for the exchange of knowledge and for what today's EU strategists are fond of calling – often somewhat euphemistically – 'knowledge-based international cooperation'.

In terms of a 'knowledge-based' international cooperation and commercial trade emerging from the Silk Road, simply keeping the road open did of course mean, first, that the essential routes, areas and oases had to be firmly and sustainably secured. From the Eastern (mainly Chinese) perspective, this meant the emergence of tributary networks of Han Chinese polities towards the innumerable peoples, ethnicities and tribes living along the way. Gelber (2007: 87) describes this situation very aptly as a 'necklace of Chinese strong points'. Chinese strategies ranged from military measures to toleration and accommodation. More often than not, a network of tributary relationships emerged, by means of which Han Chinese merchants and scholars were supported by, or inter-married with, local and regional chiefs and their clans. The vagaries of these inter-related tributary systems and the fluctuating power-relationships with China, and within the Confucian Han Empire (206 BCE–220 CE) itself, dynamically affected the ways in which trade routes were accessible to the West.

Following the mostly indirect exchanges of silk and other goods between the Roman and Han Chinese Empires around 50 BCE, the Roman Empire dispatched an embassy to the Han Court in 166 CE. Since losses via middlemen were significant, the alternative route, via India and the sea-link, seems to have been used from the second century CE long before Europeans 'discovered' it. In terms of intellectual exchange, a significant early asymmetry, or knowledge dichotomy, appears to have emerged from these early contacts: Western interest in China was often met by Chinese indifference towards the West (Gelber, 2007: 36). Notwithstanding this, knowledge transfer from China to the West, along the Silk Road and other channels – is the subject of many comprehensive studies, and prominent scholars such as Joseph Needham and Donald Lach have devoted their lives to this issue, with results that remain unrivalled. Their work will be examined in this book where the context demands it.

Second, in later centuries, perhaps the most important determinant for the vagaries of the Silk Road was the *Pax Mongolica*, the amalgamation of vast swathes of Central Eurasia under the rule of the Mongols from 1200 to 1368. Like the *Pax Romana* and the constitution of Achaemenid Empire of the Persians from Cyrus (559–529 BCE) to Darius (336–330 BCE), the rule of Tamerlane and his Mongol successors safeguarded a sustained period of peace and regional stability: Mongol rule of the Timurid Empire rendered Central Asia unified, making trade and travel in all directions safe and frequent. Shagdar (2000: 134) claims: 'no doubt that the Mongols, having monopolized East–West relations, not only gave a new lease of life to the traditional Silk Road, but also played a key role in the way it functioned'. To which can, perhaps, be added that the exchange of *intellectual innovation* played as much a role in its functioning as the political power and prestige of the 'Great Khans' (Shagdar, 2000: 138). It was at this time that the Polo brothers are said to have journeyed from Italy to China; the *Catalan Atlas* of 1375 contains an eloquent depiction of the travellers, seen by some as a first depiction of an emerging East–West 'globalization'.[6] A first cluster of Western missionary-scholars and traders were subsequently dispatched to the steppes. When the Mongol Empire fell to the Ming in 1368, this relative ease of overland travel ceased and commerce became more difficult; for some time, it halted altogether.

Consequently, the formerly plentiful channels of European information about Asia dried up. When Middle Eastern merchants and middle men imposed expensive monopolies on the commerce with the East, Europeans had to look for an alternative to overland travel, which they found through the Portuguese and other European maritime nations exploring sea routes around the southern tip of Africa, and to India (see Chapter 3). Moreover, Millward (2013: 113–114, 117) has shown how later geopolitical developments, such as the Russian and Qing 'enclosure' of the steppe from the sixteenth century and the evolution of mankind's dependency on fossil fuels in our own time, re-focused – but by no means ended – the geopolitical 'centrality' of Central Asia. The argument, advanced by many, that the rise of the European maritime trade extending to the Indian Ocean, the Straits of Malacca and the South China Sea abruptly rang the death knell for the overland Silk Roads is now generally not accepted as holding water (pardon the pun) any more. The intense, and more recent, study of the Ming Records in regard of the Xinjiang Region, for example, contradicts many earlier assumptions, showing that the overland trade continued until at least the sixteenth century (Millward, 2007: 76–77).

Third, from the European perspective, the desire to exploit the Silk Road routes, as and when they were accessible, was impelled by other intentions too: it was a complex and powerful array of commercial and religious motives that sent Europeans East during the various aspects of Silk Road travel. A key concern of the Europeans was the rise of Islam throughout the Middle East. Muslim advances from the seventh century onwards resulted in significant territorial gains. This gave rise to an increasingly urgent European desire to protect the pilgrimage routes to Jerusalem. Wood (2009: 7) argues that:

> as Muslim rulers took control of more and more territory, rather desperate attempts to form alliances with the Mongols, whose homeland lay beyond the Muslim strongholds, were contemplated by Christian rulers in Europe, despite the fact that, in 1242, a Mongol army had reached the gates of Vienna.

The desire to find allies among the peoples of the Silk Road, and pious hopes of alliances with the Great Khan, thus provided the impetus for many an eastward-bound missionary caravan. The concept of a counter-balance to expanding Islam fuelled European Silk Road ventures from the earliest times – the Great Game starts here, and it is still unfolding.

However, many travellers also went East to see whether there was even a grain of truth in the many stories and romances of Marco Polo, Sir John Mandeville, Prester John and Alexander the Great, which had come down in oral tradition and literature through the ages and which had been expanded and embellished so many times, especially in regard to the Mongols and to China (cf. Stoneman, 2008, for the Alexander legends; also: Pagden, 2008: 292–293). Others were motivated by the search for the fabled art treasures and riches of the East, and by the prospect of adventure and – importantly for this book – by the desire to learn, make contact and absorb. Later, numerous 'Orientalist' travellers went in order to understand the complexities of religious faith they encountered on the Silk Roads – predominantly Hinduism and Buddhism. I have sought to trace this fascinating history of the European revelation of these two faiths elsewhere (Wiessala, 2011: 38–50) inspired by Roger-Pol Droit's extremely valuable work on what many early Europeans viewed as a *Cult of Nothingness*.

Fourth, and finally, in assessing the enabling and inhibiting conditions of the Silk Road as a nexus between East and West, the role of religious exchange – and of what we would, perhaps, term 'faith-based learning' today, cannot be

22 *Theoretical aspects and historical predecessors*

overestimated. Many Silk Road scholars have focused on trade, material culture and missionary activity, and, as Millward has shown (2013: 18), it was religions that provided the 'intellectual connective tissue' of all these. In a great number of instances, this has provided valuable research agendas, leading to significant insights into the dynamics of the Silk Roads in different ages. However, it is only recently that the study of religiously mediated knowledge acquisition, international study, religious syncretism and knowledge dissemination is being explored to a more meaningful degree. This recent scholarly activity has many roots in the availability of hitherto unknown translations, sources, artworks and documents which are now being assembled – for example, in the context of the further study of Nālandā University, the inter-cultural activities of the Indian Emperor Aśoka and especially the Dunhuang Project.

Box 2.1 Emperor Aśoka and European Orientalist science

The Emperor Aśoka (r. 274–236 BCE), grandson to Chandragupta, the founder of the Mauryan dynasty, had a magnificent *stupa* built at Nālandā, the ruins of which can still be discerned (Asian Civilizations Museum/Krishnan, G.P., 2008: 58; Wiessala, 2011: 45–46). Aśoka had introduced Buddhism to the region around 250 BCE and had also raised a prominent 'rock edict' with magnificent lion capitals to his own memory. The towering figure of Emperor Aśoka reverberates in the present in two different ways: first, in the debate about the universal validity, or otherwise, of human rights and fundamental values, this prominent figure of Asian history has, at times, been hitched to the universalist cart of analysts who have seen – in Aśoka's dramatic turning away from violence and subsequent conversion to Buddhism – an early, and unique, form of Asian global humanism (Wiessala, 2006: 44). Second, Aśoka appears to have been a symbol of the 'discovery' of the East by many of the European 'Orientalists' of the late nineteenth and early twentieth centuries CE – most of whom arrived via the intellectual conduit of the Silk Route at places such as Gandhara, Dunhuang (Wood, 2003: 95–101; Hansen, 2012: 167–197) and Bamiyan, and further south at the cave-temples of Ellora[7] and Ajanta. Scholars and explorers arrived, often in order to plunder priceless treasures with impunity. However, many also came to unlock, to the Western collective mind, the depths of Asian philosophies, cultures and religions (cf. Wiessala, 2011: 45–46). The translations of the rock edicts of Emperor Aśoka, in particular, have at times been interpreted as a crowning achievement in the revelation of India's ancient history (Allen, 2003: 189–190). More than that, however, Aśoka has become the pivot around which has accumulated a significant, and growing, amount of scholarly speculation and analysis, in regard to early diplomatic exchanges between the Seleucid Empire of Alexander the Great's successors and Aśoka's realm. These exchanges included many Western students at Nālandā.

This chapter is mindful of placing a particular emphasis on the faith-based aspects of East–West learning and looks at the role of what one may call 'inter-religious dialogue' in modern parlance, in the creation and exchange of knowledge and in Europeans' perceptions of (Central) Asia. Curiosity about other religions, practices and traditions, in other words, prospered for significant periods, and along all branches of the Silk Road. In this context, it was actually paper, rather than silk, which was of much higher importance in these processes than has been hitherto assumed. In what follows, I will look at books, documents and scrolls, universities and libraries along the Silk Road, in two ways: first, in line with the cult of the book, common to all parts of the Silk Road touched by Buddhism. Morgan and Walters (2012: 139) encapsulate this aspect very eloquently:

> Buddhist sutras came to be worshipped as sacred objects, rather like relics. Respect for the written word existed in China long before Buddhism arrived – it was an element of Confucian teaching. China has long respected books not just for their content but for their calligraphy too. But the Buddhist veneration of the book as a religious object – what today is termed the cult of the book – was a new development.

Second, and next to their sacred functions, books and writings are placed here in the context of their value as inter-cultural transmitters of knowledge, and in connection with dedicated 'spaces', 'sites' (and 'seats') of learning. This approach is conceptualized, and expanded, most recently by Burke (2000: 7) and others. The Silk Road, from this angle becomes more than a locale for religious syncretism and exchange: it is also a model of an early, globalized, 'information superhighway'; this concept, as we shall see, seems possessed of a renewed intellectual currency at the end of the first decade of the twenty-first century. Let us now turn to some of the earlier travellers on this venerable cultural highway.

Nomads in search of the East and the West

The many Silk Road itinerants, past and present, include diplomatic envoys, military personnel, brides sent abroad in consolidation of treaties and alliances, merchants, monks, poets, explorers, artists and many more. Many of these personalities have come to light, and their activities have been scrutinized, as one important result of a small number of high-profile, global, Silk Road research projects, such as the *Orient-Occident Major Project* (UNESCO, 1957–1966), the *Silk Road: Roads of Dialogue* (UNESCO, 1988–1997) and, more recently, the *International Dunhuang Project* (Elisseeff, 2000: 12–16).

Box 2.2 Peripatetic monks, Han and Hun: some early Asian Silk Road scholars[8]

Arguably, some of the earliest embassies along what was to become known as the 'Silk Road' were the missions of the Han courtier **Zhang Qian** (Chang Ch'ien) between 138 and 115 BCE. It occurred because of the desire of the Han Emperor Han Wudi (141 or 157–87 BCE) to secure his realm and to expand its lucrative caravan trade in silk and horses with the Western regions; this has already been noted as one of the key geopolitical drivers behind the emergence of the Silk Road (see above). Zhang Qian's 13-year journey took him across the Taklamakan desert, deep into the then *terra incognita* of Ferghana, Bokhara and Samarkand in Central Asia.

His task was to establish whether an alliance would be possible between the Han Empire and the Yuezhi ('Meat Eaters') tribes, against the nomadic Xiongnu ('Fierce Slaves') (Wood, 2003: 50–51). The Xiongnu are thought to be precursors to the Central Asian 'Huns' (Millward, 2013: 13). The Han Emperor had been engaged in a succession of wars with them between 114 and 91 BCE. Described by Smith (2010: 73) as the 'first true empire-builders on the steppe', by contrast, the Yuezhi are said to have been nomadic-pastoralist tribes threatening China's northern borders. They founded the Kushan Empire, an approximate contemporary of the Roman one, to control Silk Road trade. Zhang Qian's main contribution to both Western and Eastern learning was his report on his voyage, which, in the interpretation of Howgego (2009: 20), 'opened the eyes of the Chinese for the first time to a civilized world beyond their borders', contributing to the opening of the Northern and Southern 'branches' of the Silk Road, and to more Chinese contacts with Persia and Europe.

Arguably, the most significant early Chinese travellers along the Silk Road were the Buddhist monks **Faxian** (Fa Hsien, travelled 399–416 CE), **Xuanzang** (Hsuan Tsang, 602–664 CE; travelled 629/630–645 CE) and **Yijing** (travelled 671–695 CE).[9] Their peregrinations were motivated by a spiritual quest for enlightenment, and a desire to take the Buddhist sacred texts known as the *vinaya* (or monastic rules) back to China. Their peregrinations happened across modern Uttar Pradesh and Bihar, at a distance of two hundred years. The reports both of these travelling monks compiled contributed significantly to Western knowledge about ancient seats of learning in Central Asia, South East Asia and India. Both writers departed from the Han capital, Chang'an (now Xi'an, Shaangxi). **Yijing**, for example, was the author of the *Record of the Buddhist Religion as Practiced in India and the Malay Archipelago*.

In addition to this, the records the Buddhist teacher **Faxian**[10] kept during his journey from 399 to 416 (a map is at: Hansen, 2012: 162–163) survive as the *Foguo-ji* (*A Record of Buddhistic* [sic] *Kingdoms*; Eliseeff, 2000: 5–6). Faxian visited the kingdom of Kroraina, which was at its height from 200–400 CE (Hansen, 2012: 26). Faxian also 'crossed the Pamir plateau and proceeded to the Indus valley. He visited many scared Buddhist sites in the northwest, before descending to the Ganges plain, the birthplace of Buddhism' (Xinru, 2010: 85). He stayed in the Gandhara region, and he travelled to the four most iconic sites connected with Sakyamuni Buddha (*Lumbini, Bodhgaya, Sarnath* and *Kushinagara*). On his way back home, Faxian prayed at many Buddhist sites in (modern) Sri Lanka, where he stayed for over two years, noting the presence there of many 'scholars' and 'merchants' (Hansen, 2012: 160).

The Buddhist monk **Xuanzang** – 'one part Christopher Columbus, one part St. Jerome, one part Samuel Pepys' (Morgan and Walters, 2012: 90) – visited key Silk Road oasis towns such as Kucha and Turfan, stopped in the Sogdian capital Samarkand (in modern Uzbekistan), stayed at Bagram and viewed the famous Buddhas at Bamiyan in today's Afghanistan (Howgego, 2009: 26; Xinru, 2010: 64; Hansen, 2012: 113).[11] In Samarkand (Hansen, 2012: 113), 'Xuanzang entered the cultural sphere of the Iranians, whose languages, religious practices and customs, although equally old and equally sophisticated, differed profoundly from those of the Chinese'. He explored key Indian seats of ancient learning, such as Taxila and Nālandā Universities, in search of Sanskrit texts, Buddhist relics and enlightenment. Xuanzang's travels have been rightly seen to 'embody the universal elements of a hero's quest' (Wriggins, 2004: 17). The pilgrim wrote extensively about what he found along the way – much of it devoted to intellectual exchange and international learning, and he translated thousands of Buddhist scriptures. Wriggins argues, citing Anthony Yu, that 'the sheer volume of Buddhist literature translated by Xuanzang and many other monks, and the resultant infusion of Sanskrit words into Chinese, has been compared to the influence of Shakespeare on the English language'.

However, Xuanzang also found time to relate anecdotes, such as the story of the Silk Road Princess (see Chapter 7). His main work, *Da Tang Xiyo Ti*, or *Records (of Travels to the Western Regions at the Time of the Tang Dynasty)*, became, in Allen's words (2012: 219), 'a popular classic of Chinese literature'. Moreover, Fisher (1993: 86–88) argues that his account revealed to archaeologists 'a thousand-year subculture of remarkable achievements, with artistic remains of surprising range and quality'. For Morgan and Walters (2012: 85), Xuanzang's *Records* are a 'seventh-century *Lonely Planet* guide'. Eventually, Xuanzang brought back to China more than 644 sacred Buddhist texts. In the nineteenth century, Xuanzang became one of the Hungarian–British archaeologist Aurel Stein's 'heroes', his 'patron saint' (Morgan and Walters, 2012: 16).

Last but not least, **Yeh-lü Ch'u-ts'ai** (travelled 1219–1225) was a great Kitan statesman and poet who became an advisor to Genghis Khan and his successors. He travelled with Genghis Khan and his army to Central Asia in 1219, and he journeyed to Altai, Ili Valley, Talas, Samarkand and Bukhara. His impressions can be read on some of his poems. He returned via Tienshan, Urumqi, Turfan and Hami. His key travel book is entitled *Xi Yue Lu* (*The Travel Record to the West*).

Europeans on the Silk Roads

The earliest Western travellers on the Silk Road were, invariably, missionaries. In 1245, Pope Innocent IV dispatched the Franciscan Giovanni da Pian Del Carpini (Jean du Plan Carpin, John of Plano Carpini, 1180–1252) to the Mongol court, in order to convert the Great Khan Güyüg (r. 1246–1248) and explore the feasibility of political alliance. Geopolitical considerations, once again, lay at the heart of emerging European–Asian contacts via the Silk Road. Khan Güyüg, of course, firmly rejected the papal requests for 'submission' (Pagden, 2008: 292).

However, European wishful thinking notwithstanding, Friar John's book *Historia Mongolorum* (on *The History of the Mongols*) became a key resource for Europeans seeking knowledge of Central Asia, and China, the country the Mongols were then taking on. Pagden argues (2008: 292) that this work was the 'first detailed and perceptive piece of writing about an Asian people to have appeared in Europe since Herodotus'.

The Flemish Franciscan Willem Van Ruebroek (Ruysbroeck) (William of Rubruck) too went to the Mongol capital, Karakorum, sent by King Louis IX of France between 1253 and 1255, for similar reasons of fact-finding and mission. Pagden reports (2008: 293) how he found himself drawn into inter-religious debate and dispute, and Howgego points out (2009: 36) that 'Rubruck's detailed report, sympathetic and observant, survives in full, and, in certain respects, remained unsurpassed until the nineteenth century'. It contains references to Europeans living in Karakorum, and a detailed account of *Great Cataia* (China).

This notwithstanding, many of these early Asian accounts by Europeans dated quite quickly, in the light of later, predominantly commercial, travellers – above all, the voyages of the jewel merchants Niccolò, Maffeo and Marco Polo (1254–1324; the latter's travels of 1260–1269 and 1271–1295). Lach and Van Kley (1994, Vol. II, Book 1: 36) point to some of the reasons for this: 'the great commercial prosperity of Venice in the thirteenth and fourteenth centuries led to a growth of interest there in collecting exotica from the East'. When the Polos arrived at the court of Kublai, it is reported that the 'Great Khan' requested them to bring 'men of learning' to educate his followers in Western methods.

Given the iconic status that Marco Polo's book *Il Milione* (better known as the *Travels*, or *The Description of the World*) achieved throughout much of Europe, and in the light of the many debates about the book's authenticity and use of sources, it is perhaps surprising that this text added but little to the store of knowledge in European geography and map-making (Jackson and Jaffer, 2004: 20; Pagden, 2008: 294–295). The book certainly excelled in terms of the 'romance' and the mythology of the East, not unlike the Alexander romances and the *Travels of Sir John Mandeville*. Nevertheless, Columbus is said to have taken it along to plan his journeys of exploration two centuries later (cf. Howgego, 2009: 38).

In the era following the Polos' travels, there were many other European Silk Road travellers. Few of them, however, left detailed accounts; even fewer are remembered now, whose writings covered the subject of intellectual exchange between Europe and Asia and the transmission of Western learning to the East. One of the notable exceptions, once again, was a Franciscan friar, who departed Europe in 1316, benefiting, like others before him, from the long Mongol peace (see above).

The Paduan Minorite Friar Odoric of Pordenone (travelled 1316–1330) is famed for his writings about the Christian communities he found in India, about Chinese customs and Tibet. His book, *De Rebus Incognitis et Itineris (Of Unknown Things and Ways*, published 1513) survives in more than 100 manuscript copies (Wood, 2009: 10–11). Last but not least, John of Monte Corvino is believed to have been the first European missionary to enter China in 1294, reporting back to Europe on matters of religion and the potential for conversion.

Later still, the Portuguese Jesuit, traveller and diarist Bento (Benedict) de Góis (alternative spellings: 'de Goes', 'Benoit de Goës', 1561–1607, see Chapter 3 on the Jesuits) was tasked with exploring Central Asia on behalf of his order, to establish whether the fabled 'Cathay' described so vividly in Marco Polo's account and elsewhere was anywhere to be found, whether it related to China or Tibet and whether there were Christians in Central Asia (Ross, 1994: 122; Lach and Van Kley, 1998, Vol. III, Book 4: 1773). Fr. de Góis is said to have been 'the first Jesuit to find a land route between India and China via Lahore and Kabul, between 1603 and 1607' (Lach and Van Kley, 1998, Vol. III, Book 1: 338; Wright, 2004: 46; Millward, 2013: 112). From the merchants de Góis encountered en route, he learnt about Matteo Ricci in Beijing. It was but a small step from there to make the link between the mythical 'Cathay' and the 'real' China of his day.

De Góis accompanied an embassy the Mughal Emperor Akbar dispatched to Goa. He died during his travels in 1607, but not before having written prolifically about his experiences and encounters. Matteo Ricci was later to edit de Góis's diaries into a book. It appeared also in Nicolas Trigault's text *De Christiana Expeditione* in 1615. An interesting contemporary geopolitical assessment by de Góis can be found in Trigault's incorporation of de Góis's text, and is quoted by Lach and Van Kley (1998, Vol. III, Book 4: 1768–1769): 'The Saracens on the Chinese frontier are not a warlike people. They could very easily be conquered by the Chinese, if the Chinese were interested in subjugating other nations.' Europeans would learn much more about the Silk Road politics of the day through the extensive writings of the Jesuits (see also Chapter 3).

East meets West: learning and syncretism in art and culture

In his survey of *Buddhist Art and Architecture*, Robert E. Fisher points out (1993: 86) that:

> despite centuries of commercial activity along the Silk Road, bringing Chinese goods to the Roman empire and causing numerous cities and small, independent, states to flourish, knowledge of the artistic heritage of this vast area remained largely unknown until the early twentieth century.

The art originating from along the Silk Road is, indeed, a revealing medium, showing that knowledge and skills truly travelled both from East to West and vice versa. Arguably one of the best examples of a Silk Road-mediated Western influence on the East is found in object number 41 in the 2010 landmark exhibit-cum-radio programme *A History of the World in 100 Objects* in 2010 by the British Museum.

It is a unique fusion of Eastern and Western aesthetics: a Buddha figure[12] from the Gandhara region – then part of a wealthy kingdom connected to the Silk Road, and now the region around Peshawar in Northwest Pakistan.[13] Gandhara was: 'where Eastern ideas met Western art, where Buddhism, migrating west from its Himalayan birthplace, encountered the legacy of Alexander the Great' (Morgan and Walters, 2012: 21). Referenced for the first time in the Hindu *Rig Veda* in the tenth century BCE, the kingdom of Gandhara was subject to numerous incursions from all directions and thus grew into a melting pot of cultural and religious influences and inter-cultural learning. Following Alexander the Great's appropriation of Northwest India (327–326 BCE), Greek princes from Bactria – itself the easternmost province of the Greek Empire – ran Gandhara from the third century BCE onwards.

The Persians were here; the Mauryan Emperor Aśoka (r. 274–236 BCE), grandson of the dynastic founder Chandragupta, introduced Buddhism to the Gandhara region around 250 BCE and raised a prominent 'rock edict' with magnificent lion capitals to his own memory. During the first and second centuries CE, the area was controlled by the kings of the Kushan ethnicity in Northern India. The Kushan domain,[14] in the strategically placed northwest of South Asia, extended from modern Kabul to Islamabad and was linked to both the overland Silk Road and ports on the Arabian Sea (Patry Leidy, 2008: 37–38; MacGregor, 2011: 265–268).

The Metropolitan Museum in New York, which holds a significant collection of Gandhara art, comments on the Gandhara Buddha sculptures as follows:

> Much can be learned about Gandharan Buddhism from the depictions of the Buddha and related beings that survive today. Buddhism in the region was truly multi-faceted and images of the Buddha changed considerably over the course of the Kushana reign, most notably with an increasing emphasis on the transcendent nature of the Buddha. Many of the concepts characteristic of Mahayana Buddhism – the form of Buddhism which later spread widely across East Asia – appear to have developed in Gandhara.

These sometimes show the Buddha as deified or multiplied. For the first time, bodhisattvas are depicted as enlightened beings, choosing to remain 'active in the world', in order to help others, compassionately, along the path to enlightenment.[15]

The British Museum Gandhara figure, sculpted by expert hands some time in between 100 and 300 CE, represents something unique: it is one of the first representations of the Buddha in human form, all future Buddha images have their template here (Wriggins, 2004: 68–69; Lowenstein, 2006: 43; Van Alphen, 2010: 98). The Buddha ('Enlightened One') had previously only been depicted in a 'un-iconic' manner, through symbols such as a deer or a wheel.

Here, he sits in serene meditation, displaying the *dharmachakra mudra*, a hand-gesture, indicating the 'setting in motion of the wheel of (Buddhist) law' by the Buddha, who here articulates with his hands a sacred iconography as a teacher and universal monarch. The pose hints both at the Buddhist path and the importance of Gandhara as a centre of learning, religion and mission with many Western links.[16] The Buddha figure itself is unusual, in that its features and toga-style robes appear realistic; they owe as much to the Greek and Roman style templates as they do to Indian ones.[17] Morgan and Walters report (2012: 21):

> Never before had he [the explorer–archaeologist Aurel Stein] seen such an extraordinary collection of ancient Buddhist statues. Some had features

more European than Asian, indeed many resembled Greek gods. Here were Buddhas with round eyes and wavy hair and moustaches, wearing what looked more like Roman togas than the patched robes of monks...

Robert E. Fisher (1993: 30) hints at some of the reasons why this new, Indo-Hellenic, style emerged:

Alexander the Great's destruction of the Persian Empire and disruption of society just prior to the [Indian] Mauryan Dynasty, caused artists to seek patronage elsewhere, and, judging from the Mauryan remains, some found work further east, in India. Alexander's activity across western Asia, late in the fourth century BC, increased contacts with India and was followed by the opening of the Silk Road between China and Rome, two events of great consequence in the subsequent history of Buddhism.

Alexander the Great had invaded the Kushan realm in around 329–326 BCE. Here, at the terminus point of his Eastern campaigns, Buddhist iconography was altered in the aftermath of Alexander's campaigns and the subsequent Hellenization of the area. Van Alphen shows (2010: 95) that the descendants of the Achaemenids (Persians) and Seleucids (Greeks) in this part of Central Asia were called Greco-Bactrians and continued to uphold Hellenistic culture in their cities (Wood, 2003: 39). In addition, Fisher points out (1993: 44) that the ensuing artistic and sculptural styles derived from 'Roman colonies and from the commerce between West and East, which passed [along the Silk Road] just to the north of the region'.

The resulting Buddha images are representations of the human figure – among the first in human shape – clad in Roman and Greek togas and sport elaborate jewellery, European-model curly hair styles, flowing locks and elegant, decidedly Western, moustaches. It is therefore not altogether improbable that the first human depictions of the Buddha in this region of Central Asia may have been inspired by Western portraits and templates. In architecture, too, Western classical motifs amalgamated with Indian ones (Fisher, 1993: 53–54). Patry Leidy (2008: 38) comments on this, remarking that:

the Greek themes and styles Alexander helped to introduce remained popular through contact with the expanding Roman Empire (27 BCE–393 CE). Under the Kushans, these influences joined Indian traditions and those associated with the Iranian world and Central Asia in a great pool of stylistic forms available to artists.

Object 50 in the *History of the World in 100 Objects* series is, arguably, even more illuminating.[18] This (wooden-board) painting entitled *The Legend of the Silk Princess* from Xinjiang[19] was made five centuries later than the Gandhara Buddha (above) – between 600 and 800 CE. It portrays what Neil MacGregor (2010: 319) calls 'one of the greatest technology thefts in history'. This splendid

30 *Theoretical aspects and historical predecessors*

artwork from the former Silk Road oasis-kingdom of Khotan was among the nineteenth-century finds by the archaeologist Aurel Stein (see above, and Morgan and Walters, 2012). It narrates how the Chinese secret of silk production – for so long jealously guarded as a monopoly – was supposed to have travelled west, to Khotan and further.

It escaped China, hidden in the head-dress of a princess, who had been married off for dynastic-political reasons, to a realm far west of China (Whitfield, 2004: 7; Norell *et al.*, 2011: 75; Morgan and Walters, 2012: 95). The enterprising bride chose to smuggle out of China all that was needed for silk making – including silkworms and mulberry seeds – as a wedding present for her new people. MacGregor surmises: 'the Silk Princess may not be quite on a par with Prometheus, who stole fire from the gods, but she is firmly in the tradition of great mythological gift-givers, bringing knowledge and skill to a particular people'. Apart from the painting, there are written versions of this story too. The Chinese monk and Silk Road traveller Xuanzang (see elsewhere in this chapter) included the story in his writings as follows:

> In the olden days, the people of the rocky land of Khotan knew nothing about mulberry trees, nor silkworms. But they heard that these things existed in the East, in China. Therefore they sent a delegation to ask for the secret of producing silk. The emperor laughed at them. 'This is a secret,' he said. 'It is forbidden to let outsiders find out how silk is made.' He had all border stations watched and allowed neither mulberry seeds nor silkworm eggs to be taken out of the empire. The king of Khotan then had an idea. As a sign of his veneration for the Chinese emperor, he asked if he could marry a princess of the emperor's house. The emperor kindly agreed to this wish. The king of Khotan then sent an envoy to the princess to tell her that Khotan had neither mulberry trees nor silkworms. If she wanted to wear silk, she would have to bring some seeds and eggs, with which they could make her beautiful dresses. The princess heard this and considered it. Secretly she got some mulberry seeds and silkworm eggs which she hid in her huge head dress. When the princess reached the border gates, the guards searched her thoroughly, but they dared not touch her hair. The princess was taken with great pomp to the royal palace and brought her mulberry seeds and silkworm eggs there. In the spring the princess had the mulberry seeds sown. When it was time for the larvae to hatch, leaves were gathered for them. At first they had to eat any kind of leaves, before the real mulberry leaves were available. The queen had an inscription made on a stone which said: 'It is prohibited to kill the silkworm.' In this way the secret of making silk was taken from China, and the people of Khotan began to wear not only furs but fine silk clothes.[20]

It is, perhaps, not surprising that, against this background of commercial, artistic, military, literary and religious exchange on the Silk Roads, a number of important 'nodes', or 'seats of learning' (see Chapter 1), should have sprung up and established themselves along the way, in order to provide spiritual and intellectual sustenance, in addition to the material sustenance of the oasis towns. These sites were ancient seats of learning, pre-dating European universities by many centuries. The diverse religions travelling the length and breadth of the Silk Roads were chief catalysts for these establishments, foundations, monasteries, universities and libraries, in both East and West (see below, and Elisseeff, 2000: 10).

Religions and seats of learning as catalysts for Asia–Europe knowledge transfer

> The gods that travelled the Silk Road were, like the traders themselves, happy to share accommodation.
>
> (MacGregor, 2010: 324)

Representing many other scholars, Lowenstein (2006: 56) clarifies that:

> Buddhism was not the only religion to travel the many arid wilderness tracks, to the North and South of the Tarim Basin, that constituted the Silk Road; Christians, Jews, Manichaeans, and, by the eighth century, Muslims also followed these paths.

Sørensen (2000: 27) is justified in claiming that:

> it is important to recognize the significance of religion, not only as a general component of human civilization in the societies that flourished along the Silk Roads, but as the single most important factor in the cultural dissemination and exchange that took place in Central Asia from the beginning of the Christian era up to approximately A.D. 1000.

There are, perhaps, three key points in connection with religions[21] on the Silk Road, which it is useful to call to mind at this stage. One of them has already been hinted at throughout this chapter: the religiously inspired travels along the Silk Road, by both Asian itinerant Buddhist monks and European Christian missionaries, have vastly increased the store of knowledge Asia and Europe have built up about one another over the centuries. Whether these spiritual journeys – in both a physical and a transcendental sense – occurred out of a mere zeal for proselytizing, or a desire to simply increase one's scriptural wisdom, they have led to encounters between Christianity (itself, arguably, an Asian religion) and the other three great 'Asian Faiths' of Buddhism, Islam and Chinese Religion(s).

These encounters have forever altered perceptions of learning in East and West. They have shifted the goalposts of perception in respect of what 'East' and 'West' have actually come to mean, in terms of intellectual identities and pedagogies. These processes of exchange continue to have a direct and measurable impact on the teaching and learning in the discipline of European Studies in

Asia. Thus, the many contemporary learning activities being organized under the very modern rubrics of 'inter-faith dialogue', 'inter-civilizational encounter' or just 'people-to-people-dimension' are direct academic descendants of these earlier religious West–East journeys.

Second, there is an aspect legacy of the multi-faith religious encounter on the Silk Roads which has, hitherto, received comparatively little attention, but which, nevertheless, should not be underestimated by those thinking about what 'European Studies' can mean in Asia today. This is the effect of non-Christian religious meetings on (European) Christian views of Central and South East Asia. Elverskog (2013) has recently illustrated this point with powerful reference to both the obliteration of Nālandā University at the turn of the twelfth to the thirteenth centuries (see the next section) and the more recent annihilation of the Bamiyan Buddhas (Morgan, 2012) by Taliban fundamentalists. Both acts of wanton destruction had their roots in Muslim agency in the region. It is, therefore, not really surprising that European Silk Road 'explorers' and travellers should have perceived the two faiths as strongly antagonistic and widely different. Westerners were not struck, or surprised, by the story of a Buddhist–Muslim 'clash of civilizations'; they expected to see evidence of it.

And yet one issue needs to be borne in mind: tragic as the destruction wrought upon both Nālandā and Bamiyan have been without a shadow of a doubt, they have, in the more long-term perspective, been the exception rather than the rule, in the exchange between Islam and Buddhism. The rule, as more recent scholarship is beginning to show (Millward, 2013; Elverskog, 2013), was comprehensive inter-religious learning between Buddhists and Muslims through dialogue, mutual scriptural exegesis and syncretic art production on a scale comparable to that of the centuries-old Christian–Buddhist encounter. However, as Elverskog shows (2013: 276), it was precisely this framework of supposed Muslim–Buddhist 'antagonism', which, in European eyes, seemed to explain most convincingly some of their greatest 'discoveries', such as the ruined monuments of the Silk Road – they were ruined *because* the Muslim armies had destroyed them since the times of Nālandā. Perhaps there is a lesson from history here, for those who are examining the contemporary Muslim–Buddhist encounters in 'newly democratizing' Myanmar (Burma) or mapping ethic-religious tensions along the modern Thailand–Malaysia border.

Third, in choosing to point to the possibility of framing 'European Studies in Asia' through an angle of religious exchange, mediated by a number of small but significant monastic universities, seats of learning and institutions, I am consciously connecting this investigation to more 'holistic' conceptualizations of international intellectual exchange, for which scholars such as J.J. Clarke (1997) and Peter Burke (2000) have so eloquently laid the groundwork. I am also arguing that, first and foremost, this epistemological-religious angle is not just a possibility – it is a necessity. In the perspective of this book, 'European Studies', and 'European Studies in Asia', are, first and foremost, academic disciplines and inter-civilizational, scholarly encounters, with a personal dimension, for which inter-faith dialogue can be the central vehicle.

It will become clear, I hope, at various points in the subsequent text that one of the key contentions of mine in this book is that the discipline as a whole is, at times, in danger of 'losing itself' – or being deliberately 'lost' – in the pseudo-academic fog recently created by debates about the 'impact' of academic work, especially in the contemporary humanities. The rhetoric involving constructed realities such as 'employability', 'economic usefulness' (with a nod to Newman, cf. Collini, 2012) and 'knowledge-driven international relations' can all too easily divert away the focus of the relatively young 'European Studies in Asia' discipline from its roots in intellectual and personal collaboration, research driven by religious curiosity, adaptation and syncretism, and learning for learning's sake in a liberal arts frame.

In teaching the subject across Asia for near on 25 years now, I have found (see Chapters 7 and 8) mounting, worrying, evidence of a rising instrumentalization of the subject, subjugation under a plethora of political and budgetary demands. Thus it becomes possible, for instance, that once thriving resource collections for European Studies in Asia are dispensing with their archives, in order to transmogrify into 'European Business Centres'. While it is fair to say that politics and economics have of course, to some degree, driven 'European Studies' in all ages, as the 'history' chapters in Part I of this book attempt to show, our own 'globalized' times are, perhaps, uniquely destructive in the way academic disciplines are in danger of being straight-jacketed by the c-words of modern Higher Education – commercialization, commodification and consumerization. This seems true at least for the Anglo-American, neo-liberal, 'knowledge-society' contextual discourse, which, it appears at the time of writing, is being relentlessly adopted across Asia as well.

While I am not arguing that one should close one's eyes to the economic realities of our day and age, I am proposing here that it would add much-needed value to the development of European Studies in Asia (and in general) if the focus of attention were turned once again, and much more sharply, on notions such as 'localities', 'seats of learning' and 'centres and peripheries' of knowledge. Since there are notable, countervailing, measures to the above trends being undertaken by many Asian countries and institutions who teach European Studies in a more wholesome and holistic way, it can be assumed that, at this stage, the irrevocability of the 'tipping-point' has not been reached, and that there is not, as yet, an overwhelming, international, consensus to the effect that inter-cultural education is a mere product, to be bought and sold. Therefore, I am conscious in offering here a case study from Asia, in the shape of the ancient Indian University at Nālandā.

Overcoming the suffering of ignorance: Nālandā University and its modern legacies

> Both in Europe and in India, monasteries had become Temples of Learning. But, whereas in Europe, educational activity passed out of the hands of the monks to those of secular clergy, with the spread of knowledge in the

34 *Theoretical aspects and historical predecessors*

outside world, in India, the monks were rather fortunate in retaining it. They saw, as we noticed above, what was coming, and they responded to growing needs. Therefore, instead of being swept away totally by the on-coming wave of reforms, they deemed it wiser to relax the rules of their order. The doors of the Buddhist Sangha, which were open before only to those who had forsaken the world, were now thrown open to the students as well, who, if they chose, were at liberty to leave the monastery and embrace once more the life of a householder, after their education was over. It is in this transformation of the monasteries that we find the seeds of the University of Nālandā.

(Hasmuth Dhirajlal Sankalia, 1972: 35)

Nālandā, with her learned men, famous on account of their (knowledge of) good scriptures and arts, mocks, as it were, at all the cities of great emperors.
(From a stone inscription, originally at Nālandā, quoted in Ghosh, 1939: 34)

Amartya Sen reminds us[22] that:

when the most ancient European University, the University of Bologna, was founded – this was in 1088 – the centre for higher education at Nālandā was already more than six hundred years old [...]. The destruction of Nālandā happened shortly after the beginning of Oxford University, and shortly after the initiation of Cambridge.

And Amulyachandra Sen, placing Nālandā in a wider, civilizational, context, reminds us of something that should make the ears of all those ring who are seriously concerned with devising and delivering 'European Studies' in Asia today:

This was no make-believe show, for the honour paid to learning and piety was no less than that to royalty in India of old, and it was done with a wholeheartedness worthy of an age when the cultivation of the mind ranked as the highest of all human possessions.

(Sen, 1954: 99)

Wriggins (2004: 120) provides a comparative perspective, looking at Nālandā as an academic foundation:

what Cluny and Claivaux were to medieval Europe, Nālandā was to medieval Asia – a cloister for Buddhists from all over the world (see also: Sankalia, 1972: 234). It was also the most distinguished of all the monasteries and universities in India.

Sankalia (1972) has investigated the process through which a Buddhist monastery (Sanskrit: *vihāra, saṅghārāma*) could develop into a 'university', collecting 'learned men' under one roof, and providing spaces for meditation and study – first at regular intervals, during the annual Buddhist 'rain-retreats', then permanently.

The university appears to have been similar to a Postgraduate School today, a 'university of Universities' (Sankalia, 1972: 170). Nālandā, in Northern India, stands out, first and foremost, by means of its religious-pedagogic importance to Buddhism. The site lies in the Buddhist Holy Land of Northeast India, near to Pataliputra (modern-day Patna). The monastery was founded in the fifth century BCE by the Indian Gupta dynasty. It can be interpreted, on one level, as the embodiment in stone of the Buddhist *Nidāna-sūtra* or *Pratīttyasamutpāda-sūtra*, in which Gautama Buddha taught about the 'chain of causation', in which 'ignorance' is at the heart of all human suffering (Ghosh, 1939: 36).

The (historical) Buddha himself stayed in Nālandā in the sixth century BCE, and one of his chief disciples, Sāriputta (Shariputra), hailed from there. D.G.E. Hall reports (1981: 21) that Nālandā attracted pilgrims from abroad who arrived on the Nālandā-trail, driven by a thirst for learning and enlightenment. Next to its role as an iconic place of (Buddhist) learning, it was the degree of academic weight, and of what some now call 'internationalization' which rendered Nālandā a truly international academy between the fifth and twelfth centuries, with more than 10,000 students (Morgan and Walters, 2012: 93).[23] I have referred to it elsewhere as the 'Oxford of Buddhist India' (Wiessala, 2011: 48–49) and an early catalyst for the evolution of the Asia–Europe intellectual exchange in our day.

It is this function as an intellectual marketplace of ideas for East and West alike that has led some to see Nālandā as the 'greatest centre of Buddhist learning' in Asia (Lowenstein, 2006: 55; Allen, 2012: 3). This evolution is vividly recalled in a publication accompanying the exhibition *On the Nālandā Trail*, at the Asian Civilizations Museum (ACM) in Singapore, in 2007 (ACM/Krishnan, G.P., 2008: 53): 'In due course, the mango grove and other *vihārās* (monasteries), originally meant as dwellings for wandering monks, developed into places of long-term stay, higher learning, and spiritual activities.'

In the process of imparting higher knowledge, these *vihārās* were gradually converted into academic institutions where the spread of knowledge was regarded as the noble and holy duty of the monks. The University of Nālandā blossomed from modest beginnings, growing from a place where a small group of monks lived a life of meditation and contemplation, into a fully-fledged centre of advanced study and research, funded through royal grants, payments from branch campuses and other regional hubs of learning,[24] and through endowments by wealthy laypeople (Wriggins, 2004: 124).

A look at the old Nālandā curriculum reveals not only its syncretic Buddhist orientation, but also a division into the three key areas circumscribed by the terms *pariyatti* (theory), *paripatti* (practice) and *parivedana* (experience), aiming to 'acquire knowledge both mundane and supra-mundane' (ACM/Krishnan, G.P., 2008: 53). This tri-partite curriculum was mirrored in the presence of three libraries, the *Ratnasagara* ('Sea of Jewels'), *Ratnadathi* ('Ocean of Jewels') and

Ratnaranjaka ('Jewels of Delight') (Sen, 1954: 105). Subjects taught included Buddhist philosophy, arts, medicine, logic, epistemology, grammar, mathematics, astronomy (Sankalia, 1972: 98), politics, international studies and war/conflict studies – a wide-ranging curriculum, even by today's standards. Early twentieth-century sources (e.g. Ghosh, 1939: 42) stress that Nālandā was 'bustling with literary activities' – all of which sounds astonishingly modern (see also: Sankalia, 1972: Part I, Chapters IV and VII).

What Europeans, from the early missionaries to the twentieth century 'Orientalists', came to know about Nālandā (see Wiessala, 2011: 16–50, esp. 45–46) emerged, in part, from the excavations of British archaeologists such as Francis Buchanan and Alexander Cunningham at the site throughout the nineteenth century (Allen, 2012: 78, 254). Much of it can be traced back to the detailed written observations of Chinese travelling monks such as Faxian (Fa Hsien) and Xuanzang (Hsuan Tsang; old spelling: *Hiuen Tsang*), who visited fifteen centuries earlier (see Box 2.2). Both were motivated by the acquisition of (Buddhist) scripture and extremely impressed by what they saw. Xuanzang, in particular, it is reported in some earlier sources, was 'accorded a reception at the University almost befitting royalty' (Sen, 1954: 99). It is primarily to these curious Chinese travelling monks that we owe the description of Nālandā's history, construction, funding strategy and student discipline.

What we might call the 'admissions policy' of Nālandā was succinctly outlined by academic visitors like Faxian and Xuanzang:

> of those from abroad who wished to enter the schools of discussion, the majority – beaten by the difficulties of the problems – withdrew; and only those who were deeply versed in old and modern learning were admitted, only two or three out of ten succeeding.
> (Ghosh, 1939: 42–43; Sen, 1954: 102)

Sen reports, based on Xuanzang's writings, that:

> many students who failed to secure admission in Nālandā went through some kind of a course of education elsewhere (or perhaps schooled themselves as best as they could) and, on returning home or going elsewhere, gave themselves out as graduates of Nālandā. Pseudo-scholars, or 'bogus degree-holders', are, therefore, no innovations [sic] for modern times only.

Nālandā grew into an international academic hub; it had achieved a 'celebrity spread all over the East, as a centre of educational activities' (Ghosh, 1939: 43). Here was an institution which not only provided Higher Education, but also imparted cultural and artistic skills, such as metal-casting and carving (Sen, 1954: 102). Xuanzang himself was instructed by the outstanding scholar-artist *Acharya Śīlabhadra* (Sen, 1954: 105; Sankalia, 1972: 131; ACM/Krishnan, G.P., 2008: 55). In keeping with its Buddhist rationale, all instruction at Nālandā connected with the idea of a 'journey' – academically and through life-cycles.

Tutoring aimed at shaping the holistic individual through comprehensive training. Instruction was by team-teaching, tutorials and learner-centred investigation – in seminars and through vivas (Sen, 1954: 103).

The outlook of Nālandā, as an example, perhaps, to many of our modern institutions of higher learning, was truly international; Sen reports (1954: 105) that 'no provincial or parochial spirit entered'. Student cohorts were Buddhist as well as secular, and hailed from Greece and Persia, China and Tibet, Japan, Korea, Europe and South East Asia (Sankalia, 1972: Chapter IX; Morgan and Walters, 2012: 93).

Many came from the *Śrivijaya* (*Shrivijaya*) maritime empire, a significant centre of learning in its own right, whose capital was at Palembang, on the island of Sumatra. The rulers of the *Śailendra* dynasty, which were ruling Śrivijaya, made large donations to Nālandā as early as 860 CE (ACM/Krishnan, G.P., 2008: 64; Hall, 2011: 117). The largest Buddhist monument in the world – the temple of Borobudur on the island of Java (MacGregor, 2010: 379–384) – has been described as 'an impressive and convincing textbook of Buddhism as taught by the Nālandā school' (Hall, 1981: 54). K. Hall (2011: 117) outlines the artistic and scholarly networks of the day stretching between Palembang, the capital of the Śrivijaya empire, and Nālandā: 'Chinese pilgrims regularly studied and worked on their Sanskrit and Pali language skills at Palembang prior to travelling on to Nālandā in northeastern India, which was the foremost epicenter of Buddhist scholarship of that age' (on the artistic influence of Nālandā eastwards, see also an older source: Ghosh, 1939: 21)

Although destroyed in the course of Muslim invasions, between 1192 and 1203 (but see above), Nālandā *māhavihara* became the very model for all European, and British, 'Learned Societies', which emerged in the nineteenth century. Its very demise inaugurated a long period of 'knowledge loss', from Asia to the outside world, especially in regard to ancient Indian and Central Asian history (Allen, 2012: xvi).

Guided, perhaps, by a heightened awareness of this, in 2006, Singapore, China, India, Japan and other nations finally announced a plan to restore the ancient site of *Nālandā*, as Nālandā International University (NIU) as a 'pan-Asian intellectual catalyzer [*sic*]' (De Prado, 2009: 4). Allen reports (2012: 400) that, 'in 2010, a highly unusual bill was placed before the Indian Parliament, enabling the formation of NIU, to be built beside the ruins of ancient Nālandā in modern Bihar State'. Perhaps politicians were, at last beginning to heed the calls by scholars for a new Nālandā, published as early as 1954 (Sen, 1954: 122).

Chapter conclusions

This chapter has undertaken a critical journey along the 'Silk Roads' for the intrepid intellectual traveller in all matters concerned with teaching European Studies in Asia. I have attempted to demonstrate that many European conceptions of this most famous of all channels of European–Asian interaction are essentially flawed or one-sided; this was neither all about silk, nor was it all a single road.

The vagaries of geopolitics, both from the Chinese and the Western ends, have been shown to be of high significance for the opportunities the Europeans had to export early forms of 'European Studies' to Asia along the Road. The geopolitical enabling conditions – the 'Four Freedoms', as it were, of movement of the Silk Road – were thus dependent on Mongol conquests and on the ever-changing dynamics of interaction between 'sedentary' and 'nomadic' peoples in Central Asia. The chapter has also emphasized the – often underestimated – role of written evidence, documents, material culture and religious exchange in the transmission of knowledge from West to East and vice versa – with a slight preference for the written word, so often overshadowed by examinations of art objects from the Silk Roads.

Millward's twin-concepts of 'convergence' and 'diffusion' have been found to have lasting implications for the modern European Union's cooperation with Central Asia today, which stands out by inter-faith dialogue, and by means of a (higher) education dimension which appears out of proportion, in a positive way, to the general place of Central Asia on the ladder of preferences propping up EU–Asia policies.

Last but not least, I have found that 'learning' and 'knowledge exchange' can be conceptualized, following Burke, by investigating the importance and impact of 'seats' and 'locales' of knowledge. In this context, I argue that it is possible to interpret ancient universities such as Nālandā in India, to some significant degree, as a 'seed' and a 'seat' of knowledge – a timeless model for modern curriculum design in the discipline of European Studies in Asia.

Notes

1 British Library Silk Road map: www.bl.uk/onlinegallery/features/silkroad/pdf/silk-roadmap.pdf; the 'Silk Road Links' website is a very extensive resource: www2.kenyon.edu/Depts/Religion/Fac/Adler/Asia201/links201.htm.
2 See, e.g. the evocative recording *Orient-Occident: A Dialogue of Souls* (1200–1700), *Alia Vox* AVSA 9848.
3 See: www.dhm.de/ausstellungen/tsingtau/katalog/auf1_4.htm.
4 On trade on the Silk Roads in antiquity, see: www.metmuseum.org/toah/hd/trade/hd_trade.htm.
5 Some of the diverse goods and artefacts traded in this area were shown in BOZAR (2010: 78–91).
6 For example: http://art.unt.edu/medieval-symposium/2010_papers/Holland_2010.pdf.
7 The *Ellora Symphony*, by Japanese composer Yasushi Akutagawa (1925–1989), is a brilliant, contemporary invocation in sound of the atmosphere around the ancient site.
8 A good overview is at: *Ancient Silk Road Travellers*, www.silk-road.com/artl/srtravelmain.shtml.
9 On the Chinese pilgrim Xuanzang, see: www.iep.utm.edu/xuanzang/. All three monks are described here: http://afe.easia.columbia.edu/special/travel_records.pdf; see also the website on 'Buddhist Pilgrims' maintained by the Victoria and Albert Museum: www.vam.ac.uk/content/articles/b/buddhist-pilgrims/.
10 See the dedicated website on Faxian at: http://acc6.its.brooklyn.cuny.edu/~phalsall/texts/faxian.html.

An ocean of emptiness – and a steppe in time   39

11 These were destroyed, in one of the greatest acts of myopic cultural vandalism, by the Taliban in 2001; see UNESCO website on the Bamiyan valley, at: http://whc.unesco.org/en/list/208.
12 A similar figure appears in Patry Leidy (2008) at Fig. 2.8, page 42 and Fig. 2.10, page 44; a Gandhara bodhisattva (Buddha-in-the-making) is in Lowenstein (2006: 41); many other examples of Hellenistic art in Central Asia are collected in BOZAR (2010: 100–105). The British Museum has a Gandhara bodhisattva (OA 1880.72) The Ashmolean Museum displays a Gandhara-style Buddha figure in Gallery 12 (*India to AD 600*). See also: www.metmuseum.org/toah/hd/haht/hd_haht.htm.
13 The Asia Society Museum, New York showcased Gandhara art in an exhibition on *The Buddhist Heritage of Pakistan: Art of Gandhara*, between 9 August and 30 October 2011 (http://sites.asiasociety.org/gandhara/).
14 On the Kushan Empire, see the article at: www.metmuseum.org/toah/hd/kush/hd_kush.htm.
15 See: http://sites.asiasociety.org/gandhara/exhibit-sections/buddhas-and-bodhisattvas/.
16 Collecting Gandhara sculpture was popular with British soldiers and officials on the Northwest Frontier.
17 Another fine example is in the Ashmolean Museum in Oxford (EAOS.26).
18 Other Silk Road-related objects in the collection may be found, for instance, at numbers 49, 55, 59, 74.
19 See: www.britishmuseum.org/explore/highlights/highlight_objects/asia/t/silk_princess_painting.aspx.
20 See: 'Women in World History': www.womeninworldhistory.com/silk-road-13.html.
21 The 'Religions on the Silk Road' website is instructive: http://depts.washington.edu/silkroad/exhibit/religion/religion.html.
22 At: http://nalandauniv.edu.in/abt-chairman-msg.html.
23 Earlier scholarly estimates (e.g. Sen, 1954: 100; Sankalia, 1972: 195–196) give a figure of between 3,000 and 5,000 students.
24 Such as *Vikramaśilā, Somapura, Odantapuri* and *Jaggadala* (Sen, 1954: 109; Sankalia, 1972: 196).

3 Hearts and souls – silver and spice – missionaries and Mandarins

Portuguese knowledge management and Jesuit missionary enterprise in Asia

Introduction: mission and diplomacy in the age of 'empires'

This chapter seeks to evaluate whether some roots of modern 'European Studies in Asia' can conceivably be found in the experiences of the Jesuit Order in the East from the sixteenth to eighteenth centuries, and through the impact of Jesuit missionary leaders, and their disciples. The main focus here is on China, India and Japan, and there is a deliberate emphasis on the activities of *Portuguese* Jesuits during the first European Empire in Asia. I am highlighting the Lusitanian mission since the Portuguese represented the largest contingent of Jesuits in Asia. Owing to the *padroão* system (see below), Portuguese Jesuits were sent to Asia more swiftly than those of other nationalities. Notwithstanding this, it should be borne in mind that many prominent Jesuits were *not* Portuguese.

In addition to reasons of numbers and national origin, I chose to emphasize the activities of Portuguese missionaries on account of the rich body of Portuguese resources, and because the Portuguese form of colonialism and Jesuit mission have, in the view of some observers, made the 'greatest contribution to the scientific knowledge of the world since Roman times' (e.g. Newitt, 2009: 65). Furthermore, the Portuguese Empire both showcases and prefigures the role of concepts like 'globalization' and 'knowledge transfer', germane to the study of pre-modern international and Asia–Europe relations. Thus, Wright finds (2005: 69–70) that it was the missions and the contemporary European debates about European expansionism 'which laid the groundwork for all scholarly meditations about international relations that came afterwards'.

In addition to this, the closer investigation of the Portuguese Seaborne Empire can connect notions of cultural exchange with wider ideas, such as 'power', 'control' and 'censorship', which, in today's political parlance, may be subsumed within a social-constructivist research programme focusing primarily on 'values' and 'ideas' (see Chapter 1). Last but not least, the Portuguese colonial model of crown-monopoly (and private) capitalism provided important templates for the later commercial ventures of the Dutch, English, French and other Europeans, even though those were operated on the basis of different monopolies and 'East India Companies'. Last but not least, this chapter examines two larger aspects of 'learning' and 'knowledge-based exchange', which have essential repercussions for the success or failure of European Studies in Asia in our own time. The chapter highlights the production, dissemination and control of 'Asian' knowledge by Europeans of this period. This will be done through the lens of the Portuguese Empire, and the study of both religious and non-religious sources which became keystones of a Portuguese European Studies legacy.

Jesuit presses and libraries, colleges (*colégios* and smaller *casas*), seminaries and school foundations played a vital part in this, from the foundation of the Jesuit Order in September 1540, to the reforms of Sebastião de Carvalho (the Marquês de Pombal) from the mid-1750s onwards, following the Lisbon Earthquake of 1755. The Society of Jesus was abolished in 1773, by decree *Dominus ac Redemptor noster* of Pope Clement XIV (Davies, 1996: 594). This left the missionary activity of the Jesuits in disarray, but also opened up opportunities for the subsequent foundation of secular schools and universities. Moreover, the abolition of the order never entailed the complete disappearance of Christianity in Asia. Following the restoration of the order in 1814, Jesuit educational and publication activities continued. The power of religion and of the written word still helps to determine agendas of European Studies in Asia.

The chapter also offers an analysis of what may be called the 'education of the educators', i.e. the training of the Jesuits themselves. The starting point here is the attitude of many Jesuit missionaries which sometimes stood in contrast to official Crown priorities and laws of the time: the view that Europe had much to learn from the cultures and civilizations of the East. Many Jesuit commentators understood that Asia had its own antiquity, although Eastern historical legacies were sometimes mis-attributed to Western agency in the euro-centric manner common at the time (Lach and Van Kley, 1994, Vol. II, Book 1: 191; Vol. II, Book 3: 565). The Jesuits, nevertheless, pioneered a teaching technique in Asia that may be popularly summarized as *going native*: accommodation, adaptation, integration, peaceful penetration and persuasion became the fulcrums of educational and cultural exchange with the East during the Lusitanian Empire. This was aided by what may well have been the first-ever unified curriculum underpinning European Studies in Asia, the *ratio atque institutio studiorum Societas Iesu*. This demanding academic programme was experienced by all Jesuits at first hand – and passed on in lecture theatres in Asia by those who went there.

Both this curriculum and the method of accommodation proved highly contentious. However, they both also helped to produce a wider legacy of cultural relativism which has contributed to the modern shape of European Studies in Asia. It may be précised like this: teaching the West in the East will be successful where it exhibits local relevance and an informed, yet critical, familiarity with regional conditions. A closer scrutiny of Jesuit techniques can unlock the ways in which modern European teachers can successfully interact with international and Asian learners from various pedagogic, cultural and religious backgrounds.

The Portuguese Empire as a channel of East–West knowledge transfer

The enabling conditions which allowed the small nation of Portugal to maintain an empire stretching to South America, Africa, India, South East Asia, China and Japan have already been investigated in a previous context (Wiessala, 2011) and cannot be repeated here. However, a few key points may be recalled, before examining some sources. Although, the Lusitanian activities in Asia never exceeded 10,000 men at any time, these men benefited from the existence of very advanced maritime technology (Cotterell, 2010: 3–10, 19), which enabled them to insert themselves readily into existing Asian trade patterns.

Furthermore, the Portuguese undoubtedly gained from the presence of an exceptional number of charismatic, resourceful, Iberian–European individuals, such as Fernão Gomes, Diogo Cão, Bartolomeu Dias, Fernão de Magalhães, Vasco da Gama, Francisco d'Almeida, Alfonso de Albuquerque, Ferdinand Magellan, Pêro da Covilhã, Pedro Alvares Cabral, Matteo Ricci and Ignatius Loyola, to name just a few of the traveller-explorers to Africa, India and beyond (Cronin, 1961; Fritze, 2002: 188; Howgego, 2009: 48–52). The southward, then eastward, imperial progress of these individuals would always be marked by the erection of a carved stone pillar, called a *padrão*.[1] The actions of these figurehead-explorers were underpinned by support structures of Portuguese law and governance, and heavily promoted by royal patronage of figures like Prince Henry ('The Navigator', 1394–1460), Dom João III and his brother Dom Luís.

This chapter argues that they were also controlled by strict censorship of 'Asian' knowledge, and furthered by the arrangement of the geopolitical investiture of royal patronage (known as *ius patronatus*, *patronato real*, *padroado* or *padroão*), which Pope Leo X had granted to the Portuguese in 1514. The term denotes a symbiotic relationship of 'patronage' between the papacy, the Portuguese Catholic Church and the Portuguese Crown of the time. In this arrangement, many rights and rewards of colonial industry were shared out for mutual, often exploitative, benefit, and the Iberian powers received the right to control both trade and clerical appointments.

All key participants in the *Estado Português da Índia*, centred on Goa, were paid servants of the Crown, which was afforded the revenues and privileges in Portugal and overseas, in return for financing the overall missionary enterprise. Lach illuminates this shrewd reciprocal relationship as follows:

> The Crown was granted the use of certain ecclesiastical revenues within Portugal, and the right to propose candidates for the papacy for the Sees and ecclesiastical benefices in Africa and the Indies. Such a concession hinged on the condition that that the Crown would assume responsibility for providing good missionaries and the appropriate financial support for the religious establishments and activities in the territories acquired by conquest.
> (Lach and Van Kley, 1994, Vol. I, Book 1: 230; see also: Newitt, 2009: 70)

This initial trading system of royal monopolies later changed to free trade and then into a system of voyage 'concessions' (D'Ávila Lourido, 1996: 85). At the beginning of the sixteenth century, however, the *padrão* ruled supreme: it was legitimized by the Bull *Inter Caeterae Divinae* by Pope Alexander VI, and further underpinned by successive treaties at Alcáçovas (1479), Tordesillas (1494) and Saragossa (1529). These 'sliced the world like an orange' (BOZAR, 2010: 167), created new jurisdictional boundaries and divided all 'un-explored' global spheres of influence between Spain and Portugal, the powers of the day, until they were united under the same king, Philip II of Spain, in 1580 (Brotton, 2002: 164; van der Cruysse, 2002a: 19; Newitt, 2009: 80).[2] Brotton (2012: 186) calls the treaty 'one of the earliest and most hubristic acts of European global imperial geography', while Russell-Wood (1998: 20–21) stresses an important consequence of Tordesillas: the Portuguese ability to 'put to good use the enormous data bank they had accumulated' – often through diplomacy.

The results of this global Portuguese maritime diplomacy were assiduously compiled in books such as the multi-volume *Livros das Pazes e Tratados da India*, which enclosed all the treaties signed by the Portuguese with rulers in India, East Africa and Asia, as well as with European powers from 1571 to 1856. As to the Portuguese Empire's methods of conquest, Gordon (2008: 160) distinguishes Portuguese strategy from the Ming naval voyages of the Chinese admiral Zheng He, a century earlier (1405–1433), comparing them, instead, to the methods of Genghis Khan (see Chapter 1): 'seize the trading cities, and the important resources, destroy resistance, tax trade and make conquest pay for itself'.

Finally, Newitt argues (2009: 69) that the Portuguese maritime empire (*Estado da Índia*) which emerged from 1505, did, in fact, bring forth a new, and truly revolutionary, international relations concept, in which *the Oceans themselves* became part of Portuguese *Staatsgebiet* (realm, territory). The resulting legal constructs of maritime sovereignty and *mare clausum* (a 'closed' sea) were tested by events such as the Dutch capture, in 1603, of the Portuguese carack *Santa Catarina* (van der Cruysse, 2002a: 37–38). The *Santa Catarina* incident shaped the work of a generation of European jurists – for example, of Hugo Grotius. A vehemently anti-Portuguese Grotius argued in his essay *De iure praedae commentarius* ('Commentary on the Law of Seizure', 1868) that the sea was, indeed, a *mare liberum*: open and free to all[3] (van der Cruysse, 2002b: 271). Challenging Portuguese naval supremacy, his work, later published as *Mare Liberum Sive de Iure Quod Batavis Competit ad Indiana Commercia* ('The Open Seas, or the Right of the Dutch to Trade in the Indies') laid important foundations stones for international law – reaped mainly by the later Dutch entrance into the East India trade (see Chapter 4).

God's soldiers[4]: empire, the Jesuit missionary enterprise and its educational context

From its inception at the *Collège de Sainte-Barbe* in Paris and its foundation in 1540, the Catholic Jesuit Order (Society of Jesus, *Societas Iesu*) formed an integral part of both empire and the European Counter-Reformation (c.1600–1650). Jesuits have often been called the *corps d'élite* of Catholic reform (Davies, 1996: 496) and they had 'mission new worlds' enshrined at the very heart of its constitution. Wright (2004: 31) reminds us of one of the order's 'mission statements' of 1552: 'to search out the hidden venom of heretical doctrine and to refute it, and then to re-plant the uprooted trunk of the tree of faith'. Proselytizing thus promised a harvest of souls in Asia. It could also offset the 'losses to heresy in Europe' (Mitchell, 1980: 75).

Against this background, the order operated in a military manner, under papal command, and in parallel with the Council of Trent (1545–15623). Like the Council, it aimed at the religious invigoration and a 're-Catholicization' of the empire. Pope Paul III had convened the Council in 1545, at the insistence of the Holy Roman Emperor Charles V. Its aims were 'to reform the Church from within and formalize a coherent refutation of the Lutheran Reformation' (Brotton, 2002: 121). Ringmar (2007: 163) formulates the Council's theological climate-change as follows: 'What previously had been regarded as doctrines tentatively entertained now became official dogmas, and many ideas that hitherto had been freely discussed were banned.'

The Inquisition set to work, rooting out heresies and one author after another was placed on the *Index* of forbidden books. The Council's conclusions significantly expanded papal powers; they were largely conservative.[5] The Jesuit Order was to be both instrumentalized and controlled much more tightly. Next to the papacy, Jesuits had always been linked to imperial Portuguese expansion. Disney (2009: 201) characterizes the 'special relationship' between Jesuit missionaries and Portuguese colonial bureaucracy very perceptively:

> As an international organisation with special loyalty to the Pope, the Society of Jesus had its headquarters in Rome; but in Asia and East Africa in the sixteenth and early seventeenth centuries, it was obliged to work within the context of the Portuguese *padroado*, and to co-operate closely with the secular authorities of the *Estado da Índia*.

The establishment of the 'Holy Inquisition' in Europe from 1536 undoubtedly influenced the levels of tolerance and coerciveness towards Hindus and Muslims in Asia of both the Crown and the government, and of the missionaries themselves, albeit to a lesser degree in the case of the latter. Nevertheless, in official Portuguese policy of the time, the European mediaeval religious loyalty principle of *cuius regio eius religio* transferred easily into the mind-sets of many who worked in the Asian context of this period (Boxer, 1969: 73). Calculating the 'religious component of Empire', as Wright reminds us (2004: 102), 'has always been a messy business'. In the Portuguese case, the term *missionary enterprise* designates the inter-woven legal, religious and mercantile dimensions of power.

Furthermore, Lusitanian culture of the time embraced a powerful identification with the aims and objectives of Portuguese colonialism, nationalism and missionary effort. This was, perhaps, most persuasively expressed by the poet and traveller in Asia Luiz Vaz De Camões (1524–1580) in his epic poem *The Lusiads* (*Os Lusíadas*) (Camões, transl. White, 1997: ix, xvii; Severy and Stanfield, 1992). Others, such as the humanist, chronicler and 'publicist of empire' (Lach and Van Kley, 1994, Vol. II, Book 2: 15) Damião de Góis (1502–1574), became influential in communicating the successes of the Portuguese overseas endeavours to a wider European intellectual public, not at times without falling foul of the Portuguese Inquisition, it seems (Newitt, 2009: 119, and below).

Portuguese nationalistic notions also transferred to a wider context, in which Europeans of the period perceived the East in imaginary – rather than real – terms, guided by the wishful thinking and the fantasy-literature of the day. They were looking for allies in the struggle against Islam among the Mongols or within the realm of an imaginary Christian ruler in India, a favourite staple of mediaeval folklore (*Prester John*) (Wright, 2004: 104; Pagden, 2008: 292–293; Wiessala, 2011: 31–32). The *Prester John* myth was based on a (faked) letter of 1165 and is linked to similar imaginings like the *Travels of Sir John Mandeville*, and the romances surrounding Alexander the Great (Stoneman, 2008: 83–84). Thus, in the Portuguese spice race (*Carreira da Índia*), Lusitanian identity, global commerce, mythology and mission went hand-in-hand: 'God was omnipresent, as well as mammon' (Boxer, 1969: 65).

The Jesuit letter-books: word-pictures for Europe and the Republic of Letters

The written contributions which the Catholic Orders, especially the Jesuits,[6] made to the systematization, transmission and interpretation of 'Eastern' knowledge cannot be underestimated: 'in all climes and vicissitudes, Jesuit pens were busy scribbling reports of unique value' (Mitchell, 1980: 161). Jesuit notions about curricula and teaching sowed the seeds of many modern European education systems, and of the discipline of European Studies in Asia. The Jesuits, it has often been said (e.g. Clarke, 1997: 40), were the 'first Orientalists', whose writings profoundly affected the European mind of the Enlightenment. Their practice of regular reporting and letter-writing, Hsia claims (2009: 14–15), was deeply engrained in the Jesuit foundation document, the *Constitutions*. They were also an institutional management-tool which helped to knit together a growing, complex organization. Moreover, as Laven (2011: 13) adds, 'the order's sense of community and identity was energetically reinforced through the practice of letter-writing'.

McNeely and Wolverton (2009: 29, 122) emphasize a third, important, aspect: Jesuit epistolary communications formed an integral part of the European 'Republic of Letters' (*Respublica Litteraria*), and the Jesuits were both its citizens and its mediators. This concept denotes an early version of educational globalization: an international community of learning connected by letters, printed books, journals and other sources. The Republic of Letters may have been 'largely an imagined community' (Burke, 2000: 19–20, 48). However, the exchanges within this figurative polity during the European Renaissance and

Reformation transcended religious and national boundaries, and helped to delineate what it was like to be 'European', 'Western' and a 'Scholar'. The concept also explained how the West could learn from the East. The Republic of Letters was thus about the spread of knowledge, personal encounters and locations, seats of learning and meeting places as crossroads of knowledge. This chapter, as well as those that follow, aims to demonstrate how this concept played out in the context of early modern international relations between Asia and Europe.

In terms of the writings of the Jesuit Order, Pope Paul III had mandated the Basque soldier-mystic Íñigo López de Recalde (Ignatius Loyola, 1491–1556) in 1540 with its inauguration, through the Bull *Regimini Militantis Ecclesiae*. Loyola, author of the *Spiritual Exercises* and first 'General' of the order, assembled a group of ten fellow restless spirits, among them Francis Xavier (1506–1552), the 'Apostle of the Indies'. Xavier lost no time, and, following mediation by King João III of Portugal, left for Goa, the Portuguese stronghold in India, in 1542, taking with him pictures and statues as teaching aids. The order realized the 'tremendous potential of pictorial images as a means of propagating their faith' (Kao, 1991: 252–253, 255; Laven, 2011: 228), and key Jesuits such as Giuseppe Castiglione (Lang Chining, 1688–1766), Francis Xavier, Michele Ruggieri (1543–1607) and Nicolas Trigault employed devotional art, and were linked to a 'sinicized', Western painting style embodied in the figure of missionary-artist Castiglione (Kao, 1991: 267–269; Witek, 2011: 171).[7]

Francis Xavier also recommended that the Office of the Holy Inquisition be brought to Goa, 'in order to check the morals and religion of the Portuguese' (Mitchell, 1980: 81). It arrived in 1560, and developed intense activity. Murphy reports (2013: 166) that the Inquisition conducted some 16,000 trials in Goa, sentencing some 3,800 people and burning 114 of them at the stake. Francis Xavier's personality cult began in the Saint's lifetime. In Mitchell's words (1980: 78), he was 'early encrusted with legend'. Freeman (2011: 256) reports how one of his arms was brought back to Rome as a relic, while Wright (2004: 1) reports the apocryphal – slightly gruesome – story of the Portuguese noblewoman who bit a toe off Xavier's corpse in 1554 – a memento well worth having at a time when relics were a vast, lucrative industry (Freeman, 2011). In terms of Xavier's legacy, Lach proposes (Lach and Van Kley, 1994, Vol. I, Book 1: 247) that, 'it was with Xavier's appearance in India that the Jesuits became the acknowledged leaders of the Christian missionary effort within the *padroão*'. A militantly Christian but accommodative, action-oriented, scholastic approach to evangelizing, and the aim of instruction for 'spiritual renewal', emerged early on as twin foci of the Jesuit enterprise; its principles were based in the order's Constitution.

More than 200 of Francis Xavier's own epistles, diaries and letter-books survive. They are a mirror of both Portuguese society and Jesuit missionary attitudes at the time. Francis Xavier, for example, emerges from his writings, as 'an early discoverer of the moral contradictions at the heart of Western Christian evangelism within a framework of colonial exploitation' (Mullet, 1999: 98). Other Jesuits, such as Alessandro Valignano (1539–1606), the Jesuit Vice-General

('Visitor') who arrived in India in 1542, shaped the mission in Goa, Malacca, Macao and Japan, where he landed in 1549. He did so through his individual efforts and by his writings, especially his *Apología* (1598), his three volumes entitled *Summaria* (1577, 1580, 1583) and his longer works like *De missione legatorum Iaponensium* and *Historia del principio y progresso de la Compañia de Jésus en las Indias Orientales*. These works, and many others like them, were infused by their author's deep conviction that all Jesuit activities in Asia should benefit from an infrastructure, a curriculum and language study, modelled on Jesuit organizations in Europe.

The Jesuit letter-books (i.e. compilations of letters written by the Jesuit missionaries), reports, diaries, travelogues, mission histories, epistolary communications and other collateral data published from the *colégios* in Évora, Coimbra, Alcalá, Lisbon, Paris, Bruges, Rome, Goa and elsewhere from the middle of the sixteenth century onwards are a veritable treasure-trove of information on the products, arts, cultures and societies of Asia. The establishment of the Congregation for the Propagation of the Faith (*Sacra Congregatio de Propaganda Fide*) in 1622, by Pope Gregory XV (r. 1621–1623), while it facilitated independence, centralization and dissemination of Jesuit sources, also maintained surveillance over Catholic teachings abroad (Lach and Van Kley, 1994, Vol. III, Book 1: 132).

Antwerp and Amsterdam, in particular, became marketplaces for commodities and ideas; nodes in the network formed by the trade in knowledge, especially in Jesuit materials (Burke, 2000: 63). For observers, such as Maillard (2008: 22–23), the Jesuit epistolary sources 'opened up a way to an era of interreligious dialogue' (*ouvraient la voie à une ère de questionnement interreligieux*). Moreover, Hobson comments (2004: 200): 'the many Jesuit books infused the European imagination, from the intellectual to the layperson and from the masses to some of Europe's monarchs'.

Whilst the Jesuit sources were more significant at the time than the few, contemporary, pictorial representations of the arts and cultures of Asia, the Jesuit letters (Maillard [2008: 22] uses the more precise term *récits épistolaires*) constituted, nevertheless, revealing *word-pictures* for Europe. These depictions truly stood out through their comprehensiveness, depth and vividness of coverage. Lach and Van Kley (1994, Vol. II, Book 1: 70; Book 2: 251) offer an insightful summary, providing a flavour of content and contradiction in the Jesuit chronicle-narratives:

> they were usually hostile to India, while appreciating the fact that the Hindus opposed Islam as well as Christianity. They blamed the 'delights' and 'delicacies' of India, like many Portuguese themselves, for undermining the virility and character of the Portuguese nation. They were unabashedly curious about the islands where most of the spices grew. Japan, which had been little more than an imaginary island to Ariosto, became a concrete reality by the end of the century. Until 1587, hopes ran high that Japan was about to accept Christianity, but Hideyoshi's change of attitude produced an

almost instantaneous spate of criticisms about the island empire. The success of the Jesuits in being received at the court of Akbar again raised hopes in the 1590s for the success of the Jesuit enterprise in India. Still, all of the states of Asia, like the nations of Europe, were judged by both the Jesuits and the [European] *letterati* to spend too much of their energy and substance on useless war [...].

This wide-ranging Jesuit reporting and correspondence system shows the Jesuit missionaries predominantly as transmitters of written information, only rarely as sources of knowledge about Asian visual arts, objects, products and culture. The framework of epistolary communications was meticulously managed and monitored by a central distribution office at the Jesuit church in Rome (the *Gesù*). The communications and their administration and (selective) publication constituted an early, fully networked, intelligence system unparalleled anywhere in Europe, except perhaps for Venice (Lach and Van Kley, 1994, Vol. I, Book 1: 315; Burke, 2000: 123–124). McNeely and Wolverton (2009: 146) describe the German Jesuit Athanasius Kircher (1602–1680), who 'sat like a spider at the centre of the world's largest missionary and correspondence network in Rome, that of the Jesuits'. Key documents were collected, in annual series (*litterae annuae*) and unauthorized versions, by European intellectuals; they were translated into Latin and other European languages. Many were illegally intercepted, often at great risk and in the face of Iberian censorship (see below). The *cartas* (letters) of Évora, for instance (1598), remain a noteworthy collection, even today. Some of these compendia were collectively known as *Indian Letters* and *Japan Letters* (see Chapter 4).

Lach and Van Kley (1994, Vol. III, Book 3: 1546) note another significant aspect of the Jesuit letter-books:

> the more detailed accounts were intended for the enlightenment of the Jesuits in Europe who were potential recruits for the mission. The shorter versions were issued in larger numbers for popular consumption. To appeal to their readers, the Jesuit letters, and the books compiled from them, include mundane, as well as missionary materials.

These latter versions, in particular, conveyed to the European public a new picture – albeit an incomplete one – of the 'East', displacing some entrenched stereotypes of the day. In the context of the Counter-Reformation, they also possessed significant propaganda-value, seeking to demonstrate the continuing dynamism and outgoing appeal of the Catholic Faith vis-à-vis Lutheranism and the perceived threat of the Ottoman Turks and other foes. Jesuit missionary reports, as Mitchell states (1980: 74), could thus be used, 'to bring funds, recruits and prestige' (See Appendix 1: *The European revelation of Asia and the odyssey of the Orient: selected Portuguese writings on the East*).

The power of knowledge: Lusitanian information control and censorship

Knowledge, as the saying goes, is power. The Portuguese colonial authorities maintained a strict system of censorship and information control in regard to what they learned in the East, maintaining, with varying success rates it has to be said, an 'information-monopoly', next to a religious and economic one (Curtin 2000: 16; Lach and Van Kley, 1994, Vol. I, Book 1: 151, 154, 230). The controlling mechanisms of the *Estado da Índia*, the *padroão* system, the Jesuit curriculum (*ratio studiorum*), the (Portuguese) Inquisition (from 1540) and the Treaty of *Tordesillas* worked hand in glove, as it were, to keep the rest of Europe in the dark about the world beyond their borders. The frequent collusion of royalty in this censorship – for instance, by King João II (r. 1481–1495) and Prince Henry the Navigator (1394–1460) – thus sustained 'a system of discovery and commerce that was exclusive and monopolistic' (Lach and Van Kley, 1994, Vol. I, Book 1: 151–152). The portolan-charts, *mappae mundi* and ships' logs detailing Portuguese routes to the East became *Herrschaftswissen* (power-bestowing-knowledge), whilst, at the same time, Portuguese galleons maximized the advantages of Europe's gunpowder revolution and artillery (Severy and Stanfield, 1992: 79; *Der Spiegel*, 2009: 56).

Secrets such as these materials were jealously guarded in the *Casa da Índia*, in the Lisbon chartrooms on the River Tagus and at Henry's headquarters-cum-naval academy in Ságres (Severy and Stanfield, 1992: 72). Much historical evidence does, indeed, point to a near-total 'news-blackout', covering even specialized branches of knowledge, such as botany (Russell-Wood, 1998: 154–155; Febvre and Martin, 2010: 278). In 1504, King Manuel decreed the penalty of death, over betraying issues of Portuguese navigation. Consequently, during the first half of the sixteenth century, not a single work on the Portuguese discoveries in Asia is known to have been published in Portugal.

In terms of books, the (Portuguese branch of the) Inquisition, as well as civil authorities, colluded in the construction of what can be seen as a three-tier filter system: any books, reports and other new materials were subjected to the control of the Portuguese High Court of Justice (*Desembargo do Paço*), the bishops and the 'Holy Office' of the Inquisition herself. This scheme was in force for nearly 300 years. It was applied especially strictly to materials shipped in from abroad, both from Europe and from the Lusitanian Eastern Empire. Some unfortunate writers, such as Fernão Lopes de Castanheda, even had to withdraw publications about Asia which were already in print (Lach and Van Kley, 1994, Vol. I, Book 1: 152–154). The books which did appear were, more often than not, translations into other European languages, and Portuguese originals, diverted and smuggled out of the country by paid informers and spies – often under dramatic, and adventurous, circumstances.

'Barbarians for the love of god'[8] – Jesuit accommodation and religious salesmanship

The missionary enterprise of the Jesuits in Asia has rightly been described as comprehensible only against the background of some important foundational principles derived from both Italian and European humanism and from the *Spiritual Exercises* of Ignatius of Loyola (Ross, 1994: 204). Following Jesus entailed *missio*, i.e. 'outreach', and being a missionary implied cultural adaptation, because Jesus adapted himself to the human condition.[9] The resulting Jesuit version of humanism, which prospered from the late fifteenth century, accentuated discursive methodologies such as disputation and adaptation. Moreover, integration and acquisition of language competence were vital evangelical tools (Ross, 1994: 204; Lach and Van Kley, 1994, Vol. I, Book 1: 279; Pina, 2001: 63; Kiechle, 2009: 32–33; Brockey, 2007: 7–8).

The missionaries' inter-cultural approach aimed at sustained, flexible dialogue with Asian elite and at the parallel conversion of the masses; a dialogue that was, furthermore, adapted to local conditions as required (see below, and Brockey, 2007: 7–8, but also 47–48; Clements, 2005: 15–16). Da Silva Tavares (2004: 128) has characterized Jesuit missionaries as 'cultural intermediaries' (*Os Jesuítas como Mediadores Culturais*). Scholars like Ross and Hsia (Ross, 1994: 170–171, 203; Hsia, 1998: 186–187) derive the intricacies of the Jesuits' method of 'sweet conversion' (*il modo suave*) largely from the writings of Alessandro Valignano – for instance, his *Il Ceremoniale per I missionary del Giappone*. The Jesuit approach contrasted starkly with the uncompromising Spanish methods of enforced 'Hispanicization' in the Philippines, aiming to make them an *almacén de la fe* (a 'storehouse of the faith'; Villiers, 1998: 128). Mullet (1999: 24–25) argues that the Jesuits were simply proficient users of the mass media and 'social media' of the day, adept at deploying advanced techniques of salesmanship, promotion, advertising and publicity.

Christine Maillard (2008: 22–23) quotes the Italian Jesuit Roberto de Nobili (1577–1656) as a prime example of the Jesuit approach. In his two principal texts on India, *Informatio de quibusdam moribus nationis indicae* (1613) and *Narratio fundamentorum quibus Madurensis institutum caeptum est et hujusque consistir* (1616–1619), de Nobili warns against imposing unto autochthonous cultures what is alien to them, advocating instead a measured cultural assimilation – through dress, diet, way of life and the adoption of indigenous names – in order to adapt Western teachings to Eastern audiences and gain admission to the autochthonous, mental universe. (Maillard's French text [2008: 23–24] is much more precise: '*afin de gagner les indigenes au message chrétien, il convient de ne pas leur imposer ce qui leur est étranger, mais de s'assimiler à eux afin de mieux acceder à leur univers mental*').

De Nobili was, perhaps, a more extrovert example of 'going native' – Russell-Wood reports (1998: 201) that, in attempting to reconcile Christian and Hindu teachings in South India, he went as far as dressing as a Hindu *sannyasi* guru, calling himself a Brahmin, learning Tamil and Sanskrit and anointing his body.

Clarke (1997: 51) remarks that de Nobili's chosen way of linguistic/hermeneutic accommodation between Eastern and Christian scriptures was inevitably, unusually, transgressive of the bounds of religious orthodoxy of the time (see also: Lach and Van Kley, 1994, Vol. III, Book 1: 150–151; Vol. III, Book 2: 1012–1017, 1095; Mullet, 1999: 194–195). Finally, Mitchell (1980: 160) is more direct: 'a wild, almost Faustian, streak of intellectual arrogance made him a liability to the Society...'

Notwithstanding numerous individual idiosyncrasies, many Jesuit missionaries strove hard to *be* Chinese, Hindu or Japanese; in the process, they became, in Mitchell's memorable phrase, 'chameleons of God'. They both embodied and promoted a key aspect of pedagogy which cannot be underestimated: Peterson states this most clearly (2011: 79): 'they presented the essentials of their learning as universal', claiming a worldwide understanding. By the end of the sixteenth century, the Jesuit missionaries had become convinced that cultural association was the one indispensable key to acceptance amongst the contemporary Asian elites.

The fact that this cultural affiliation was frequently mutual can be seen in the development of a distinct, Baroque-inspired, 'Jesuit' art style in this period. Rome became 'a honeycomb of commissions and a beehive of artistic energy' (Hsia, 1998: 155). Missionaries used murals and paintings to convey their messages in Asia. In addition to this, many artworks borrowed heavily from Eastern architecture, and Hindu and Chinese art, as indeed Asian art borrowed from Europe (Lee, 1991a). Notwithstanding this Jesuit concern for the didactic value of art in the service of religion, the members of the order actually did little to disseminate the visual representations of life and cultures in the East available at the time (Lach and Van Kley, 1994, Vol. II, Book 1: 62, 67; Bailey, 2001; see also above, and Chapters 4 and 5). Lach and Van Kley (1994, Vol. I, Book 1: 250) offer the following précis of the Jesuits' 'peaceful penetration' of Asian societies:

> to win Muslims and Hindus to Christianity, they preached in the squares; they disputed publicly with Brahmans and Mullahs; they sang the catechism to a popular tune in public places; they permitted heathens and Muslims to attend mass; and they had their students hold sermons in Konkani on Sundays and holidays.

Many Jesuit *colégios* and *casas* (smaller teaching establishments) began by teaching basic skills and literacy, before moving on to subjects like theology, mathematics, music and philosophy – all the time transmitting key Catholic tenets. Jesuit teachers such as Alessandro Valignano advocated a policy of accommodation in China and Japan (albeit, notably, not in India; see below). Boxer (1969: 66) critiques the 'carrot-and-stick-methods' of the Portuguese colonial administrators, in Asia and at home. In seeking to work with the colonial bureaucracy, the Jesuit mission displayed varying degrees of collusion, accommodation, toleration and resistance, both overt and covert. The terms of the *padroão* system necessitated a Church that displayed both military vigour and economic acumen. In the Spanish Philippines, the Jesuit *programme of cultural affiliation* was directly challenged and rivalled by the *doctrine of direct action* preferred by many Spanish conquistadors and missionaries (Boxer, 1969: 64, 78; Lach and Van Kley, 1994, Vol. I, Book 1: 299, 329; Brockey, 2007: 106–107). Ross (1994: 206) concludes his study with a critical assessment of the impact of the Jesuits' integrationist approach: 'what is certain is that the Europe of the Eighteenth Century, whether Catholic, Protestant or Deist, was not ready for it and could not understand it. To the arrogant imperialist expansionism of Nineteenth Century Europe it was nonsense.'

Box 3.1 Life of the mind[10] and life of the spirit: the Jesuit *ratio studiorum*

The Jesuits were known as the 'Schoolmasters of Europe'. Boxer points out (1969: 345), that: 'apart from their privileged positions at Coimbra and Évora, the Jesuits had a virtual monopoly of Higher Education through the network of the Higher Education *colégios* which the order established both in Portugal and throughout her maritime empire – from the Maranhão to Macao'. Russell-Wood (1998: 198) states that, 'other than the Colleges of the Society of Jesus, and religious orders, there were no institutions of higher education'.

The humanist education provided by the Jesuits through their colleges, especially in India and America, provided a formal setting for the transmission of ideas and concepts, albeit towards a limited audience. In classrooms and lecture theatres, the Jesuits both expanded and capitalized on their solid educational reputation by importing and consolidating a unified approach to learning (and thought control) which pervaded Jesuit seats of learning and presses world-wide. This approach was enhanced by the *esprit de corps* among the Jesuits. The pedagogical twin-challenges of having to 'go native' and to present 'universal' Christian truths at the same time became a key theme in Jesuit pedagogy in Asia and elsewhere. Bridging this intellectual gap was helped by the production of the main Jesuit pedagogical manual, the *ratio studiorum* ('plan of studies'), finalized in 1599.

This compendium of guidelines for Jesuit education formed part of a 'distinctive and influential pedagogical system' (Wright, 2005: 50). Its curriculum changed little throughout the sixteenth to the nineteenth centuries. It rested in the near-monopolistic influence the Jesuits gained in the educational arena in Portugal, for example, through control over colleges and public teaching, and by means of elevation of Jesuit colleges into universities (Boxer, 1969: 345). The *ratio* betrayed the classical roots of Jesuit learning and was also an expression of a widely propagated Jesuit principle – *give us a boy and we will return you a man – a citizen of his country and a child of God.*[11] At final graduation, this would yield good Christian-Humanists, virtuous citizens and 'eloquent, elegant, members of the secular world' (Wright, 2005: 51).

Instruction according to this programme was in Latin. For Brockey (2007: 8), this standardized syllabus demonstrates that 'the communal life of the men of the Society of Jesus in their colleges was as much a life of the mind as a life of the spirit'. The *ratio* was sub-divided into 'cycles', covering all the skills the missionaries would need for disputation and conversion 'in the field': 'Letters' (Latin, grammar, rhetoric, dialectic, poetry, history), 'Arts' (philosophy and science) and theology. The latter was deliberately deferred to the end in order to put in the 'ground-work' first, as it were. Brockey points out (2007: 222–223) that for the novice missionaries on an initial period of probation, it was teaching experience, above other techniques, that was seen as a vital preparation.

The similarities and differences between the *ratio studiorum* and the civil service examination system the Jesuits encountered, for example, in Ming and Qing China, was not lost on them. Matteo Ricci (1552–1610) and others commented on this extensively. The rules on examinations, for instance, of the *ratio studiorum*, stressed the public nature of the many *viva-voce* style exams. The Jesuit teaching method of the Paris Method (*modo parisiensis*) prized teaching and learning in the shape of 'pious competition' (Brockey, 2007: 215), through debates, role-plays, recitations and dialectic. In Laven's analysis (2011: 135), 'the transparency of this system was to be ensured by openness rather than seclusion'. But it seemed logo-centric.

By contrast, the Chinese placed a much higher emphasis on the written word. Many observers connect this to the nature of the Chinese polity: 'in the quest for order, debate was deemed counter-productive' (Laven, 2011: 137, 141). Nevertheless, Lach and Van Kley (1994, Vol. II, Book 3: 528) report that, into the official reading list for the *ratio studiorum*, kept at the Vatican Library and Printing Press, the Jesuit Michele Ruggieri asked the librarian in charge to incorporate his own, highly positive and influential, 'moral portrait' of the Chinese.

But the Jesuit *ratio studiorum* was also frequently dogmatic, inflexible, pedantic and formulaic, and it often relied on censorship (see above, and Boxer, 1969: 346). Perhaps this programme can be said to pre-refigure the scholarly debates about universities of our own time; for whilst it provided, for those who submitted to a Jesuit education, a set of what we may call 'transferable skills', it was far from encouraging a deep, independent analysis, debate and an intellectual independence and emancipation commensurate with the philosophical and scientific demands of the day. *Plus ça change...*

The Jesuits in India

The Jesuit mission in India was facilitated by Vasco da Gama's pioneering sea voyage, via the Cape, in 1498. It developed, from its bases in Goa and Malacca, captured by Alfonso de Albuquerque in 1510–1511, and it advanced on the back of the wider Lusitanian commercial project of the *Carreira da Índia* (the main Lisbon–Goa round-trip). The dynamic ascendancy and decline of the Catholic mission occurred in the 'wake of imperial incursion' (Wright, 2004: 4). It shadowed the rise and wane of overall Portuguese political and military power. The Portuguese carracks and frigates (*náos*) carrying silver, goods and missionaries to India included armed vessels such as the *Madre de Deus*. The Goa mission was greatly aided by the existence of the Saint Thomas Christians in India, who were believed to have been converted by Saint Thomas himself (Pearson, 1987: 119). Jesuit evangelizing was distinct by the family policy of the Portuguese, which encouraged the emergence of Luso-Indian families, to the consternation of many high-caste Hindus. But the Indian Jesuit presence was unique within the global Jesuit enterprise of the time, in at least three more ways.

First, the Indian case field demonstrated many of the discrepancies between the *padroão* Jesuits' approaches and those of the Portuguese Church and state. While the missionaries concentrated on making converts and building schools, rectories and colleges, the Church and Crown implemented many harsher policies, especially towards Muslims and those who were considered as 'heathens'. Lach and Van Kley (1994, Vol. I, Book 1: 237) argue that the presence of the latter could only be seen as a threat to the body politic of Portuguese India. Luiz Vaz De Camões (1524–1580) spent more than a decade in India, and he seized upon these tensions in his satirical work *Disparates na India* ('Follies in India').

Second, the stereotypes, racism and ignorance of the Jesuit missionaries, with regard to ancient Indian learning, often hampered a constructive missionary policy. Pearson (1987: 117) finds that, after 1540, 'intolerance became the theme', and Mitchell (1980: 158) speaks of an evolving Jesuit 'conquistador mentality'. There were exceptions, such as Francis Xavier, who arrived in 1542 (Mullet, 1999: 94–97). Overall, however, figures such as Alessandro Valignano thought little of Indian civilization; a deeper accommodation with Indian elites was thus not attempted.

By contrast with the Japanese, the Indians, as Alessandro Valignano saw them, had a limited capacity for 'the intellectual presuppositions of Western civilisation' (Moran, 1993: 97; Ross, 1994: 204–205; Lach and Van Kley, 1994, Vol. I, Book 1: 259; Mitchell, 1980: 158–159). Valignano did think more highly of the Japanese, believing them to be 'a people noble and rational' (Moran, 1993: 99, 101). He oversaw an official Japanese embassy to Europe in February 1582 (Moran, 1993: 6) in order to win support for the Jesuit mission. In spite of his bias, Valignano insisted the Japan Jesuits learn languages, organizing training seminars for this purpose. Moran points out (1993: 182) that this tangibly changed European attitudes to Japanese culture. Valignano also instructed those under his care 'not to yield to the desire to convince the Japanese of the superiority of European ways – for that is the seed-plot of much discord' (Moran, 1993: 176). Similarly, in India, he encouraged his missionaries to improve the accuracy of their letters and epistolary communications home.

Third, and notwithstanding these cultural stereotypes, Jesuit teaching at the Goa College and in other parts of India had a multi-cultural audience; a 'cosmopolitan lot of adolescent youths: Hindus, Sinhalese, Moluccans, Chinese, Japanese, Kaffirs and Ethiopians' (Lach and Van Kley, 1994, Vol. I, Book 1: 263). The Jesuits had brought a printing press – the first in Asia – to Goa in 1556, in a year in which the Jesuit college of St. Paul had 110 students (Mullet, 1999: 194). Ten years earlier, 11 nations were represented amongst the students of St. Paul's College, and there were many other mission stations throughout India and Ceylon.[12]

This was significant in terms of teaching Europe in Asia, since it gave the Jesuits posted there abundant opportunities to pursue policies of adaptation and to engage with remote, non-Western cultures. The overall, colonial Portuguese irruption into Asia shows a familiar pattern of presence in the periphery and minimal concern for the interior of countries such as China, India and Japan. The Jesuit missionaries, by contrast, reached numerous locations far away from the main Portuguese centres; the missionaries had little alternative other than to learn about the values and ways of others, thus developing a major character trait for teachers in Asia, which continues to reverberate today.

The relations between the Jesuit missionaries and the third Mughal Emperor, Akbar (r. 1556–1605; *Great Mogul*),[13] which commenced around 1580, represent, arguably, the most eloquent example of Jesuit approaches to knowledge transfer, expectations and misunderstandings which the Jesuit approach would engender in Asia. They also expose the underlying productive tension between 'identity' and 'alterity' (*tension productive entre identité et alterité*), which Maillard identifies (2008: 22). Emperor Akbar was genuinely curious, syncretic (or eclectic), in his religious choices, proclaiming that 'all religions are either equally true or equally illusionary'. Doniger (2010: 532–533) reports that:

> on one occasion, Akbar proposed to a group of Jesuits and Muslim theologians the test of walking through fire (somewhat like the test that a South Indian Shiva had proposed to the Jainas) in order to determine which was the true religion. But unlike the Jainas, the Jesuits (in the person of Father Aquaviva) refused. Sometime later, Hindus, seeking revenge for the destruction of some of their temples by Christian missionaries, murdered Aquaviva.

Claudio Aquaviva left behind numerous letters and was, arguably, one of the most prolific contemporary Jesuit writers on India, second only to Francisco Cabral (1528–1609). In 1601–1602, Akbar, who had first welcomed the Jesuit fathers, granted the Christians the right to proselytize, abolished the poll-tax on non-Muslims, sponsored art and built houses of worship. However, he never lost sight of a potential conquest of the *Estado da Índia* (Lach and Van Kley, 1994, Vol. III, Book 1: 147; Vol. III, Book 2: 631; Farrington, 2002: 56–57). Much like in the case of Japan (see Chapter 4), the Jesuits introduced European engravings, printing presses and paintings to Akbar's domain, during three missions in 1580–1583, 1591 and 1595–1605. They hoped the Emperor might be a potential convert – and become more prone to their influence – until they realized that Akbar continued to worship in both mosques and Hindu temples, and to participate in traditional fire rituals. His son Jahangir (r. 1605–1627) continued an artistic and intellectual tradition of exchange with Europeans.

Constantinian conversions and canonical controversies: the Jesuits in China

> Though the Jesuits essentially failed in their goals for the conversion of China, the mission remains an enlightened phase for East–West interaction.
> (Reed and Demattè, 2007: 67)

> Fine words and an insinuating appearance are seldom associated with true virtue.
>
> (Confucius, *The Analects* 1:3 and 17:17, found in: Laven, 2011: 138)

The first contingent of Portuguese had set foot on Chinese soil in 1513. Four years later, King Manuel I (r. 1495–1521) appointed Tomé Pires (see above) as first ambassador to the Ming Court. Pires arrived in 1520. His successors gained a tentative foothold in Macao, renting the peninsula from the Chinese from around 1557. Eventually, the Portuguese acquired a near-monopoly of the China–Japan silk and precious metals trade, circumventing the prohibition by the Ming dynasty (1368–1644) of direct Chinese trading with Japan. Chinese demand for inexpensive Japanese silver remained strong, as did, conversely, Japanese demand for silks and Chinese luxuries. Consequently, 'by ferrying Chinese silk to Japan, and Japanese silver to China, Portuguese merchants creamed off extraordinary profits from two nations that refused to do business directly' (Laven, 2011: 37). Subrahmanyam (1993: 277) even claims that:

> without the Society of Jesus, and Japanese silver, the history of the Portuguese in Asia would have been quite different in the Sixteenth and Seventeenth centuries; and in the final analysis, the Jesuits and Japanese silver came to have a complex historical interaction…!

This lucrative trading monopoly was in the hands of both the Macao merchants and the Jesuits, who reaped significant profits from the *nao do trato*, the ship sailing the Macao–Nagasaki route (Moran, 1993: 43–44); this was mirrored by a virtual Jesuit religious monopoly in Japan (see below). Wills (2011: 43) comments that, in Macao, 'the most powerful establishment – that of the Jesuits – was a great asset in diplomacy with the Chinese and controlled so much wealth that it became a major investor in foreign trade'. Like other observers (e.g. Laven, 2011: 102), Wills sagaciously emphasizes the importance of exchange of both intelligence, and objects, to construct the future cultural terrain of modern Asia–Europe diplomacy. The idea of the exchange of objects as a *conditio sine qua non* – an essential condition – of international relations will be taken up again in Chapter 5.

In relation to diplomacy, the overall rise and fall of the Jesuit mission in China was both inhibited and enabled by the outlook of successive Emperors in the transition from the Ming (1368–1644) to the (Manchu) Qing (1644–1911) dynasties. Responses ranged from toleration (by edict of the Kangxi Emperor in 1692) to tacit accommodation, to persecution. Waley-Cohen (2000: 57) suggests that among other aspects conditioning the reception of the Jesuit mission were the transition from the Ming to the Qing, the Jesuit method of 'scientific evangelization' – employing science as a 'lure' towards conversion – and the degrees of compatibility between Chinese and European intellectual traditions. Wright (2005: 65) has characterized this as 'accommodationist strategy' plus a 'pastoral of technology'. The mission was initially led by Alessandro Valignano and

Michele Ruggieri in Macao and Zhaoqing, to the west of Canton, and by Matteo Ricci in Peking.[14] Subsequently, mission centres were established in Hangzhou, Nanchang, Nanjing, Shaanxi and Shanxi (maps in: Brockey, 2007: 88, 122; Howgego, 2009: 112).

The China mission has been called the 'most distinctive and renowned of all the Jesuit enterprises of the 17th Century' (Lach and Van Kley, 1994, Vol. III, Book 1: 175), and it straddled the era from the Ming (1368–1644) to the (Manchu) Qing dynasties. There can be little doubt that it benefited from the Jesuits' Japan and India experiences, which had begun some decades before, although conditions in Ming dynasty China (1368–1644) could not have been more different from Japan and India in many ways. Wills (2011: 63) shows that the European missionaries 'gradually expanded their enterprise on the basis of a very Chinese network of publishing, friendship and patronage'. China was a unified Empire, with an ancient, assured and cohesive culture. The Jesuits' attempts to integrate Christianity into that high culture rested largely on the missionaries' view that the Chinese Empire 'could easily be fitted into Christian views about history, the universe and God' (Gelber, 2007: 124).

Jesuit evangelizing in China has been understood by most analysts as standing out, by means of its 'trickle-down-from-the-top-approach', targeting the elite. Notwithstanding the fact that this may be too simplistic an interpretation (Brockey, 2007: 47–48), the Jesuits went to great lengths to establish dialogue on equal terms with Chinese literati, in a culture which was declared to be at least as sophisticated as Western Christendom (Clarke, 1997: 41) and was 'bursting with otherness' (Wright, 2005: 84). Reed and Demattè (2007: 48) comment that, 'the Jesuits generally approached the Chinese as the equals of Europeans, both in the discourse they framed for European audiences and by their behaviour in China'. To this end, it was only natural that many Jesuits should become literati; many 'changed into Chinese dress and appearance, learned the Chinese language and manners, and studied Confucianism' (Gelber, 2007: 102).

The encyclopaedic writings of the Jesuit translator and musicologist Jean-Joseph-Marie Amiot (1718–1793)[15] are an eloquent testimony to this approach. Amiot was the official translator of Western languages for the Qianlong Emperor. His main work was the *Mémoires concernant l'histoire, les sciences, les arts, les moers, les usages &c. des Chinois, par les missionaires de Pékin* (publ.: 1776–1814; BWB, 2009: 72). Wright (2005: 85) quotes Amiot's writings in order to pin down the overall Jesuit pedagogic method:

> thus we try, in the interests of our religion, to gain the goodwill of the prince and to make our services so useful and necessary to him that in the end he will become more favourably inclined towards Christians, and persecute less than he has done.

The China mission was further distinguished by its artistic dimension, its anti-Buddhist and anti-Taoist tenor and its tolerant position in the 'rites controversy' (Lee, 1991b: 3–4; Wright, 2004: 118; Mormando and Thomas, 2006).[16] The emergence of the Chinese rites controversy has been traced (e.g. Hsia, 1998: 190–191) to the arrival of rival, Spanish missionaries from the Philippines from the 1630s onwards. The term is applied to the repercussions of the Jesuit toleration of Chinese ancestor-veneration, rituals in honour of Confucius and ritual rites of sacrifice (see below).[17] J.J. Clarke (1997: 41) points out that this policy of accommodation was in fact part of a much deeper hermeneutical engagement by the Jesuits with the religious ideas and practices of China – the 'appropriations of Chinese values, in order to bolster the Christian cause' (Laven, 2011: 202). This appeared necessary, since merely seeking to 'supplant' Confucianism with Christianity was too simplistic a method for dealing with a society as developed as the Chinese. The vexatious debate over what the Jesuits proclaimed were civic, not religious, rites causes disbelief even today. Witek, for example (2011: 177), comments, 'that the principles on in-culturation divided, so harshly at times, those who preached the love of God to the Chinese, perhaps, is difficult to fathom centuries later'.

This issue was by no means a light matter, since it touched on the very legitimacy both of the Chinese governing scholar-gentry class and of Chinese Emperors, who relied on an astronomical system called the *Grand Concordance* to order the realm. Both derived their ultimate authority from the twin wellsprings of Confucianism and ancestor worship. This conflict affected the Jesuit mission in China in many ways and, perhaps surprisingly, was only fully resolved with a decree issued by Pope Pius XII in 1939 (BWB, 2009: 13). Boxer (1969: 240) quotes the anger and bemusement of the Kangxi Emperor of the new Qing dynasty (r. 1661–1722)[18] upon reading a Chinese translation of the papal decree *Ex illa die* (1715) – which condemned the Chinese family rites as a form of idolatry:

> After reading this decree, I can only say that the Europeans are small-minded people. How can they talk of China's moral principles when they know nothing of Chinese customs, books or language which might enable them to understand them? Much of what they say and discuss makes one laugh. Today, I saw the Papal Legate [*Mezzabarba*] and the decree. He is really like an ignorant Buddhist or Taoist priest, while the superstitions mentioned are those of unimportant religions. This sort of wild talk could not be more extreme. Hereafter Europeans are not to preach in China. It must be prohibited in order to avoid trouble...

Notwithstanding threats, the Kangxi Emperor decreed the toleration of Christianity in 1692, and missionaries (except those serving at the court) were only expelled from China some time later, in 1717 (Kao, 1991: 261). The main Jesuit missionary figures of Michele Ruggieri (1543–1607), Matteo Ricci (1552–1610), Ferdinand Verbiest (1623–1688), (Johann) Adam Schall (von Bell, 1591–1666; see Chapter 1 and Appendix 2; Gelber, 2007: 103–105; Wiessala, 2011: 35–36; Witek, 2011: 135) and Francis Xavier loom large over the history of Jesuit evangelizing in China. However, there are also significant lesser-known Jesuit personalities, among them the musician, clock-maker and engineer Tomé Pereira (1645–1708; see Saraiva and Jami, 2008: xiii, 187–204). The impact of these missionaries continues to inspire a significant body of Asia–Europe scholarship. Beyond these debates, the evangelization of China demonstrates many unique features of the global Jesuit method and mythology. Lach encapsulates this ethos well, by stating:

> Nothing was more moving to the Jesuits and their artists in Europe than the conquests of Xavier in Asia and the story of his tragic death off the coast of China. This Christian Alexander, who fought the good fight without an army, died alone, almost like Christ himself, within sight of his ultimate goal. Episodes from the life and martyrdom of Xavier were painted on the walls of Jesuit chapels, houses, and colleges, as reminders to the faithful of the efficacy of sacrifice in realising the church triumphant.
>
> (Lach and Van Kley, 1994, Vol. II, Book 1: 71–72)

A closer scrutiny of the endeavours of the Jesuits in Macao, Beijing and rural China exhibits the same methods applied in the missions to India and Japan. Key figures like Matteo Ricci and Adam Schall (see Chapter 1 and Appendix 2) became linguistically competent and culturally literate in their host environments (cf. Pina, 2001: 63). Arriving in Chao-ch'ing, near Canton, in 1583, Ricci translated both Confucius and Euclid and compiled a first Portuguese–Chinese dictionary. He later created a world map, the *Kunyu wanguo quantu* (*Complete Map of all the Nations of the World*, 1602), suffused by Christian cosmology and the Ptolemaic system. Reed and Dematté (2007: 55, 71–87, 190–195) explain his motives: 'influenced by his understanding that the Christianization of the Roman Empire followed the conversion of the Emperor Constantine, Ricci believed that the conversion of China would likewise happen from the top down with the emperor's sanction'.

Serving this very purpose was Ricci's *magnum opus*, The True Meaning of the Lord (Master) of Heaven (T'ien-chu shih-I, Tianzhu shiyi), in 1596 (Lee, 1991b: 4; Pina, 2001: 65; Disney, 2009: 202; Gelber, 2007: 102, 123; Laven, 2011: 195–226).[19] This didactic catechism was organized dialogically, involving a Chinese and a European *literatus*. It has been said to have reflected the Jesuits' attempts to 'Catholicize' Confucianism (Mitchell, 1980: 156), presenting Christianity as a 'system of social ethics and individual morality profoundly consonant with Confucianism' – a 'fulfilment of Confucianism' (Ross, 1994: 166; Hsia, 1998: 187). Pagden claims (2008: 296) Ricci may have been 'responsible for the image of Confucianism we have today'. Reed and Dematté (2007: 30) posit that 'Confucianism in the strict sense was also regarded by some Jesuits in China much like a pre-Christian classical philosophy that was adapted in the mediaeval Scholastic synthesis – as a teaching that foreshadowed the Christian revelation'. In this context, it is perhaps not difficult to see how the main flaw of Ricci's *True Meaning of the Lord of Heaven* may have been his 'superimposition' of a 'personal god' onto the impersonal 'supreme heaven' of Chinese Confucianism (Laven, 2011: 221, 223).

That notwithstanding, the target audience of the text was elites and rulers, first and foremost, and the 'masses' at a later stage (Reed and Demattè, 2007: 30). Gregory (2003: 37) portrays the Jesuit method of this kind of 'Constantinian conversion' in China as follows: 'The Jesuit approach to the immense challenge of converting a sophisticated, highly literate culture such as China's was to present their Christian message in terms as far as possible consistent with the dominant beliefs and practices of that culture.' In doing so, the Jesuits made some high-profile concerts to their Learning from Heaven (*Tianxue*) among the Chinese literati and government officials, such as the literati Xu Guangqi (1562–1633), Li Zhizao (1565–1612) and Yang Tingyun (1557–1627). These men were known as 'Three Pillars of the Early Christian Church in China' (*kaijiao san dazhushi*) (Elman, 2008: 18; Waley-Cohen, 2000: 65–66; Peterson, 2011: 102–111, 118–128; Laven, 2011: 208). Li Zhizao became famous as the editor of the *Tianxue chuhan* (First Collection of Heavenly Studies, 1626), which contained the *Xixue fan* (Summary of Western Learning), a work outlining the European university curriculum (Reed and Demattè, 2007: 56). Hsia shows that many Chinese sympathizers of Catholicism can be traced to the Tunglin Academy, which encompassed those opposing the conservative officials: to these scholars, 'Christianity promised to offer personal and collective regeneration and a restoration of cosmic and social order' (Hsia, 1998: 188), whereas high-profile conversions secured patronage, rendering Christianity mobile amongst travelling scholars (Brockey, 2007: 59).

Here, as elsewhere in the *padroão*, the Jesuit letter-books and other written sources provided numerous comprehensive, first-hand accounts of China to Europe. Lottes points out (1991: 65–66) that the Jesuit missionary reports which reached Europe were often far more positive than later, eighteenth-century materials, and that they were often the basis upon which the high esteem of China prevalent in the early Enlightenment was based. The reports were also to inform other European writings: the text *China Illustrata* (1667), by the prominent Jesuit Athanasius Kircher (1602–1680), is a comprehensive example of this. Mormando and Thomas (2006: 58) argue that (see also Reed and Dematte, 2007: 148–149):

> Kircher is today one of the most famous and studied Jesuits of the Early Modern period. He is often compared to Leonardo da Vinci for his insatiable curiosity about the world, inventive imagination, and the broad scope of his many works encompassing disparate fields of knowledge and inquiry.

Beyond individuals, Wood stresses (2009: 47) that one of the most significant contributions of the Jesuits to the emerging European picture of China of this period was the Jesuit description of the Chinese academies and civil service examination systems, which promoted a *carrière ouverte aux talents* (a career-bureaucracy based on merit). McNeely and Wolverton (2009) show how Jesuits such as Matteo Ricci (1552–1610) conceived of the Chinese academies as *academia di letterati*, who were, therefore, part of the Chinese, rather than the

European, *Republic of Letters*. Wood also points out how the ideas of a country governed by well-read philosophers found their way into the sinophile writings of Voltaire (1694–1778) – for example, through his *Lettres Chinoises et Indiennes*. And is the Chinese system of the time really a million miles away from today's *concours* organized annually by the EU institutions?

These apparent commonalities notwithstanding, the depth and methods of engagement by the China Jesuits renders the China mission quite distinct from India and Japan, and it reflects the flexibility of the Jesuits' approach to educational matters, in at least three ways: first, as observers like Russell-Wood argue (1998: 199), China represented 'one of the rare instances, possibly unique, of the dissemination of European ideas beyond the religious sphere and actually reaching indigenous intellectual élites [...]'. This was embodied in the Jesuits' top-down approach, targeting exactly those elites, although Brockey (2007: 47–48) warns against understanding this style as the Jesuits' only method.

Second, the Jesuit missionary enterprise was fuelled by books, reason and science. Secular knowledge and natural science (especially mathematics, calendar science and astronomy) were consciously employed as vehicles of proselytizing and evidence of Western supremacy. In fact, Brockey (2007: 215) argues that 'no other category of Western erudition is as closely associated with the China Jesuits as natural philosophy, or, more specifically, mathematics and astronomy'. The method received official acknowledgement across Asia because it was aiming at rendering the Jesuit mission not just acceptable, but also useful. Astronomical knowledge in China at this time meant political legitimacy, since the Son of Heaven was 'responsible for the accuracy of the calendar and the harmony of the celestial movements' (Reed and Demattè, 2007: 54). Ferdinand Verbiest's armillary spheres[20] and his observatory in Beijing can still be appreciated today (Reed and Demattè, 2007: 60–67; Saraiva and Jami, 2008; BWB, 2009: 13).[21] Astronomy and the resolution of the late Ming calendar crisis constituted a 'win-win situation', increasing Jesuit credibility and legitimacy, as well as helping to augment the station of the Emperor himself, as 'Son of Heaven' (Hsia, 1998: 189; Elman, 2008: 16–19). Wright (2005: 85) quotes Verbiest, exclaiming: 'as a star of old brought the Magi to the adoration of the true God, so the princes of the Far East, through knowledge of the stars, would be brought to recognise and adore the Lord of the stars'.

Moreover, Lee states (1991b: 3) that 'what actually made Ricci and his followers appear attractive to the educated Chinese was their knowledge of science'; and, in Elman's words (2008: 15), 'the Jesuits added precision to the investigation of things, by exposing seventeenth-century literati to early modern European classifications, forms of argument, and organisational principles for specialised knowledge – that is *scientia*'. Last but not least, Wills (2011: 56) stresses that 'the astronomical and calendrical [*sic*] work of the Jesuits turned out to be their most secure justification for a presence in Beijing'.

Jesuit scientists were subsequently to serve Chinese Emperors of the Ming (1368–1644) and succeeding Qing (Manchu, Tartar, 1644–1911) dynasties, as tutors, astronomers, painters and architects for over 150 years. Jesuit academics like Matteo Ricci produced *mappae mundi*, introduced star charts and assembled clocks. They cultivated their influence through their skills, making friends with officials and scholars (Saraiva and Jami, 2008: 81–98; Gelber, 2007: 102; Wood, 2009: 36). At times, they were involved in making cannon and using their military know-how for the benefit of Chinese power (Lach and Van Kley, 1994, Vol. III, Book 1: 187; Wiessala, 2011: 35–36). They thus aroused curiosity and hostility in equal measure.

Third, the Jesuits' presence in China, as well as the resulting written sources, helped to generate a China-image throughout Europe that was largely sinophile in character. The works of Voltaire have already been mentioned in this context, and many of the China Jesuits in the mission field also wrote extremely favourably about their host nation. It is significant to note that the China-friendly tendencies of the time were frequently used, in the form of a kind of 'counter-identity' to Europe, in order to criticize conditions back home, and that Jesuit writings from the Middle Kingdom played a large part in the evolution of this intellectual and political tendency (Wiessala, 2011: 34–35). To quote Gelber, referring to Matteo Ricci's manuscripts on China (2007: 102):

> Here was a very large and unified realm, well-ordered and with a central orthodoxy, namely Confucianism. Social life was regulated by rituals and manners that produced a harmony only too likely to be disturbed by foreigners. Administration was through a professional bureaucracy, selected on merit. It was all a stark contrast to the fragmented and embattled state of Europe after the Reformation.

The 'pastoral of the intellect': the Jesuit mission to Japan

This one, half-hidden, facing the coast
Of China, from whence it may be reached,
Is Japan, with its reefs of silver ore,
And soon to be illumined by God's law.
                    (Luiz Vaz de Camões, *The Lusiads*, Canto 10, verse 131)

Whilst Japan is, by and large, the subject of the next chapter, the arrival of Iberian (Portuguese and Spanish) and Italian Catholic missionaries in the Japanese archipelago deserves special emphasis in this one, for three, inter-connected reasons. First, as Dunn points out (1972: 7), the perceived threat of foreigners affected Japanese society in many ways, helping, for instance, to forge, among the Japanese, an 'improvement in public spirit'. Others, as Screech argues (2004: 313), adopted the new ideology of 'Just War', imported by the foreigners, in order to change an unstable domestic context. Second, it was the agency of (mostly) Iberian Jesuits which constituted the main channel of knowledge transfer from Japan to the West at this time (De Bary *et al.*, 2006: 128).

There appears to be a wide consensus that European traders had first stumbled upon the Japanese archipelago involuntarily, in 1543, when a few very emaciated

Portuguese traders became stranded on Tanegashima, south of the island of Kyūshū (see Severy and Stanfield, 1992: 89). Some argue that this may have marked the initiation of 'Western' studies in Japan; others point to the arrival of the Basque knight-cum-priest Francis Xavier (1506–1552), in Kagoshima in 1549 as the start (Burke, 2000: 59; Goodman 2006: 289–290). Xavier,[22] a close confidant of the Jesuit founder Ignatius de Loyola (1491–1556), was keen to reach Japan, believing, like Alessandro Valignano, the Japanese to be the 'best people yet to be discovered in Asia' (Moran, 1993: 97, 99, 101; Cotterell, 2010: 45). Mitchell finds (1980: 155) that the conversion of Japan, for Xavier, was the key to the Catholicization of Asia, 'a mirage which continued to shimmer tantalizingly on the Jesuit horizon'. Pina (2001: 60) writes that it was 'in Japan that Xavier perceived the lacunae of the traditional model of the *tabula rasa* method', based on a pattern of 'Europeanization'.

Xavier's arrival inaugurated what Saraiva (2007: 159) terms Japan's 'Christian Century' (*Século Cristão*), lasting from 1540 to 1630; by the end of the 1500s, there were perhaps around 300,000 Japanese Christians. Hsia argues (1998: 181) that the Christian presence in the Japanese islands depended on two key sets of circumstances – Portuguese trade from Macao, and the instabilities of domestic Japanese politics. The Christian Century ended in anti-Catholic persecutions and in the resolve of successive Japanese shōguns to 'eradicate forever the despised religion from the island empire' (De Bary *et al.*, 2006: 290).

Before that expulsion, however, and prior to the arrival of the more acceptable Protestant Dutch (see remainder of this chapter), the activities of Xavier and his Portuguese successors in Japan became 'Europe's most important representatives in the first encounter between the two cultures' (De Bary *et al.*, 2006: 128). The Jesuits, who had been granted Nagasaki in 1580, became a key channel through which Europe learnt about Japan and Asia. There were other orders already active in Asia – for instance, the Augustinians, Franciscans and Dominicans (Disney, 2009: 201). However, Japan became a virtual missionary monopoly of the Portuguese, until challenged by the Spanish from their stronghold in the Philippines.

The Jesuits had come, courtesy of Portuguese merchants, who arrived from Portuguese Macao, from where both groups were controlling the silk trade at the time, and which was the most lucrative of all Portuguese operations in Asia (Cotterell, 2010: 44). On the Goa–Macao–Nagasaki run to Japan, commerce and the Cross supplemented one another well: in the words of Luís de Camões, Japan to the Portuguese had 'reefs of silver ore' and was 'soon to be illumined by God's law' (Camões, transl. Landeg White, 1997, *Canto Ten*, 131). A merchant base sprang up at Hirado in the northwest of Kyūshū Island; it was later also to be used by the Dutch and English. The Iberians confronted Japan with their culture, with tobacco, knowledge of castle architecture, firearms (Man, 2011: 67) and moveable type.

However, the missionaries encountered a sophisticated, written culture and an 'indigenous printing process already highly developed' (Febvre and Martin, 2010: 213). Shíba Kōkan's biographer, Calvin French, points out (1974: 4–5)

64 *Theoretical aspects and historical predecessors*

that the Jesuit printing press, set up in Nagasaki by four returning Japanese envoys to the Vatican from 1590 (Masanobu, 1978: 25), to full-scale anti-Christian repression in 1614, tapped into a rich intellectual climate. The press became the focal point in opening up a short era of unrestricted cultural intercourse between Japanese and Europeans, which lasted for 50 years, and extended to comparative language studies, the dissemination of devotional manuals, translations of books such as *Aesop's Fables* (in 1593) and the introduction of copperplate print-marking and engraving. This initiated a mutual artistic influence which helped to give rise to the wider *rangaku* ('Dutch Studies') movement, which is the main concern of the next chapter (Screech, 1996: 67; Febvre and Martin, 2010: 213–214; Kamei-Dyche, 2011: 274). Through their writings the Jesuits contributed to the formation of the overall picture that Europeans gained of the Japan of the sixteenth to eighteenth centuries. Some prominent examples are briefly discussed here, in order to provide a wider framework for an appreciation of the artistic exchange between the later Dutch and the Japanese, which informs the rest of this chapter. The Jesuit Luís Fróis followed Xavier in 1563 and became, arguably, the most prolific of all Jesuit authors on Japan. Lach singles him out as 'probably the greatest of the Jesuit letter writers' (Lach and Van Kley, 1994, Vol. I, Book 1: 249). His *Historia de Japan* and his treatise on *Contradictions and Differences of Customs between the People of Europe and of this Territory of Japan* are key resources for European Studies in Asia, even today (De Bary *et al.*, 2006: 141–144).

Other, culturally sensitive Jesuit texts on Japan were the *Advertimentos* and *Summary of Japanese Matters* by Alessandro Valignano, and the works of Fernão Mendes Pinto (1510–1593). Further Iberian sources are the *Historia de las Missiones* (1601) by Luis de Guzman, the *Historia de las islas del archipielago Filipino y reinos de la gran China, Tartaria, Cochin-China, Malaca, Siam, Cambodge y Japon*, by the Marcelo de Ribadeneira (1602), and Fernão Guerreiro's five-volume work *Relaçam* (1603–1611) (Lach and Van Kley, 1998: 1829–1888). These writings were complemented by later non-religious sources such as François Carron's *Beschrijvinghe van het machtigh coninck-rijk Iapan* (1646) and the *History of Japan* (1727) by Engelbert Kaempfer, a German surgeon in the employ of the Dutch (see elsewhere in this chapter). Many of these sources contain vivid descriptions of the economics, customs, people and the art in Tokugawa Japan.

Black legends and hagiographies: resistance to the Jesuits' approach

Wright (2004: 8) states that, 'whether loved, or loathed, the Society of Jesus could never be ignored'. The Jesuit programme of cultural accommodation, in particular, was never without difficulties and critics, and it often provoked envy, heated discussion, hate and suspicion in equal measure, in Rome and elsewhere. In the eyes of many, cultural accommodation, indigenization and adaptation, as promulgated in Valignano's *Advertimentos* and elsewhere, could all too easily grow into inappropriate syncretism, the 'thin end of the wedge' dissolving Christian dogma. The Jesuits were seen as popish plotters, international power-brokers, 'king-killers, poisoners or practitioners of the black arts' (Wright, 2004: 9). Boxer (1969: 347) singles out one of the charges most frequently levelled against the order: it seemed to have been more important to them to produce 'good Christians and Catholics, rather than good Latinists' (*mais cristãos e catolicos, ainda que menos latinos*).

The Jesuits' efforts to learn, and communicate in, a variety of Asian languages and dialects, both alphabetic and ideographic, brought to the surface of intellectual debate the *Terms Question*: the challenge of conveying Christian words, instructions, prayers and concepts in a language in which there simply existed no idioms for many of those 'Western' concepts? The debate over whether it was preferable to tolerate the Chinese terms *Shang-di* (*Shangde*, 'God on High') and *T'ian* ('God'/'Heaven'), or better to transliterate Latin words or invent new terms, such as 'Lord of Heaven' (*Tianzhou*), exemplified this dilemma (Ross, 1994: 155; Hsia, 1998: 188; Waley-Cohen, 2000: 77; Pina, 2001: 66–67; Reed and Demattè, 2007: 30). Some wider issues were intimately connected to this, as Wright observes (2005: 75):

> why would someone living in 16th century China, a place where the punishment of crucifixion was reserved for bandits, want to worship a person who, 1500 years earlier and half-way across the world, had been hung on a cross like a common criminal...?

To the Jesuits' many detractors, the Chinese *Rites Controversy*, over doctrinal pliability – the level and depth of accommodation to local religious practices and ancestor rites of potential converts – was a bitterly fought, significant discourse in Europe and Asia (see above, and Lach and Van Kley, 1994, Vol. I, Book 1: 250–251; Clarke, 1997: 41). Disney states succinctly (2009: 343): 'at issue was whether the traditional ceremonies, performed by cultured Chinese in honour of Confucius and their ancestors, were compatible with Christianity'. The Augustinian, Dominican and Franciscan Orders, for example, utterly rejected the Jesuit stance on the 'secular' character of the Chinese ancestral rites, and they were supported in this stance by Spanish missionaries in the Philippines.

Hsia (1998: 191) points to the difference between the India and China missions in this respect: 'unlike China, the acrimonious exchange in the India mission took place within the Jesuit Order, whereas, in the Middle Kingdom, it pitted the Jesuits against the mendicant orders, especially the Dominicans'. Religious orthodoxy won the day in the end: the two Apostolic Constitutions *Ex illa die* (1715) and *Ex quo singulari* (1742) settled the issue *against* Jesuit practices of cultural, religious, hermeneutic and linguistic inculturation. However, many Jesuit missionaries found many ways of getting around the papacy in this matter (Boxer, 1969: 239).

Chapter conclusions

In spite of the limitations of the *ratio studiorum*, and of the 'cultural myopia' (Boxer, 1969: 82) which affected many of the Jesuit missionaries, many others were much more broad-minded, and they became significant cultural catalysts between Asia and Europe. In his early analysis of 1969, Boxer (1969: 352) summarizes the Jesuits' educational achievements: 'The Jesuits persisted, and they must be given full credit for the remarkable, if intellectually rigidly circumscribed, educational work which they performed in the tropical world until the catastrophe of 1759/60.'

Analysts of the interaction between Jesuits and Chinese offer a nuanced assessment of the Jesuit legacy. Lackner (1991: 132), for example, finds, 'in spite of censorship tactics, the image which was communicated to Europe by the Jesuits during the Seventeenth and early Eighteenth Centuries was based on several affinities between the religion and the language of the two cultures'. In terms of the 'embedding' of the Jesuit mission in its context of empire, the Portuguese case shows that 'mission' and 'colonialism' cannot *always* be equated with wholesale *Europeanization*. Learning and exchange, artistic and cultural influence did work both ways, and many more Europeans became aware of Asian contributions to world history, broadening their intellectual horizons.

However, Lach stresses a first, important, limitation (Lach and Van Kley, 1994, Vol. I, Book 1: 322): 'the extant corpus of Jesuit letters is not of equal value for the various parts of Asia. It is likewise much better for some epochs than for others.' It is worthwhile recalling a second constraint regarding the (European) reception of Jesuit-mediated, 'Eastern' knowledge in the Europe of the period: it is expressed most eloquently by Burke (2000: 196):

> the appropriation of exotic knowledge naturally included a process of *domesticating* or *stereotyping*. Even Western observers in the 'field' perceived unfamiliar cultures in terms of stereotypes. Some, like those of American cannibals and oriental despots, exaggerated the cultural distance between the foreign culture and that of the observer. Others did the exact opposite.
>
> (italics added by me)

To which may be added that the Jesuits saw the Asian cultures, religions and practices they encountered through the mirror of their own religious project – that of conversion.

It is the perspective of actual conversion rates and missionary successes that leads to another qualification of the assessment of the Jesuits' successes, and of their reception in the Asian context of the period. Mullet summarizes this as follows (1999: 195): 'the oriental societies that Europeans most esteemed tended, at least in the long run, to prove most resistant to the allure of Europe's religion, or religions'. Laven expresses one of the underlying reasons for this phenomenon as follows (2011: 66):

For whereas the Jesuits, who believed those in ignorance of the true faith to be destined to damnation, were committed to *conversion*, the Chinese, who considered their spiritual lives to be enriched by the *addition* of new devotional strands, took a syncretic approach to religion. Paradoxically, the only reason the foreign priests were accepted within Zhaoqing was that their cult was viewed as an enhancement to existing religious practices.

In the context of this dynamism between *syncretism* and *conversion*, especially through the mirror of the European *Learning from Heaven* brought to China, Peterson (2011: 132–134) delineates three overall legacies this period has had in producing the future keystones of European Studies in Asia: first, the importance of acculturation – adapting to the 'knowledge universe' of another cultural tradition; second, the importance of the methodologies of *comparison* and *contrast* in teaching and exchange; and, third, the ideas of universality and cultural specificity, especially in the context of a subject that involves religious doctrine.

Notwithstanding these observations, the Jesuit letter-books transmitted to Europe reveal a wide range of topics of interest to the Jesuit missionaries, and they played a significant part in the exchange of knowledge and objects between Asia and Europe from the late fifteenth to the early eighteenth centuries and beyond. Laven (2011: 29) summarizes: 'from out of this rich field of scholarship, a single theme came to dominate: the exchange of ideas between East and West and the hybrid intellectual world that grew up around the missionaries'.

Although many of the works that reached Europe were censored by the Portuguese colonial authorities (for a time), from the mid-seventeenth century onwards they found their way out of Portugal by means of translators, intellectuals, academics and collectors in a number of European countries. The scope of the knowledge contained in the pages of these works was vast: it ranged from naval and geographical information and detail about Asian flora, fauna and ethnography, to comprehensive information about Asian customs, religions, philosophies, arts, products and much more. In this manner, through Portuguese traders, seafarers and other intermediaries, the mediaeval, Ptolemaic, European image of Asia was substantially added to, often significantly corrected – and always enriched.

One final aspect deserves to be mentioned here: in the choice of their methods of accommodation and adaptation, in 'becoming' Indian, Japanese or Chinese, in 'going native' as it were, the Jesuits, in particular, changed both themselves and contributed to change in the minds of those – Europeans and others – who consumed their research. Mullet comments (1999: 194):

> the European educational experience in Asia was far from being solely that of one-way European propagation of teaching, for in such societies as India, China and Japan, the missionaries and colonists found, and in some cases admired, ancient, complex and advanced civilisations.

In the process of the developing exchange with these civilizations, identities were altered and horizons widened, on either side. Laven (2011: 45) claims that 'going native' often resulted from local conditions too, as well as from 'tactical' considerations. Peterson provides a telling example of this (2011: 91): 'Learning to speak Chinese led to reading, which led to writing. Writing Chinese entailed using Chinese vocabulary to express non-Chinese concepts, and losing important distinctions in the translation. The boundary shifted.'

Can being 'lost in translation' actually be a good thing?

Notes

1 The Portuguese term *padrão* (plural: *padrões*) can also mean 'model', 'standard', 'gauge' and 'pattern'.
2 On the Spanish–Portuguese dispute over the 'Spice Islands', see: Brotton (2002: 164); Curtin (2000: 172–178); Milton (2002: 28–29).
3 Richard Hakluyt subsequently translated Grotius's work into English.
4 This epithet is borrowed from Wright (2004).
5 The Council of Trent met during three sessions: 1545–1547, 1551–1552 and 1562–1563.
6 See the 2007 *In Our Time* programme radio podcast on BBC Radio 4: www.bbc.co.uk/podcasts/series/iotr/all.
7 Asia House UK organized an event on Castiglione: http://asiahouse.org/exhibitions-and-events/detail?id=233.
8 This heading was inspired by Laven (2011: 47).
9 http://epicworldhistory.blogspot.co.uk/2012/06/jesuits-in-asia.html.
10 This term has been borrowed from Brockey (2007: 8).
11 See Hastings's engaging first-hand account of Jesuit education at *Stonyhurst College* in Lancashire (Hastings, 1971).
12 On other Jesuit mission stations in India and Ceylon, see Lach and Van Kley (1994, Vol. I, Book 1: 262–280).
13 Antonio Vivaldi (1675–1741) named his Violin Concerto in D major RV 208 *Il Grosso Mogul*, in memory, perhaps, of Akbar and the Mughal Empire.
14 www.ibiblio.org/expo/vatican.exhibit/exhibit/i-rome_to_china/Jesuits_in_China.html.
15 Amiot is the composer of the *Mass of the Jesuits at Peking*: http://classical-iconoclast.blogspot.co.uk/2009/04/jesuits-in-asia-chinese-baroque-music.html.
16 Some sources on the rites controversy can be found at: www.fordham.edu/halsall/mod/1715chineserites.asp.
17 Chinese and Japanese sources on this issue are commented on in Lee (1991b: 21, fn 2).
18 The Kangxi (*K'ang-hsi*) Emperor was the first to benefit from the Jesuit introduction of (anti-malarial) quinine into China (Wood, 2009: 39).
19 The *Mass of the Jesuits in Beijing*, composed by the Jesuit Jean-Joseph-Marie Amiot, is a unique product of this cultural encounter, combining, as it does, Chinese and European musical and religious idioms (Naïve E8910, re-issue of Auvidis-Astree E-8642).
20 One of Ferdinand Verbiest's armillary spheres could be seen in the exhibition *Zoon van de Hemel* (Son of Heaven) in Brussels, 10 October 2009–24 January 2010, as part of the europalia.china event (www.bozar.be/activity.php?id=9132) (see: De Coster, 2009).
21 The exhibition *Heaven on Earth – Missionaries and the Mathematical Arts in 17th Century Beijing*, at the Museum of the History of Science in Oxford (24 May–7 September 2008) illustrated this aspect of Jesuit 'missionary tactics'.
22 In 2011, Xavier's arrival in Japan was aptly commemorated on the CD *Hispania & Japan: Dialogues* by the Ensemble *Hespérion XXI*, under the direction of Jordi Savall (*Alia Vox*: ASIN: B0055U9LAA). There is also a related recording of *Francisco Xavier e la Ruta de Oriente*, on the same theme and by the same artists (*Alia Vox*, ASIN: B000XIJ3OI).

4 Finding Europe in Nagasaki and Ayutthaya

The Japanese Leonardo and the Siamese falcon

Introduction: a word-picture and a journey to Tokugawa Japan

The image is, perhaps, the most iconic work of art we commonly associate with Japan. It contains a striking blue: *Preußisch Blau* (or *Berliner Blau*), which has the idealized formula Fe7(CN)18. The colour was first *manufactured* in Berlin in 1706, and it is often seen as the first anorganic colour pigment that is *not* found in nature. It is a deeply satisfying, almost visceral, hue. *The Great Wave*, painted around 1831 by Katsushika Hokusai (1760–1849), part of a series of woodblock prints called *Thirty-six Views of Mount Fuji*, has loomed large in the Japanese public conscience since the tsunami and earthquake at Fukushima in 2011.

The Great Wave was chosen as one of the pieces in the British Museum's hugely successful 2010 exhibition *A History of the World in 100 Objects*.[1] The 'Prussian Blue' (*berein burāu*) which is so astounding in this print is not, however, really a *Japanese* blue. The pigment was imported to Japan via China, or by Dutch traders on Deshima, an island in Nagasaki Harbour, from the eighteenth century onwards. British Museum Director Neil MacGregor writes: 'the blueness of *The Great Wave* shows us Japan taking from Europe – and with absolute confidence' (MacGregor, 2010: 610).

In so taking, Hokusai used 'Western perspective' in his print, and has been said to have gone through an 'apprenticeship' with Shība Kōkan (1747–1818) in the 1790s (Masanobu, 1978: 126), although many doubt this claim. Shība Kōkan, a painter from the capital Edo ('River Gate'), was fascinated by all things Dutch, many of whom he encountered at Deshima (Wiessala, 2011: 1–7). Some say this was a first, tentative inkling of 'European Studies' in East Asia. The almost three centuries of Japanese history which are commonly referred to as the *Tokugawa* (or *Edo*) period (1600–1868) followed the *sengoku jidai*, the internecine clan warfare of mediaeval Japan, and the 90-year interlude of Portuguese missionary presence (1540–1630; see also Chapter 3). In Edo Japan, a single Japanese political space was achieved through the agency of the 'Three Unifiers', Oda Nobunaga (1534–1582), Toyotomi Hideyoshi (1537–1598) and Tokugawa Ieyasu (1543–1616).

Tokugawa Ieyasu reorganized the Japanese regional hegemons and promoted Confucian and Buddhist Studies (Jansen, 2000: 45). He built a system of 'bureaucratic nobility' (Hiroshi, 2006: xxiv), while corresponding with King James I of England. He also deployed European gunpowder and shot to widen his control (Curtin, 2000: 157). Tankha and Thampi (2005: 39–40) posit that the era named after him irrevocably transformed the previous foreign policy concept of *sankokusekaikan* ('three-country view', i.e. Japan, China/Korea and India). The new thinking now accommodated Europeans[2] – referred to as 'Southern Barbarians' (*nanbanjin*, Masanobu, 1978: 17).[3] His victory at the battle of Sekigahara in September 1600 and the capture of Osaka Castle in 1615 enabled this first shōgun of the Tokugawa *bakufu* (literally: 'tent-government') to gain control, from Edo, over the feudal lords (*daimyo*) (Goodman, 2000: 3; Yoshiteru and Bytheway, 2011: 84–86). Whether Tokugawa Japan was, indeed, a fully centralized state, rather than a 'pacified and bureaucratized' confederacy (Jansen 2000: 33, 60–62, 201) or a 'federation of virtually independent' regions (*han*) (Curtin, 2000: 160), is still debated in controversial terms.[4]

What does seem certain is that Ieyasu consolidated his power by means of a land survey based on estimated annual rice yields (*koku*) (Dunn, 1972: 15).This *sankin kôtai* system, enforcing alternate attendance of all feudal lords in Edo for long periods of time, was a pillar of government, ensuring loyalty, stability – and the permanent bankruptcy of most nobles. To consolidate his control further, Ieyasu afforded stipends and ideological support to the elite warrior class (*samurai*), leaving many of them enough leisure time to pursue hobbies such as fine art – and learning about the 'West'. The shōgun also brought the imperial court into his service and styled himself into a virtual equal of the Emperor (*tennō*) (Gordon, 2003: 14; Goto-Jones, 2009: 25–26). Evidence for this contrived 'dual sovereignty' (Hiroshi, 2006: xvii) lies in the dichotomy between the contemporary imperial-ceremonial centre at Kyoto and the political heart in Edo (Macfarlane, 2008: 109–110) (see Appendix 3: *The sankin kôtai system; stability, balance and constraint*).

Much of the Japanese artistic activity during this time can be interpreted as a countervailing and de-centring dynamic to the officially sanctioned Confucian culture, the established social hierarchy and the Tokugawa government's policies of isolation (*sakoku-jidai, sakoku-seisaku*, 1630–1853). The *sakoku* policy[5] was designed to keep Japanese in Japan, tighten prohibitions on Christianity and yoke trade to government control (Yoko, 2009: 26–29).

How much of the *sakoku* idea(l) actually transmuted into systematic, governmental policy remains open to debate. Many point out that Japan was never hermetically sealed, and that there is evidence the country sought to re-structure her relations with China, South East Asia and Korea at this time, aiming to control foreign trade and the flow of information (Subrahmanyam, 1993: 26; Hobson, 2004: 93; Hiroshi, 2006: 3; Michel, 2007: 286). In addition to limited contacts with foreigners, deepening changes to the Japanese class system of the period provided both a challenge and a significant stimulus to Edo intellectuals (see Appendix 4: *The class system and the politics of art in Edo period popular culture*).

One aspect of the Edo period with a direct bearing on subsequent Japanese–European cultural encounters[6] was the availability of new information through media and books. Prints, an avid reading public, itinerant book lenders and dealers, printing presses and thriving publishing businesses all thrived in the urban centres. Book titles ranged from popular novels and instruction manuals, to long philosophical treatises (Dunn, 1972: 154–155). All were driven by new demands for literary entertainment by the townspeople (*chōnin*: merchants and artisans) (Nishiyama, 1997: 73–75; Bullen *et al.*, 2009: 1; Kamei-Dyche, 2011: 274). A 2010 Tokyo exhibition on *Information and Media in the Edo Period* (see Chapter 5) outlined these tendencies as follows:

> As the city of Edo (present-day Tokyo) developed, publications such as the Guide to the Townships of Edo, which introduced the locations of the city's great many townships, and the Edo Shopping Guide appeared, reflecting efforts to streamline social information. In other publications such as the Directory of Prominent Persons Residing in Edo, the fields of expertise and even the addresses of scholars and literary figures were collated as information, broadening networks of interpersonal knowledge transmission.[7]

Some scholars assert that it was during those 250 years of *Pax Tokugawa* that Japan grew into a 'true' nation (Huffman, 2010: 55; Goto-Jones, 2009: 28). This provided a fertile soil in which the seeds of cultural, scientific, literary and artistic activities could readily grow, including the engagement with European foreigners – especially the Dutch (Guth, 1996: 15).

Tokugawa intellectual life and the 'red-haired Gaijin' on Deshima[8]

The 'state ideology' of the Tokugawa polity was derived from Sung dynasty (960–1279) Chinese models of (Neo-)Confucianism, especially those of the philosopher Zhu Xi (Chu Hsi, 1130–1200), the intellectual originator of the (Chinese) Sung dynasty philosophical Renaissance. Zhu Xi thought has been labelled a 'rationalizing influence in the sphere of ethics' (Bellah, 1985: 55, 69) (See Appendix 5: *Chinese Zhu Xi thought and its influence on Japanese intellectuals of the Edo period*)

Literacy rates in Tokugawa Japan were higher than that of (most of) Europe at the time – nearly everyone in Edo could read and write (Curtin, 2000: 160; Bullen *et al.*, 2009: 17). Woodblock prints (*ukiyo-e*, 'xylography'), depicting landscapes and the 'Floating World' of actors, 'courtesans' and 'townspeople' were popular; they represent, arguably, *the* unique, innovative, economic commodity and 'cultural currency' of Edo aesthetics – although they were not seen as 'art' at the time (Dunn, 1972: 169). In his *A Tale of the Floating World*, the Buddhist cleric and author Asai Ryōi, sketches some of the significant, socio-political, aspects of the 'Floating World' in a powerful manner, bordering, perhaps, a little on the satirical:

*Living only for the moment, turning our attention to the pleasures of the moon,
the snow, the cherry blossoms and the maples,
singing songs, drinking wine, and diverting ourselves
in just floating, floating, caring not a whit for the poverty staring us in the face, refusing to be disheartened,
like a gourd floating along with the river current:
this is what we call the floating world*

In this ephemeral world,[9] encounters of a kind could, and would, occur which were all but impossible elsewhere. It was in the 'Floating World' also that publishers such as *Suwaraya Mohei* and *Suwaraya Ichibei (Ichibee)* met many literati and scholars of 'Western Learning' (Masanobu, 1978: 34; Nishiyama, 1997: 67, 69–70). The creative, discursive and promotional activities of agents, unofficial 'salons', writers, artists, publishers, book-lenders and collectors contributed to business, and to the intellectual climate of the time, shaping the 'foreign interests' of many Japanese intellectuals.

Yoshimune (1684–1751), the eighth shōgun of the era, and 'perhaps the most important after Ieyasu' (Jansen, 2000: 46), was a pragmatic reformer (Goodman, 2000: 62). He had books and military knowledge imported from both China and Holland to help solve Japan's problems and to promote progress (Boxer, 1968: 61–62; Masanobu, 1978: 20, 29; Goodman, 2000: 35; Johnson, 2005: 97, 139; Shiori, 2009: 65). Beyond books, the battle over the epistemological merits, or otherwise, of 'Western Learning' (*rangaku*)[10] was carried into 'almost every imaginable field' (Keene, 1969: 61) by a group of scholars and artists who sought to deepen their knowledge of Western art and science among their associates (see below). They were, in Masanobu's memorable words (1978: 13), 'a group of sometimes brave and often lonely students of the world beyond the barrier'. Others referred to them, less flatteringly, as part of *rampeki* (the 'Dutch Craze'; Sansom, 1963: 189).

The *rangakusha* are often said to have represented a self-conscious 'counterculture' (Guth, 1996: 12) to the officially revered Chinese neo-Confucian templates. Guth argues that the attitudes of the Tokugawa shōgunate towards art embodied the Confucian tenet that 'personal practice and promotion of the arts by the ruling élite served to legitimate [sic] the regime, impart the proper moral values to the nation, and ensure cosmic order'. There were many outstanding personalities in this time of intense intellectual and artistic achievement: Arai Hakuseki (1657–1725), for example, is said to be the first to separate (Western) natural sciences from ecclesiastical authority (Goodman, 2000: 47–48). Some have called this time, during which Japan transmogrified from militarism to intellectualism, a 'Japanese Renaissance', during which artists like Shíba Kōkan became a 'Japanese Leonardo'.

Buddhism was the 'established church and arm of the state' (Harvey, 1990: 168). However, the Tokugawa government largely co-opted religion into politics (Bellah, 1985: 51; Goodman, 2000: 3, 43; De Bary *et al.*, 2006: 29; Leidy, 2008:

296; Ellwood, 2008: 158–159). Confucian ideals of 'benevolent government', loyalty, orthodoxy, duty, obligation, harmony, discipline, obedience, serving the group and filial piety, and the five human-moral relationships of Confucian thought (ruler–subject, father–son, husband–wife, elder–younger, friend–friend), chimed well with a Tokugawa polity which aimed not only at consolidating power, but also at regulating moral-educational standards and popular behaviour (Lach and Van Kley, 1998: 1652; Jansen, 2000: 191; Goodman, 2000: 3; Laven, 2011: 113). Collcutt (1993: 134) asserts the significant point that 'Confucian influences during the Edo period were most powerfully and broadly felt in the field of education and scholarship'.

Moreover, Goodman posits (2000: 4) that, by embracing Shu Hsi Confucianism, the shōgun hoped to 'promote a spirit of learning, while, paradoxically, discouraging free enquiry'. Notwithstanding this, a variety of schools of thought competed with one another at this time, and thinkers like Suzuki Shōsan (1579–1655), Kaibara Ekken (1630–1714) and Ogyū Sorai (1666–1728) rose to great prominence. Competing epistemologies were motivated by 'ancient learning' (*kogaku*) or the study of medicine, botany and herbs (*honzōgaku*) (Masanobu, 1978: 68; De Bary *et al.*, 2006: 46; Jansen, 2000: 199).

There were counter-currents, of course, to the predominant Confucian templates (Hall and McClain, 1991: 402); the 'Native Learning' School (*kokugaku*) was one of them, and so was the science which the red-haired foreigners brought in (*rangaku*). Jansen points out (2000: 209) that this did not, however, automatically equate with a 'love of foreigners': some scholars of the time were openly contemptuous of the Dutch at Nagasaki. Nevertheless, Shiba Kōkan and the scholars of Western learning were inspired by the exposure to European books and linked to the small number of Dutch traders – perhaps never more than 20 (Effert, 2000: 9) – kept isolated on the island of Deshima (Dejima: 'the island that juts out') in Nagasaki Harbour.

Built in 1636 for the Portuguese, it became the Dutch East India Company's (Vereenigde Oostindische Compagnie, VOC) only factory in Japan between 1641 and 1859. The Japanese called the strangers *Gaijin*, or 'red-haired barbarians' (see Appendix 6: *Samurai William*). The 'Hollanders' were more tolerable, since they were Protestants, more interested in trade than proselytizing. They were keen to break into the lucrative trade in Chinese silk and Japanese silver. The island of Deshima was 150 feet by 500 feet in size – roughly the extent of *Dam Square* in Amsterdam.[11] In spite of this, Deshima developed into a stepping stone between civilizations, quite out of proportion to its size, 'one of the most curious plots on the face of this planet' (Boxer, 1968: 116). In the international history of ideas, Deshima has been conceptualized as an example of 'locating knowledge', a 'micro-space of exchange', a 'seat of knowledge' and a template for 'knowledge transfer' between 'centres and peripheries' (Burke, 2000: 53–60).

The island was an (artificial) microcosm of Europe, but also a conduit for increasing East–West awareness – a rare window onto Europe.[12] It was from here, it was said by some Japanese, that *oranda kaze seken wo fukiwatarū* ('the wind of Holland blew through the land'; Sansom, 1963: 189), touching subjects such as medicine and art, botany and astronomy, literature and military engineering. David Mitchell's novel *The Thousand Autumns of Jacob de Zoet* offers a vivid evocation of the daily routine on Deshima at this time, and of the intellectual ferment in Tokugawa Japan. Mitchell's depiction of the *Shirandô*, a private Japanese Academy of Western Learning, although entirely fictional, evokes something of the intellectual commitment of its students (Mitchell, 2010: 199–200):

> [...] the answer is 'Belief' – Beliefs that are ignoble or idealistic; democratic or Confucian; Occidental or Oriental; timid or bold; clear-sighted or delusional. Power is informed by Belief that this path, and not another, must be followed. What then, or where, is the womb of Belief? What, or where, is the crucible of ideology? Academicians of the *Shirandô*, I put it to you that we are one such crucible. We are one such womb...

Under the spell of the West: Shíba Kōkan (1747–1818) and the Rangaku Movement

'Dutch Studies' (*rangaku*), or the 'Red-Hair-Learning' (*kōmō bunka*) movement,[13] found a prime exponent in Shíba Kōkan – or, perhaps, it was the other way around. *Rangaku*, in my view, brought something new, and rather radical, to Japan: 'history was to be controlled in the present in relation to *nature* and not to ancient models or moral philosophy' (Hall and McClain, 1991: 633). 'Western' medicine and 'read-head-style surgery' (*namban igaku/ishigaku, kômôryû geka*) were good examples of this new approach, entering Japan via Nagasaki and Edo (Horiushi, 2003: 161).[14]

The dissemination of *rangaku* was mediated by Dutch traders, German pharmacists, and Japanese physicians and interpreters. The latter, in particular, were important catalysts; however, their central contributions are often underrated (Boxer, 1968: Ch. IV; Horiushi, 2003: 149; Michel, 2007: 285). *Rangaku* spread to the Japanese provincial domains (*han*) and was adopted by private schools under the patronage of *daimyō* and *samurai* (Goodman, 2000: 32, 147–189). Jansen (2000: 211) characterizes *rangaku* in Tokugawa Japan as 'one of the most extraordinary chapters in cultural exchange in world history'. It was to have far-reaching effects. An office for the translation of foreign books (*banshowagegoyo*) was established in 1818, and many future leaders of the Meiji Restoration received their education in private *rangaku* schools.

However, *rangaku* grew into more than the collective activities of some native naturalists: many intellectuals were also interested in, and critical of, the international relations of Japan, circulating and debating amongst themselves the official annual reports submitted by the Dutch to the Tokugawa shōgunate – papers such as *oranda fūsetsugaki* ('Annual Report on Foreign Events'; Hiroshi, 2006: 24–25; Shirahara, 2008: 197). Moreover, many of the Japanese scholars experienced government hostility since they also often harboured anti-Buddhist (and anti-Chinese) sentiments. Shíba Kōkan, for instance, is known to have produced numerous anti-Buddhist tracts. He also used his 'Western' knowledge to challenge Buddhist cosmology, preferring instead the 'new', 'Western', heliocentric theory (Goodman, 2000: 102).

Rangaku can thus also be seen as expressing a political agenda, representing Europe as a superior moral order of great antiquity, whilst subtly criticizing at the same time deficiencies and shortcomings in Japan, the anachronistic seclusion policies and the domineering influence of Chinese ideas on Japanese culture (Keene, 1969: 59; Nishiyama, 1997: 14; Goodman, 2000: 71–72). This process appears to mirror the cultural-relativist attitudes espoused by the eighteenth-century European Humanists who used models drawn from Asia or China in order to criticize the political situation in Europe (French, 1974: 129–131; Wiessala, 2011: 33–34).

In the context of examining what 'Holland' may have meant to these intellectuals, Screech (1996: 7) describes Europe – especially Holland – as a 'cluster of concepts, not a place'; a 'discourse' and 'willed construct', separate from the concept of the 'West', and 'Europe', and having to do rather with the Japanese 'self'. These concepts were embodied in a new cultural middle class composed of all traditional social strata – *samurai*, merchants and artisans (*chōnin*; Nishiyama, 1997: 48), farmers and scholars (Johnson, 2005: 130, 148). This bourgeois group sponsored art and forged what has been described as a 'new mentality culled from imported things' (Screech, 1996: 7).

The *rangakusha*, who organized *salons* exhibiting Western-style (*yōga*) painting, embraced artists, scientists, aristocrats, mapmakers and writers, some employed by the government (for example, Aōdō Denzen [1748–1822]). Others, like Shíba Kōkan, worked independently. Among the most prominent of the literati was the medical pioneer Sugita Genpaku (1733–1817), who famously organized a public dissection on 3 March 1771 for a small coterie of Edo physicians, and guided by Dutch anatomy books (Ranzaburō, 1964: 264; Jansen, 2000: 212–213; Keene, 2006: 27–29). The body on the slab was that of one *Aochababa* ('Green Tea Hag'), a woman of around 50 and a convicted criminal (Goodman, 2000: 82; De Bary *et al.*, 2006: 296).[15]

The painters Satake Shozan (1748–1785) and Hiraga Gennai (1729–1779) are seen as significant influences on Kōkan. Moreover, Odano Naotake (1749–1780) and Sō Shiseki (Soshiseki, Kusumoto Sekkei, 1715–1786/1787) were his instructors. Kōkan's wider social network encompassed the physician Ōtsuki Gentaku (1757–1827), the mathematician Honda Toshiaki (1744–1821), who commented on European-style division of sunlight into light and shade, and the engraver Aōdō Denzen (1748–1822), who achieved (Lee, 1983: 191): 'a successful melding of Western modelling and atmospheric perspective with characteristic Japanese compositional modes, format and medium'[16] (see Appendix 7: *Watanabe Kazan, the 'frog in the well' and the 'risky' business of Rangaku*).

Within this network, the artists of the domain of Akita command special attention: they were much admired, not least by Shíba Kōkan, who promoted their work. The style was named the *Akita Ranga School* (秋田蘭画), in honour of Satake Shozan (1748–1785), the lord (*daimyō*) of Akita province. Akita was also home to the Western scholar Odano Naotake (1749–1780). The style encompassed painting and copperplate engraving in European style (Keene, 1969: 17; French, 1974: 4; Yamada, 1976: 73–74; Johnson, 2005). Akita Ranga artists like Odano Naotake (1749–1780) were among the first to embrace the 'European' use of shadows and reflections, implied light sources, *chiaroscuro*,[17] linear perspective,[18] three-dimensionality, receding space and use of horizon lines. They aimed at an 'uncompromising realism' (Parthesius and Schiermeier, 2000: 84; Shiori, 2009: 73). Johnson (2005: 65–71) identifies the key European-inspired compositional elements which became hallmarks of these artists: the use of a *horizon-line*, the use of *reflections on water* and the placement of a *large object* in the foreground (a stylistic device commonly known as *repoussoir*).

However, Shíba Kōkan's, and his contemporaries', admiration of European cultural and artistic templates was frequently uncritical; it fed off an unbridled enthusiasm for Western history and culture and an earnest attempt to employ 'useful' elements from Western realistic art in developing Japanese styles. This method was in line with official Japanese attitudes towards the West. It was focused on the perceived capacity of 'Western' art to *accurately represent* the external appearance of its objects – that is, on quasi-photographic realism. For Shíba Kōkan and plenty of his contemporaries, art had a didactic, pedagogical purpose – 'it had to teach the viewer how to see and understand reality in ways the viewer was not used to' (Plutschow, 2006: 202). To spread this message, Kōkan, who had, at one point, wanted to become a sword-smith (Parthesius and Schiermeier, 2000: 16), became a 'word-smith', penning several art books – for instance, *Seiyōga Dan* (Seiyō Gadan: 'Discussion of Painting', 1799) (French, 1974: 81–82, 171–174; Johnson, 2005: 115, 146; Goodman, 2006: 310). Shíba Kōkan used a *camera obscura* (*shashinkyō*) and was fascinated by optics, glass and the scientific instruments of his time, such as hot air balloons, orreries[19] and quadrants, all of which he wrote about meticulously. Other *rangakusha* too, published widely (see Appendix 8: *Original works and translations by prominent Rangaku scholars*).

But Shíba Kōkan clearly stands out among this crowd. Born Kichijiro Andō, or Katsusaburō (勝三郎), he is seen as an intellectual, a self-confessed forger of the works of Suzuki Harunobu (1725–1770), the 'father of "Western-style" oil painting in Japan' (Yamada, 1976: 73), the key exponent of European realism and an eccentric, who published his own obituary before he died, to 'rid himself of unwanted friends' (Plutschow, 2006: 19, 203). The Tokugawa equivalent of 'un-friending' someone on *Facebook* today, it seems. He is acknowledged as the first[20] Japanese artist to 'resurrect' the copperplate engraving technique, lost since the closure of the Nagasaki Jesuit printing press in 1610 (See Chapter 3, and Boxer, 1968: 111; Febvre and Martin, 2010: 213–214).

An Amsterdam exhibition in 2000 characterized him as being *in 'de ban van het Westen'* ('under the spell of the West'; AHM, 2000). Shíba Kōkan and his circle of *rangaku* painters both 'baptized' Japan with European art and produced a large number of inspiring Japanese paintings at the same time. Hiroko Johnson

(2005: 71) describes the result as 'a hybrid of western engraving and traditional Japanese painting techniques'. Shíba Kōkan is remembered today because, as Keene puts it (1969: 69), 'of his influence on later Japanese artists, including Hokusai', who shaped the visual sensibility of many late nineteenth-century European artists, and were thus making the 'circle of borrowing' complete (Masanobu, 1978: 14; Tanaka, 1995: 256; Nishiyama, 1997: 71; Johnson, 2005: 154–155; Shiori, 2009: 80).

Peripatetic painters and Europeans on progress: the idea of the 'journey' in the meeting of Japan and Europe

Travel was an important mode of exchange during the Edo period, and Guth (1996: 150) summarizes that Tokugawa Japan was 'a nation on the move'. A paper scroll – more than seven metres long, and drawn in Shíba Kōkan's own hand – is an eloquent testimony of this artist's own journeys into the Japanese countryside, in the course of which he showed people from diverse regions of Japan examples of his art, or demonstrated optical instruments (AHM, 2000). The scroll was a highlight of the 2000 Amsterdam Kōkan exhibit. Shíba may have produced the first copperplate print in the history of Japan, and a few years later (1792), he became the first person to make a *copperplate-printed* world map (*Yoshi Zenzu, Chikyū Zenzu*). This, together with his unique etching of the sun, showed his interest in Copernican heliocentricity (Masanobu, 1978: 68; French, 1974: 121–124; Screech, 1996: 95; Shirahara, 2008: 123, 197–199; Clark, 2011: 29).

In spite of his interests apparently encompassing the whole world, and even the solar system, his own, personal world seems rather small. The highlight of his *Wanderjahre* was a trip Kōkan undertook to Nagasaki in 1788, aged 41.[21] Some scholars (Bell, 2004: 208–209, French, 1974: 53–77) have noted that Kōkan had hoped to find a teacher at the Dutch trading post; however, the Dutch in Nagasaki were traders, not artists, and in the event, Kōkan had to learn what he could from illustrations in Dutch books. He did, however, manage to get onto Deshima, disguised as a carrier, and even onto a Dutch ship – where he lost no time sketching. A woodcut illustration he made of the house of the *opperhoofd* in 1788 survives in Leiden (Boxer, 1968: Plate XII, after p. 124; French, 1974: 53; Masanobu, 1978: 72; Effert, 2000: 59; Screech, 2004: 314).

His travelogues, *Saiyū Ryodan* and *Gazu Saiyudan* ('Story of a Western Journey', 1794, 1803) and *Saiyū Nikki* ('Diary of a Western Journey', 1815), paint a very vivid picture, illustrated with sketches in his own hand. They are best read in conjunction with his other journal, *Shumparō Hikki* ('Notes by Sumparo', 1811), to convey a fascinating picture of broader social and intellectual conditions in Edo Japan at the time of his travels (Parthesius and Schiermeier, 2000: 13). *Saiyū Ryodan* and *Saiyū Nikki* stand in a tradition of Edo period Japanese travel writing that has received only modest critical attention in English so far. This seems surprising, since the travels of Edo intellectuals and artists allow contemporary analysts to draw important inferences as to whether the kind of 'Enlightenment' of Tokugawa times can in any way be compared with the conditions 'similar to those in Europe' (Plutschow, 2006: 3, 9).

Shíba Kōkan's travel diaries reveal him as an entrepreneurial, critical, observant, creative and eccentric individual. He self-funded his journey by demonstrating Western scientific instruments, by showing his *camera obscura* and his 'Dutch' paintings (*oranda-e*) to people in the provinces, by lecturing on Holland, geography and international relations (French, 1974: 55; Guth, 1996: 146) and by undertaking small commissions and portraits on the spot – many of which consciously imitated 'Western' conventions. The significance of Shíba Kōkan's 1788 Nagasaki trip lies in the fact that it consolidated his preconceptions about the visual impact of European art, and the accomplishments of Western learning. He is said to have become a 'full-blown' *rangakusha* after his return home (Shiori, 2009: 75–76). Therefore, Shíba Kōkan's travels become a first metaphor for many wider intellectual journeys undertaken by both Japanese and Europeans in Tokugawa times. The journey, therefore, is one of cultural *rapprochement* between Japan and Europe, the *Far East* and the *Far Away West*, seen through the window of many Dutch–Japanese meetings (Plutschow, 2006: 10).

The second paradigm of inter-cultural encounter is *De Hofreis naar Edo*,[22] the annual trip the Dutch had to make from their tiny trading outpost on Deshima to the seat of government in Edo, to pay their respects to the shōgun. Both kinds of journey are well-documented, mainly through Shíba Kōkan's own diaries, and in contemporary sources, like the official daily records (*dagregisters*)[23] of the Deshima Factory and the written output of some of its more enterprising Directors-turned-Japanologists, such as Isaac Titsingh (1745–1812), Jan Cock Blomhoff (1779–1853) or François Caron (1639–1640). Boxer (1968: 167) states that Isaac Titsingh has a 'double claim to fame', as a pioneering interpreter of Japan to Europe, and also of Europe to Japan. And François Caron, the author of *Beschrijvinghe van het machtigh Coninck-rijk Iapan* (1646), is credited with providing the most authoritative account of Japan in the seventeenth century, and steering the Dutch factory through waves of anti-foreign hysteria, which occurred at regular intervals (Lach and Van Kley, 1994, Vol. III; Book 1: 458–459; Book 4: 1855–1856).

The yearly ritual of the VOC's round-trip from Deshima to Edo and back was made a total of 166 times (Masanobu, 1978: 30). This was the only time that the Dutch and a few other European foreigners (see Appendix 9: *Dutch, Germans and Swedes in Tokugawa Japan*) were allowed to leave their small island-prison. The conveying of the *fūsetsugaki* – an early *International Relations Digest* (Ishii, 1971: 166–167) – during the court journey is easily underrated. Keene (2006: 24) observes:

> The summaries prepared by the head of the Dutch trading station of events in the world outside Japan during the previous year, the *fūsetsugaki*, as they were called, were essential to the *bakufu* because they provided information it could not obtain in any other way about developments abroad that might threaten Japanese security.

Contemporary Japanese reports about Siam are a case in point (Ishii, 1971: 169–171, 173), linking, as it were, both the Japanese and the Europeans to Siam (modern Thailand), whose relations with Europe can be said to be another precursor of 'European Studies in Asia' and are the subject of the remaining part of this chapter.

In conclusion to this section, there can be little doubt that the hollandophile *rangaku* movement was pivotal in both Japanese cultural history and the development of Asia–Europe exchange, with profound consequences for future international relations, knowledge transfer and art history. Keene (1969: 122) argues that it was precisely the 'receptivity on the part of Honda [Toshiaki, 1743–1820], Shíba [Kōkan] and other advanced men of their time that made it possible for Japan alone among Asian nations to rise to the challenge of the West'. There is more than a grain of truth in this assertion, since the way the Japanese reacted to Western learning influenced both Japanese science and art. Plutschow (2006: 17) cites the Swedish botanist and taxonomist Carl von Linné (Linnaeus, 1707–1778), whose binomial plant classification system came to Tokugawa Japan through his Dutch students and his Swedish colleague Carl Peter Thunberg. The wider philosophies of René Descartes, too, are also said to have reached Japanese shores through Linnaeus's work.

Therefore, it is possible to perceive some individual Japanese intellectuals of the period, such as Arai Hakuseki (1657–1725), as founders of something akin to a proto-European Studies discipline in Japan. Shíba Kōkan, too, on account of his publicly critical stance on Japan's isolationist policies, has invariably been described as a 'global thinker of sorts' (Plutschow, 2006: 201). He was ahead of his time, and even predicted Japan would have to open up to foreign influence in order to prevent colonization. Pedagogically speaking, there is much evidence to conclude that he was also an inspiring teacher, able to explain what must have seemed to most of his audience a very alien culture, in accessible terms – a skill indispensable to his modern contemporaries in this field.

However, a few significant qualifications need to be made to the overall picture: many views of the West, Holland and Europe, which were readily adopted and promulgated by artists-in-the-Western-manner like Shíba Kōkan, were unquestionably unreflective and uncritical. French (1974: 77) points out that Kōkan's enthusiasm for the West may have 'precluded doubts or criticisms of his Utopia'. Furthermore, the *rangakusha* were not revolutionaries; *rangaku* was never a 'grass-roots movement'; it never represented a mainstream of Tokugawa thought; the scholars of Western ways did not displace the Tokugawa feudal system or topple all conventions of Japanese art. Thus, 'Dutch Studies' did not emerge as a widespread novel theoretical framework. It represented a 'natural ontology' (Hall and McClain, 1991: 634), and an 'applied science', emphasizing practical experience and 'useful' knowledge.

Goodman (2006: 8, 291) summarizes it as 'a utilitarian technical supplement to a well-ordered, harmonious, intellectually-satisfying ethical system derived from Zhu Xi Confucianism'. 'Western art' was assimilated, in order for the Japanese to help grasp the truths of nature. Goodman (2000: 103) cites Shíba

Kōkan's work as being 'as much an appreciation of western science as it was more information on the technique of European painting'. In this qualifying view, acts such as the relaxation on the ban of Western books by the Tokugawa shōgun Yoshimune opened the door to foreign knowledge for its assumed utilitarian worth, but was never anything else but 'supplementary', and it re-enforced the power of shōgunal government (Ranzaburō, 1964: 264; Goodman, 2000: 65). This power was never significantly changed, and many scholars did not abandon their Confucian ethos.

If, as Roberts (2009: 65) argues, the wider adoption and adaptation of European knowledge was, ultimately, 'directed by local interests', it is nevertheless possible to see that, in the final analysis, the Dutch Studies scholars created a significant legacy for future Asia–Europe relations which it is impossible to overlook. Jansen (2000: 215) terms it a 'mind-set': 'a delight in the new, the different and the difficult'. The movement can also be said to have been a form of 'adaptive' or 'defensive' modernization. Keene (1969: 31) makes this point, arguing that 'these men were interested not so much in Dutch medicine or astronomy as in discovering how the European example could help keep Japan safe from invasion by making the nation strong and economically sound'.

This is a process which mirrors the kind of modernization pre-modern Siam went through in the nineteenth century, in its relations with Western powers, before it became Thailand (see the next section). It seems certain to me, though, that the intellectual debates in Tokugawa times, regarding what knowledge is for and what 'kinds of knowledge' are 'useful' and 'economically purposeful' to learners and to society as a whole, pre-figure the discourses of our own age in respect of such ideologies as 'employability' and the 'knowledge economy', and the way these concepts are defined, instrumentalized and disseminated.

Japanese diplomats, Siamese falcons and white elephants in the Venice of the East

> Some found it odd that King Chulalongkorn had a Dane to run his navy, a Belgian to manage the legal system, an Englishman in charge of the police, and many more suchlike; but it was a system adopted by Siamese kings in time of need since the days of Ayutthaya, and generally it served them well.
> (Garnier, 2004: 65)

Tokugawa Japan (see above) and Europe encountered one another not just on Japanese soil, but also in those 'indianized' (Acharya, 2013) areas of South East Asia in which merchants from both hemispheres did business. The Siamese capital of Ayutthaya was a prime location: a geographical nexus of exchange and pre-modern international relations. In addition to the European influence, Ayutthaya was also the destination for Japanese Christian refugees in times of persecution in Japan (Dhivarat, 2011: 149–150). The Japanese diplomat Yamada Nagamasa, in particular, embodies this 'hinge-function' of South East Asia in the meeting of Asia and Europe, as indeed does William Adams from a Western perspective (see Appendix 6: *Samurai William*). Yamada became a key diplomatic figure: as governor and head of the Japanese community, he was officially recognized by the Japanese and Siamese authorities as one of the Thai King's ministers (*okya senaphimuk*; Ishii, 1971; Yoko, 1999; Iwamoto, 2007). He maintained extensive contacts with the Europeans. Ayutthaya was an early Asia–Europe *cosmopolis*.

Kenneth R. Hall (2011: 20, 234) places the emergence of the cosmopolitan realm of Ayutthaya (1351–1767) on the lower Chao Phraya river in Siam (modern Thailand) in the context of classical 'geographical statehood' in early South East Asia. This embraced both 'riverine' and 'wet-rice-plain' regional polities. Peleggi (2013: 58) stresses the 'dual nature' of Ayutthaya, as both an agrarian state and a maritime entrepôt, whose monarchs used naval leadership and its possibilities. And Garnier (2004) situates Ayutthaya within the wider Chinese trade and tributary system before and after the Mongol conquest, and especially during the Ming dynasty (1368).

Irregular rhythms of involvement: early European–Asian encounters in Siam

Ayutthaya was an elite-run, rice-plain-based, kingdom. It was chosen as the Siamese capital in 1350 by King U-thong (Ramathibodi I; r. 1351–1369), in line with Buddhist geomantic-cosmological rules. The *Annals of Ayutthaya* show that Siamese suzerainty subsequently consolidated vis-à-vis smaller adjacent kingdoms like Sukothai. Ayutthaya became a communications and trans-shipment node for the intra-Asian trade, a transmission belt in the Asian state system of the period, as well as a centre of exchange with Europe, China, Macao, Korea and Japan (D'Ávila Lourido, 1996: 79ff.; Breazeale, 1999: 44; Garnier, 2004: 17; Yoshiteru and Bytheway, 2011: 91; Frey, 2011: 169).

In traditional (royal) Thai historiography, Ayutthaya is characterized as a 'port-polity', resembling Angkor (in Cambodia), Srívijaya,[24] Majapahit (on Sumatra and Java) and other realms. It was strategically located at the confluence of three rivers (Chao Phraya, Pasak and Lopburi) (Sternstein, 1965: 86–87; Breazeale, 1999: ix). Control of trade, production, agricultural hydraulics and overall irrigation was shared between jealously guarded, lucrative royal monopolies and Buddhist temple networks. The name 'Ayutthaya' is a reference to 'Ayudhya', the (mythological) city of the Hindu epic, the *Ramayana*. Ayutthaya – both a religious-royal town and a trading kingdom – is often exoticized as the 'Venice of the East' (Garnier, 2004: 51), but its riverine location and proximity to the sea made Ayutthaya the greatest emporium of the East for centuries.

The kingdom's geographical extent, social strata and political make-up was well known to Europeans, through contemporary accounts by European visitors. In fact, Europeans wrote more about Ayutthaya than anybody else (see below, and Sternstein, 1965: 106–107; Smithies, 1993: 116–118; 1995: 76–78; Villiers, 1998: 120–122; Garnier, 2004: 20; Baker, 2011: 38–39; Frey, 2011: 163). Ayutthaya's maritime connection, and a tendency towards toleration of foreigners and the faiths they imported[25] was noted by Europeans (Smithies, 1993: 121; Villiers, 1998: 123). The King saw himself as the sovereign of just his subjects' bodies, not also of their souls. This religious freedom facilitated inter-cultural communication, allowing diasporas to establish themselves and to 'reconstruct important coordinates of meaning and belief in a foreign environment' (Frey, 2011: 173). However, it also laid Ayutthaya open to European proselytizing, which was embedded in a geopolitical context of monopoly capitalism: the elimination of 'indigenous and resident diaspora intermediaries who had controlled trade in Southeast Asia since its inception' (Hall, 2011: 35). Ayutthaya's location allowed it to exploit international trade, via the Chao Phraya Delta and the Maritime Silk Road, throughout South East Asia, and into the networked Indian Ocean trade areas to Melaka (Malacca, in modern Malaysia), China, Indochina, India and the Philippines (D'Ávila Lourido, 1996: 76–77; Lach and Van Kley, 1998, Vol. III, Book 1: 233). Although (nominally) a 'vassal' state of China, Ayutthaya became powerful enough to attack the adjacent Angkor realm around 1369 and in 1431; however, the royal capital was itself besieged by Burmese armies in 1568–1569 and 1583, and finally sacked in 1767.

Maritime and trade engagement was essential to the legitimacy of Ayutthaya monarchs such as Trailok (r. 1448–1488). In 1458, Trailok consolidated his position by, amongst other measures, the promulgation of key Thai law codes and the reform of the Siamese *sakdina* system (commonly understood as 'feudalism'). Investigating the linguistic provenance of this term, Reynolds (2006: 107–108) defines *sakdina* as 'a social formation' and as 'the political, social and cultural order that characterized Thai society for some five hundred years'. It was a way of controlling people and resources by institutionally tying them to class and social structure.[26] The parallels with Tokugawa Japan are, indeed, striking. The Siamese King also expanded his realm into the Northern Malay Peninsula (Dhivarat, 2011: 147–148).[27] The *Patani Sultanate*, which extended by that time also to the areas of Kedah, Kelantan and Terengganu (in today's Malaysia), became a semi-independent vassal kingdom, a tributary to the Siamese Empire of Ayutthaya, with repercussions even today.

Ayutthaya had 200,000 inhabitants (Baker, 2011: 41; Peleggi, 2013: 59), not least as a result of its foreign contacts (Hall, 2011: 331–332). To the Dutch and English, Ayutthaya afforded the potential to tap the China and Macao trade, 'whence came supplies of silk and porcelain' (Hall, 1981: 323). Ayutthaya also connected with the Japan trade (Yoshiteru and Bytheway, 2011). It became a locale of early, non-indigenous, 'expatriate' communities in South East Asia (Osborne, 1997: 102). Thai documents such as the *Athibai phaen thi phranakhon si ayuttahya* ('Description of Ayutthaya'; Baker, 2011: 38, 58) testify to the presence of a plethora of foreign traders. Frey (2011: 162) examines twin-phenomena of Ayutthaya's economic social and political transformation and the presence of foreigners, in the context of a more 'connected' interpretation of Asia–Europe history, including art history (Appendix 10: *The writing on the wall: foreigners and Europeans (falang) in Thai art*).

Following the capture of Melaka (Malacca in modern Malaysia) in 1511, by Alfonso de Albuquerque, the Portuguese sent some envoys to Siam.[28] D.G.E. Hall (1981: 264) claims that Duarte Fernandez was the first European in Ayutthaya in that same year (D'Ávila Lourido, 1996: 77; Trakulhun, 2011: 183). Breazeale (2006: 54, 62–65) narrates an early Portuguese embassy to Siam under Father Francisco de Anunciação and describes a 'cavalcade of diplomats' sojourning between Ayutthaya and the Portuguese Government in Goa; many more Portuguese were later to enter Siam as merchants, missionaries[29] and mercenaries, even establishing a gun foundry at Ayutthaya. However, Siam was never a significant part of the *Império Português* (Villiers, 1998: 119; Breazeale, 1999: 44; 2006: 58).[30] Garnier (2004: 69) claims that 'only a few ripples of the [Portuguese] tidal wave of curiosity and discovery which surged across the oceans of the world in the 16th Century seemed to travel into the Gulf of Siam'. The English and Dutch presence too is, at times, best described as an 'irregular rhythm of involvement' (Dhivarat, 2011: 145) and of inactivity.

European sources and the 'burden of Higher Education'

The Portuguese (see also Chapter 3) have left us many sources on early Siam–Europe relations. Balthasar Sequeira (1551–1609) was the first Jesuit to be sent in 1606. João de Barros reported on the Luso–Siamese mercantile-military treaty of 1518, the presence of Islam, Siamese gifts to Portugal (Lach and Van Kley, 1994, Vol. II, Book 1: 10) and the liberal-arts oriented monastic curriculum offered in Buddhist monasteries, which reflected that of Nālandā University in India (see Chapter 2). Other Iberians too, like Marcelo de Ribadenaira (*Historia*, 1601), commented on education in Ayutthaya, on legal training and, interestingly, on the presence of foreign students in local law schools (Lach and Van Kley, 1998, Vol. III, Book 3: 1171). Luiz Vaz De Camões (1524–1580) has the kingdom of Siam explained to the Portuguese in *Canto X* of his epic poem *Os Lusíadas* (The Lusiads). Portuguese and Malay became *linguae francae* for foreigners in Ayutthaya, and Tomé Pires, Duarte Barbosa, João de Barros, Fernão Mendes Pinto and other Portuguese authors (Smithies, 1995: 59) wrote about the Siamese capital (Lach and Van Kley, 1994, Vol. I, Book 2: 522–531; Villiers, 1998: 121–123).

Mendes Pinto, writing on the eve of a Burmese aggression, reports how King Naresuan (r. 1590–1605) cajoled the Portuguese into his army by holding out privileges, land-grants and honours if they rallied to his colours. In Mendes Pinto's words, 'out of the 130 of us Portuguese who were there at the time, 120 agreed to go with him' (Smithies, 1995: 60; Cotterell, 2010: 33; Trakulhun, 2011: 183–186). Next to the Portuguese, other Europeans too became, at times, willing mercenaries: Dutch vessels, for example, aided King Prasat T'ong (r. 1629–1656) against both the Cambodians and the Portuguese (Hall, 1981: 339). Frey (2011: 168) interprets this as one reason for the privileged status of the Dutch in Siam, when compared to other Europeans. Valuable contemporary accounts of Ayutthaya come from the French priest Jacques de Bourges, the

84 *Theoretical aspects and historical predecessors*

German physician Engelbert Kaempfer (en-route to Japan; see above), the Portuguese Diogo do Couto and Dutchmen Cornelis van Nijenroode (Frey, 2011: 163–164; Ten Brummelhuis, 2011: 196), Joost Schouten and Jeremias van Vliet, all of whom directed the Dutch factory between 1617 and 1641. Van Vliet is, perhaps, best known among the Dutch for his testimony, the *Description of Siam* (Smithies, 1993: 113; 1995: 63; Villiers, 1998: 119ff.; Garnier, 2004: 39–40; Dhivarat, 2011: 143–144; Frey, 2011: 169; Peleggi, 2013: 60).

This wealth of historical European sources notwithstanding (Breazeale, 1999: x), Trakulhun employs the cases of the Frenchmen Nicolas Gervaise and Simon de la Loubère as illustrative examples in identifying a significant perceptual limitation affecting early European accounts of Siam. He calls this the 'burden of Higher Education', explaining that, 'steeped in classical learning, La Loubère's knowledge and intellectual capacity determined his mode of categorization of his observations' (Trakulhun, 1997: 80). There can be little doubt that this was true, to a greater or lesser degree, of many Europeans who reported on Siam (and wider Asia) in this period. (European) classical antiquity frequently looms large over these accounts. Another, stereotypical, theme emerging in European writings is the recurring view that successive Siamese monarchs are adroit at playing Western commercial and religious rivalries off against one another. Peleggi (2013: 59) sees this as follows: 'the Siamese sovereigns manipulated foreign rivalries to offset the demands of individual European countries for exclusive commercial and diplomatic rights'. This was to influence later Siamese–European (and Thai–EU) relations deeply (see Appendix 11: *Contemporary European accounts of the Kingdom of Ayutthaya and related modern publications*).

A microcosm and a Siamese game of thrones: law, science and diplomacy

Ayutthaya became a vibrant, multilingual and cosmopolitan microcosm of European (and East Asian) activities in Asia, where Chinese, Persians (Iranians), French, English,[31] Dutch, Danish, Russian, Portuguese, Luso-Asians, Malays, Japanese, and other nationalities and ethnicities all established a presence. The background to this visibility was unstable, and the politics of Europe remained dynamic and in flux. This resulted in cut-throat competition among Europeans *in situ* in Asia (e.g. Lach and Van Kley, 1998, Vol. III, Book 3: 1203). As a means of ensuring control (Ruangsilp, 2009: 147), Europeans were made to settle in quarters (*ban* or *baan*; cf. Smithies, 1995: 65) located beyond the city-limits formed by the three rivers encircling Ayutthaya (Sternstein, 1965: 104–105).[32] Many of them, for instance, from among the French Jesuits, became quite entangled in Siamese wars to the North (Chiegmai, Sukhothai, Lan Na), East (Cambodia, Angkor) and West (The Mon Kingdom, Pegu; Trakulhun, 2011). Dutch merchants were involved in freebooting against the Portuguese, in the Bay of Bengal and the Straits of Malacca (Hall, 1981: 185–200; D'Ávila Lourido, 1996: 78–79; Villiers, 1998: 120; Borschberg, 2002: 61–63).

Finding Europe in Nagasaki and Ayutthaya 85

The French Catholic *Société des Missions Etrangères* arrived in 1662, sending Jacques de Bourges, to make Ayuttaya into the base of French Asian evangelization and to seize the mantle of the declining Portuguese mission (Smithies, 1993: 113; van der Cruysse, 2002b: 52–55, 352). Lach and Van Kley (1998, Vol. III, Book 1: 252) describe the Siamese capital under King Narai (r. 1656–1688) as a 'French Macao'. The French Orientalists of the nineteenth century, like Henri Mouhout (1826–1861) and Francis Garnier (1839–1873), would later re-construct, in the euro-centric terms of their age, many aspects of life at Ayutthaya (King, 1995).

Among the aspects of Siamese–European relations highlighted as noteworthy by the missionaries and other Europeans, three themes are recurrent: they deserve special emphasis because they reverberate strongly down the centuries, and remain influential on contemporary European Studies in modern Thailand, and elsewhere in Asia. First is the interaction of Europeans with – or their perceived immunity to – Siamese law, a subject on which Simon de la Loubère comments extensively (Trakulhun, 1997: 81). From what was perceived to be the 'secretive' nature of the ways in which Siamese law codes were promulgated, many Europeans drew inferences as to the 'mystifying' nature of Siamese people, and of Asians. The euro-centric stereotype of European 'mutation' and Siamese (Asian) 'inconvertibility' (Trakulhun, 1997: 81) may well have one of its origins in actual and perceived divergences of legal systems, when compared to European yardsticks and discourses.

The so-called 'Van Vliet incident'[33] of 1636 is a good illustration of this: on 10 December 1636, some employees of the VOC, 'in a state of drunkenness', desecrated one of the holiest Buddhist temples in Ayutthaya, a transgression for which they were sentenced to death by being trampled on by an elephant – a standard execution method at the time (van der Kraan, 2000: 1). The Dutch – like other Europeans – sought extraterritoriality for their citizens, i.e. immunity from the application of Siamese law. This was eventually granted, 30 years later and only under threat of violence (Frey, 2011: 170). The incident had repercussions for future European (and Thai) Studies. It not only showcased the diplomatic skills of the Dutch factor Jeremias van Vliet in obtaining a pardon for the culprits; it also brought to the fore issues which were to inform later diplomatic and legal relations between Asia and Europe, and the syllabus of many a European Studies course in Asia.

Bhawan Ruangsilp (2009: 156) expounds:

> The Dutch-Thai case was not unique in the whole context of the cross-cultural interactions between Asia and Europe in the early modern period. A plurality of legal systems did, indeed, exist in practice in many places in Asia, upheld by the approval of indigenous rulers, as well as overseas European authorities, as a response to the cosmopolitan environment of its time, when a nation-state that enforced the monopoly of order and justice was still merely a concept.

Yoko (2009) has investigated the parallel case of foreigners in Japan, as a 'reverse' of how Japanese were administered. These legal questions can, arguably, be said to have an impact comparable to the work of Hugo Grotius's on the 'Freedom of the Seas' (*mare liberum*; see Chapter 3).

Astronomy and natural sciences form the second backbone of early diplomacy between Europeans and Siamese. Smithies (2003) shows how both lunar and solar eclipses, in 1685 and 1688 respectively, gave the Jesuits, who were in Siam, in transit to China, a unique opportunity to use the Siamese monarch's fascination with the heavens. In Ayutthaya, as well as China and Japan, Europe–Asia discourse was thus often framed by science, and by connections that were made between science, conversion and dynastic politics, all against the background of various machinations by the European factions. The Siamese Jesuits did not 'hide their light under a bushel' and 'selected to impress' the King with their knowledge (Smithies, 2003: 190–192). Euro-Asian astronomical activities were also a temporary leveller of status since, during observations with the Jesuits, King Narai 'did suffer them' to be at the same height as himself – a rare privilege indeed (Smithies, 2003: 191). The representation of the eclipses of 1688 – a revolutionary year of 'regime change' in Siam – assumes a changed significance when seen as tools of diplomacy: they were opportunities for the Siamese King to interact with Europeans; conversely, here were some chances for Europeans to access and influence the monarch in a game of power, trade and diplomacy. Exhibitions and cultural events are fulfilling much the same purpose in the Asia–Europe relations of our own time (see Chapter 5).

Diplomacy is, indeed, the third *leitmotiv* of European–Siamese relations in the sixteenth and seventeenth centuries. The extraordinary levels of diplomatic activity sets this exchange apart from all others investigated in this book. More so than, say, in Tokugawa Japan, diplomatic missions and the Europeans' desire to secure influence at the Siamese court became a hallmark of the interaction. An embassy from Ayutthaya to The Hague in 1608–1609 was amongst the first diplomatic missions (Hall, 1981: 380), building on an early Dutch visit to Siam in 1604. Other (Siamese) embassies followed, for instance, to France and Portugal (1608, 1615–1617, 1684), with the purpose of finding allies against Siam's neighbours.

The Siamese envoys dispatched to Lisbon in 1615–1616 and 1684 never arrived; they were either unable to proceed from Portuguese Goa (Breazeale, 2006: 68) or shipwrecked in Africa. However, their journeys are noteworthy for the detailed instructions they had received, covering such diverse matters as trading, learning, Siamese–European protocol, the international relations of Siam with the Muslim world and China, and the situation of Europeans working for the Siamese monarch (Smithies and Dhivarat, 2002: 126–133). A further diplomatic train, led by Pero Vaz de Siqueira, was dispatched from the Portuguese viceroy at Goa to Ayutthaya in 1685, seeking to, once again, ensure 'extraterritoriality' for the Portuguese in Siamese law (see above, and Smithies and Dhivarat, 2002; Seabra, 2004).

A Siamese progress to the Court at Versailles in 1686, under the Siamese commoner-turned-noble (*khunnang*) Kosa Pan, did reach its destination. It became 'one of the best-documented diplomatic receptions in East–West relations' (Guy, 1999: 88).[34] It inaugurated significant diplomatic exchange between France, wider Europe and Siam (van der Cruysse, 2002a, 2002b). Building on the work of the *Société des Missions Etrangères*, founded in 1658, Louis XIV of France (r. 1643–1715) had dispatched an embassy in 1680; it was shipwrecked off Madagascar. A further embassy in 1685, under the Chevalier Alexandre de Chaumont (c.1640–1710), the Jesuit Guy Tachard (1648–1712) and François-Timoléon (1644–1724), the Abbé de Choisy, did arrive in Siam. This mission was accompanied by Jesuit-astronomers (Smithies, 2003: 190).

Another progress departed in 1687/1688 under the diplomat Simon de la Loubère (1642–1729), to whom we owe the book *Du Royaume de Siam* (Paris, 1691). De la Loubère's book contains unparalleled detail of Ayutthaya, but, as Trakulhun (1997: 76) argues, is coloured by euro-centric 'perceptual schemes' and 'pre-existing interpretive schemas', as regards diplomatic protocol, ritual and ceremony practised by Siamese kings (see also Peleggi, 2013: 60). The role of the Jesuit Fathers in the embassy was to 'impress the Siamese court with European culture, learning and religion' (Guy, 1999: 88) and to spread the Catholic faith *in partibus infidelium* (Lach and Van Kley, 1998, Vol. III, Book 1: 253–254; Brockey, 2007: 156).

This 'scientific' approach to missions in Siam was similar to the one adopted in China (see Chapter 3), in that the Jesuits concentrated on the conversion of the elites. The hope was that King Narai might be converted – an endeavour in which Narai's polyglot European aide, Constantine Phaulkon (see below), attempted to become involved. Taking the 'Asian' point of view, Garnier (2004: 120) examines Siamese diplomatic techniques of the time vis-à-vis many European embassies: 'it sometimes seems as though foreign emissaries were rewarded by the Siamese in direct proportion to the success the Siamese had in thwarting their aims'.

The 1688 Siamese Revolution curtailed the French presence in Siam, and subsequently all Europeans, bar the Dutch, were expelled from the realm (Lach and Van Kley, 1998, Vol. III, Book 1: 103; Garnier, 2004: 91). A letter by William Soame (an English merchant in Siam) survives; in it, Soame comments on the turbulent events of 1688, such as the accession of King Phetracha, the execution of Constantine Phaulkon, the demise of King Narai and the French military defeat of Siam.[35] Thongchai Winichakul (2011: 30–32) sees the 'watershed-year' of 1688 as 'instrumental' in that it altered the direction of Thai historiographical discourse, towards a stronger emphasis on 'ancient' Thai capitals and their monarchs, framing Siam's struggles for continuing independence, with lasting repercussions for the modern Thai–European diplomatic interaction.

Legacies, historiography and the power of personalities in the 'Wild West of Asia'

Following the destruction of Ayutthaya in 1767, and the end of the reign of the last Ayutthayan monarch (Boromoraja, 1758–1767), the new (Chakri) dynasty established Bangkok as the capital. From the mid-1800s, successive Thai

88 Theoretical aspects and historical predecessors

monarchs such as Rama IV (Mongkut,[36] 1851–1868) and Rama V (Chulalongkorn 'the Great', 1868–1910) are said to have set Thailand on a path to modernity, fed mainly from three wellsprings: Buddhism and the monarchy, an international relations strategy of 'defensive modernization' (Curtin, 2000: 151) and the historical-cultural templates defined by a Thai concept of 'civilized antiquity' (*siwilai*), especially by the former royal capital of Ayutthaya, as 'the mark of Siam's beginning' (Winichakul, 2011: 37).

Chulalongkorn, the King after whom Thailand's oldest university is named, is often seen as an important pre-cursor of 'European Studies' in Thailand. Today, Ayutthaya is a popular tourist destination on a day trip from Bangkok (Saipradist and Staiff, 2007); however, it has also become a key cultural template. Askew (2002: 16) points out that the name 'Ayutthaya' was included in the first city title given to the city of Bangkok ('Krung Thep Therawadi *Sri Ayutthaya*') in 1782. Although the title was later revoked, the art, architecture and the very layout of modern Bangkok has been found to derive much of its 'Thai-ness' from the old royal capital.

In this context, Askew analyses the ideological aspects of the 'imperative to re-build Ayutthaya' (2002: 17): 'the general desire to reproduce the familiar spatial and symbolic signifiers of the royal city as an embodiment of king-centered polity is clear'. In the same vein, Thongchai Winichakul (1994: 162–163) demonstrates how the 'traditional' elements of Thai history, embodied in the 'great historical centres' narrative were also very consciously woven into the fabric of modern Bangkok, supporting and legitimizing what he terms the 'geo-body' of modern Thailand. This refers, in particular, to the iconography of some of today's best known cultural heritage sites within Bangkok, such as *Rattanakosin* Island, *Wat Phra Kaeo* ('The Temple of the Emerald Buddha') and the 'Grand' (Royal) Palace complex (*Chakri Mahaprasad*) (Van Beek and Tettoni, 1999: 165–196). Modern Thailand and her students of European Studies sometimes continue to interpret 'Europe' through the looking-glass of Thailand's historical-ideological geo-body.

Thus, the predominant Thai historiographical discourse of a 'defensive', 'timely' or 'adaptive' modernization, referred to in this book, and undertaken by 'benevolent' Siamese kings has been criticized by observers such as Thongchai Winichakul (2011: 29), who argues that the phenomenon also served Siamese royalist-political and expansionary interests. However, the way modern Thai governments view Ayutthaya (and European *falangs*) is still, arguably, pervaded by a sense of determination to preserve the country's monarchy, sovereignty and territorial integrity, collectively known as the *Royal Imprint on International Relations*.[37] This text is a prerequisite for anyone teaching European (Union) Studies in Thailand (see also Welch, 2013).

In fact, the role of Ayutthaya as a core foundation stone of modern Thai identity, reinforced through politicians, the media and (school) curriculum reform in both the 1960s and the 1990s has been shown to have altered according to the changing requirements of the governments of the time, be they military-dictatorial or, more or less, democratic. Ayutthaya has, therefore, been imagined, and re-imagined, numerous times, with an emphasis, at times, on concepts of monarchy, strong leadership warrior-kings and military prowess, at other times on antiquity and civilization, local history, de-centralized historiography and regional centres (Vanichviroon, 2004: 59–60).

It is with reference to Ayutthaya that Saipradist and Staiff (2007) illuminate:

> the strong nexus between Thai heritage (*moradok*), nationalism (and its insistence on the historical narrative of the modern nation-state that draws a line between Sukhothai, Ayutthaya and Bangkok), and the so-called three pillars of Thai cultural and social identity: Buddhism, the Monarchy and the State (symbolized in the Thai flag). This relationship is both represented and enacted, over and over, by tourism to Ayutthaya – in the guidebooks, and in the way the tourist experience is constructed at the site.

This political 're-fashioning' of Ayutthaya into the lead-narrative of Thai identity, disseminated, for example, in schoolbooks and university texts from the 1960s to the 1990s, has also deeply affected the ways in which Europeans are written into – or out of – the bigger picture: as 'reflectors' of Siamese/Thai 'glory', 'confirmers' of the state's equal place in international relations, 'yardsticks' of modernity, visitors and business partners, and, most recently, as, more or less culturally literate 'tourists' (Saipradist and Staiff, 2007) and foreign exchange students from Europe. Ayutthaya's former European traders have become today's FDI (foreign direct investment) providers. At the time of writing, perceptions of a 'rise' of Asia and of a Europe 'stagnating' in a 'Euro-crisis' are once again causing the 'Ayutthaya past' to be re-evaluated and re-interpreted, in terms of modern Asia–Europe/EU relations.[38]

In terms of a more personal Asia–Europe 'people-to-people exchange', 2011 marked the five-hundredth anniversary of the arrival of the first Europeans in Siam (Smithies, 2011).[39] From among the many remarkable figures, two key personalities have been selected for closer inspection, because they vividly illustrate the overlap between knowledge transfer and pedagogy, influence and diplomacy, personal adaptation, acculturation and accommodation that has provided the historical templates for modern Europeans living, working and teaching in Asia. Constantine Phaulkon (1647–1688, real name Constantinos Gerakis, Κωσταντής Γεράκης)[40] was the son of an innkeeper on the Greek island of Cephalonia. Cabin-boy and assistant gunner-turned-merchant-adventurer, he arrived in Ayutthaya in 1678 with Richard Burnaby, the factor of the East India Company, whom Phaulkon was later powerful enough to help make governor of Mergui, an important province (Smithies, 1994: 147). Phaulkon was converted to Roman Catholicism in 1682 by the Flemish Jesuit Antoine Thomas (1644–1709). He was a gifted interpreter and persuasive adviser, who rose to unique prominence under King Narai, becoming 'Superintendent of Foreign Trade', obtaining the ministerial rank of *phrakhlang* in 1683 – and jealously guarding his privileges. Hall observes (1981: 387–388) that Phaulkon's influence had consolidated to such a degree that he had become 'the controlling factor in its [i.e. Siam's] foreign policy' – quite a career for a *falang*.

First employed to promote English interests in Siam against the Dutch, the Greek, who married a Catholic of Japanese-Portuguese-Bengali descent, later switched to support – then undermine – French interests, making enemies in the process, such as the French Chevalier de Fo(u)rbin and many Thai courtiers (Smithies, 1994: 151; Garnier, 2004: 126–127). The Siamese dynastic revolt in 1688 brought a new king to the throne (Petraja, 1632–1703); the over-ambitious Phaulkon fell out of favour and was beheaded – news of which event eventually travelled as far as Japan (Ishii, 1971: 169).

Farrington (2002: 77) assesses Phaulkon's ambiguous legacy as follows: 'for ten years, Ayutthaya [...] became the free-trading "Wild West" of Asia, under the influence of Constantine Phaulkon, a former [EIC] company employee of Greek origin who became Siamese Minister for the Affairs of Foreigners'. Robert Bruce simply described Phaulkon as the 'Greek Dictator of Siam' (*History Today*, Vol. 32, Issue 2, February 1982). D.G.E. Hall (1981: 397) points to the aftermath of Phaulkon's scheming:

> the reaction against the policy of King Narai and Constant Phaulkon had caused such a powerful upsurge of anti-foreign sentiment that, until the days of [king] Mongkut in the middle of the Nineteenth Century, Siam was to be very chary of granting privileges to Europeans.

Is this a good theme, perhaps, to explore in modern European Studies?

Second is English merchant Ralph Fitch (*c.*1550–1611). 'Portugal produced no Marco Polo, or even a Ralph Fitch', Lach and Van Kley (1994, Vol. I, Book 1: 204) claim. Fitch, England's commercial agent and trade pioneer to India and Burma from 1583, and a prolific author on Asia in his own right, is a frequently neglected figure. A London leather trader, he is said to have been the first Englishman to visit South East Asia and record what he saw (Lach and Van Kley, 1994, Vol. I, Book 2: 499; van der Cruysse, 2002a: 54; Garnier, 2004: 98).

The significance of Fitch's testimony about Burma (e.g. the *Shwe Dagon* Pagoda), India, Malacca, Siam (Ayutthaya and Chiang Mai) and elsewhere is threefold: first, he seems to have explored many 'interior places' which other Europeans had not reached yet; second, Fitch's accounts deal with Asian history at a time when Jesuit sources (see Chapter 3) were still few and far between; and third, the recollections of his peregrinations – imprecise as they may be – nevertheless constitute examples of stories of personal experience of Europeans in Asia, set against the backdrop of the Siamese wars with the kingdom of Pegu (in modern Myanmar) throughout the sixteenth century (Breazeale, 2006: 54–57). This afforded Europeans an insight into the vagaries and webs of early South East Asian international relations.

The great English collector of travel literature, Richard Hakluyt, included Fitch's account in his account of travel, geography and global trade, the *Principal(l) Navigations, Voyages, Traffiques and Discoveries of the English*

Nation of 1589[41] (Hall, 1981: 297). Perhaps Fitch's peregrinations are also referred to, albeit indirectly, by Shakespeare in Act 1, Scene 3 of *Macbeth*, where the first witch cackles about a sailor's wife: 'Her husband's to Aleppo gone, master o' the Tyger' (van der Cruysse, 2002b: 268; Garnier, 2004: 99). Fitch reported that he had seen the white elephants of the King of Pegu. Since no one, bar the king, was allowed to own them – and since he demanded money from the people for their upkeep – they were considered expensive and useless (hence the expression 'White Elephant').[42]

In conclusion to this section, the pre-modern relations between Siamese Ayutthaya, as a hub of trade, religion and education in South East Asia, her European residents and their governments contain many lessons for the teaching of European Studies in modern Thailand and wider Asia. Among them, the role of identities and legitimizing historical narratives of nations is, arguably, the most significant one, when comparing Asian historiographies with the teaching of foundation-narratives of such modern constructs as the European Union. Siamese–European interaction from the fifteenth to the eighteenth centuries can also reveal valuable insights about the 'obstacles' a 'Western' education can represent to a fuller understanding of (South East) Asian modes of thought, aesthetics and political practices. Furthermore, the impressions which the many European traders, missionaries and envoys have left us in their reports and narratives, travelogues and accounts, in regard to the thorough (monastic) education system they encountered, are opening up many avenues and case studies for later visitors, teachers, lecturers and observers to engage in modern cross-cultural pedagogies without condescension, and in a spirit of open enquiry. Last, but by no means least, the history of Europeans in Ayutthaya and Siamese in Europe, which is replete with embassies, good-will missions and much exchange on the borders between the scientific and the diplomatic, contains many valuable insights in how to train diplomats in Europe and Asia today – this thread will be taken up again in Chapter 8, dealing with contemporary diplomacy training in Brussels.

Chapter conclusions

By way of conclusion to this chapter, both cross-cultural encounters put under the spotlight here – Dutch–Japanese and European–Siamese – have made essential contributions to the history of knowledge and ideas in Asia–Europe relations. They have pointed to lessons to be learned about both the potential and the limitations to inter-cultural exchange at different points in history. More so, perhaps, than the cases of Central Asia/Silk Road and the Portuguese Empire and Jesuit proselytizing, European–Asian meetings from Japan to Ayutthaya show the limits, and the politics, of educational exchange and learning in action.

What modern educators, lecturers and planners of European (Union) Studies (in Asia) may learn from these early encounters may be either the importance of diplomacy and 'people-to-people meetings', or the respect for cultures, faiths and identities. Siamese, Europeans and Japanese have shown us how to penetrate and seek to understand another culture and to thus encourage intellectual curiosity, trade, knowledge exchange and cooperation. More so than the case studies of the Jesuits and Central Asia, the examples of Ayutthaya and Japan show us that much fruitful dialogue between civilizations is possible without the religious dimension, although this has never been far from the surface in bringing 'Europe' to 'Asia'. In common with the West–East encounters of Portuguese Asia and the Silk Routes, the educational meeting of Europe and Asia in Nagasaki and Ayutthaya has also demonstrated the significant impact that art has had in the context of these exchanges.

Bringing one culture into another, by means of art-related events, exhibitions and such like, is of course a central tenet of 'European Studies in Asia' and should not be absent from the syllabi and module outlines of today's lecturers and Professors. The next chapter will cast some more detailed light on how public art exhibitions have risen to this task of bringing Asia and Europe closer to one another, and of providing a channel for artistic expression and cultural collaboration to get onto the relevant timetables of European Studies in Asia, and into Asian classrooms led by Europeans.

Notes

1 See the podcast at: www.bbc.co.uk/ahistoryoftheworld/objects/MAPlqOEHRsmI1awIHQzRSQ.
2 Foreigners from Europe, especially Portuguese, are often depicted on *Namban* folding screens (*byōbus*) of the period (see Severy and Stanfield, 1992: 86–87, for a prime example). In 2010/2011, the *Museu do Oriente* in Lisbon held an exhibition entitled *Namban Commissions – The Portuguese in Modern Age Japan* (www.museudooriente.pt/).
3 For a general overview of Edo-period historiography, see Hall and McClain (1991).
4 The (rather idiosyncratic) *Samurai Archives* is at: www.samurai-archives.com/.
5 As opposed to *kaikoku* (meaning: 'opening the country').
6 On the Edo period: Victoria and Albert Museum: www.vam.ac.uk/content/articles/t/the-edo-period-in-japanese-history/.
7 See: www.tnm.jp/modules/r_free_page/index.php?id=685&lang=en.
8 The exhibition *Red-haired Barbarians: The Dutch and Other Foreigners in Nagasaki and Yokohama, 1800–1865*, at the *International Institute of Social History* in Amsterdam illuminated the stereotypical Japanese perceptions of the Dutch through a selection of 40 Japanese prints (www.iisg.nl/exhibitions/japaneseprints/).
9 The ambiguous spaces of the 'Floating World' were ingeniously evoked in music, for example, in *Meditation on Ukiyo-e*, by Alan Hovhaness (1911–2000), and in Evelyn Glennie's masterpiece, *Fantasy on Japanese Woodprints* [sic] *op. 211*.
10 The term *rangaku* derives from the Japanese *O-ran-da* – the linguistic rendering of 'Holland' (Keene, 1969: 17).
11 For a modern take, see 'Deshima Re-emerges', at: www.uwosh.edu/home_pages/faculty_staff/earns/deshima.html.
12 The exhibition *Holland and Japan – 400 Years of Trade* at the *Schiphol Rijksmuseum* celebrated the legacy of 400 years of Dutch–Japanese relations in 2009 (http://api.rijksmuseum.nl/tentoonstellingen/holland-en-japan?lang=en).
13 Goodman (2000: especially 118–146) offers a satisfyingly detailed account of the movement.
14 *Rangaku (Tome 1) La Cité sans Nuit*, by Luca Enoch and Maurizio Di Vincenco

(2007) is a brilliant evocation of this – in comic-strip manga-style (Paris: Les Humanoïdes Associés).
15 An interesting You Tube video on *Rangaku* is at: www.youtube.com/watch?v=9Ns4n 5AEFRA.
16 The characters for 'Aōdō' in Denzen's name stand for 'Studio (or 'Hall') of Asia and Europe' (Keene, 1969: 67–68; Masanobu, 1978: 93; Lee, 1983: 187; Nishiyama, 1997: 70–71; Goodman, 2000: 111, 128).
17 Lit.: 'light/shadow'. The traditional Asian technique to indicate depth had been the (Chinese) *kumadori* (lit.: 'dark smudging', 'giving shade').
18 Although it is inaccurate to say that traditional Japanese artists knew nothing of the effect of distance (Stewart, 1979: 71; Jarves, 1984: 106).
19 An orrery is a globe or a sphere illustrating the mechanics of the heavens. Copernicus is said to have made the first one.
20 Although Kōkan's erstwhile teacher Aōdō Denzen made a rival claim to the discovery (Masanobu, 1978: 98).
21 A map of this journey is in French (1974: 56–57).
22 Effert (2000: 52) has a wonderful painting of (part of) the journey by Kawahara Keiga, from the National Museum of Ethnology in Leiden, Netherlands (Siebold Collection 1–4488–23); see also: www.geheugenvannederland.nl/?/en/items/KONB11 xxCOLONxx1-4488-33.
23 See: www.hendrick-hamel.henny-savenije.pe.kr/Dutch/bijlagene.htm.
24 The Maritime Empire of *Śrīvijaya*, located around Palembang (on the island of Sumatra), lasted from the seventh to the fifteenth centuries; *Majapahit* existed from the thirteenth to the sixteenth centuries (source: National Museum of Malaysia).
25 A good, general booklist on the subject of 'Europe and Siam' can be found at: www.museumvolunteersbkk.net/pdf/2011/books_realted_500symp_web.pdf.
26 This system was described by many Europeans, e.g. Dutchman Jeremias Van Vliet (Garnier, 2004: 55–56).
27 Askew (2002: 24) explains this as follows: 'The *sakdina* structure [...] linked the social ranking and status of a state-appointed nobility (*khunnang*) to a means of control over the labour and economic surplus of commoners (*phrai*) through the divisions (*krom*) and their graded functionaries'.
28 The five-hundredth anniversary of Thai–Siamese relations in 2011 was widely commemorated in Bangkok – for example, through Academic Seminars at the *European Studies Centre of Chulalongkorn University*, an exhibition at *Museum Siam* and a range of events and publications mediated through the *Portuguese Cultural Center – Camões*, Bangkok. Some key websites in regard to this event are: http://eeas.europa.eu/delegations/thailand/documents/more_info/chulalongkorn500years_en.pdf (university); www.mfa.go.th/main/en/media-center/14/8094-500-years-of-Diplomatic-Relations-between-Thailand.html (MFA); www.bba.bus.tu.ac.th/upload/student/news211/500years.pdf (project proposal with useful background information); https://sites.google.com/site/pccbkk/in-the-news/bookspublishedin2011about500yearsportugal-thailand (books).
29 The main Orders were Dominicans, Franciscans and, especially, Jesuits (see Chapter 3).
30 Bernades de Carvalho (2011) offers an extensive treatment of the Portuguese presence in Ayutthaya.
31 The English factory at Ayutthaya was, however, closed between 1622 and 1674, with one, brief, interval in 1662.
32 For example: www.ayutthaya-history.com/Settlements_Dutch_BaanHolland.html.
33 Sometimes, this incident is called the 'Dutch Picnic' (Ruangsilp, 2009: 142–143).
34 J. Hainzelman's famous engraving, *The Siamese Embassy Processing a Letter from Phra Narai to Louis XIV at Versailles, 1 September 1686*, can be viewed in Jackson and Jaffer (2004: 89).

35 See: www.siamese-heritage.org/jsspdf/1991/JSS_080_1e_LetterByEnglishMerchant 1688.pdf.
36 Mongkut is, perhaps, best known as the King in the 1951 play and 1956 film *The King and I*, based on the 1946 film *Anna and the King of Siam*, which was based on the 1944 novel about Anna Leonowens' years at his court, from 1862 to 1867.
37 See, for example, the Thai Foreign Office Public Relations Department website, at: http://thailand.prd.go.th/ebook/imprint/page3.php.
38 See also *Ayutthaya: Past, Present and Future of a Heritage City*; Final Report: www.ayutthaya-history.com/files/AyutthayaHeritageCityReport2011.pdf (2011).
39 This anniversary was commemorated by *Bangkok's National Museum Volunteers (NMV)*, who organized a symposium entitled *500 Years: Europeans in Siam* on 24 February 2011 (see: *Bangkok Post*, 9 February 2011). www.museumvolunteersbkk.net/pdf/2011/Lecturers_and_topics_5feb.pdf.
40 γεράκι ('geraki') is the Greek word for 'falcon'.
41 See Claire Jowitt: 'The Tudor Guide to Colonising the World', in: *History Magazine*, 14/1 (January 2013).
42 From: www.bbc.co.uk/radio4/history/empire/episodes/episode_12.shtml.

Part II
Contemporary representations and actors

5 Travels of the mind

Exhibitions, websites and public events connecting with European Studies in Asia

Introduction: the subject of exchange and learning in Asia–Europe relations through the prisms of public 'blockbuster' exhibitions, smaller events and museum displays[1]

Museums are texts and sub-texts, narratives and displays, stories and shop-windows, all at once, rolled into one package. When the museum visitors come through the door, they enter a world of myth and wonder, reality and fantasy, subtle message and gentle deception. If it is a good museum, that is. But what is a 'good' museum? Every museum, every show, be it real-world or virtual-reality, seeks to draw us into a framework, which is more of less alien to us, and in which the priorities and conditions, the leitmotivs and connections have been made by someone other than us. Is a 'good' museum, therefore, the one that leaves the 'thinking' to us? Do the more 'thought-provoking' exhibitions leave us enough private 'head-space', in order to make our own connections and define our own questions?

When researching museum exhibits on the subject of Asia–Europe intellectual exchange, the journeys of knowledge and the roles of religion, trade, science and politics in shaping *what* and *how* we learn from one another, I found that this is, indeed, so. I felt I was becoming more sensitive to those missing links, the unspoken sub-text and the subtle connection that suggested itself only after a repeat visit or two. With this chapter, I am attempting to convey an impression of a range of exhibitions on the broad subjects of this book, and especially on the topic of how 'Western', European, knowledge travelled to Asia, and how it was received in the East. The time-frame of the chapter covers exhibitions over, approximately, the last decade, in both Europe and Asia, and I am approaching this area by means of a range of short case studies and a brief look at 'on-line' presentations towards the end of the chapter.

Over the last decade, I have been privileged to visit a large number of museums, events, lectures and exhibits on three continents, and I continue to do so. Looking back at my own perspective over those years, I would have to say that I observed matters as a 'European Studies' scholar, a lecturer on the EU in Asia, a frequent visitor to Asia, Australia and New Zealand, and someone who has thought and written a great deal about the area of Europe–Asia political exchange and the vagaries of the EU's Asia policies. I feel, however, that there has always been another dimension, and I hope that it comes to the surface in this chapter, and throughout the rest of this book. This is the cultural, artistic, side of East–West knowledge transfer; those aspects of Asia–Europe which underlie the politics of the day. Consequently, in what follows, I wish to emphasize the roles of cultural assumptions and values, artistic absorption of – and response to – the 'Other', mutual development through creativity, and learning through in-acculturation and integration. I hope that my choice of key exhibitions reflects this (See Appendix 12: *A selection of exhibitions and museum displays on Europe–Asia relations*).

Four 'blockbuster' exhibitions with high relevance to European Studies in Asia (2000–2010)

Encounters: The Meeting of Asia and Europe 1500–1800
Victoria and Albert Museum, London, 23 September–5 December 2004

A Passage to Asia: 25 Centuries of Exchange between Asia and Europe; Palais des Beaux Arts
Brussels Centre for Fine Arts, Brussels, 25 June–10 October 2010

Japanse Verwondering (Japanese Amazement): Shiba Kōkan 1747–1818: Kunstenaar in de ban van het Westen (Artist under the Spell of the West)
Amsterdams Historisch Museum (Historical Museum of Amsterdam, [now: Amsterdam Museum]), 2000

Westerse Reizigers in China: De Ontdekking van het Rijk van het Midden – Voyageurs Occidentaux En Chine: La Découverte de l'Empire du Milieu (Western Travellers in China: Discovering the Middle Kingdom)
International Arts Festival: europalia.china, Bibliotheca Wittockiana, 28 October 2009–10 January 2010

The *Encounters* exhibition at the V&A in 2004 was, arguably, the most relevant show in the context of this book, in terms of its legacy, relevance, impact and scope, and in the context of the period it showcased. Foregrounding as it did the processes and results of the inter-cultural *meeting* of East and West, *Encounters* was also one of the most written-about and reviewed events in this area.[2] The exhibition touched on all the three priority areas of Asia–Europe history which I have chosen to highlight in Chapters 1–3 of this book, offering texts and exhibits on the Portuguese age of 'discovery', religious enterprise and the early Europe–Japan knowledge transfer and technological exchange of the Dutch and the *rangaku* scholars (see Chapter 4).

The principal subjects of *Encounters* were subsumed under the categories of 'discoveries', 'encounters' and 'exchanges'. Instead of presenting a chronological, narrative, view of the historical Asia–Europe interaction, this exhibition raised important questions in early international relations, such as on whose 'terms' these early meetings took place, what the 'impact' of European presence in the East was, and which 'roles' the concepts of 'East' and 'West', 'Orient' and 'Occident' may have occupied in one another's imagination during the period 1500–1800 and later. A secondary theme was represented in the idea of 'personal encounters', between Asians and Europeans, which occurred for a number of reasons.

The events, lectures and publications which accompanied *Encounters* – in particular, a parallel conference (12–13 November 2004) – placed the exhibition in a wider geopolitical, mainly economic, context analysing, for example, the collapse of the Mughal Empire in India and the role of the British East India Company, and the Opium Wars in China. *Encounters* also made a link with broader concepts which demonstrated the lasting impact of Asia–Europe relations on world history and the legacy of those early meetings for our 'modern' notions of 'globalization', 'hybridity' and 'fusion' (Jackson, 2004: 20–22).

In terms of educational exchange, *Encounters* established a number of important narrative themes and topoi which were both confirmed and contradicted by different exhibitions on this subject (see below). Among them were the ideas of 'control' and 'exotic' other-ness: In his exhibition review in the *Independent*, Michael Church wrote, quoting the exhibition's curator: 'the foreigners were controlled. And, just as Westerners saw the East as exotic, so Asians saw these curiously dressed, big-nosed, Westerners as exotic.' In an article in a thematic issue of the *V&A Magazine*, Sanjay Subrahmanyam (2004: 34–42) discussed evidence of the European personal, diplomatic and pedagogic technique of 'going native' in Asia, by adopting Eastern dress, manners and habits (cf. Jackson and Jaffer, 2004: Chapter 12; Open University, 2010: 14–15). Mark Kennedy in the *Guardian* saw this behaviour, rightly or wrongly, as 'unintentionally hilarious'.[3] However, this form of adaptation became an important *modus operandi* for both missionary (see Chapter 3) and general methods of bringing Europe to Asia.

A further message emerging from the objects chosen for this exhibition, and foregrounded in the accompanying literature, was the idea of a 'moving of goalposts'; a very perceptible shift in assumptions and the gradual emergence of more 'rigid' stereotypes and attitudes of both Eastern and Western interlocutors. In later times, these appeared to replace many formerly much more flexible civilizational and mental boundaries. At the time, the *Economist* commented as follows, in a piece called 'East meets West':

> [...] the irresistible conclusion is that this was an age characterized not, or not chiefly, by hostility and incomprehension, but rather by a fluid, hybrid fusion of cultures, underscored by mutual fascination and even respect. The West's hostility towards Asians, the racism, the power politics and even brute oppression—that was largely for later.
>
> (www.economist.com/node/3285860)

A number of objects shown in in *Encounters* resonated strongly with the idea of 'European Studies' in Asia. Among them was Shíba Kōkan's hanging scroll depicting *The Meeting of Japan, China and the West*, a map depicting the famous pilgrimage of the Chinese Buddhist monk *Xuanzang* (*Hsuan Tsang*, 602–664 CE; see Chapter 2) to India from 629/630 to 645 CE, and a number of objects bearing testimony to early diplomatic encounters between Asia and Europe, such as an engraving showing the visit by the German physician Engelbert Kaempfer to the shōgun of Japan (see Chapter 4; Jackson and Jaffer, 2004: 1, 27–28, 98).

Two items which spoke, perhaps, most eloquently of the pedagogic and didactic aspects of early European encounters with Asia are the page illustrated by Odano Naotake, from the *Kaitai Shinsho*, the 1774 translation by the Japanese *rangaku* scholar Sugita Genpaku of a Western anatomical atlas, and the 1757 Korean astronomical screen bearing testimony to the presence of Jesuit astronomy in Korea (Jackson and Jaffer, 2004: 182, 300; see also Chapters 2 and 4).

In summary, the 2004 *Encounters* exhibition at the V&A deserves a central position in the depiction of the intellectual side of Asia–Europe relations. It established a number of sharp foci which were developed in a range of later shows and publications. One of the key ideas developed here was the centrality which concepts of 'learning' and 'teaching' assumed in all forms of the Asia–Europe artistic, diplomatic and religious exchange, especially from the sixteenth century onwards. A number of intellectual and pedagogic modalities of Asia were expressly showcased in this show – for example, the European 'teachnique' of 'going native', of 'in-culturation' and adaptation, and the Asian response to, and development of, European artistic and scientific models and templates.

Last but not least, *Encounters* was successful in demonstrating that pedagogic exchange, and the export of 'European' knowledge to Asia was embedded in a much wider geopolitical framework of trade and power, domination and control, mission and religion, the components of which were never solely determined by the Europeans. What this means in terms of what one may now call 'European Studies in Asia' was that the processes of both learning and myth-making worked both ways – arguably, they continue to do so in our own time.

Herman Van Rompuy described the display on *A Passage to Asia: 25 Centuries of Exchange between Asia and Europe*, at the *Palais des Beaux Arts* (Brussels Centre for Fine Arts) in Brussels, from 25 June to 10 October 2010 in the following terms:

> *A Passage to Asia – 25 Centuries of Exchange between Asia and Europe* is a project close to my heart. The word 'passage' speaks to me. You feel the movement, you almost smell the sea air. Your ears are full of the din of the trade routes, the hustle and bustle of centuries of travel to and fro. To this travel, there is no end. We remain on the go, from Europe to Asia and back; from Asia to Europe and back – after 25 centuries, we are still in transition, passage, progress...
> (Herman Van Rompuy, President of the European Council, in: BOZAR, 2010: I)

This major exhibition, it seems, brought out the more 'poetical' tendencies of Council President Van Rompuy – otherwise well in evidence through his well-known publication of *haiku*-style poetry. There was more than a hint to E.M. Forster's (1924) novel *A Passage to India* in this title, and more than a little of the history and the 'romance' of Asia–Europe exchange present in the objects chosen for exhibition, as well as in the catalogue. A visitor leaflet accompanying this exhibition sought to further evoke the traditional leitmotif of the 'exoticism' of the Asia–Europe encounter:

> Europe and Asia have had close relations for thousands of years. Commercial and political networks developed, both on land – via the Silk Road – and on sea. Conquerors like Alexander the Great, Attila, and Genghis Khan set out in search of glory, wealth, and power; travellers like Marco Polo, Zheng He, and Magellan were fascinated by riches, silk, spices, porcelain, etc. Trade opened the way for the spread of major religious and philosophical trends, inexhaustible sources of inspiration for art and culture. A Passage to Asia throws light on 2,500 years of exchanges between Asia and Europe and also between different Asian peoples. The exhibition presents an exceptional selection of over 300 decorative and artistic objects never previously shown in Europe: burial urns, bronze ritual drums, gold jewellery, ivories, old maps, and unique textiles, as well as extraordinary cargo recently recovered from shipwrecks at the bottom of the sea. Both the exhibition and a festival will coincide with the ASEM (Asia–Europe Meeting) 2010 summit.

The overall presentation, as the curators explained (BOZAR, 2010: VIII), was organized around the subliminal constants of 'faith' and 'trade'. However, it also exhibited a rich symbolical value and political background, in that it was organized to coincide with ASEM 8, the eighth Asia–Europe summit meeting, during the Belgian EU Presidency,[4] from 4–5 October 2010. Like the cultural festivals which accompanied it, this display was meant to bring home the messages of both the legacy and the on-going nature of the larger East–West meeting of peoples and cultures. It appears that the *leitmotiv* of an 'encounter of cultures through people' chimed particularly well with the modern (ASEM) political parlance of a 'people-to-people dialogue' between civilizations. Thus, the event clearly aimed at introducing, through selected objects, a brief history of some of the milestones of Asia–Europe cooperation.

At the same time, it seemed a matter of political expediency that this history was linked to more contemporary ideas of the free 'passage' of goods, people and information, 'diversity' and 'equality' – all concepts at the very heart of EU foreign policy towards Asia, and elsewhere. A stated aim of this exhibition – contemporaneous as it was with ASEM 8 – was, therefore, to offer a strong source of inspiration to the heads of state and government of the participating 16 Asian ASEM countries and the 27 Member States of the European Union. Using historical pattern and precedent as inspiration for modern synergies is not a new method of interpreting relations, as we shall see in other sections of this book.

A Passage to Asia was possessed of a nuanced ideological subtext. It sought to emphasize the significance of the 'open passage' of 'knowledge, science, art, religion and commerce' (BOZAR, 2010: II). To this end, it stressed some of the traditional modes and themes of East–West exchange, among them trade (both intra-Asian and with the West), the geopolitical role of China then and now, the function of art in intellectual exchange, the 'mythology' of Asia–Europe and, last but not least, the place of people from East and West learning with, and from, one another. This latter aspect was evident in the choice of exhibits with a connection to cultural 'crossroads' of one kind or another, both over-land and of a maritime nature.

This method underscored how knowledge and understanding of each other's culture and history continue to be 'paramount to the success of our mutual undertakings' (BOZAR, 2010: IV). Through the prism of the material cultures of jade, gold, clay and bronze, and through the artistic modes of sculpture, fresco and painting, the exhibition shed light on the concept of connectivity, shown in such examples as the (maritime) Srivijaya empire of early South East Asia, early Indo-Roman trade (BOZAR, 2010: 38–40) and, of course, the Silk Route in Central Asia (see Chapter 2).

The art connected with the *Dunhuang Caves*, which captivated so many of the European Orientalists of the nineteenth and twentieth centuries CE was a further interesting highlight of this event (BOZAR, 2010: 71–92; see also the *Silk Road* exhibition, below). Another emphasis of *A Passage to Asia* was evident in the stress on ideas of artistic syncretism and inter-civilizational artistic dialogue. Thus, Hellenism, Gandhara art and the objects made by the Greco-Bactrians in Asia were much in evidence in this exhibit, as was Indo-Portuguese devotional (Jesuit) art (see Chapter 2). This was meant to highlight 'connections' between empires, such as the Achaemenid (Persian), Han, and Indian and Roman ones.

Reinforcing this idea, many map exhibits and hanging scrolls bore testimony to the role of diplomatic and scientific exchanges between China, Korea, the Middle East and Europe. Last but not least, the knowledge-enabling function of religious exchange – mainly Christianity, Islam and Buddhism – and of spiritual epistemologies in East and West inter-cultural exchange was foregrounded, for instance, through the case of Nālandā University and the spread of both Indian and Islamic art throughout South East Asia (BOZAR, 2010: 127, 149).

The ideas of 'adaptation', 'influence' and 'syncretism' in teaching and learning, in both East and West, ran through this exhibition, as though it had been a red thread of guidance, woven into its fabric. This was not limited to religion either, as the examples and objects of material culture showed. Many exhibits here represented eloquent evidence of a fusion of styles, ideas and concepts. This fusion, as this exhibition showed, served both the purpose of the export of popular commodities and the exchange of learning.

A great number of exhibitions over the last few decades have been expressly dedicated to the influence of Japanese on European art, to the nineteenth and early twentieth century Western artistic phenomenon of *Japonisme* or to some of the outstanding, and well-known, individual Japanese artists, such as Andō Hiroshige or Katsushika Hokusai. This would suggest that European public interest in Japanese modes of artistic impression continues to be high. This appears to be the case, in particular, in regard to Japanese woodblock prints of the Edo (Tokugawa) period (1603–1868; see Chapter 4 and King, 2010; Marks, 2010).

Among the occasions which have placed a specific emphasis on lesser-known Japanese personalities such as Shíba Kōkan, there were, as far as I can see at the beginning of 2013, only three public exhibitions of note, of which the one at the Museum of Art History in Amsterdam in 2000 is highlighted here. It was entitled *Shíba Kōkan 1747–1818: Kunstenaar in de ban van het Westen (Artist under the Spell of the West)*. The other end of the decade, 2009, saw a range of related exhibitions and public events in Holland to celebrate 400 years of trade and diplomatic relations (1609–2009) between the Netherlands and Japan – for example, the exhibition *400 Jaar Handel*, at the *Rijksmuseum* in Amsterdam.[5]

Furthermore, Shíba Kōkan was in the spotlight during a 1996 exhibition, *Shíba Kōkan hyakkaji (Shíba Kōkan: A Versatile Life)*, organized by *Machida City International Woodblock Art Museum* and *Kobe City Art Museum* in Japan. The *Rangaku* (Western Learning; see Chapter 4) movement had been showcased during other events, for instance, the *Japan und Europa* exhibition in Berlin in 1993, whilst the contemporary intellectual background of *Media and Information in the Edo Period* in Japan was highlighted during a short, eponymous, gallery exhibit at the Tokyo National Museum in 2010.[6]

The exhibition *Japanse Verwondering (Japanese Amazement): Shíba Kōkan 1747–1818: Kunstenaar in de ban van het Westen (Artist under the Spell of the West)* was held at the Amsterdams Historisch Museum (Historical Museum of Amsterdam [now Amsterdam Museum]) in 2000. It was accompanied by an exceptionally thorough catalogue-cum-book (AHM, 2000, see Fig. 7.), providing much of the context of Japanese–European relations in the period of the Tokugawa shōgunate. Most of the literature cited in Chapter 4 (e.g. Keene, 1969; French, 1974; Guth, 1996; Goodman, 2000) provide useful background reading to Shíba Kōkan, and in regard of the exhibition dedicated to him in Amsterdam in 2000. However, on account of the treatment of this period's social, historical and cultural context, Effert and Forrer's title on *The Court Journey to the Shōgun of Japan* (2000) and Plutschow's *A Reader in Edo Period Travel* (2006) represent background reading to this fascinating exhibition.

The theme of this display can be encapsulated in the phrase of looking at something *different*, and looking *differently* at something *familiar*, in other words, learning processes and the impacts of inter-civilizational exchange. To this end, *Japanse Verwondering* can be said to have showcased, through the example of Shíba Kōkan, the ideas of 'isolation', 'curiosity', 'imitation', 'inspiration', 'trial and observation' – and what we call today the various domains and areas of 'learning', and of acquiring competencies.

Though the artistic merits and qualities of Shíba Kōkan, were, perhaps, a little over-stated in the catalogue (AHM, 2000), there can be no doubt that the purpose of the event was to demonstrate exactly those epistemological debates which were so characteristic of many parts of the new urban culture of the Edo (Tokugawa) period of Japanese history (see Chapter 4). A strong accent both in the exposition and throughout the background materials which accompanied this exhibition was, therefore, placed on the 'correct' models and artistic templates in Japan at the time; the life-story of the artist Shíba Kōkan, including his travels, social and personal encounters, was being employed here, in order to demonstrate in which ways this remarkable artist's own biography strongly reflected those wider debates.

The retrospective, in approximately chronological fashion, narrated Chinese, Confucian, Japanese and European forms of learning, strands of influence and choices of artistic expression on Kōkan, analysing this painter's journey – both literal and mental – 'in search of the world behind the art' he encountered (AHM, 2000: 37). An important secondary theme of the exhibition was encapsulated in the ideas of wider 'learning-journeys' and of the value of 'travelling'. Shíba Kōkan's own, personal, journey to Nagasaki, for example, was presented as strongly redolent of the annual 'court journey' (*de Hoofreis*) of the Europeans (Dutch) on Deshima (see Chapter 4; Effert and Forrer, 2000; Plutschow, 2006: 203).

In addition to this, the displays connect well with the wider concepts of 'geographies' and 'locales' of learning, 'seats of knowledge', 'discoveries' in a global context and 'centres and peripheries' of inter-cultural exchange – all of which strongly inform the work of cultural historians such as Burke (2000: 53–80; see also Chapter 1). Moreover, the presentation, and the objects and documents of *Japanse Verwondering* pointed to the role of (text-) books as inter-cultural 'carriers' and 'mediators' of knowledge, to the significance of templates, both scientific and artistic, and to the concept of a 'transfer' or 'metamorphosis' of scientific materials, instruments and sources into the artistic domain.

It was, perhaps, for this latter purpose that maps were suggested here as the ideal 'hybrid' objects, standing in between science and art. One of the key artworks of this exhibition was the Chikyū Zu (*Wereldkaart*, map of the world), which Shíba Kōkan produced in 1793 using Pierre Mortier's map of 1721, which his Edo friend Sugita Genpaku owned, as a (European) template (AHM, 2000: 101–104). As in the knowledge transfer mediated by the Portuguese (see Chapter 3), the *Japanse Verwondering* exhibition also offered the important subtext of the limitations of intellectual curiosity and inter-cultural learning: although Shíba Kōkan was not prevented from drawing his maps, he was not allowed to sell them, since in Tokugawa Japan information pertaining to foreign countries was privileged, state-controlled knowledge (*Herrschaftswissen*, AHM, 2000: 101). He did, however, show his world maps to people he met in his travels (Plutschow, 2006: 221).

Voyageurs Occidentaux En Chine: La Découverte de l'Empire du Milieu was a small but thoroughly researched and presented exhibition in Brussels, which bound together, in a number of pictorial and documentary ways, a number of the themes and strands of Asia–Europe intellectual exchange which are at the heart of this chapter and of the overall book. It was organized in the framework of a larger event – the 21st *Europalia.china* Festival. This event, which was dedicated to China, offered four key themes: 'Eternal China', 'Contemporary China', 'Colourful China' and 'China and the World'. According to the exhibition catalogue, all festival exhibitions aimed to 'put the cultural richness and diversity of China under the public spotlight'.[7]

The festival showed not only popular art, but also the national heritage and Chinese contemporary art, in 48 exhibitions and 519 events, at 75 cities in five countries. The *Western Travellers in China* exhibition can be linked, thematically, and in its foci, with a 2007/2008 exhibit called *China on Paper: European and Chinese Works from the Late Sixteenth to the Early Nineteenth Century*, at the J. Paul Getty Museum in Los Angeles, USA,[8] which placed a particular emphasis on the scientific and cartographic work, in the service of religion, undertaken by China Jesuits like Ferdinand Verbiest. This event interrogated the artistic and written evidence of the Jesuits' assimilation policies in China. In an accompanying publication, the curators remind us that the Jesuits' approach 'led to an intellectual and visual production that proposed China and Europe as mirror civilizations: mutually distant and exotic but with common moral values and equally long histories', and that 'books and prints were central to the ways in which Europeans and Chinese communicated between 1500 and 1800' (Reed and Dematté, 2007: 5, 48).

The smaller Brussels display in 2010, showcasing *Western Travellers in China* at the *Bibliotheca Wittockiana*, offered valuable background information and inspiration on the theme of East–West learning through the prism of European contacts with China, and in terms of a variety of texts, the majority of them travelogues and photographs taken by European travellers and 'adventurers' in the 'Middle Kingdom' in the course of almost seven centuries. It proved highly advisable to 'read' this exhibition in conjunction with the study by Reed and Dematté (2007), especially as far as the Jesuits in China are concerned. Frances Wood's title *The Lure of China* (Wood, 2009) can provide further, in-depth background information on the motives and achievements of the European travellers, while the earlier 2008 exhibition *Heaven on Earth: Missionaries and the Mathematical Arts in 17th Century Beijing*[9] was an excellent preparation for the understanding of the Jesuits in China (see also Chapter 3).

The exhibits themselves, as well as the materials which accompanied them, naturally enough sought to place *Western Travellers in China* in the context of prominent 'national' travellers, originating from what is now Belgium, such as the Franciscan Willem Van Ruebroek (Ruysbroeck), who travelled in 1253, and the Jesuit Ferdinand Verbiest, leaving for China in 1656. The exhibition thus offered an extremely wide temporal perspective, ranging from Ruebroek and Marco Polo in 1275, to European photographers well into the twentieth century. The catalogue placed a special emphasis on the activities of the European Franciscans, Jesuits and others, stating that 'the missionaries certainly succeeded in strengthening the ties with China' (BWB, 2009: 12).

In the *Bibliotheca Wittockiana* exhibit, priority was afforded to images: next to the (later) photographic records, the exhibits were all writings which contained engravings and drawings. This succeeded in bringing to the fore the ways in which learning and exchange occurred between China and the West through the observation and description of material cultures, in the shape of everyday objects, plants, costumes and customs. *Western Travellers in China* was a unique exhibition on account of its range, and it comprised of texts and images pertaining to all three areas of historically documented exchange chosen for Part I of this book. Next to the vital written letter-books and testimonies of key Jesuit figures, such as Jean-Joseph-Marie Amiot and Athanasius Kircher, the exhibition contained several crucially relevant Portuguese writings, such as Álvaro Semedo's *Histoire Universelle de la Chine* (see Chapter 3; BWB, 2009: 41).

In terms of teaching European Studies in Asia, the value of this exhibition lay in the fact that it successfully traced a significant part of the oral, pictorial and written histories of Europeans becoming more aware of the breadth and sophistication of Chinese civilization. In terms of China learning from Europe, there can be little doubt that key items in the exhibit, next to the Jesuit resources, were the photographs from the nineteenth and early twentieth centuries, many of which bore rich testimony to the curiosity of contemporary Chinese from all backgrounds and occupations about – literally and metaphorically – the 'image' of China, and of themselves to the outside world, as well as about the photographic process itself. One extremely eloquent example are the pictures taken around 1898 by the Austro-German aristocrat Ernst von Hesse-Wartegg (1851–1918), during the short time which became known as 'Deutsch-China' (Qingdao, German: 'Tsingtao'; BWB, 2009: 155).

German colonial ambitions – such as they were – were based on the work of the geographer Baron Ferdinand von Richthofen (see also: Chapter 2), who was particularly ambitious as to the establishment and development of an educational system for Chinese and Europeans in Shantung province, under the aegis of the German Imperial Navy of the time (as opposed to the *Kolonialamt*, the Colonial Office). The exhibition *Tsingtao: A Chapter of German Colonial History in China, 1897–1914*, at the German Historical Museum in Berlin, threw some light on this brief episode:

> The German administration was able to prevent land speculation on the Bay of Kiaochow with modern land-use laws, which allowed for the organized planning and construction of Tsingtao, the German colonial city. Through this successful policy, German politics was able to achieve in China what the land-reform movement was calling for in Germany. Tsingtao, a trading and naval post, was divided into various functional zones: residential, business, educational, health care. In addition, the town's recreational facilities and infrastructure were built with the highest standards in mind. The Chinese population from surrounding areas showed its approval of the ambitious planning and realization of the city by moving to Tsingtao in large numbers, thus creating a lively working and business environment. After completion of the Shantung railroad, which connected Tsingtao to the interior of the province, the city's port flourished and quickly became one of the

most important on the Chinese coast. Turn-of-the-century German architecture still defines the face of the former European quarter of Tsingtao.[10]

Four smaller exhibitions with relevance for European Studies in Asia (2002–2013)

Trading Places – The East India Company and Asia, 1600–1835
The British Library, London, 24 May–15 September 2002

The Silk Road – Trade, Travel, War & Faith
The British Library, London, 7 May–12 September 2004

Encompassing the Globe – Portugal and the World in the 16th and 17th Centuries (Autour du Globe: Le Portugal Dans Le Monde aux XVIe et XVIIe Siècles)
Brussels, Palais des Beaux Arts ('Bozar'), 26 October 2007–3 February 2008

Mughal India: Art, Culture and Empire
British Library (PACCAR Gallery), 9 November 2012–2 April 2013

Trading Places – The East India Company and Asia, 1600–1835 was one of a number of events organized around the beginning of the final decade of the twentieth century, in order to commemorate the foundation of, and the evolving balance of power between, European 'East India' trading companies 400 years earlier. It coincided, within a time-frame of around two years, with similar events in the Netherlands, Denmark, France, Spain and Portugal, the five current EU Member States with a colonial legacy spanning a range of countries in South and South East Asia. The title of the London exhibition, *Trading Places*, encapsulating, as it did, a deliberate ambivalence, in doing so also sketched some of its key themes: first, the event invited interpretation of the roles of 'trading-places' in Europe, such as Venice, London, Lisbon and Amsterdam, and across Asia, for example, Bantam and Batavia. In this way, the exhibit offered food for thought, albeit to varying degrees, pertaining to the dual nature of European trading at the time – direct trade with Asia, in, for instance, porcelain, and involvement in existing, intra-Asian, trade patterns, exemplified in the Jesuits' involvement in the Macao-Nagasaki trade in silver (see Chapter 3). However, it was, arguably, the second meaning of the exhibition's title which was most thought-provoking in the context of this book, and in terms of the 'learning-dimension' of Asia–Europe relations: Europeans and Asians 'trading places' and, in doing so, attempting – sometimes, and with various degrees of success – to 'go native', but always learning, translating, writing about each other, compiling dictionaries, teaching, disputing and publishing.

As one case in point, this exhibition offered fascinating material relating to information about the Malay language, as well as other tongues in widespread use as *lingua franca* in South East Asia from the fifteenth to the seventeenth centuries (Farrington, 2002: 36). Last, but not least, the emphasis *Trading Places* placed on *Asia in Britain* raised awareness not only of the exchange of commodities and its legacies, but also of the growing impact of the wealth generated by the 'Eastern trade' on art, architecture, intellectual life and consumer patterns in Britain at the time and beyond. Asia was thus shown to change both the physical and the mental landscapes of Europe and the Europeans.

The Silk Road – Trade, Travel, War & Faith, at the British Library, London, from 7 May to 12 September 2004, followed an organizing principle followed in many publications on the Silk Road before and after (cf. Hansen, 2012): linking locales and regions in Central Asia with themes relevant to the Asia–Europe commercial and intellectual exchange on this early information-super-highway. In his review for the *Independent* (*Independent*, Review, 3 May 2004: 18), Michael Church stressed that the show was telling the 'quotidian, human story' of the Silk Road. He also opined that the presentation truly represented a 'journey to the heart of Asia' and that 'under brute persuasion from political realities, the penny is at last beginning to drop: Central Asia, which the West has always viewed as merely an exotic travel destination, is one of the most significant regions of the world'.

The exhibition ostensibly revolved around the life and work of Sir Marc Aurel Stein (1862–1943), an Anglicized Hungarian, and one of the key European Silk Road explorers between 1900 and 1930 (Whitfield, 2004: 16–17; see also Chapter 2). However, it also drew much wider circles, using the four labels of 'trade', 'travel', 'war' and 'faith' to invite visitors and readers to explore the key drivers for this pivotal channel of historical Europe–Asia exchange.

One of those drivers was the aspect of 'security', exemplified in the erection of Chinese garrisons along the Silk Road, as one of its 'enabling-conditions' (see Chapter 2). In our time, the issue re-surfaces in the debates about the relationship between the Chinese state and the *Xinjian Uighur* region. The exhibits chosen for *The Silk Road – Trade, Travel, War & Faith* not only foregrounded the Silk Road's connections to our own era; they also underlined major external historical and cultural influences on Central Asia from Europe and the Persian West, in the shape of, for instance, the Hellenism of Ghandara art and the travels of Roman art motifs deep into Central Eurasia (see Chapter 2).

In terms of 'European Studies' in Asia, and of the travels of ideas and knowledge, this British Library display was among the most thought-provoking in the scope of this chapter. Appealing, perhaps, to the senses to a lesser degree than other presentations studied here, it was nevertheless special: concentrating, as it did, on written documents, scrolls and paintings from Central Asia, it seemed to deliberately encourage a questioning of the different ways of acquiring ancient knowledge – and of the diverse inquisitive, as well as acquisitive, archaeological methods of both European archaeologists such as Aurel Stein, Heinrich Schliemann, Ferdinand von Richthofen or Flinders Petrie, and their Asian collaborators (Whitfield, 2004: 8–9). Comparisons of the degrees of 'aggressiveness' and 'subterfuge', with which artefacts were acquired, would inspire much of the later

Travels of the mind 109

post-colonial discourse about science and knowledge transfer as tools of 'imperialist' appropriation and expansion.

Beyond these issues, *The Silk Road – Trade, Travel, War & Faith* pointed to another concern at the heart of the 'Europeans Studies in Asia' phenomenon: by showcasing the earliest Chinese star charts, and a copy of the *Diamond Sutra* – the earliest dated, printed book in the world (868) – the exhibition's emphasis on religion, the role of printing and written cultures as drivers of knowledge and ideas between Asia and Europe was unmistakable (Whitfield, 2004: 35–38; see also: MacGregor, 2010, and, especially: Hansen, 2012).

Autour du Globe: Le Portugal dans Le Monde aux XVIe et XVIIe Siècles (Encompassing the Globe – Portugal and the World in the 16th and 17th Centuries), open to the public in Brussels, from 26 October 2007 to 3 February 2008, emphasized the identity of the Portuguese Empire; however, it also covered the wider international connotations of Portuguese exploration. Perhaps this was an appropriate strategy for an exhibition showing in Brussels, the self-styled 'capital' of Europe. The publicity materials of the exhibition stated that:

> By bringing together more than 160 extraordinary masterpieces, this exhibition has the purpose to explore the unity and diversity of the cultures that contributed to Portugal's trading empire. From Africa to Brazil passing through China, Japan and the Indian Ocean, it provides a wide-ranging and unforgettable image of the new world's great age of discovery. If the centerpiece of this event will focus more on Portugal itself, on the tracks of the Portuguese conquests between old maps, navigational instruments and manuscripts, the main interest of this exhibition remains in its indubitable diversity.[11]

Mughal India: Art, Culture and Empire, at the British Library in 2012–2013, offered an extraordinary display of Mughal paintings, manuscripts and other works of art. A number of objects here related well with the twin-themes of 'Europeans and their influence on Asia' and 'Asian inspiration on Europe and the Europeans'. As an example of the former, the display included Mughal miniatures betraying the influence of 'Western-style', linear, perspective, introduced to the Mughal Empire through the intermediaries of the Jesuit missionaries (see also Chapter 4 on this issue in Japan), and through figures such as Thomas Roe, the British ambassador (1615–1618) to the Court of the Mughal Emperor Jahangir, whose journal became a valuable supply of information for the Europeans of the time. *Mughal India* included key, 'cross-cultural' artworks, such as *A Scene with European Figures*, attributed to the artist *Sanvala* (c.1600, Johnson Album 16.6).[12] The four foreign figures in the painting look curiously out of place, in their obviously Indian surroundings. Moreover, it is visible that some motifs and figurative templates in the painting have been borrowed, not quite seamlessly, from templates in European Christian Art (e.g. John the Baptist, top-right).

The painting speaks volumes about the Mughal Emperors' knowledge of foreign (European) cultures, including their own perceptions and interpretations of those cultures. The painting links well with other works of art of this period, which had been part of previous exhibitions – for example, *A European Lady and Gentleman in Elizabethan Costume* and others (*c.*1620–1630; Farrington, 2002: 58–60, 115). Conversely, a painting reappeared in the *Mughal India* exhibition which had also featured in the context of the *Encounters* exhibition at the Victoria and Albert Museum in 2004: *Sir David Ochterlony in Indian Dress and Smoking a Hookah and Watching a Nautch in his House in Delhi*[13] is a splendid example of the fact that the Europeans of the time who went to India had been, in William Dalrymple's words (2004: 169), 'acculturating themselves to India in a kaleidoscope of different ways'. In this anonymous watercolour, Ochterlony represents the 'European going native'. By all accounts, the Boston-born Sir David (1758–1825) was seen as more than a little eccentric: it appears he preferred to be addressed by his full Mughal title (*Nasir-ud-Daula*, 'Defender of the State'), and enjoyed life to the full – as a Mughal gentleman.

The picture, painted in Delhi in around 1820, shows him in full Indian dress, smoking the *hookah* and surrounded by some of what are reputed to have been his 13 wives. The portraits of Ochterlony's venerable ancestors, aligned on the ceiling in the upper half of the painting, form a wonderful, and somewhat incongruous, contrast with the resident-gone-native. However, and on a more sombre level, the painting also bears testimony to some personal and religious issues pertinent for Europeans in India at the time, such as the question of in which faith to raise the children from combined European–Indian relationships (Dalrymple, 2004: 169).

Smaller exhibitions, permanent displays, research projects and key publications

Ashmolean Museum of Art and Archaeology, Oxford, UK

Asian Civilizations Museum (ACM), Singapore

The British Museum, London: Japanese Galleries (2013)

Asian Art Museum (Muzium Seni Asia), Universiti Malaya, Kuala Lumpur, Malaysia

The British Museum, London/University of Oxford: 'Empires of Faith' Research Project (2013)

The Ashmolean Museum of Art and Archaeology, Oxford, UK

The distinctive *Crossing Cultures, Crossing Time* (orientation-) gallery of the *Ashmolean Museum of Art and Archaeology, University of Oxford*, arguably, represents an 'orientation' in two key meanings of the term: visitor guidance, as well as an inquiry of cultural interchange with the East. The theme pervades a number of spaces in the museum (Brown, 2009: 25). As a leitmotiv, *Crossing Cultures, Crossing Time* embraces a number of thought-provoking exhibits, connections and ideas on the theme of Asia–Europe 'conversation' and 'learning'.

The (refurbished) museum's emphasis on links and learning through material cultures is embodied in the idea that 'cultures interact with, and influence, one another' (Brown, 2009: 23). Within this framework, the museum's Buddha statue from Gandhara (see above) assumes a special meaning as an object symbolic of the *Crossing Cultures, Crossing Time* didactic method of the museum, linking, as it were, Hellenistic, Indian and Greco-Roman artistic templates in dependence on the trade routes and exchanges which connected people.

In a political climate which all too often dwells on the differences between cultures and civilizations for the sake of political expediency, this approach not only reflects academic debates over the last few decades (Brown, 2009: 25), it also reverberates strongly with the idea of prolonged, and fruitful, scholastic communication between East and West, which is at the heart of this book. The new, permanent exhibit at the Ashmolean – the world's first public museum – takes the idea of *Crossing Cultures, Crossing Time* to the people-to-people level, allowing a glimpse at the ways individuals shaped the dynamics of East–West trade, religious exchange and diplomacy through the Japanese tea ceremony in Japan, the Gandhara Buddha in Pakistan and the Bactrian camel on the Silk Road.

In terms of the idea of the development of a 'European Studies in Asia' academic discipline, the Ashmolean both builds on its historical and colonial traditions in the nineteenth and twentieth centuries, and offers pointers for the didactics of teaching 'Europe' in the East in the foreseeable future. What a modern European Studies pedagogy may learn from this can be encapsulated both in the method of seeking 'commonalities' across civilizations, and in the choice of a focus on 'objects' and 'materials culture' as learning materials. The latter focus specifically links the Ashmolean conception with related educational packages of the British Museum, such as *A History of the World in 100 Objects* (MacGregor, 2010; see also above).

The Asian Civilizations Museum (ACM), Singapore

On the other side of the globe, the Asian Civilizations Museum (ACM) in Singapore[14] shares with the Ashmolean Museum (see above) both a history of recent refurbishment and a strong educational focus with an East–West flavour, as well as a strong catalogue of pedagogical outreach events, accompanied by relevant scholarly activity. As one of the successors to the erstwhile *Raffles Museum*, the ACM has strong conceptual and cultural links with Europe, by means of the British colonial connection. In her overview of museums in South East Asia, Kelly (2001: 63) states:

> the British instilled a healthy sense of history and a respect for material culture in the countries they colonized in Asia, and it is not surprising that

112 *Contemporary representations and actors*

some of the most advanced museums in South East Asia are located in former British colonies.

The ACM appears, by and large, to confirm this assertion. It has inherited a vast, and relatively young, collection and now successfully combines the British colonial heritage linked with Sir Stamford Raffles, and the former *Raffles Museum and Library* (ACM, 2003: 11–15), with a contemporary, wide-ranging, overview of the key cultures in the region. The result is a confident assertion of the conscious construction of modern Singaporean national identity over many decades. The museum first opened in 1997 and moved to a second building in Singapore's colonial quarter ('civic district') by the Singapore River in 2003.

The ACM has four foremost regional foci on China, South Asia, South East Asia and West Asia/Islam. In spite of this key emphasis – or, perhaps, because of it – the ACM is regularly offering a number of exhibitions which interrogate the themes connected with the history of thought, religion, ideas and education and international and Asia–Europe exchange. Perhaps the most prominent among those was the Silk Road exhibition *On the Nālandā Trail – Buddhism in India, China and South East Asia* in 2007/2008 (see above).[15] Other temporary displays have placed a spotlight on international trade in export textiles and ceramics, and on photographic art, bridging the gap between 'East' and 'West'.

In its permanent displays and galleries, the ideas of 'Europe in Asia' and 'Asia in the making of Europe' are evident in a number of materials, artefacts and cultural displays. The *Dehua* enamelled wares from China, for example (ACM, 2006: 84–87), bear eloquent testimony to the popularity of Chinese decorative items and figurines ('Blanc de Chine') in European houses around the eighteenth and nineteenth centuries. They point also to the trade routes and to the Dutch East India Company (*Vereenigde Oostindische Compagnie*, VOC), who transported many of these much sought-after items to the West. Paintings, such as the one on *Europeans Visiting the Vishnupada Temple*, not only allow conclusions as to how Asians have perceived Europeans as 'traders' and 'tourists' in the past, but also display a 'highly eclectic blend of Indian and European styles, revealing an element of realism, adapted from European paintings' (ACM, 2006: 104, see also Chapter 4).

'Technocrats with art sense': the Asian Art Museum (Muzium Seni Asia), Universiti Malaya, and National Museum of Malaysia (Muzium Negara), Kuala Lumpur, Malaysia[16]

The collection at the Museum of Asian Art (*Muzium Seni Asia*, MSA)[17] is located inside the campus of Malaysia's oldest university, Universiti Malaya (UM). The roots of the museum can be traced to the establishment in 1945 of the *Asian Art Museum* at the then University of Malaya located in Singapore. Until 1969, the collection was housed in Singapore, and a substantial number of artefacts (Collections 1–3) remain in the museum of the National University of Singapore (NUS).[18]

At the time of writing, UM was the only university in Malaysia to own a museum. It holds four paintings by M.F. Husain. Next to objects donated or bought at auction, the MSA also embraces archaeological finds from Tioman Island and many beaches of Peninsular Malaysia (Port Dickson, Johor Lama, Malacca, etc.), where very significant quantities of European ceramics shards were found. This was seen as clear evidence of the country having been a meeting point of cultures and business activities during the seventeenth to nineteenth centuries CE. Today, the UM Museum of Asian Art appropriately complements the presence of the *Asia–Europe Institute* (cf. Chapter 7) nearby at the university; both institutions have a tangible concern with matters of 'exchange', 'learning', 'culture' and 'creativity'.

The purpose of the UM collection is pedagogic, and the objects on display here appear to adhere to the same narrative which also underlies the predominant political discourse in contemporary Malaysia, regarding the country as a multicultural nation, embracing Chinese, Indian, Malay and tribal heritage. In the Director's own words, MSA is pursuing an academic 'ideal', aiming at a more 'holistic' museum pedagogy for students and visitors: 'technocrats with an art-sense' was how he phrased it. This theme can be detected also in the National Museum of Malaysia (Muzium Negara) in Kuala Lumpur (see below).[19] Although Muzium Seni Asia does not, at first sight, divulge a strong narrative of Europe–Asia relations, it nevertheless allows many glimpses at the history of the trading routes which bound the Malay world to Europe, the Middle East and Persia and, further afield, to China, Korea and Japan.

It is thus, perhaps indirectly, in the remarkable ceramics and porcelain collections of this site that a history of East–West aesthetics, trade, imitation and influence is subtly revealed, through the display of export-oriented wares which were, of course, based on perceptions of what was, and what was not, considered 'fashionable', 'saleable' or 'tasteful' in markets such as Europe. Next to social strata and market forces, what is also reflected in the displays of *Muzium Seni Asia* is the effect of the Asian politics of the past on Europe, through the character of ceramics. For example, against the background of an unstable situation in China following the collapse of the Ming dynasty, the Dutch traders, who were the key carriers of Chinese porcelain to Europe at the time, began to encourage new Japanese artists, instead of the traditional Chinese ones, to produce export ware such as *Kakiemon* (see above). An augmented Japanese porcelain manufacture, in turn, was one of the enablers of later Dutch–Japanese mercantile, scientific and cultural contacts (see Chapter 4).

At MSA, one example of inter-continental artistic patterns 'crossing over' (in more ways than one) is the museum's delicate *Kraak* ware,[20] a kind of Chinese export-porcelain, produced mainly during the reign of the Wanli Emperor (1563–1620), and until around 1640. It was among the first Chinese export porcelain ware to arrive in Europe in large quantities and can frequently be seen in Dutch still-life paintings of 'foreign luxuries'. MSA has a significant collection of around 280 Malay *Kendi* (from Sanskrit: *kundika:* 'pure-water dropper') ritualistic drinking vessels. *Kendi* are unique and embody the 'local genius' of

114 *Contemporary representations and actors*

Malay invention They also testify to a busy technology-transfer and trade with Europe, Siam, China and Vietnam through entrepôts such as Johor, Malacca and Ayutthaya (see Chapter 1, and: Khoo Joo Ee, 1991: 13–18).

By showcasing a wealth of other 'inter-cultural' objects as diverse as jars from Martaban (in modern Burma/Myanmar) and European plates with Arabic calligraphy designs (UM 76.12), the MSA exhibits in Kuala Lumpur speak eloquently of trade-routes, profits, networks and entrepôt bases which developed into meeting places of cultures, bearing testimony of fashions of mercantilism, as well as changing mindsets. The MSA website explains:

> This porcelain eventually lost its popularity towards the end of the 17th century during the transition period between the Ming and the Ching Dynasty. With the English taking over the trade with China, products from the Jingdezhen kilns began to face competition from manufacturers in Swatow, whose products were relatively cheaper and bore newer designs known as san sui or willow pattern. Traces of this porcelain were discovered in areas along the silk routes (sea) such as the coasts of Africa, Middle Asia, Kamakura in Japan, the Philippines, the Pahang River, Tioman Island, Kota Tinggi and Johor Lama in Johor and also in Kedah.[21]

When I met the Director of the MSA on 15 March 2013, I queried him at length about what the museum's exhibits can reveal in the context of a 'European Studies in Asia' academic discipline. In response, Dr Abd Aziz Rashid mentioned Portuguese and English influence on indigenous *itik pulang petang* ('duck-like') wood-carving patterns, or on Malay floral porcelain designs (*bakul pung*) to render them less repetitive. Much of this influence would have been mediated through the port city of Malacca, captured by the Portuguese in 1511. Last but not least, as a footnote almost, it is revealing that, next to European figurines (e.g. UM), the *Muzium Seni Asia* collection also displays a fascinating statue of a *Central Asiatic Foreigner* (No. UM 58.19) – possibly originating from the Sogdian Empire (see Chapter 2).

Box 5.1 The National Museum of Malaysia (Muzium Negara) in Kuala Lumpur

Compared to *Muzium Seni Asia* on the Universiti Malaya campus, the – better known – National Museum of Malaysia (Muzium Negara) has a wider scope and ambition, but shares MSA's pedagogic approach to Museum Studies. As of May 2013, Muzium Negara offered four permanent, themed displays, covering, respectively, *Early History, The Malay Kingdoms, The Colonial Era* and *Modern Malaysia*. Whilst the first and last of these galleries focused almost exclusively on domestic matters – especially on the creation of post-independence Malaysian national identity – the displays in the remaining two galleries contain much of interest to the scholar interested in European influence in Asia, especially when interpreted through the lens of trade, European cartography of the region and the

Travels of the mind 115

> Portuguese Empire (Chapter 3). The *Malay Kingdoms* galleries offer a glimpse of how entrepôts such as Melaka (Malacca, see above) or regions like Johor and Sabah became both trade hubs, locations of significant European expatriate communities and desirable geopolitical spheres of influence in both the intra-Asian trade, in which many European nations became lucratively involved, and wider commercial networks in the Bay of Bengal, South China Sea and beyond. For students and teachers tracing the history of the discipline of European Studies in Asia, the ancient European maps on display inside the *Malay Kingdoms* galleries are, arguably, among the most instructive items, since they serve to narrate both the evolution of European perceptions of South East Asia and the formation of the acquisitive attitudes, with regard to Asian political spaces, of the later, colonial age (see above); in connection with the latter, I found the *Malay Kingdoms* displays conveyed a far more powerful testimony of the levels and branches of Asia–Europe interaction than the perhaps rather narrow conceptual focus of the dedicated *Colonial Era* galleries in the museum (Visitor Guide [*Panduan dan Peta*] and see Muzium Negara website).

The British Museum, London: Japanese Galleries (2013)

Many works of art included in the British Museum's series *A History of the World in 100 Objects* have already been commented on in other chapters and sections of this book (e.g. Gandhara art, in Chapter 2, on the Silk Roads), and this will not be repeated here. A number of particular events and gallery displays in the British Museum (BM), however, have highlighted selected aspects of the 'exchange' dimension of Asia–Europe relations. One recent example, at the beginning of 2013, was the display *Japan: From Prehistory to the Present*, in the *Mitsubishi Corporation Japanese Galleries* of the BM.[22] The display sought to show how Japan's development of a thriving, modern, high-tech society was entirely compatible with the celebration of many aspects and elements of Japanese 'traditional' culture (BM Brochure: Japan, 09/2012). The BM's connection with the acquisition of many objects for its founding collections of 1753 is through objects and manuscripts brought back by Engelbert Kaempfer from Nagasaki in 1692, and subsequently acquired by Sir Hans Sloane.

In spite of the wide range of the gallery theme, the portion dedicated to Edo Period Japan was memorable in its focus on the concept of four 'gateways', through which Edo-period Japan both interacted with, and was influenced by, external influences. The gateways, to be conceived of in both a geographical and a cultural understanding, were Tsushima, Satsuma, Nagasaki and Matsumae. Next to the links with the *Ryūkū* Islands and the domain of the *Ainu* (*Aynu, Aino*) indigenous people of the North, Nagasaki was represented as the focal point of Japanese–European interaction (see Chapter 4). That this interaction was both artistic and mercantile in nature was in evidence through the display of contemporary export-porcelain, such as a pair of elephant sculptures by the Japanese potter *Kakiemon* (1660–90, BM: JA 1980.3–25.1,2). These had previously been included in the British Museum's project *A History of the World in 100 Objects* (No. 79, MacGregor, 2010: 511–515).[23]

The British Museum, London: 'Empires of Faith' project (2013)

The research project entitled *Empires of Faith*, which started at the British Museum in 2013 and ran in conjunction with the University of Oxford, encompassed a number of leitmotifs which also appear as key subjects in this book – for example, trade and migration, religion, art and iconographies, diplomacy and the contact between cultures. The cross-over, Gandhara-style, religious art and statuary, for example, which had already played a part in the British Museum's project *A History of the World in 100 Objects* (MacGregor, 2010), and which also informed the Ashmolean Museum's *Crossing Cultures, Crossing Time* orientation-display, resurfaced once again, quite deliberately, in *Empires of Faith* (see also Chapter 2). There was, in fact, some overlap between *Empires of Faith* and *A History of the World in 100 Objects*, in the choice of objects and research orientations.

A certain amount of duplication notwithstanding though, at the heart of *Empires of Faith* was, arguably, one of the most relevant clusters of enquiry in all Europe–Asia intellectual, cultural and artistic exchange. It may be phrased like this: did religious imagery and iconography emerge separately, in different traditions across Asia and Europe, or was there mutual influence and inspiration? In terms of regions and themes, the event was described as ranging 'from the cults of the Roman Empire to Manichaeism, from Britain and Spain in the west to the Indian subcontinent and the borders of China in the east'.[24]

The project's wide scope of investigating 'religious change, self-assertion and identity through visual means' harmonized with the idea of bringing 'European Studies' to Asia, since one of the key foci here was the critical interrogation of pertinent matters of conflicting religious, cultural and social identities, and the desirability, or otherwise, of seeking to contain 'multiple identities' within a single state or group of states. The 'conceptual leap' required to move from the project's examinations of diplomacy, religion and art in, for instance, the Roman and Sassanid Empires, and the Chinese, Gupta and Kushan realms, to more modern political entities and polities such as 'Europe', the 'EU', 'ASEAN' (The Association of South East Asian Nations) and 'Asia' was not a difficult one to undertake.

In addition to this, the focus of this event was on what may be termed the instrumentalization of power, government, political and spiritual authority, and of religious 'truth', as constructed and disseminated through images and myths, which bore more than just a passing resemblance to modern notions of 'constructing', and teaching about, 'Europe' for Asian contexts, to debates about the development of 'identities' in regional and inter-regional frameworks (see Chapter 1) and to contemporary discourses surrounding religious education and politics.

Ayutthaya Historical Studies Centre and Study Annex, Ayutthaya, Thailand: conscious collectors of identity

In Thailand, public exhibitions, and displays at museums and galleries such as the Bangkok National Museum,[25] the *Chan Kasem* National Museum, *Chao Sam Phraya* National Museum and the Ayutthaya Historical Study Centre (AHSC),[26] have become essential sources of authenticity for historiography, both domestic and foreign, regarding Thailand. They frame the history of Siamese/Thai interactions with foreign countries in the changing contexts of indigenous, dynastic evolution, royal and military history, foreign exchange and, last but not least, learning. The focus of the desired narrative has undergone changes in dependence on the shifting political context and national interest in modern Thailand. However, the separate Museum Annex (AHSC Research Institute), built away from the main AHSC location but located close to the site of the former Japanese settlement, is solely dedicated to Ayutthaya's commercial relations with foreigners.

The small but eloquent display celebrates Ayutthaya's interaction with both East and West, with Europe, China and the Muslim world.[27] Like the two-centre AHSC as a whole, it embodies a 'curriculum', a desirable collective memory – to be read much like a school textbook. It has been said to have been designed to represent and reinforce certain aspects of Thai national identity, such as successive rulers' legitimacy, the 'civilized', international status and 'antiquity' of the country in the concert of nations, and the cosmopolitan heritage of historical

---

Box 5.2 Some on-line museums and interactive Asia–Europe installations (2013)

(For weblinks, see 'Selected websites' at the end of the book.)

Special permanent displays

Islamic Arts Museum, Kuala Lumpur, Malaysia
Portuguese Presence in Asia, Museo Fundação
The Spice Trail, British Library

On-line exhibitions

Art of the Silk Road
ASEMUS: Asia–Europe Museum Network
Connected Histories, Shared Future (ASEF Travelling Exhibition, in 2012, on the occasion of ASEF's fifteenth anniversary)
Europalia India (2013/2014)
Japan–Netherlands Exchange in the Edo Period
On-Line Museum: Resources on Asian Art
Virtual Collection of Masterpieces (ASEMUS)

templates such as Ayutthaya, representing peaceful commercial relations with foreign nations. Vanichviroon (2004: 118) posits that 'the commoditization of Ayutthaya's new image as an international entrepôt has proved to be a very successful industry'; however, standing in the cool shade of the Museum Annex and pondering the themed displays, I could not but conclude that, apart from officially sanctioned identity-construction, here was a history also of people from Asia and Europe, trying to come to terms with one another's customs, morals and ways.

Chapter conclusions

This chapter has approached 'European Studies in Asia' from, perhaps, a slightly different angle, seeking to demonstrate the wealth of information inherent in public exhibitions, special gallery displays and virtual museums, all of which can be used to both inform and build the curriculum in European Studies in Asia further, and in new directions. The chapter has found that some of the shows and displays coalesce around recurring themes, such as 'East–West history', 'cross-cultural influences' and 'transmission and localization of knowledge', which not only directly 'connect' with key research agendas in the European Studies in Asia discipline, but form a near-nigh inexhaustible store of knowledge which can be utilized to introduce new lectures, modules, case studies and thematic strands to the European Studies timetable in Asian classrooms.

In terms of Asian and European Studies, and of Museum Studies, these exhibitions, plus many smaller spaces and events, are, of course, 'texts' in the pedagogic sense, which can be fully – and meaningfully – integrated into the teaching of Europe across Asia. The choice of exhibits in this chapter has been both aligned to the preceding 'historical' examples in earlier chapters of this book (Chapters 2–4), and chosen to form a conceptual and pedagogic bridge to the chapters dealing with contemporary matters or teaching experience (Chapters 6–9). This has been done to encourage the reader, and the European Studies Professor in Asia, to make use of the materials which inevitably accompany these shows, and which often represent the results of painstaking and meticulous research on art and art history.

Notes

1 An excellent overview of exhibitions and related events on the theme of 'Asia–Europe Exchange' can be found at: http://afemuseums.easia.columbia.edu/cgi-bin/museums/search.cgi/topic?topic_id=170;page=1 and at: http://afemuseums.easia.columbia.edu/cgi-bin/museums/search.cgi/topic?topic_id=170.
2 See, for example, Michael Church, in *The Independent (Review)*, Monday, 13 September 2004: 18.
3 *Guardian*, Wednesday, 17 March 2004: 7.
4 ASEM 1, the inaugural Asia–Europe Meeting, took place in Bangkok in 1996 (cf. Wiessala, 2002a: 74–87).
5 For the *400 Jaar Handel* exhibition, see: www.codart.nl/exhibitions/details/1918/; see also the informative Dutch Embassy website, at: http://japan.nlembassy.org/you-and-netherlands/dutch-japanese-relations.html.

6 *Historical Collection: Speaking to the Future Series – Information and Media during the Edo Period*, Tokyo National Museum, Room 16, Honkan, 3 August–5 September 2010.
7 *Europalia India* took place from 4 October 2013 to 26 January 2014.
8 www.getty.edu/art/exhibitions/china_paper/.
9 24 May–7 September 2008: Museum of the History of Science in Oxford: www.mhs.ox.ac.uk/heaven/.
10 See: www.dhm.de/ausstellungen/tsingtau/tsingtau_e.html.
11 See: www.bozar.be/activity.php?id=7340&lng=en.
12 See: http://pressandpolicy.bl.uk/Resource-Library/A-scene-with-European-figures-Attributed-to-Sanvala-c-1600-c-British-Library-Board-Johnson-Album-16-6-647.aspx.
13 See: www.bl.uk/onlinegallery/onlineex/apac/addorimss/s/zoomify54784.html.
14 Website: www.acm.org.sg/home/home.asp.
15 Website: www.acm.org.sg/exhibitions/eventdetail.asp?eventID=186.
16 My sincere thanks go to Abd Aziz Bin Abdul Rashid, for an interview granted on Tuesday, 19 March 2013 and for his kind help with checking and editing the final text of this section.
17 Muzium Seni Asia; Universiti Malaya; 50603 Kuala Lumpur; www.museum.um.edu.my/.
18 www.nus.edu.sg/cfa/museum/index.php; according to the MSA Director, the collection of the Asian Art Museum, University of Malaya in Singapore, was taken to the University of Malaya, Kuala Lumpur. The impact of the dividing of the university was that the artefacts of the museum have been divided too. For example, artefacts which acquisition numbers 1–3 still remain in the NUS Museum in Singapore.
19 www.muziumnegara.gov.my/main/.
20 The name is believed to be a phonetic corruption of the word for the Portuguese merchant-ships (carracks).
21 Source: www.museum.um.edu.my/.
22 See: www.britishmuseum.org/about_us/news_and_press/press_releases/2006/japanese_galleries_reopen.aspx.
23 See: www.britishmuseum.org/explore/highlights/highlight_objects/asia/p/kakiemon_elephants.aspx.
24 See: www.britishmuseum.org/research/research_projects/all_current_projects/empires_of_faith.aspx.
25 Bangkok National Museum Volunteers: www.museumvolunteersbkk.net/html/museum.html.
26 The latter three are all located in Ayutthaya; see: www.ayutthaya-history.com/.
27 See: www.ayutthaya-history.com/Historical_Sites_MuseumChaoSamPhraya.html, and: www.ayutthaya-history.com/Historical_Sites_AHSC.html.

6 Contemporary actors, networks and institutions in the European Studies in Asia discipline

Co-constructed curriculum leadership and Higher Education regionalism

Introduction: European Studies in Asia – 'soft power' and product placement?

The paradigms and ideological *leitmotivs* of the European Union's Foreign Policy, as pertaining to Higher Education exchange with Asia, are not hard to find. They are in line with a neo-liberal view of HE which strongly promotes the tenets of 'internationalization', 'global competitiveness', 'people-to-people exchange' and 'inter-cultural learning' (Stokhof et al., 2004: 3).

What De Prado (2009) is calling 'Higher Education regionalism' is an important part of this. The *Framework 7 Programme*, the *Europe 2020* Strategy[1] and *Horizon 2020*, the Commission's new *Framework Programme for Research and Innovation*, for instance, as well as blueprints like *Rethinking Education* (COM (2012) 669)[2] – while managing to remain largely 'humanities-free' – are, however, stressing the role of Higher Education in creating new knowledge in society. It appears, though, that this knowledge is mainly conceived of as being useful only where it 'fosters innovation' and 'socio-economic' outcomes.[3]

The second pillar, as it were, of the European Studies (or EU Studies) curriculum in Asia can be said to derive largely from the study of educational concepts and international pedagogy. Thus, the politically desirable outcomes, which are informing the Commission's strategies – for example, the ideas of an EU 'Research Area' and 'Higher Education Area' – are complemented by more abstract ideas, such as an 'Asia–Europe educational space', which underlies much of the work of the Asia–Europe Foundation and many other agents (see below). The strategies of educational managers and policy-makers in regard to 'knowledge-based' international cooperation and 'knowledge-economies' (Letta, 2003: 482) thus find their equivalent in the analysis by educationalists on topics like 'learner perspectives' and 'teaching methodologies', seeking channels to put the abstract concepts on Higher Education, proclaimed, for example, by the EU and ASEAN, into practice.

Specifically for the European Studies in Asia context, this has led to the construction of some interesting intellectual bridges and models, such as an 'Asia–Europe partnership of knowledge' (Archibugi and Coco, 2005; Wiessala, 2011), or as an example of 'epistemic communities' linking Asian and European lecturers and students (Van der Geest, 2006: 149). The European Studies in Asia discipline may thus be said to spring from the two theoretical wellsprings of political strategy/foreign policy and pedagogic theory. A third inspiration may well be the related concern for (Higher) Education as an instrument of the successful projection of 'soft power' to Asia, by means of 'people-to-people exchanges'; much like China, for example, has long done through the Confucius Institutes (Hong, 2013: 10–11).

In general, most of the EU's educational collaboration with the Asia-Pacific comes under the rubric of *Cooperation with Industrialized Countries* and the relevant policy instruments (cf. note 5). According to those, educational dialogue has three cornerstones: the promotion of joint/double degree projects, the furthering of more mobility projects and the parallel conduct of a wider policy dialogue.[4] In connection with the latter, Higher Education and the construction and dissemination of a 'European Studies in Asia' syllabus are, therefore, political actions and part of the official toolkit of EU diplomacy and foreign policy (Wiessala, 2011: 83), complementing the EU strategies on Youth, Culture, Development and Vocational Training.

In the context, therefore, of what the EU – and the Council of Europe[5] – see as an 'inter-cultural dialogue', Higher Education and the discipline of 'European Studies in Asia' are manifesting EU presence, visibility, and 'normative' vision and identity as a 'soft' international power in Asia (Wiessala, 2006: 13, 54, 61–87; Pace, 2007: 1041–1064). This much was clear from at least *Towards a New Asia Strategy*, the Commission's inaugural Asia policy of 1994 (see above).

According to the Commission's numerous 'Asia Policies' and 'Country Strategy Papers since *Towards a New Asia Strategy*,[6] the 're-oriented' (Wiessala, 2006) Higher Education experience of 'European Studies in Asia' must also serve the purposes of poverty eradication, economics and commerce, energy-related, scientific and environmental policies, civic responsibility, human rights and social cohesion and progress (see, e.g. Reiterer, 2004: 368; Wiessala, 2006).

Aside from these, 'knowledge construction', 'academic communities' and the realization of 'knowledge economies', 'learning societies' and 'knowledge-based international cooperation' have become much-vaunted tenets of both the EU and many academics working in European Studies in Asia (Zhou, 2004; Archibugi and Coco, 2005), especially in the liberal arts and the study of social policy and the humanities. Higher Education is seen as part of the increasing globalization of the trade in goods and services, an 'internationally tradeable service' in the sense of the World Trade Organization (WTO), regulated, for example, in the case of Malaysia (see Chapter 7) quite strictly by legislation (McBurnie and Ziguras, 2001: 85, 92–99).

It may be hypothesized, therefore, that next to those general directions and guidelines, the European Commission's more specific 'declaratory diplomacy' towards Asia – its policy blueprints, 'strategies' and other papers – constitute a key element in the genesis and evolution of the 'European Studies in Asia' discipline. Three of them, in particular, have had a somewhat wider impact: the following short extract from the Commission's paper on *The Role of the*

Universities in the Europe of Knowledge (COM (2003) 58 final) provides an idea of – some would say exposes the central fallacies in – the EU's thrust in (Higher) Education policy:

> The European Union therefore needs a healthy and flourishing university world. Europe needs excellence in its universities, to optimize the processes which underpin the knowledge society and meet the target, set out by the European Council in Lisbon, of becoming the most competitive and dynamic knowledge-based economy in the world, capable of sustainable economic growth with more and better jobs and greater social cohesion. The European Council in Barcelona recognized this need for excellence, in its call for European systems of education to become a 'world reference' by 2010.

In (the annex to) its *A New Partnership with South East Asia* (COM (2003) 399 final), the Commission provided some clues as to a more region-specific rationale of its HE cooperation in South East Asia, balancing EU 'branding' with cultural awareness. According to the paper, cooperation in Higher Education is the key to:

- improving mutual understanding and increasing awareness of Europe in South East Asia and vice versa;
- re-positioning Europe as a major HE partner and as a centre of excellence in South East Asia;
- promoting scientific and technological development, thus enhancing growth and competitiveness;
- strengthening the economic and cultural presence of Europe in South East Asia (and vice versa).

The Commission's proposal for a *European Parliament and Council Decision on Establishing a Programme for the Enhancement of Quality in Higher Education and the Promotion of Intercultural Understanding through Cooperation with Third Countries (Erasmus World) (2004–2008)* involves European MA courses but also bemoans:

> Europe's status as a centre of excellence in learning is not always appreciated or understood by third country universities, nor by students looking for an international education. One of the reasons behind this situation is the lack of a European higher education identity. Another factor is the lack of transparency of quality assurance procedures. Increasing attractiveness of our universities requires an assurance of quality that is widely understood in the world.

A number of the Commission's strategy papers contain specific references to the subject area of *European Studies*, including curriculum matters, most notably (but not exclusively) the following:

- *A Long-Term Policy for China–Europe Relations* (COM (1995) 297 final);
- *Report from the Commission to the Council and the European Parliament on the Implementation of the Communication 'Building a Comprehensive Partnership with China'*;
- *Europe and Asia: A Strategic Framework for Enhanced Partnerships* (COM (2001) 469 final);
- *A Maturing Partnership: Shared Interests and Challenges in EU–China Relations* (COM (2003) 533);
- *Strengthening Cooperation with Third Countries in the Field of Higher Education* (see above);
- *Country Strategy Papers on China* (2002–2004 and 2007–2013);
- *EU–India Strategic Partnership* (COM (2004) 430).

An analysis of some of the later EU papers by the Commission and the Committee of the Regions (Wiessala, 2011: 85–86)[7] reveals a more specific focus on 'European Studies', or 'European Studies in Asia', as a subject of 'added value', a 'research cluster', an 'interdisciplinary subject', a tool of 'augmented culture' and 'intercontinental mobility', an instrument of EU human rights promotion[8] and wider Asia–Europe interaction, and an extension of the established presence in Asia of such traditional cultural–pedagogical multipliers as the *British Council*, the *Alliance Francaise*, the *Instituto Cervantes*, the *Instituto Camões* or the *DAAD* (*Deutscher Akademischer Austauschdienst*, or *German Academic Exchange Service*).[9]

There is, of course, a balance to be achieved here, between the precepts of 'officially sanctioned' European Union ideas for the deliberate 'projection' of EU agendas into Asian teaching contexts, and the diversity, heterogeneity and fragmentation resulting from a persisting, Member-State-driven 'Europeanization' of Asian learning experiences. I would posit that the curriculum for the evolving discipline of 'European Studies in Asia' is the *preferred locale* for this balance to be constructed, debated and fine-tuned. Is there any evidence in practice that the EU's papers on Higher and Further Education do, indeed, influence the content of lectures in Asian theatres? I would say from my own experience (see Chapters 7–9) that there is.

Thus, the production of students who co-construct their learning, and who become able 'knowledge mediators' of the future, can be said to be as much a determining factor of curriculum construction as are the Commission's evolving concepts relating to enhanced international collaboration between Asia and Europe, a stronger focus on cross-cutting issues (poverty, energy, environment, human rights [including the right to education], gender equality, access to justice, access to [primary] education, electoral empowerment) and enhanced 'capacity-building' in Asia, by means of knowledge transfer and student/staff mobility.

If one accepts the underlying assumption that the European Studies lecturer or Professor in an Asian classroom is thus, indeed, some kind of 'ambassador' for the Commission's, and by extension the European Union's, political priorities in Asia, then there is one aspect which is, perhaps, of enhanced importance in choosing what one includes in one's 'European Studies' modules: this is the 'shifting sands' of external influences which, to an exceptionally high degree, have steered – sometimes led astray – EU Higher Education priorities towards Asian interlocutors. Thus, concerns over terrorism and human rights, values and stereotypes, awareness deficits, student mobility and the intended 'character' of interdisciplinary subjects, such as 'European Studies' or 'EU Studies', have, over time, been promoted as essential or desirable content of the 'European Studies in Asia' syllabus.

This is evident from an analysis of a wide range of EU Asia blueprints, which have, over more than two decades (1994–2014), referred the curriculum-development aspects and learner needs of the discipline with increasing frequency and, importantly, with more and more 'detachment' from the international crises and concerns of the day that so often distracted the early policies.[10] Many of the later, country-specific, Commission papers fleshed-out and fine-tuned this picture – for example by referring to European Studies as a vehicle for human rights concerns, by 'connecting' earlier, informal forms of European academic exchange with Central Asia, India or China to a more 'unified' European Studies curriculum across the (Asian) board, or by contributing to the foundation of new EU Representations (now: Embassies) across Asia, and of new seats of learning, such as the *Asia–Europe Institute* in Malaysia (see Chapter 9) the *China–Europe International Business School (CEIBS)* in Shanghai, and the *EU–China Higher Education Programme*.

Next to country-specific political agendas and priorities that were 'embedded' in these Country Strategy Papers and related documents, a curriculum for 'European Studies in Asia' can be said to have been constructed, institutionalized and progressively further defined, promoted and expanded in this way, especially in terms of the addition of more 'legal' content in European Studies courses across Asia. In terms of human rights, however, this focus disappeared again at a later stage, especially in the EU's HE relations with China. Human rights content is the *Stiefkind* – the neglected adopted child that is hidden away in the backroom – in the 'European Studies in Asia' curriculum – a lacuna that casts a pall over the whole endeavour, even in 2014, and in spite of much tokenism over 'local' democracy initiatives in the People's Republic of China.

In terms of the development of learning and teaching content in relation to the European Union, the Union's declaratory strategies on China, India, Central Asia, Australia and New Zealand are not just remarkable for the steady expansion of flagship projects like *Asia Link*,[11] the (older) *ASEAN–EU University Network Programme*[12] and *ERASMUS Mundus*,[13] with a burgeoning range of projects relating to Asia[14] and China (Hong, 2013). These and other Commission papers, programmes and projects have further constructed what Gadman and Cooper (2009: 30) have termed 'reciprocal interactions in open-source communities': interactive networks of knowledgeable lecturers and students who have shared ideas and information, becoming a creative source of curriculum development, freely using social media, such as LinkedIn Groups, to co-construct and reform the European Studies curriculum in Asia.

Thus, through the 'integrative interactions' (Gadman and Cooper, 2009: 70) of many, the intellectual ownership properties of what constitutes the learning space of European Studies in Asia have shifted; they are now not confined any more to the pages of Commission strategies – important as these continue to be to provide stimuli. On-going European Studies curriculum planning, in both the physical and the exploding 'virtual' domains, has become a product which is now greater than the sum of its many parts. My case study of European Studies in New Zealand and Australia (Chapter 9) provides many clear examples of communal ideational creativity, distributed between many institutions and actors across large and geographically diverse countries. Some of the former and current academic networks on Europe–Asia relations, India and China are another case in point for this phenomenon. Many of them have their roots in early academic collaboration between China and the EU.

Box 6.1 Key 'knowledge-multipliers' and intellectual networks

(Also, and for weblinks, see 'Selected websites' at the end of this book.)

ERASMUS Mundus Student and Alumni Association
EU4Asia Programme (2009–2011)
EU Network of European Studies Centres in Asia (EU-NESCA, 2006–2008): Research Dialogue
Eurasian Silk Road Universities Consortium
European Institute for Asian Studies (EIAS)
European Policy Centre (Brussels)
European Union – Asia Centre (Brussels)
European Union Centres Network (EUC, New Zealand)
European Union Studies Association Asia-Pacific (EUSAAP)
Europe-China Research and Advice Network (ECRAN)
Finnish University Network for Asian Studies
International Institute for Asian Studies (IIAS)
Network for South East Asian Studies
Nordic Institute of Asian Studies (NIAS)
Regional EU–ASEAN Dialogue Instrument (READI – Education)
Singapore Institute of International Affairs (SIIA)
SOAS Centre of South East Asian Studies
South East Asian Ministers of Education Organization (SEAMEO)

In its more recent (multi-annual) *Indicative Programmes (MIP), National Indicative Programmes (NIP)* and *Country Strategy Papers (CSP)* on Asia and China,[15] the EU appears to recognize these processes through fostering a discourse on 'internationalization' through European Studies, 'knowledge-driven, broader, international collaboration' and similar concepts, by promoting the 'multiplication effect', inherent in contacts with universities teaching European Studies courses, and by further widening the circle of stakeholders – for example, through the encouragement and support of alumni of EU cooperation programmes.

At the time of writing, the newest Commission pronouncements on Higher Education in EU–Asia relations on the teaching of European Studies largely stay within the 'people-to-people' and 'dialogue-of-minds' discourse exemplified by the work of the Asia–Europe Foundation (see below). This has predominantly meant increasing participation in European Higher Education exchange programmes such as *TEMPUS* and *ERASMUS Mundus*,[16] with the three-fold aim of teaching the EU, engendering changes in 'host' societies and networking researchers.

This is also true for the *(Higher) Education Initiatives* and *Joint Declarations on (Higher) Education*, where they exist (Wiessala, 2011: Chapter 6).[17] Occasionally, like in India, the EU adds more manifest political agendas, referring, for instance, to European academics in Asia as 'policy-thinkers' or providers of an 'informal network of checks and balances within civil societies' in Asia; thus, the former *Jawaharlal Nehru University – European Studies Programme* (JNU–EUSP, 2002) was singled out in this context – although the key Commission line on India has long been one of commonality in democratic development. The pedagogic issue of learner preferences is a relatively new concern for some of the Commission's papers.[18]

One aspect deserves to be mentioned separately: an 'organic' connection between the, more or less, 'abstract' EU policy papers and the actual experiences of European Studies lecturers 'on the ground' in Asian universities can be found in the one interest that is common to both the supra-national and inter-governmental varieties of EU Higher Education interaction with Asia, and to both the Commission's papers and the Member States' own individual endeavours; this is the desire to commercially *position* European Higher Education, and European universities, including their cultural–political manifestations such as the *European Union Higher Education Area (EUHEA)*, the *'Bologna' Process*, the *European Union Research Area (EURA)* and the growing number of European branch campuses (especially in Malaysia) as a world-class 'brand' in Asia, in the face of growing competition from such 'Western' nations as the USA, Australia and New Zealand. This commercial dimension of 'learning' and 'pedagogy' (Pang, 2006; Edwards and Usher, 2008) links wider discourses on 'globalization' to the topics of curriculum design and reform of tertiary education in Australasia and Europe (James and Mok, 2005; Pang, 2006; De Prado, 2007, 2009).

The development and delivery of a well-designed 'European Studies in Asia' curriculum, including – as it almost inevitably does – high-profile educational conceptual frames, such as *Asia Link* and *ERASMUS Mundus*, visits by its Asian students to Europe, internships and work experience elements, seems to many European Studies Professors like a fairly 'natural place' to pursue this 'branding' exercise. *Asia Link*, for example, has encompassed projects on topics close to the European Commission's key Asia priorities, such as Asian–European Management (Ref. No.: VN/Asia Link/007) and European Studies in

China (Ref. No.: 98/679–02). Consequently, 'European Studies' constitutes not just an ideological and pedagogic 'laboratory' for key EU political and cultural notions: it may also be understood also a kind of 'product placement' of the EU as a major global HE partner for Asia. I argue here that this a consequence of a much-changed international Higher Education landscape; it also points to much wider debates about what universities, or fully commercialized 'multi-versities', are in fact for (see, for instance, Collini, 2012), which cannot be argued out in detail in this book.

Finally, a recent *ERASMUS Mundus*/ASEMUNDUS/DAAD[19] 'Good Practice Report', on *Succeeding in European–Asian Higher Education Cooperation*,[20] provides a glimpse of the 'networking' and curriculum planning dimension of European Studies in Asia.[21] The report highlights a range of relevant seminars, the promotion of joint study programmes (ASEMUNDUS Report: 8) and the involvement of the Asia–Europe Meeting of Ministers of Education (ASEMME,[22] cf. below and Chapter 7), as well as reporting a number of case-studies which bear eloquent testimony of joint curriculum and programme content development, as well as a more synergistic teaching methodology (*ASEMUNDUS Report*: 23)

The Asia–Europe Foundation, Singapore

Having emerged from the bi-annual summitry of the Asia–Europe Meetings from 1996 onwards, the Asia–Europe Foundation (ASEF) in Singapore[23] may seem quite an obvious candidate to include in a book on European Studies in Asia; and, indeed, ASEF offers a wealth of activities which seem tailormade for the advancement of EU–Asia intellectual exchange.[24] Prominent among them is a 'European Studies in Asia' (ESiA) initiative, based, in part on the *EU Through The Eyes of Asia* study, linked to the NCRE in New Zealand (see Chapter 9).[25]

And yet the key research agendas suggested by much of the recent academic literature on ASEF continue to reflect either an, often overstated, interest in the mechanics and political theories which would explain ASEF as an 'institution' of the Asia–Europe Meeting – a physical emanation establishing itself, 'big-bang-like', of a mere process, and growing 'pillars', much like the EU itself. Alternatively, some writers have left this convenient model behind and have sought to identify the more long-term issue of (regional) 'identity-formation' with a purpose, looking less at the scaffolding of ASEF's structure and plethora of initiatives, and focusing more on the Foundation as an example of the interdependence of political actors and of ideas surrounding the perceived values of exchange and inter-continental dialogue – social-constructivism applied to the *dialogue*, rather than the *clash*, of civilizations paradigm (Wiessala, 2011: 162).

It seems surprising then that, against this background, from among the forest of theorizing about the structure, process orientation and identity of ASEF, one tree has received so relatively little attention: the examination of ASEF as a key *driver of the European Studies curriculum in Asia*. Perhaps this area is easily obscured by other, more pressing, political concerns. The questions of how the

Foundation arose in the midst of the Asian Financial Crisis of 1997/1998, how it is rooted in the European Commission's first *New Asia Strategy* of a few years earlier and how it is strategically aligned with every major Commission blueprint on EU–Asia relations ever since are certainly worth investigating, and the answers yielded by research in this direction will bring important clues of the relationship between politics, culture and Higher Education. However, I would posit here that ASEF is more than a mere instrument of EU foreign policy, or a vehicle for the promotion of other EU policies on, for example, democratization, human rights and development.

ASEF has been all the above, of course, but the organization has now also become, arguably, the most prominent amongst only a handful of regional bodies with the remit and power to shape the very notion of what 'European Studies in Asia' actually means. There are a number of developments, including the evolution of the 'cultural–educational' pillar of the Asia–Europe Meeting summitry itself, which strongly prefigure the role of ASEF as 'curriculum builder' for the discipline of European Studies in Asia. The themes of 'interdisciplinarity' and 'cross-cultural networking', inherent in the design of all of ASEF's programmes are, of course, a strongly enabling background condition for Area Studies, including those covering Europe and Asia, as is what, with Chartsuwan (2004: 178), may be seen as a balance between direction from the 'top-down', and contributions from the 'bottom-up' in the ASEM way of working. The resulting wealth of ASEM exchange activities do not just express the much-vaunted 'people-to-people' ideology of the forum, they also, by and large, fill in the picture of what should actually be taught about 'Europe' in 'Asia'.

One advantage of this curriculum development is that it is co-constructed. In the context of the *ASEF Lecture Tours*, *ASEF Universities* (including ASEFUAN, the ASEF Universities' own 'alumni-network'[26]), *ASEF Education Workshops* and many similar intellectual encounters, participants are taking the opportunity to engage critically with EU, ASEF and ASEM priorities, as regards the East–West exchange, and to express for themselves what should be on the timetables of European Studies in Asia. Leaving aside, for the moment, the significant collaborative research dimension ASEM has accumulated, for instance, through the *Asia Europe Journal*, the combined efforts of many participants in ASEM activities can be said to constitute a 'civil society', in the best sense of the word. A 'society', of like-minded people – often future leaders – who 'civilize' educational policies, by questioning its political foundations, enriching the goalposts of EU priorities through many perspectives of their own, which find their way, eventually, into 'European' lecture theatres in Asia. In this way, ASEM provides an indirect 'filter', a conceptual lens made up of many participants, who modify the officially sanctioned neo-liberal language and ideology of the 'knowledge economies', thus translating the political priorities into a more practical pedagogic product on the ground. Therein, I would posit, lies the real value of ASEF – the real meaning of an East–West 'people-to-people' dialogue.

I have seen, as I hope will become evident in the subsequent chapters about my own teaching experience in Asia (Chapters 7–9), how this dynamic process of a co-constructed European Studies curriculum works: on the basis of an ASEF Summer University, a new course on the EU emerges in a European Studies Centre in Thailand or Malaysia; an event in the *Asia–Europe Dialogue on Cultural Policies*[27] can lead to the introduction of a new module on European fashion in New Zealand; as a result of dialogic diplomatic interaction in the course of an ASEF University programme, an ASEM *Inter-Faith Dialogue*, an ASEM *Talk on the Hill* or a conference of the *Asia–Europe Young Leaders' Symposium*, the syllabus of a postgraduate course on the EU in India is amended.

There are many examples of such direct links between the exchange activism of ASEF and concrete impact on courses on the EU across Asia, either directly or by means of the (alumni, classroom[28] and other) networks the ASEF programmes have spawned. The institutional alphabet soup of ASEM activities is easy to criticize, in terms of 'symmetry', 'decline' (Camroux, 2006) and 'cooperation fatigue', but its influence on the identity and nature of curriculum development of European Studies in Asian universities, professional organizations and think-tanks is undeniable, and much more long-term than any individual ASEF University programme, ASEF Education Hub and Asia–Europe Colloquium on University Cooperation – important as these initiatives may be, of course, in kick-starting processes and bringing people together.

The Asia–Europe Meeting, ASEM Ministers of Education Meeting, ASEM Rectors' Conference and South East Asia–Europe: Higher Education and Research Forum

If the Asia–Europe Foundation (ASEF, see above), as the only official physical institution of the ASEM process, can thus be said to have both direct and indirect influence on the development of the 'European Studies in Asia' curriculum, then it would be natural to make the assumption that the ASEM summitry itself is possessed of a similar intention, or at least that a direct effect on the shaping of the ESiA discipline would have arisen as a side effect of the interactive relationships between Asian and European scholars, produced in between, and during, the main ASEM every two years. Perhaps it may be hypothesized that there is a relationship here, akin to the one between the European Council and the Council of Ministers in the European Union, where ASEM sets the general policy direction, and the many groupings and sub-fora it has instituted fill in the details of actual intellectual cooperation and academic development.

To this may be added the additional input provided to ASEM by both its Member States and their education ministries, and the universities and university consortia linked to it. To test this rather convenient model, it is useful, following a quick overview of the 'pedagogic' aspects of ASEM, to narrow the search a little, as it were, and to home in on two or three of the dialogue and discussion platforms which have arisen out of ASEM, especially in the field of Higher and Further Education. I have argued elsewhere that the intellectual DNA of ASEM has represented, from the beginnings of the forum in 1996, a strong 'learning dimension', articulating the intellectual 'software' of societies on both continents, and, more often than not, strongly reflecting the national (Higher) Education systems of the individual member states whose history has, after all, contributed to making ASEM what it is (Wiessala, 2011: 159).

In the three years since I wrote this, this trend has been further strengthened and has also undergone further re-direction towards a neo-liberal understanding of universities, with which many institutions in Asia are grappling in 2013/2014. As one result of these processes, there is now a bewildering variety of both intra-ASEM and external agenda-setting fora and events, which I am arguing can, in themselves, be said to have had a direct impact on which aspects of 'Europe' and the EU are being included in the teaching in Asian classrooms and lecture halls. By involving many educational policy-makers, officials from national education ministries and academics in the process of giving the 'cultural and educational' pillar of ASEM further direction, the summitry has not only produced a permanent institution (the Asia–Europe Foundation; see above), it has also sought to exercise a kind of 'distributed educational leadership', consulting and involving its main stakeholders, civil society, professional organizations, school and academic communities and national governments.

The DEEP database,[29] ASEM Education Secretariat, ASEM Education Hubs and Education Workshops, Asia–Europe Colloquies on University Cooperation, ASEM DUO Fellowships, the ASEM Education Hubs Education and Research Network (AEH-EARN, 2000) and initiatives like the Asia–Europe Classroom (AEC) and ASEM Rectors' Conferences have ensured that peer-influence (Niemann, 2001: 33) is still one of the deliberate drivers of ASEM activity, in HE and elsewhere. The ASEM Rectors' Conferences, in particular, are standing out in seeking to empower (European Studies and other) students in fora such as an *Asia–Europe Students Forum*,[30] and by focusing on 'enabling' themes such as *Students as Future Leaders*.[31]

Furthermore, the *South East Asia–Europe: Higher Education and Research Forum* was an off-shoot of ASEM 8 in 2010, aiming to highlight EU–South East Asia cooperation achievements in the field of HE and facilitate knowledge exchange.[32] It complements the *ERASMUS Mundus* document, *Strategies to Strengthen Collaboration in Higher Education between Europe and South East Asia*, of October 2010,[33] which was derived from a 24-month *ACCESS* (Academic Cooperation Europe South East Asia Support) project and survey.[34] The resulting ACCESS paper hinged on notions of educational 'transformation' and 'diversification', and advocates the parallel 'de-coupling' of the processes of 'regional' and 'international' integration, in order to facilitate more efficient ways of East–West Higher Education long-term collaboration (ibid.: 4).

While the ideas of spinning a 'web of learning' and 'networking', and of creating a pool of critical academics – who would nevertheless disseminate 'European' ideas about education in Asia (Chirathivat and Lassen, 1999: 43; IEEM, 2001: 77, 81, 160–166; Meissner, 2002; Wiessala, 2002a: 121) – remain reasonably persuasive metaphors in explaining ASEM agency in Higher Education, there are now many new aspects of the ASEM rationale which influence the development of the academic discipline of 'European Studies in Asia'. From an early focus on pedagogy and teaching practice, ASEM has created many dialogue platforms with a more dedicated curriculum development brief in the discipline. Among the large number of these groups, many of which are also inter-linked with other regional fora such as SEAMEO (see below), two examples may be singled out on account of their concrete concerns with matters of European Studies pedagogy in Asia: the Asia–Europe Meeting Ministers of Education (ASEMME) format and the ASEM Rectors' Conference.

The somewhat awkwardly named Asia–Europe Meeting Ministers of Education (ASEMME) meetings may well have taken their initial cue from the experiments of the early ASEM Education Hubs, in their intention to create a process of exchange and a mechanism aiding the development of joint initiatives in response to problems of common concern to education policy-makers in Asia and Europe. In May 2013, at the time of the 4th ASEMME meeting in Kuala Lumpur, Malaysia, one such concern was, once again, the issue of 'balanced mobility', i.e. the deficit in the numbers of European students coming to Asia, when compared to the large numbers of Asian students making their way to Europe (*University World News*, Yojana Sharma, 14 May 2013, Issue No.: 272).

This issue, next to mutual degree recognition, research collaboration between Asian and European academics and the wider discourse regarding a 'global knowledge society',[35] had been on the ASEMME agenda since *ASEMME 1*[36] and during the first ASEM Rectors' Conference in Germany in 2008 (see below). The historical background for this imbalance in East–West learner movements remained, however, largely unaddressed by the ASEMME forum (see Chapters 1–4) – as, indeed, did the matters of underlying European and Asian 'attitudes' towards migration and education. The fact that 'student mobility' issues are but a mirror of the wider 'Cinderella phenomenon', or 'triadic' conceptualization of EU–Asia relations, in which US–Asia and EU–US relations are thriving, over and above EU–Asia contacts, also remained largely unrecognized.

Nevertheless, following the rubric of *Strategizing ASEM Education Collaboration*, ASEMME 4 prioritized 'student mobility' and educational 'connected-ness' among learners. The ASEMME 4 leaders pointed both to the mobility statistics and to the stipulations in the relevant 'constitutional' document of ASEM, the *Asia–Europe Co-operation Framework (AECF)*. No doubt, the ASEMME 4 participants were also aware of the 'competition' from American and Australian exchange initiatives and university branch campuses in South East Asia – a trend highlighted by the South East Asian Ministers of Education Organization (SEAMEO; Wiessala, 2011: 84). Since what has been termed the frequently 'disproportionate' dissemination of the 'yields of educational exchange' (e.g. IEEM, 2001: 102) was more than evident in 2013, the issue of 'balanced mobility' became pressing. The Asia–Europe Institute (AEI; see Chapter 7) at the University of Malaya was one of several concrete examples across South East Asia of a wider ASEM/ASEMME concern directly shaping the European Studies curriculum in Asia; an example, furthermore, which I have been privileged to experience first hand (Box 6.2).

Box 6.2 'Balanced mobility' and the West looking East: ASEMME 4 in Kuala Lumpur

The activities at the AEI in connection with the 4th Meeting of the ASEM Education Ministers (ASEMME 4)[37] in Kuala Lumpur on 12–14 May 2013 make for a realistic and interesting case study of a part of my typical work at the Institute. AEI was asked by the Malaysian Ministry of Higher Education (MOHE) in Putrajaya to become involved in the ASEMME 4 event, which had been themed *Strategizing ASEM Education Collaboration*, and focused on four priority areas: quality (McBurnie and Ziguras, 2001), structural convergence and recognition; engaging business and industry in education; balanced mobility; and life-long learning, including technical and vocational education and training.[38]

This initiative could refer back, among other fora, to a 2012 *ASEM Seminar on Quality Assurance*[39] and the *2nd Roundtable* of the *European Union-Asia Higher Education Platform (EAHEP)*, a (former) Commission-funded initiative, in Kuala Lumpur in 2009 – especially to its conclusions on student mobility.[40]

The key part of AEI involvement was to be to come up with a proposal to address the issue of balanced mobility, against the background of between *six and fifteen times* more Asian students going to Europe than European learners studying in Asia. 'Mobility', for the purpose of the ASEMME 4 Meeting, was defined as 'movements between locations, especially the movement of students, staff, academicians and resources'. The wider context for the issue was framed by the progressive internationalization of Malaysian Higher Education, a recent *Universitas 21 (U21)* evaluation,[41] the idea of the 'Bologna Process' and European Higher Education Area as potential 'models' for Asia,[42] and the function and role of the Asia–Europe Institute at Universiti Malaya. Other aspects pertained to the long-term impact of 9/11 on international student flows into Malaysia.

It was both exciting and instructive to work, in close association with the Visiting Research Fellows and permanent AEI staff, through different stages of a proposal which was going to be presented to ASEMME 4 by Malaysian Higher Education Department Director-General Professor Dr Morshidi Sirat on the final day of the meeting. The AEI proposal rested on the AEI's participation in an ASEM *Joint Curriculum Development Pilot Scheme*, the creation of an *ASEM Centre of Excellence (ACE)* on the AEI/UM campus and the provision of future scholarships to students who would act as *Mobility Ambassadors* across ASEM Member States.

A strong part of the proposal was the re-purposing of the existing (postgraduate) European Studies curriculum at the AEI, which was, arguably, showing signs of both 'dated-ness' and 'overlap' in its four main Masters' programmes (see the subsequent chapter for details). It was proposed, therefore, to 'streamline' the postgraduate curriculum and re-visit individual modules and programmes on the course, in order to offer new provision directly linked to the concerns expressed by ASEMME 4, and to the wider issues affecting Asia and Europe in 2013.

Thus, issues of international diplomacy, the perceived 'rise' and continuing 'dynamism' of Asia were underlying the suggestions to introduce to the AEI portfolio a suite of new Masters' programmes in Asia–Europe Relations, the Study of Terrorism/Counterterrorism, Knowledge Management and Knowledge-Based International Relations and Contemporary Asian Studies. At the time of writing,

> these proposals were still being developed, with a view to finalising them well before ASEMME 5 in Latvia in 2015.
>
> Participation in putting the proposals together and seeing them eventually adopted at ASEMME 4 was a welcome confirmation of the 'direct and tangible impact' that academics working in Asia–Europe relations can have on the development of a 'European Studies in Asia' curriculum. The Malaysian party press carried daily reports of ASEMME 4, exploring the importance of the meeting for the nation, and rendering the European Union highly visible, for a time (e.g. New Straits Times, NST, 12 May 2013: *Bridging the Gap between Worlds*; The Star, 13 May 2013: *The West Must Look East*).

Last, but not least, next to the ASEMME meetings, the ASEM Rectors' Conferences can be said to have made important contributions to shaping the teaching of an interdisciplinary subject such as European Studies, or European Studies in Asia. This has been the case because the organizers of these events have been especially adept to link the ASEM summitry to related educational agencies across South East Asia, among whose key remits is curriculum development and international relations pedagogy. Thus, the ASEM Rectors' Conferences' concerns with, for example 'e-learning'[43] offers regional and thematic synergies with the *Institute of Educational Leadership* (*Institut Kepimpinan Pendidikan*, IKP)[44] at the University of Malaya, the *Southeast Asian Educational Leadership Conference* (SEALC)[45] and, on a non-university level, the *South East Asia School Principals Forum* (SEASPF).[46]

The educational policy 'concert' of these players, with its emphasis on cultural and educational exchange, has created the 'seed bed' for curriculum planning in European Studies and related disciplines. The ASEMME meeting, since its inception in 2008, has promoted discourse surrounding a stronger focus on the idea of 'educational leadership' in Higher Education[47] in both Asian and European Institutions of Higher Education (HEIs). This has influenced the curriculum planning of the IKP and of a range of other European Studies Centres from South East Asia to Japan and China. In 2013/2014, for example, the lead provided by ASEM led to the creation of a new MA, in Educational Leadership, at Universiti Malaya, the syllabus of which examined, among other subjects, the EU Higher Education Area, EU Research Area, the Bologna Process and the training requirements for HE Leadership in European Development Policy and Human Rights promotion (see also: Wiessala, 2006).

The ASEAN University Network and the South East Asian Ministers of Education Organization

In addition to these facilitators of educational development and curriculum panning for European Studies in Asia, there are ideational mechanisms of interaction across Asia and Europe and beyond. While these do not exist predominantly for the benefit of the further development of the European Studies discipline, they nevertheless produce intellectual 'spin-off' content, inspiration, resources and advice which should influence all European lecturers and Professors working in international relations across Asian universities. A very good example, and one which has inspired regional as well as EU–Asia initiatives, are the findings of a key report issued by the Organization for Economic Cooperation and Development (OECD): *Innovation in South East Asia: An OECD Review of Innovative Policy*, of May 2013, with its focus on 'extra-regional knowledge circulation', including flows between the South East Asian region and the established centres of 'knowledge production', such as the EU.

On the basis of reports like the OECD one, the ASEAN University Network (AUN) is already either co-sponsoring or providing other input to many of the initiatives and groups looked at in this chapter. In terms of the more specific concerns of this chapter with 'modelling' the curricular future of the 'European Studies in Asia' discipline, the AUN is distinctive, in that it provides discussion platforms, such as the AUN Rectors' Meeting and the ASEAN+3 Higher Education Policy Dialogue, to address key issues such as student mobility, credit transfer and recognition of qualifications, quality assurance and leadership (Wiessala, 2011: 159), which directly impact on the kind of rules which govern the introduction and 'validation' of 'European Studies' courses in widely differing contexts in Asian (and ASEAN) universities. This is embedded in the findings of other relevant studies of ASEAN Higher Education systems, such as the Regional EU–ASEAN Dialogue Instrument (READI).[48]

In my own experience, awareness of those rules and embedding, and of the AUN's attempt to 'harmonize' them, Bologna-like, across its Asian constituency, pays many dividends in connection with the planning of a meaningful, and realistic, European Studies portfolio in Asia. This is particularly true for ASEAN Member States like Malaysia who are suffering from a disproportionately high level of interference and control from their governments and education ministries. One aspect of this, which, in my view, will both further 'liberate' the EU Studies curriculum in Asia and assume a much higher importance in medium-to long-term curriculum design, is the AUN's attempt at facilitating more 'borderless' Higher Education provision, such as the ASEAN *Cyber University*,[49] and the (science-focused) *SEA–EU-Net*, funded under the European Commission's *Framework 7 (FP7) Programme*.[50]

Many of these concerns do, of course, overlap to a greater or smaller degree with similar issues also exercising the minds of ASEM, SEAMEO or EU policymakers. There is not a world of difference, for example, between the alphabet-soup institutional worlds of the ASEM Education Minsters Meeting (ASEMME) and the ASEAN Education Ministers Meeting (ASED), or between the AUN Rectors' Meeting and the ASEM Rectors' Meeting. Despite sometimes blurred areas of innovation and competency, however, many good examples of policy platform convergence abound (see also: European Commission/ERASMUS-Mundus Project, 2010: 7). One such case relevant to the concerns of this book is the *ASEAN Curriculum Sourcebook*,[51] a key resource, which – although aimed at the schools sector – nevertheless easily transfers to the development and delivery of key European Studies in Asia content, especially in its main foci on 'identity and diversity', 'promoting equity and justice', 'connecting global and local' and 'working together for a sustainable future'. In my view, it can be used as inspiration for European Studies modules and courses, up to postgraduate level, in the same way.

This also applies to the excellent *Know Your Neighbours Teaching Guide*,[52] a similar comparative curriculum publication by SEAMEO (see below), which connects and compares South East Asia with the teaching cultures of Australia, New Zealand and the Pacific. Another example of good practice is the AUN's stated concern for 'student-driven' future leadership of these processes (e.g. AUN Student Leaders Forum 2013–2016).[53] This interfaces organically with similar, developing themes in other, interactive, Asian and European HE agenda-setters, from ASEMME to the *Graduate Student Forum* of the London-based *University Association of Contemporary European Studies (UACES)*,[54] which is – arguably and among many other things – the main curriculum discussion forum for the European Studies (and European Union) Studies disciplines in Europe.

Networking with the Bangkok-headquartered SEAMEO,[55] established in 1965 as a chartered international organization, can also yield important benefits for curriculum designers, teachers and administrators of European Studies in Asia programmes. This is true both for the SEAMEO head organization itself, which has its origins in the 1956 *Association of Southeast Asian Institutions of Higher Learning* (De Prado, 2009: 8), and for its 20 specialist educational facilities across the South East Asian/ASEAN region. SEAMEO, which is developing modalities of collaboration and convergence on South East Asian (Higher) Education with both ASEAN and ASEM,[56] attracted the attention of programme planners and centre managers for European Studies in Asia at an early stage, through some relevant and innovative, student-centred projects, such as *Connecting Southeast Asia & Europe e-Learning Models*.[57] It shares its Bangkok offices with the *UNESCO Asia and Pacific Regional Bureau for Education*.

At present, in helping to construct European studies syllabi in Asia, many Asian universities and centres, such as the Asia–Europe Institute at the University of Malaya (see Chapter 9), will not only use their own and ASEAN's experience, but will seek resources and curriculum guidance from, arguably, the most relevant of the SEAMEO regional hubs, the *SEAMEO Open Learning Centre (SEAMOLEC)* in Jakarta, Indonesia.[58] SEAMOLEC seeks to provide expertise and resources on Information and Communications Technology (ICT)-based open and distance learning. The centre's *SEA EduNet* project (now in 'version 2.0')[59] can be especially pertinent when it comes to delivering a European Studies timetable over great distances in Asia, or shared between more than one study centre/HEI in the Asia-Pacific (*SEAMOLEC e-Magazine*, July 2013, in Bahasa Indonesia, and some English).

SEAMOLEC's six-day workshops on promoting 'teaching-by-simulation', for example, whilst seeking to address, no doubt, the (distance) learning needs of a country 5,000 km in diameter, can also relate directly to international student

136 *Contemporary representations and actors*

exchange and European Studies in Asia teaching (ibid.: 7–8). In addition, the work on 'quality assurance' (Yavaprabhas, 2007: 16), 'internationalization' and 'credit transfer' of the *SEAMEO Regional Centre for Higher Education and Regional Development (SEAMEO-RIHED)*[60] in Bangkok, Thailand, effectively links AUN with ASEMME, ASEM and a web of other, international partners, providing a source of (teaching) materials for those seeking to provide a more 'rounded' study experience to students of European Studies in Asia. In conducting pre-lecture research on EU–Asia relations, for instance, a look at the SEAMEO connection, or at similar initiatives such as the 2006 *Brisbane Communiqué*,[61] on curriculum, quality, recognition of qualifications and training can enable European/EU Studies lecturers to enrich their classes with the many diverse, holistic, environmental, poverty-eradication and socially engaged international relations perspectives provided by SEAMEO and related interlocutors (Box 6.2, see also the SEAMEO Newsletter, *SEAMEO Education Agenda*, 2007–2010).[62]

Box 6.3 SEAMEO and other key resources for teaching European Studies in Asia

(For weblinks, see 'Selected websites' at the end of the book.)

ASEAN+3 Summit
Asia-Pacific Centre of Education for International Understanding (APCEIU)
Asia Regional Integration Centre
Association of Pacific Rim Universities (APRU)
Brisbane Initiative (2006)
Education Services Australia
International Council for Open and Distance Education
SIL International
Social Transformation and Educational Prosperity (STEP)
UNESCO
UNESCO Bangkok (E-Library)
UNESCO's Asia and the Pacific Education for All (EFA) website
University Mobility in Asia and the Pacific (Australia)
World Bank (Education)

The National Centre for Research on Europe and the 'perceptions' projects: a successful 'dual embedding' of the European Studies discipline

The National Centre for Research on Europe (NCRE) at the University of Canterbury (*Te Whare Wānanga o Waitaha*) in Christchurch, New Zealand (*Aotearoa*)[63] is, quite possibly, the most remote European Studies Centre that it is possible to imagine in the context of a book about 'European Studies' in

'Asia' (see also Chapter 9). And yet the University of Canterbury (UC) is also an official *EU Information Centre*. Moreover, the NCRE is, arguably, the best possible example for the fact that the 'tyranny of distance' is no more: physical remoteness from Europe does not have to equal mental disengagement, or lack of interest by academics and the public.

By contrast, at the time of writing this (August 2013), the NCRE has, over a period of more than a decade, made contributions to the curriculum development in European Studies in Asia, which are remarkably out of proportion to its relatively modest size.[64] This appears all the more notable because the NCRE is a 'normal' department of the University of Canterbury (UC),[65] whilst also offering BA (Hons) and PhD postgraduate degree pathways and Jean Monnet modules in European Studies. The wider university (UC), by contrast, seems to define itself more through STEM subjects (science, technology, engineering and mathematics), rather than the liberal arts and humanities; a trend which appears to have increased following the 2010 Christchurch earthquake.

Founded in 2000, as the *Centre for Research on Europe*, a major European Commission grant helped the centre to acquire the 'national' moniker in 2002. It remains, in 2013, the only tertiary-level, dedicated EU Centre in New Zealand,[66] and intensively collaborates with four other New Zealand universities (Auckland, Victoria, Otago and Lincoln). The main research foci of the staff are strongly reflected in the teaching ethos and syllabus (see Chapter 9); both revolve around 'local' and 'regional' issues which form a 'bridge' between the European Union and New Zealand's region: thus, development policy, human rights, Pacific issues and the relations of the European Union with the 'Pacific' members of the group of 79 African, Caribbean and Pacific (ACP) states form 'natural' research 'clusters' of the NCRE.

This is an important factor in the centre's success, since – by contrast with many other, similar EU centres across Asia – it has managed to establish the 'locality' and regional relevance of its work, emphasizing issues such as 'migration', 'tourism', 'trade' 'multi-culturalism' and 'social values' as part of the underlying common rationale for taking up the study of Europe in New Zealand.[67]

More recently, and in line with many international Higher Education Institutions, the NCRE has strongly foregrounded those aspects of a European Studies degree which relate to the employment prospects of its future graduates in both the public and the private spheres in New Zealand.[68] As part of the study of the EU at the NCRE, students, furthermore, complete an internship, either in New Zealand[69] or in the European Parliament. It has also explored previously unchartered academic territory, especially through one of its key Research Projects, *EU in the Eyes of Asia* (see below).

As I have been involved with the NCRE over most of its first decade, the completion of which was duly celebrated in 2012, I have included my experiences in working with the staff and (postgraduate) students there in the 'pedagogic' section of this book (Chapter 9). I am examining the NCRE at this point solely in the context of the development of the 'European Studies in Asia' discipline, looking at the impact the centre has had on shaping and debating the learning and teaching experience, both within and outside of the core discipline, on international research, networks and projects surrounding European Studies in Asia, and on rendering the idea of 'Europe' and 'European Union' relevant to local concerns in the Antipodes.

The fact that the influence of the NCRE is disproportionately strong on determining what exactly constitutes 'European Studies' and 'European Studies in Asia' can, in my opinion, be explained by means of a combination of reasons. First, there is no doubt that the NCRE has carved out its niche on the basis of a strong academic profile and the tenacity and vision of the people who work there, in the face of significant difficulties and set-backs over time (e.g. the 2011 earthquake). The way in which staff interests have been managed and skilfully integrated into the current (and future) EU Studies curriculum sets the centre apart from many others across Asia, in which these 'alignment' and dynamic development processes are not taking place, leaving the European Studies timetable a hostage to fortune, and at the mercy of often disparate staff interests, which are challenging to reconcile in the service of pedagogy.

The effect the NCRE has had from afar on the construction and furthering of the academic field of 'European Studies in Asia' has been further consolidated by the choice of research projects, such as *EU in the Eyes of Asia*, which, once again, have had a global influence disproportionate to the shape of the NCRE (Holland *et al.*, 2007, 2010). By investigating, over a period of almost a decade, how the EU is viewed in Asia, and who are the key media and opinion-formers in the region, the NCRE has not only created data and resources which are now almost universally quoted, it has also achieved a process one may call 'dual embedding': it has embedded itself in the scholarly consciousness of European Studies academics and students across the world, and, aside from this significant reputational issue, the centre has also entrenched exactly those EU concerns, policies and activities in the political landscape of New Zealand and its region which are relevant to Pacific concerns and the practicalities of EU–New Zealand relations.

Another reason for the substantial impact of the NCRE on the contour of the wider European Studies discipline – aside from undeniable and passionate vision and a thought-through strategy – can, arguably, be detected in the range of what one may call its targeted and coordinated approach to networking and outreach, where the former relates to the centre's involvement in relevant government and NGO fora in New Zealand, Asia (such as the Asia–Europe Foundation; see below) and, indeed, beyond, and the latter pertains to the wider, 'societal' function of the NCRE inside New Zealand.

Notwithstanding the NCRE's interactions with a plethora of Higher Education, development and advocacy groups in the Pacific and internationally, the latter, 'domestic', activity, 'connecting' New Zealand citizens of all ages to the ideas of the EU as a 'partner' and potential 'model' for the region, and keeping this up in the face of a colossal geographical remoteness, will be, in my view, the more important NCRE role for the future of New Zealand and of the post-earthquake Canterbury region.

In trying to achieve this, the NCRE could look, in 2013, to its own, continuing and interactive, processes of engagement with the New Zealand Government and the EU, at the levels of policy advice and consultancy. In addition, therefore, to leveraging its political connections, the NCRE was looking, in mid-2013, at introducing entirely new EU modules (see below, Chapter 9), thus inaugurating a process of rendering the EU relevant, 'fresh' and interesting to a new generation of New Zealand graduate students, who continue to stand out by possessing an above-average level of expertise and interest in the EU.

Chapter conclusions

This chapter has shown that the modern 'European Studies' or 'European Studies in Asia' academic disciplines feed from the twin wellsprings of official educational policy and declaratory diplomacy of the EU and its representations across the region, and from the higher-than-average number of professional, governmental and NGO associations, think-tanks and regional organizations making an impact on enriching the teaching of European Studies, especially in the South East Asian region. While the EU's contributions may be conceptualized as a didactic form of educational diplomacy, foreign policy or the projection of 'soft power', other think-tanks have a more education-oriented, pedagogic orientation.

One of the central findings of this chapter is that, across the region, curricula for European Studies are increasingly 'co-constructed', involving a plethora of resources, institutions, centres and 'knowledge-multipliers', outside of official policy dialogues and networks. The work of larger organizations and processes, such as the EU, the Asia–Europe Meeting (ASEM), the Asia–Europe Foundation (ASEF) or the South East Asian Ministers of Education Organization (SEAMEO) is, of course, very significant in terms of the 'inter-cultural dialogue', (regional) 'identity-building' and 'intellectual exchange' aspects of the European Studies teaching initiatives in Asia, especially where it enables students and lecturers to meet and network across boundaries of faith, ethnicity and social class. But, significantly, there are many more, smaller, agencies, educational enablers and multipliers to hand, often with a very specific brief, which make valuable contributions to teaching European Studies in Asia, on small budgets.

These multiple platforms, networks, levels, players and processes are shaping the EU Studies teaching and research programme to a much higher degree than official documents of the EU or ASEM, since the former involve 'inspiring' processes of co-determined curriculum-building, which, to a large degree, involve learners themselves. However, there are also a large number of smaller and more specific 'side-shoots' of these bigger agenda-setters, who can provide endless inspiration, as well as a string of (often free) resources, for both the lecturer and the student of European Studies in Asia.

140 *Contemporary representations and actors*

There is, as yet, very little critical, academic, work in the emerging area of this kind of co-constructed Higher Education regionalism. De Prado's analytical comparison (de Prado, 2009: 15) offers the beginnings of a much-needed, sharper, focus on both the educational cooperation mediated by institutional and political dialogue, and the collaborative creativity housed in 'European Studies' centres in Asia and Europe (Table 6.1).

A categorization such as this one is able, on the one hand, to help explain Higher Education regionalization in terms of structures and networks, whilst also leaving room for accommodating individual activities and priorities of European

Table 6.1 Comparing regional cooperation in Higher Education in Europe and Asia (source: de Prado, 2009: 15)

Element	*Europe (EU)*	*East Asia*
Main policy frameworks	Erasmus: European Commission's efforts to promote linkages Bologna Process: pan-European intergovernmental convergence	ASEAN+3: East Asia Vision/ Study Group reports. Group on facilitation and promotion of exchange of people and human resource development Southeast Asia: joint SEAMEO-ASED ministerials Northeast Asia: ministerials developing
Academic institutions	1949–: College of Europe Masters 1975–: European University Institute 2010–: European Institute of Innovation and Technology	None yet Nālandā in India may be an external catalyser
Networks	A variety of active associations	Growing number
Student exchanges	Erasmus: aiming at three million by 2012 Bologna: allowing fuller mobility	Autonomously growing in Northeast Asia Very incipient exchanges in ASEAN
Faculty exchanges	Erasmus: tens of thousands for short periods Bologna: encouraging fuller mobility	Very limited
Content	Erasmus: ECTS Bologna Process: promoting structural homogenization in a global context	Declarations aiming to structural transformations
External linkages	Bidirectionally important	Crucial to develop
Overall assessment	**Advanced regionalism**	**Growing regionalism**

Studies Centres globally. Whereas this particular frame is focused on East Asia, and on structures and networks, it can be imagined that similar, future work will start to expand the frame to investigate also aspects of networking and collaborative, co-constructed syllabus creation in the European Studies discipline in Asia.

Notes

1 See: http://ec.europa.eu/europe2020/index_en.htm.
2 See: www.cedefop.europa.eu/EN/Files/com669_en.pdf.
3 See: SPEECH/12/863, and: http://ec.europa.eu/programmes/horizon2020/.
4 Overview: http://ec.europa.eu/education/external-relation-programmes/industrialised_ en.htm.
5 See e.g.: Council of Europe, 'Higher Education Series' No. 16; *Speaking Across Borders*.
6 *Towards a New Asia Strategy* (NAS), of 13 July 1994: COM (94) 314.
7 Among the key EU policy papers in this context are: *The Role of the Universities in the Europe of Knowledge* (COM (2003) 58); *Education, Training and Research: Trans-National Mobility* (COM (96) 462); *Towards a European Research Area (ERA)* (COM (2000) 6); *E-Learning* (COM (2000) 318; COM (2001) 172); *Making a European Area of Life-Long Learning a Reality* (COM (2001); 678 and 1939); *Inter-Cultural Dialogue and Understanding* (COM (2002) 401); *Investing Efficiently in Education and Training* (COM (2002) 779); *Teaching and Learning – Towards the Learning Society* (COM (95) 590); and *Strengthening Co-operation with Third Countries in the Field of Higher Education* (COM (2001) 385), plus a range of secondary blueprints.
8 The 13th ASEM Human Rights Seminar took place in Copenhagen, in October 2013.
9 The vital role of which, in making this author what he is, and in setting him on the career path he has chosen as a former *Fachlektor* of Law in Cardiff, it is now high time, I think, to finally fully acknowledge here – Danke.
10 *EU Industrialized Countries Instrument (Council Regulation (EC) No 1934/2006)*; *Europe and Asia: A Strategic Framework for Enhanced Partnerships* (COM (2001) 469 final, of 4 September 2001); *A New Partnership with South-East Asia* (COM (2003) 99, of 9 July 2003); *Strategy Paper and Indicative Programme for Multi-Country Programmes in Asia (2005–2006*, http://eeas.europa.eu/asia/rsp/05_06_en.pdf); *Regional Programming for Asia – Strategy Document 2007–2013* (http://eeas.europa.eu/asia/rsp/07_13_en.pdf).
11 For 2002–2005 projects, see: http://ec.europa.eu/europeaid/where/asia/regional-cooperation/higher-education/documents/asia_link_2002-05_en.pdf.
12 See: http://globalhighered.files.wordpress.com/2010/02/aunp.pdf.
13 The latter is funded to the tune of 1.3 billion euros for a total of ten years.
14 An overview of projects *relating specifically to Asia* within *ERASMUS Mundus* is available here: http://eacea.ec.europa.eu/erasmus_mundus/results_compendia/documents/projects/action_3_promotion_projects/regional/a3fiche_asia.pdf.
15 *A Long-Term Policy for China-Europe Relations* (COM (1995) 279); *Building a Comprehensive Partnership with China* (COM (1998) 181); *Report (2000) from the Commission to the Council and the European Parliament on the Implementation of the Communication 'Building a Comprehensive Partnership with China'* (COM (2000) 552 final, 8 September 2000); *Implementation of the 1998 Communication and Future Steps for a More Effective EU Policy* (COM (2001) 265); *A Maturing Partnership: Shared Interests and Challenges in EU–China Relations* (COM (2003) 533); *EU–China: Closer Partners, Growing Responsibilities* (COM (2006) 632).
16 See: http://eacea.ec.europa.eu/erasmus_mundus/documents/erasmus_mundus_0913_low.pdf.

142 Contemporary representations and actors

17 For example, in the cases of Australia, Central Asia, China and India (cf. THE, 20 May 2005 on China); also: South Africa: http://ec.europa.eu/education/external-relation-programmes/doc/jointsouthafrica_en.pdf.
18 See, for example: *EU–India Enhanced Partnership* (COM (1996) 275); *EU–India Strategic Partnership* (COM (2004) 430); *2007–2013 CSP India* (http://eeas.europa.eu/india/csp/07_13_en.pdf); *The EU and Central Asia: Strategy for a New Partnership, October 2007* (www.eurodialogue.org/eu-central-asia-strategy/10).
19 DAAD is the German Academic Exchange Service.
20 See: www.asem-education-secretariat.org/imperia/md/content/asem/asemundus/good_practice_report.
21 See also slides, at: http://eacea.ec.europa.eu/erasmus_mundus/events/cluster_asia/28-09/erasmus_mundus-an_example_of_good_practice_for_europe-asia_cooperation_wuttig.pdf.
22 See: www.asem-education-secretariat.org/en/12205/.
23 Established in February 1997; 31 Heng Mui Keng Terrace, Singapore 119595; www.asef.org.
24 ASEF celebrated its fifteenth anniversary in 2012: http://asef.org/index.php/projects/programmes/2427-15-anniversary.
25 See: http://asef.org/index.php/projects/programmes/548-european-studies-in-asia-(esia).
26 See: http://asef.org/index.php/projects/themes/education/3008-12th_ASEFUAN_AC_and_AGM.
27 See: www.asef.org/index.php/projects/programmes/524-cultural-dialogue.
28 See: http://aec.asef.org/.
29 See: http://deep.asef.org/about/index.asp.
30 See: www.asef.org/images/stories/publications/documents/ASEM-Rectors-Conference-3-Publication.pdf and: www.asef.org/index.php/projects/themes/education/2357-3rd-asem-rectors-conference ('Are You Fit for The Future'?).
31 See: http://asef.org/index.php/projects/themes/education/2357-3rd-asem-rectors-conference.
32 See: www.asem8.be/event/south-east-asia-europe-higher-education-and-research-forum.
33 See: www.menon.org/wp-content/uploads/2012/05/ACCESS-White-Paper.pdf.
34 See: http://ec.europa.eu/education/programmes/mundus/projects/action4/08asia.pdf and www.menon.org/wp-content/uploads/2012/05/ACCESS-White-Paper.pdf.
35 See: www.asef.org/images/stories/publications/ebooks/2ndasemrc_publication_web.pdf.
36 ASEMME 2 was in Vietnam in 2009, ASEMME 3 in Denmark in 2011, ASEMME 5 will be in Latvia in 2015.
37 The meeting is a biennial dialogue forum involving education ministers and senior officers from 27 EU Member States, two European (non-EU Member) countries (Norway and Switzerland) and the European Commission, with 20 Asian countries, plus the ASEAN Secretariat, a total of 51 countries and partners.
38 A short article, by Shada Islam, is at: www.aseminfoboard.org/asemin-the-news/item/1237-Asia-and-Europe-focus-on-education-partnership-.html; see also: www.asem-education-secretariat.org/en/12205/.
39 See: www.asem-education-secretariat.org/imperia/md/content/asem2/events/2012_qa_france/asem_qa_recommendations.pdf.
40 Outcome Report: www.eahep.org/images/Malaysia/annex%202%20second%20eahep%20workshop%20final%20outcome%20report_final.pdf.
41 See: www.universitas21.com/.
42 See, for example the Second Roundtable of the (now terminated) *EU–Asia Higher Education Platform (EAHEP)*, at www.eahep.org/eahep-project/round-tables/bologna-process-and-asia.html.
43 See: www.asef.org/index.php/projects/programmes/529-asem-rectors-conference.
44 For which I have the privilege of working at present (August 2013); see: http://iel.um.edu.my/.

45 See: http://go2fresnostate.com/seaconference/.
46 See: www.seaspf.org/.
47 See the ASEMME 1 publication: www.asem-education-secretariat.org/imperia/md/content/eu/asemsecretariat/chairs_conclusion_berlin_2008.pdf.
48 See: http://readi.asean.org/news/123-readi-supports-study-on-education-systems-and-policies-in-asean-in-2013.
49 See: www.aunsec.org/aseankoreaacademic.php.
50 See: www.sea-eu.net/.
51 See: http://library.stou.ac.th/sites/default/files/ASEAN_Curriculum_Sourcebook.pdf; also available on SEAMEO website: www.seameo.org/.
52 www.seameo.org/images/stories/Publications/Relevant_Publications/teaching_guide.pdf.
53 www.aunsec.org/aseanstudent.php.
54 www.uaces.org.
55 www.seameo.org/.
56 See: SEAMEO *SEA Education Access Magazine*, 1/2006: 20.
57 www.seameo.org/index.php?option=com_content&view=article&id=255:cae-e-learn&catid=112:completed-project&Itemid=582 (the project is now completed).
58 www.seamolec.org/.
59 Funded by the European Commission: www.seamolec.org/newsdetails.php?id=210 (in Bahasa Indonesia).
60 www.rihed.seameo.org/.
61 See: https://www.aei.gov.au/About-AEI/Policy/Documents/Brisbane%20Communique/Brisbane_Communique_pdf.pdf.
62 www.seameo.org/index.php?option=com_content&view=category&layout=blog&id=131&Itemid=565.
63 *National Centre for Research on Europe (NCRE)*, University of Canterbury, Kirkwood Village KD04; Tel: (0064)33642348, ext.: 6348; www.europe.canterbury.ac.nz/ (see also Chapter 9 and 'Selected websites' at the end of this book).
64 In 2013, there were four FT academics working at the NCRE, including the Director and Deputy Director. The academic staff are supported by four administrative staff on campus (Kirkwood Village K4). A large number of visiting academics have visited the centre, and there continues to be a changing body of Research Fellows, lecturers, Adjunct Fellows, graduate students, alumni, interns, advisory board members, business advisory groups and research associates linked with the NCRE, at various times.
65 www.canterbury.ac.nz/.
66 I gratefully acknowledge the kind input of my Malaysian student, Miss Munirah Mauzud, who worked at the NCRE from 29 April to 21 June 2013, in connection with piecing together the more recent 'history' at the centre. I would also like to thank her for kindly allowing me to use parts of her full 'Internship Report' in this chapter, as well as in Chapter 9.
67 NCRE Brochure: *Why Study the EU in New Zealand?* (2013).
68 University of Canterbury, Career Hub: *EU Studies* (www.careerhub.canterbury.ac.nz) (UC: 2013).
69 For example, at the European Union delegation to New Zealand in Wellington, which was established in 2004, http://eeas.europa.eu/delegations/new_zealand/.

Part III
Teaching Europe in Asia
Case studies

7 Teaching comparative regionalism and the EU in South East Asia

'Sons of the soil', student politics and European Studies in Malaysia

Political tsunamis, sultans of sting and sodomy: politics in Malaysia in 2013/2014

Whilst issues of the desirability of a critical student voice and the on-going legacies of the colonial past can be said to have set, for certain parts of 2012 and 2013, the tone of some debates about politics in Malaysia, there were other concerns with a more direct effect on the European Studies discipline here. 2013 was the year of 'GE13' – the thirteenth General Election since the creation of Malaysia in 1963. GE13 has been called the 'most closely contested' election ever (Rahman, 2013: 7); it was held on 5 May 2013.

The 'political tsunami' of the March 2008 General Election (GE) had seriously dented the power-monopoly of the ruling coalition, the *United Malays National Organization* (UMNO, see: Ooi Kee Beng, 2010)[1] and its hegemonic constituent party, *Barisan Nasional* (National 'Front', or 'Team' 'BN'), which has held power for 56 years in Malaysia's controlled democracy (from 3 April 2009 under Prime Minister Datuk Sri Tun Abdul Najib Razak). Having been released from prison (see below), opposition leader Anwar Ibrahim managed to consolidate the opposition as a coalition (*Pakatan Rakyat*, 'People's Pact') under the umbrella of his Centrist Party (*Parti Keadilan Rakyat* [People's Justice Party], PKR).[2]

In the run-up to 'GE13', there were very strong demands for electoral (roll) reform and the promotion of more democratic practice and transparency in the face of entrenched structural bias, such as a (Westminster-inspired) first-past-the-post system, a disproportionally powerful executive power, a token opposition, the *Bumiputera* preference-code (see below)[3] and a racially structured (Soong, 2012: xi), rather than integrative, thrust (some say obsession) in Malaysian politics, stemming, in part, from the pre-independence period. Other Malaysian political observers complain also of a catalogue of democratic shortcomings, including the unacceptability of the concept of *Ketuanan Melayu* (Malay dominance; cf.: Nain, 2013: 11) in the UMNO political lexicon, and the reluctance of the Malaysian government to ratify the *International Covenant on Civil and Political Rights (ICCPR)* and the *International Covenant on Economic, Social and Cultural Rights (ICESCR)* (Soong, 2012: 62–63).

Tan Sri Abdul Rashid bin Abdul Rahman, a former chairman of the Malaysian 'Electoral Commission' (EC), put the contemporary Malaysian political dilemma succinctly (Rahman, 2013: 19): 'Malaysians generally have learnt to accept that some laws which are considered "cruel" and against the principle of human rights and freedom, have contributed towards the country's achievement as a progressive, peaceful and stable democracy.' Elsewhere, he is more forthright (Rahman, 2013: 47–48), lamenting 'major abuses such as the indiscriminate use of state resources by the governing party, alleged corrupt practices, limited freedom of expression during election, imbalanced coverage by the press and so on'. To this may be added an opaque system of political party funding and an electoral register which includes a good number of deceased voters.

In addition to issues of elitism, electoral 'cleanliness' and democratic practice in politics – and possibly connected to them – a pall was cast over GE13 and Malaysian politics by the 'armed incursion' of 9 February 2013, of 235 militiamen of the 'self-proclaimed' (and now defunct) 'Sultanate of Sulu'[4] from the southern Philippines into the resource-rich[5] Malaysian state of Sabah in North Borneo, triggering an armed response by army fighter jets, as well as an upsurge in Malaysian nationalism.[6] The event resulted in casualties among both intruders and military personnel. It appeared to demonstrate that there might as yet be unresolved matters from the times of the *British North Borneo Chartered Company*,[7] and it led to a raft of publications defending the inviolability of Malaysian territory (e.g. Patail, 2013).

From the point of view of teaching International Relations in ASEAN and the EU, there could hardly have been a more suitable case study, involving, as it did, concepts such as 'de-colonization', 'self-determination', territorial 'lease' versus 'cession', referendums and conventions involving Malaysia, Spain, Holland, China, Singapore, Indonesia, Brunei, Britain, Germany, the US, the Philippines and other state actors from as far back as the 1800s, to Malaysian independence in 1963. This showed how today's Malaysian Sabah on Borneo was a strategic area on the trade routes between China and Singapore.

Arguably the most potent aspect of Malaysian politics, especially among increasingly vocal and social-media-savvy students, is the astonishing treatment meted out to Dato' Seri Anwar Ibrahim (1947–), the leader of the opposition in Malaysia's Parliament. Anwar was a former student leader at the University of Malaya (1967–1971), and became Deputy Prime Minister under former Prime Minister Tun Dr Mahatir Mohamad, who dismissed him in 1998, as a consequence of disagreement over how to handle the Asian Financial Crisis (1997/1998). Anwar was charged, on 3 February 2010 in the High Court in Kuala Lumpur, with the offence of 'sodomy',[8] following a complaint by Mohd Saiful Bukhari bin Azlan, one of Anwar's party workers.

The trial was quickly dubbed 'Sodomy 2'. In a first trial, which began in 1998, Anwar had been convicted of 'corruption' and was sentenced to six years in jail.[9] In the second one ('Sodomy 1'), he was convicted in 2000, but acquitted by the Federal Court in 2004. In the third trial, the High Court, on 9

January 2012, acquitted and discharged Anwar on the grounds that (DNA) evidence had been tampered with (Marican, 2012: 172–174); however, at the time of writing, an appeal lodged on 20 January 2012 by the Attorney-General is still pending.

Pawancheek Marican (2012: xvii–xviii), one of Anwar's lawyers in the first two trials, charts the twists and turns, alleged conspiracies, sex videos, bomb explosions and affairs surrounding the trial. Marican ponders the significance of what he calls 'highly-charged, political trials' and 'the emasculation of such civilizational concepts as the rule of law, civil society and democracy' in modern Malaysia.

All three court cases against Anwar Ibrahim are strongly reminiscent of the long-standing practice of the equally monopolistic *People's Action Party (PAP)* in neighbouring Singapore, of 'silencing-by-bankrupting' its political opponents through the domestic court system. The Anwar trials have attracted widespread, international condemnation as 'show trials', from groups such as *Human Rights Watch*[10] and the *Inter-Parliamentary Union*,[11] who have long suspected that human rights safeguards are fragile in the country, and that Malaysian courts are rarely free from interference by hidden political hands (Marican, 2012: 22, 49–50; see also: Soong, 2012).

Policy copying or policy learning? The state of Malaysian Higher Education in 2013/2014

Anthony Welch (2013: 53–83) identifies a number of key factors influencing contemporary Higher Education in Malaysia, among them a long-standing and influential tradition of Islamic learning and scholarship, which has many repercussions today, both in the structure of Higher Education institutions in Malaysia and in the pedagogic content of many courses. In addition to this, a number of issues can be seen to characterize the current state of Malaysian HE since the *Seventh Malaysia Plan* opened up the system by stipulating a higher degree of 'internationalization', in line with overall changes in the global tertiary education landscape. The changes in the *New Economic Policy (NEP)* of Malaysia since the Asian Financial Crisis (1997/1998) and an accelerating 'brain-drain' amongst Malaysian academics (and business owners[12]) are but two of the larger problems, unfolding against a background of wider shifts, from public to private HE in the country since the 1990s, and the more recent opening up of 'branch campuses' of European, US and Australian universities in Malaysia. The Malaysian government now conceives of Higher Education as a 'commoditized', export-industry article (Kassim, 2013: 47; Macfarlane, 2012: 16, 88; Tham Siew Yean, 2013) and a provider of international links, income and students for the country, as it claims to be moving towards a 'high-income' economy over the next decade.

Box 7.1 'Sons of the soil' and ethnic ideologies: racial over democratic citizenship

Even though ethnic Chinese and Indians have been in Malaysia for centuries, they are not treated as indigenous 'sons of the soil', or Bumiputeras. One way of looking at this policy is that it provides affirmative action to redress historic patterns of inequality. A less charitable interpretation is that it is an open form of racism against Malaysians of Chinese and Indian descent, who make up around one third of the population. Whereas it is possible to find many affirmative action programmes in other countries for minorities, in Malaysia this benefits the majority over the ethnic minorities. 'Malaysia, though, is just one of several countries that might be criticized as having a less than desirable policy that presents an ethical question for anyone wishing to do business there' (Macfarlane, 2012: 127).

In 2013/2014, the on-going implications of the *Bumiputera* (*Bumiputra*)[13] system continued to be, arguably, the most controversial issue in the Malaysian Higher Education system. *Article 153* of the *Federal Constitution of Malaysia* has 'legalized' a 'racial preference-strategy', aiming at the improvement of Malay treatment, especially at tertiary level. In public universities, and in the economy in general, a kind of legally sanctioned discrimination plays out in favour of the *Bumiputeras* (*Bumiputras*), the majority, Malay-ethnicity, 'indigenous', population segment (all 'indigenous' Malays, by constitutional definition, are also Muslims). Ideologically, this system is justified through the concept of *ketuanan Melayu* ('Malay supremacy', from Malay *tuan*: 'master'). *Bumiputera-ism* is today seen by its critics as an artificial, state-sponsored (and officially engineered) form of identity (Ibrahim, 2013: 301). The policy is commonly justified with reference to political stability and overall racial population proportions in Malaysia. In the view of its opponents, it is also a skewed framework of 'affirmative action'. Lee (2013: 236), for example, argues that it is used 'to justify policies and practices that have been implemented to entrench a citizenship where rights and membership are determined by race – a racial citizenship'.

Highly politicized Malay 'affirmative-action' initiatives in education, the professions and business can be traced back to the time before independence in 1957 (see *AEI Post*, Vol. 3, June 2010: 19), preceding both the current *Bumiputera* code and the *New Economic Policies (NEP)* put in place to implement it (Gomez and Saravanamuttu, 2013). The original idea seems to have aimed at 'restructuring' society, by dis-associating ethnic background from economic activity. The race riots between Malays and Chinese on 13 May 1969 provided the original impetus for successive UMNO governments to entrench *Bumiputera* preferences from 1971 to 1990, by means of the *NEP*, although the *ketuanan Melayu* idea seems at odds with the concept of former Malaysian Prime Minister Mahatir Mohamad regarding a *Bangsa Malaysia* ('Malaysian ethnicity'). Having achieved some of its economic objectives, by creating a new Malaysian middle-class, both *NEP* and *Bumiputra* preferences appear to be in direct contradiction with 'equality' provisions, such as there are, in the Federal Constitution of Malaysia.

The *Bumiputera* system, implemented originally as an 'immediate remedy' to increase Malay HE participation in relation to Malay majority share of the population, has become a permanent fixture and, some would say, a stain on Malaysia's reputation as an emerging global knowledge-hub. It mandates preferable, racial-quota-based admission to ethnic Malay students (Gomez and Saravanamuttu, 2013: 8), thus militating against a merit-based (meritocratic) admissions policy. In 2000, enrolment in public universities, by ethnic group, was 59.9 per cent Malay/ *Bumiputeras*, 32.5 per cent Chinese and 6.8 per cent Indian (Lee, 2013: 243). The *Bumiputera* method extends to the recruitment and promotion of lecturers too. HE 'massification' entails increased specialization of the Professoriate (Macfarlane, 2012: 75). In addition to this, the encroaching 'privatization' of HE in Malaysia (see elsewhere in this chapter) and a mushrooming growth of private HE providers have, in Lee's words (2013: 247) 'ethnically segmented HE along a public/private divide, as well as across public and private higher education institutions'. This toxic combination ensured that 90 per cent of student enrolment in private universities in the 1980s and 1990s was from the Chinese and Indian ethnicities (McBurnie and Ziguras, 2001: 94); even today, the figures are heavily skewed – although Malay participation in private universities' degree programmes has been elevated. This does not, however, mean that this group is more successful at finding jobs.

In summer 2013, some European media reported that the Bumiputera quota system had been officially abolished as early as 2002, quoting Malaysia's Education Ministry as stating that the system was now wider and based on 'merit'. Many doubt this.[14] In late 2013, the reality is, perhaps, best encapsulated in the following comments made to me directly by a Chinese-Malaysian student within the last five years:

> Regarding the quota thing, yes, officially it is 'supposed' to be based on meritocracy. But there is still plenty of discrimination, you know, by the people who 'sieve' applicants and what not. I think it's mostly 'lip-service'. In a way, non-Bumiputera have better chances than before – but it is not entirely equal. Myself and my Chinese friends experienced this ourselves when applying to [University X]. Back in 2006 or 2007 some friends and myself applied for a TESOL course. During the application process, the website said that, if we made it to the interviews, we would be notified by a phone call. So, what happened was we never got the calls, but, according to the website we were eligible to proceed to the interviews, which I had missed the deadline, because I didn't know, I didn't check the website every day. Now, one of my friends who did, he applied for the interview. And he was given bloody two days or something, to go to another state [a state outside Kuala Lumpur in the Federation of Malaysia], to attend the interview. He managed to get a plane ticket, flew all the way there and attended this interview. Now, when he showed me the photos, I saw that they were mostly Malay, and they were from that state, meaning they did not have to go very far. And we found out that there were actually interviews conducted in KL [Kuala Lumpur], mostly filled by Malay students. I really didn't understand why they asked him to go so far. Then my other friend told me she found out that only the Malay students received the phone calls that we were supposed to get. She was angry – she said it was very unfair. My friend, who went so far for the interview, at the last minute, finally managed to get into the TESOL course. And you know, I found out a large number of the admitted students were so bad at English. In the end I got my second choice, studying English at the Faculty [of Y]. And I was very happy. I think I was better off there. In the university I actually met one male

> Malay student who was in the TESOL course. His English exam result was what: band 2 or band 1? That means you are not proficient at English at all! He didn't seem to have his heart set on the course either. I asked him why he was studying this, and he said: 'well, the government offered me this, so I thought I might as well take it'. He dropped out in the first year. So you see, Professor, despite the government saying that they use 'meritocracy', the system is still rather corrupt; a lot of the people in it don't want to give non-Bumi [students of non-Malay ethnicity, i.e. Chinese and Indian Malays] a chance to go in if they can, perhaps they have been instructed by those in government to reject them – but this may be a 'conspiracy theory'! Anyway, I even had friends who had so many problems getting into the course they wanted, which was so sad. They tried a strategy – which was to just take any course offered, and then ask to change in the second year, apparently it would have been easier. Some of them failed to do so – so either they pushed through with a course they hated, or they dropped out. Ah, so many stories...
>
> In the face of many such comments, I witnessed, it seemed to me in late 2013, that the inequalities entrenched in this system – rather than academics' supposed failure to publish in the 'right' ISI journals – were keeping local public universities in a low position in international university rankings, as well as exacerbating the continuing exodus of staff and students from the country. Such systemic exclusion cannot but leave itself open to harsh criticism, on both linguistic and equality grounds – however, it may be covered with a historical patina surrounding ethnic imbalances, poverty alleviation, national unity, political stability and access to public goods. Critics are right in calling this a political strategy, based on racial arithmetic and underpinned by the construction of a questionable, and wholly artificial, sense of belonging (Ibrahim, 2013: 301).

In spite of the near-hegemonic hold the *Bumiputera* idea has over large sections of Malay public opinion, what Welch (2013: 78) and others call the '*Bumiputera-ization* of Malaysian public Higher Education' can have significant consequences 'on the ground', as it were, in terms of loss of quality, academic freedom, weak leadership in departments, lack of incentive and an indifference and complacency towards international linkages and funding, amounting to a process of socialization which encourages conformity and discourages lateral thinking and initiative (Kassim, 2013: 117). A system which 'guarantees' jobs to a segment of the population also entails a grossly over-inflated bureaucracy in which academic workloads are low, unspecified and frequently overlapping.

As a result of this, there are, perhaps, two wider – and countervailing – trends in Malaysian public Higher Education in 2013/2014. On the one hand, there has been a rampant 'politicization' and 'corporatization' of the tertiary sector (from 1995),[15] as well as louder political demands for its increased 'internationalization'. On the other hand, the system is its own worst enemy, in that it holds back opportunity and competition in engaging many of the best minds in the country. This framework also ensures that market conditions for the still rising number of private providers of Higher Education, and for foreign universities' branch campuses, remain vibrant – sometimes at the expense of equality and human rights concerns. Kassim (2013: 61) reports:

> disgusted with quota systems, the alleged religious, racial and political indoctrination of our kids in the public education system, and, of course, the rapidly declining standards in these institutions, many parents have opted for the private higher education sector, which has exploded on the Malaysian scene over the past couple of decades or so.

It is, perhaps, not surprising then that the 'gold-rush' – the overt and covert 'commercialization' and 'corporatization' of Higher Education in Malaysia (as elsewhere; Macfarlane, 2012: 122–124) – is also the main target for wider criticism of the system (e.g. Kassim, 2013: 121–122). The main thrust of what gets published on this appears to focus on both public and private HEIs not delivering the 'public goods' of HE, or neglecting their partnerships with local stakeholders through 'consultancy overkill', whilst at the same time making increasingly implausible claims to 'excellence', an internationally vacuous concept (Deem *et al.*, 2008; Collini, 2012: 109; Kassim, 2013: 47, 121).

Such concerns with quality, excellence and government regulation of Higher Education (McBurnie and Ziguras, 2001) are, indeed, not a million miles away from similar ones in Europe. In Malaysia, many of the critical voices regarding HE home in on the current obsession within Malaysian universities to 'shoot up the rankings' of global league tables (Nain, 2013: 111–113), on the implications of 'research clusters' and other observable restrictions of academic freedom, and on the negative consequences of a further concentration of resources, which has been characterized as 'policy-copying, but not policy-learning', harming both system and institutional diversity (Deem *et al.*, 2008: 92).

Colonial baggage and the emergence of 'European' studies in Malaysia

In addition to these questions, there were other developments in Malaysia–Europe relations in 2012/2013 that, although not noticeably influencing the EU teaching experience, nevertheless were rarely far from the surface of things. Among the most widely reported incidents was the (UK) High Court's pronouncement on what was dubbed 'Britain's My Lai' (e.g. *The Times*, 28 April 2012: 3): the killing of 24 Chinese villagers in *Batang Kali*, Selangor State, by a military patrol of the Scots Guards during the 'Malayan Emergency' (1948–1960)[16] on 11–12 December 1948. The investigation preceding the High Court judgement was said to have been inspired by the enhanced scrutiny of the killings at My Lai, Vietnam, and the *Mau Mau* Uprising in Kenya. At the time, the British colonial government had claimed the villagers of *Batang Kali* had been 'terrorists' and 'bandits' on the run – it seems political expediency ruled even before our own age of the politics of fear.

154 *Teaching Europe in Asia: case studies*

Although the High Court did rule against a full public enquiry of the incident in 2012, the decision was, nevertheless, praised as a 'moral victory', since it made public the criticism of successive British governments who had omitted to investigate – and sought to retroactively 'justify' – what is now often called a massacre. The 176-page ruling in 2012 stated that 'there is evidence that supports a deliberate execution of the 24 civilians' who were described as unarmed rubber workers.

The event casts a long shadow over Malaysia–EU relations and the High Court's verdict continues to be challenged[17] by the relatives of those killed (*Observer*, 6 May 2012; *The Times*, 5 September 2012: 20).[18] The short book *Slaughter and Deception at Batang Kali* (Ward and Miraflor, 2009) is a recent account of the event and its aftermath.[19] Meanwhile, the *New Straits Times* reported that, in April 2010, Tham Yong, 78, the last witness of the *Batang Kali* killings, had sadly passed away.

The Asia–Europe Institute, University of Malaya, Kuala Lumpur (2011–2014)[20]

Against this background of commoditization and internationalization in Malaysian universities, both private and public, a contentious system of ethnic discrimination and an accelerated pace of globalization (Collini, 2012: 14–15), the Asia–Europe Institute operates within the (public) Universiti Malaya (UM). As a public university, UM falls under the *Bumiputera* principle, perhaps the most flawed part of the hitherto accepted Malaysian model of a historical 'social contract', which forms part of the country's Constitution, history and *New Economic Policy* (*NEP*, 1971–1990) (see Box 7.1 and: Saravanamuttu, 2010; Gomez and Saravanamuttu, 2013). This means special privileges and university 'quotas' are 'reserved' for ethnic Malays to ensure, in the eyes of many, the maintenance of the socio-economic status quo (Abraham, 2006: 26–27; see Box 7.1).[21] Rahman (2013: 91) points out the obvious consequences, other than social distancing:

> lack of places for non-Malays with good results had produced anxiety among them. To ease that problem, private Colleges and Universities (more than 100 of them to-date) have been established, with most of the running courses in collaboration with foreign Universities in the 'West', some of them well-known, some of a more than dubious nature.

The AEIs' annual reports, course leaflets and other promotional literature provide evidence of high levels of compliance with government policies; too close an association, I felt, had the potential of impinging on critical enquiry, academic freedom, independent thought and the leeway available for creative, lateral thinking and teaching. The Institute seemed, in my view, sometimes in danger of being 'straight-jacketed' by too many layers of responsibility, rules and regulations, leading all the way up to the Ministry of (Higher) Education.

However, there was also strong evidence of proactive, strategic adaptation to the new, globalized educational world, and of a commitment to the necessary, concomitant changes to the various strands and programmes in the AEI's evolving academic identity. The AEI, ambitiously, aims to be 'the place where intellectual discourses are held'. Its watchword of *Building Ties Beyond Boundaries* encapsulates the constituent elements of the Institute's academic self-image as follows (AEI Leaflet: *Building Ties Beyond Boundaries*, 2009, 2013):

- a focus on postgraduate studies (MA and PhD degree level), combined with a programme of research methodology training;
- a choice of four, clearly defined Masters' routes (expanding from 2013);
- an emphasis on the academic credentials of 'the best Professors from Asia and Europe' (international teaching);
- a firm, regional, embedding through the fostering of ties with other ASEAN Member States and the ASEAN Secretariat;
- an orientation towards pedagogic internationalization, through international conferences, international 'road-shows' (recruitment fairs) and visiting scholars programmes, themed around pertinent questions, e.g. educational research (AEI Annual Report, 2007: 37);
- a programme of academic visits to potential partners in the East and West (e.g. China and 'West Asia' [the Middle East, UAE]);
- the availability of financial support to students who evidence 'appropriate personal and leadership qualities' and who have no support from their home governments or other sources (AEI IMRI Brochure, 2013: 2);
- provision of the opportunity, for learners, to undertake an 'internship' abroad.

Many of these themes were, more or less, present also in the 'academic DNA' or other, past and present, European Studies Centres in the South East Asian region, although an over-reliance on foreign academic talent is being tempered, at the time of writing, by new financial constraints. What sets the AEI apart, in my view, is the on-going attempt to keep the learning provision up-to-date and tied to evolving political concerns in both the Association of South East Asian Nations (ASEAN) and the European Union (EU), and to develop the curriculum into new areas, radiating out from the four original, 'foundation' MA degree programmes. Most prominent among the more recent developments at the AEI was the emergence of a new *International MA Degree Programme in European Studies* for 2014. The AEI is connected to both the EU and a consortium of Malaysian Higher Education Institutions, by means of past and present, multi-national projects and consortia such as 'MYEULINK',[22] SINCERE'[23] and others (cf. *AEI Post*, Vol. 3, June 2010: 16; Vol. 4, 2011: 16).

When subjected to a closer analysis, the composition of the student body in the four Masters' programmes at the AEI shows a clear trend to (a) linear growth, year-on-year, and (b) an initial phase of students of predominantly Malay/South East Asian provenance with only a few foreign participants joining, changing to a broader picture, including students from all continents, from roughly 2008 onwards (AEI Brochure: *Graduate Study at AEI*, 2013).[24] In terms of its research ethos and academic identity, the AEI identifies itself strongly with the humanities and social science disciplines, especially as regards the parallel key themes of globalization, regionalization and relevance to Europe–Asia relations, in relation to its programmes of study at MA and PhD level (in Social Sciences and Humanities). As far as I can see, there are, in 2013/2014, very few other academic centres in South East Asia which have built a research strategy around this conceptual brief (see: *AEI Post*, Vol. 3, June 2010: 35, for an overview).

The Institute links its overall research aims to the performance appraisals of all visiting staff and Senior Research Fellows – for example, by applying the (Asian) yardstick of article publication in 'ISI-rated' academic journals. The key research foci[25] of the AEI initially reveal an undeniably domestic Malaysian flavour, coupled with a strong awareness of emerging themes of internationalization. Research at AEI can be summarized as revolving around the following key areas (AEI Annual Reports, Kuala Lumpur: AEI/UM, from 2007):

- Globalization, Regional Integration and Development;
- Multi-culturalism and Community Development;
- The EU as an Exporter of Values and Norms (e.g.: *AEI Post*, Vol. 4, 2011: 15);
- Society and Gender Studies, Ethnic Relations;
- Sustainability, Governance and Social Changes;
- Business Networks, Knowledge Management and Competitiveness;
- Social History and EU Visibility (e.g. Malaysian contributions to the *EU through the Eyes of Asia* project, by means of conferences and discussion fora).

At the time of writing (May 2013), there were 18 PhD students enrolled at the Institute. This was the largest number of PhD candidates I had witnessed anywhere in similar institutions across Australasia. The PhD candidates were working on subjects as diverse as tourism, Muslim women's activism, ASEAN-5 and China, city marketing, international education policy, research collaboration, European NGOs, film and heritage in Germany (see *AEI Post*, Vol. 1, September 2007: 6–9) and Malaysia and regional economic integration in ASEAN, to name just a few.

A brief look at the theses of former PhD students reveals more recurring academic concerns, such as a study of discourse analysis, feminist studies and comparative female leadership in Asia. Importantly, the Institute's PhD cohorts seemed not to be 'stuck in their PhD room' and isolated, but rather fully integrated in AEI research training initiatives, cross-university networking circles and wider UM frameworks. They were also required to undergo an initial 'candidature defence procedure' at an early stage of their work, to a team of supervisors, resident academics and Research Fellows, and visiting academics.

'Something special to Asia': the 'glocal' perspective of the AEI management and staff

The Asia–Europe Institute began operations earlier than most of its recent regional competitors, and was up and running just one year after the first Asia–Europe Meeting (ASEM) in Bangkok in 1995, following a proposal by, among others, Malaysia's former Prime Minister, Tun Dr Mahatir Mohamad (see below). It operates directly under the guidance of the Vice-Chancellor and Deputy Vice-Chancellor of the University of Malaya (UM).[26]

Established as an Asia–Europe *Centre* (AEC) in 1997, it was subsequently upgraded to an Asia–Europe *Institute* (AEI) in 2000. Its original remit was wide; it included the idea of growing closer ties and enhancing relations with Europe, in line with both evolving ASEM priorities and Malaysian domestic policies. A recent example of the latter is the *10th Malaysia Plan*,[27] with its emphasis on 'globalization of Higher Education', a further 'internationalization' of Malaysian HE[28] and the concomitant desire to attract far more foreign students (and lecturers).

The priority themes of the *10th Malaysia Plan*, in as far as they relate to politics and development, are strongly evident in the design of the promotional materials of the AEI, and of the University of Malaya overall, especially the 2013 prospectus, *Discover UM – A World of Opportunities*, which revolves around key messages pertaining to a diverse – yet still noticeably 'Asian' – student body. Other official documents endeavour to strike an equally successful, yet difficult, balance between domestic cultural embedding, 'Malay-ness' and an open, dynamic, international orientation. At the time of writing, this 'glocal' mix was highly successful in the recruitment and retention of international postgraduate students.

Against this background, the AEI continues to interview all prospective students, both domestic and international, in order to ensure consistency and what is termed 'seriousness of purpose', and it offers intensive training in Malay, the 'native language in this country', to all foreign learners – and staff. I took the three-week course in Malay Language and Culture (*Expresi Bahasa Melayu Asas – Peringkat Rendah*) in May 2013, so as to gain a better appreciation of the ways in which students are prepared for studying at AEI. Among the other admission criteria (entry requirements) for studying one of the AEI MAs, which cost RM50,700 (for international students) and RM41,074 (for home students), are professional and vocational qualifications, as well as an 'open' category of 'other' qualifications, 'approved by the University of Malaya Senate from time to time' (*AEI Prospectus*, 2013: 26, bullet point 3).

In order to be able to get a fuller picture, as it were, of what drives the AEI and what motivates the people managing the centre, I needed to look behind the brochures and websites. I decided to conduct short interviews with the centre's Directorate, in April 2012 and again in April 2013. In that second year, my 'status' at the AEI had changed from that of a 'Visiting Professor', who was there for two weeks only in order to teach a specific module (*QXGB6101*

Multi-lateral Institutions and Asia–Europe Economic Development), to a 'Visiting Senior Research Fellow', who was more fully integrated, complete with a staff card, university e-mail address – and, of course, more responsibilities.

This, I felt, gave me much more of an insight into how the AEI functioned, though I was curious to learn more about its 'identity' and about how it positioned itself in comparison with other, similar centres in the regions, such as the European Studies Centre at Chulalongkorn University (Wiessala, 2011) and the EU Centre across the Causeway, in the nearby city state of Singapore.

The academic background of the current (2013) Directorate of the AEI[29] is extremely diverse, ranging from Malay Linguistics and East Asian/Japanese Studies, to Soil Science, Children's Literature, Postcolonial Studies and Cultural, Urban, Rural and Modernization Studies, as well as Museum Studies and Art. The three main reasons the International Master's Programme at AEI is seen as unique by those who run it are: first, the intensive, short-term engagement of a 'mixture' of international lecturers and visiting Professors from Asia and Europe; second, the linear growth of international students on the programme; and, third, the existence of a lively, high-level events programme, including a three-fold typology of public guest lectures (*AEI Lecture Series; Eminent Persons Lecture Series (EPELS), AEI Post*, Vol. 3, June 2010: 02; Vol. 4: 03; *Ambassador Lecture Series*, see *AEI Post*, Vol. 2, June 2009: 03; Vol. 4, June 2011: 04) and an ad-hoc range of seminars, debating events, research seminars, workshops and visiting lecturers (cf. *AEI Post*, especially Volumes 4 and 5). Speakers at these events have included former ASEAN Secretary-General Surin Pitsuwan (2011),[30] a wide range of Asian diplomats and ambassadors and the Institute's many visiting lecturers and visiting Research Fellows.[31]

A seminar on 13 and 14 December 2011, on *Entrepreneurship in Higher Education: Increasing Competitiveness, Enhancing Resilience*, was a particular highlight of the recent AEI events programme, linking, as it were, the Institute's activities with the discourses determined by the wider changes in the Malaysian HE landscape, such as the reduction in government support from 2015 and stronger pressures on the 'commercialization' and 'impact' factors of teaching and research (see the introduction to this chapter).[32] The conference also clearly referenced relevant aspects of the EU–Malaysia relationship in as far as they are grounded in specific policy blueprints of the European Commission. The latter's communication *Implementing the Community Lisbon Programme: Fostering Entrepreneurial Mindsets through Education and Learning*, of 13 February 2006, was one pertinent example of this.[33] A similar seminar was an *AEI Advanced Workshop* on *ASEAN Studies Teaching for Lecturers* in April 2012, which looked at pedagogy, learning styles and teaching materials. The AEI provides a range of in-house publications – for example, an *Occasional Papers* series and books linked to its key research foci, such as *Can Asians Think – Can Europeans Listen?*, by Corrado Letta, a former AEI Senior Research Fellow (*AEI Post*, Vol. 1, September 2007: 16; Vol. 2, June 2009: 24).[34]

Beyond the events and publications organized at the AEI, the Institute's fourfold structure of its MA programmes[35] is an approach I have not encountered elsewhere, in terms of their academic content, logical coherence and breadth of student choice. This structure was, arguably, the result of 'aggressive changes' (AEI Annual Report, 2008: Introduction) in the administration and structure of the Institute (and the wider university) from 2006 onwards. In 2012 and 2013, the AEI's Deputy Executive Director interpreted the enhanced attractiveness of the programme to international students in itself as a vital contribution to its inter-cultural flavour, because the student groups would indirectly, almost without trying, have to learn to accommodate difference and exchange values. This seemed to me a convincing, almost 'constructivist' rationale on which to base subject-specific learning, and which sat well with some approaches to intellectual exchange by the European Union and the Asia–Europe Foundation (see Chapter 5).

In terms of graduate destinations of UM/AEI graduates, the private sector – for example, in business, and in terms of consultancy jobs – was, at the time of writing, balanced, perhaps slightly outstripped, by employment choices of AEI graduates in a variety of Malaysian government institutions, think-tanks and ministries, as lecturers and civil servants. In a way, therefore, in terms of human resources, the AEI is an important pool of talent, and a recruitment source for future, more internationally attuned Malaysian leaders. The current head of the Razak School of Government in Putrajaya, the administrative centre of Malaysia, is a former AEI Director. However, conversely, from year two of my stay at the AEI, I also noticed that an increasing number of learners had made the bold move back from employment, for instance, in the Foreign Office in Putrajaya, back into continuous professional development (CPD) and graduate education, as 'mature' students, in order to either change direction or to improve their career prospects (see student interviews, below).

For me, this spoke of the flexibility and adaptability of the programme to diverse learner groups. The diversity of the four key pillars of the course (especially the *International Master's Programme in Small-and-Medium-Enterprises*) is, arguably, a key factor in making an AEI International Master's Degree more suitable, in terms of graduates' future employment, when compared to a more traditional MBA, which may well be too narrow. The content of the four individual, and thematically linked, MAs on offer at AEI, in as far as the subject of 'European Studies' or 'European Union Studies' was concerned, had been arrived at by means of regional marketing surveys and, importantly, also by an attempt to fulfil one of the key conditions of constructing a successful EU Studies syllabus in Asia – making it relevant, on a comparative level, to an ASEAN context. Therefore, it comes as no surprise that staff from the *ASEAN Secretariat*, in Jakarta, Indonesia, are teaching at AEI at various times. Furthermore, ASEAN colleagues are occasionally being consulted as external validators with regard to future course development at the Institute. This connection is mutual, since the current AEI Deputy Executive Director possesses significant work experience inside the ASEAN Secretariat.

These aspects continue to clearly set the programme apart from others in South East Asia, which sometimes appear to revolve around specific research interests of the respective school, or staff who happen to be there at various times. Sometimes, EU syllabi are simply constructed around a formulaic tripod of 'history', 'law' and 'politics' of the EU, making them much more earth-bound and short-lived. By contrast, the Director of the AEI emphasizes the openness and flexible multi-disciplinarity of the programme; because staff interests (and those of the visiting Research Fellows too, at the AEI, one might add) are so diverse, there can be no personal 'hobby-horses' and interests 'straight-jacketing' the development of the programme and centre. Perhaps this may help to account for the year-on-year rise in student numbers at the AEI, which seems to stand in stark contrast to steadily declining numbers at similar institutions in South East Asia.

The EU content of the programme is comprehensive, does not get lost in detail and includes – like the other MAs on offer – an internship for the students, which can take them to Europe or the Middle East ('West Asia'), but also elsewhere to Asia and as far away as New Zealand for one month (see Chapter 8). It also allows the foreign Professors the flexibility to have a significant input in the finalization of the syllabus and in the pedagogic development and delivery of the individual teaching sessions.

The centre's vision for the future rests on an envisaged programme growth and a new strategy for domestic and international staff recruitment, in the face of an expected 30 per cent government cut to its budget expected as early as 2015. An *International Master's Programme in European Union Studies* is under development for validation in 2014, as well as two other programmes, and more teaching staff are being sought, with a view to their ability to secure both research quality and external grant funding – a situation similar to, but not quite as bad as, the one in the UK in 2011–2012.

There was, as far as I could see, an initial involvement of staff from the ASEAN Secretariat in course planning, but, perhaps surprisingly, little collaboration with the EU office in Kuala Lumpur, or those of individual EU Member States. In March 2013, five posts for new lecturers were being advertised, to join the three full academic posts and three visiting Research Fellows who currently work at the AEI. Staff recruitment was an on-going exercise, since great care was taken to align the respective job descriptions with the demands of the wider university's research strategies and quality standards. These enhanced both rankings on global 'league tables' but also contributed to the further entrenchment, in Malaysia, of educational Darwinism (Collini, 2012: 163).

More so than in other European Studies centres throughout the South East Asian region, the benefits of confronting learners with different instruction styles associated with employing a small group of visiting lecturers continue to be sought out, despite tighter budgets, with the aim of enriching the AEI's course portfolio and strengthening its pedagogic ethos. When I asked the AEI Directorate how they would define future 'success', it was clear that pedagogic quality and 'legacy creation' were top of the agenda, both in terms of research and preparation of future diplomats. This was enshrined in the unique AEI suite of programmes, addressing issues like entrepreneurship and employability in a diverse and holistic manner.

Box 7.2 Political students and student politics in contemporary Malaysia

A public lecture by Dr Mahatir Mohamad, the very controversial former Malaysian Prime Minister, on 14 March 2013, reminded me of one of the key themes which had run through both the media controlled by the Barisan Nasional (BN) Government, and the comments and articles on opposition blogs, for as long as I have been associated with the AEI. This was the question of what role – if any – students (especially students of politics) ought to play in debating, critiquing and discussing the actions of the Malaysian Government. This issue may, perhaps, strike European observers as slightly odd; indeed, when told about this issue, many European colleagues commented along the lines of: 'well, of course students should critique the government'; 'that's what being a student is all about'; and 'I'd fail them if they did not become active in politics'. This point of view was prevalent among colleagues from France and Germany; not surprising, really, when seen against the backdrop of the legacies of the '*Studentenbewegungen*' of the 1960s to 1980s.

In contemporary Malaysia, the issue appears a little more nuanced, since the cause for a greater role of the 'student voice' in politics was advanced in 2012/2013, when some amendments were made to the Malaysian *Universities and University Colleges Act 1971/2012 (UUCA)*, the *Private Higher Educational Institutions (Amendment) Act 2012* and the *Educational Institutions (Discipline) Act 2012*. These more recent changes notwithstanding, significant limitations on campus-based political activism in Malaysia remain, stemming from concerns over preserving inter-racial harmony and stability in the country and deterring extremism. However, the 2012/2013 legal amendments make it easier for students to take part in politics more actively, critically and openly than before, to join political parties and to stand as candidates in General Elections, especially 'GE13' on 5 May 2013. The changed legalisation was widely reported in the government-controlled *New Straits Times* (e.g. 10 April 2012: 1, 10; 11 April 2012: 4).[36] It coincided with alterations made to Malaysian legislation like the *Sedition Act, Official Secrets Acts* and, especially, the widely despised *Internal Security Act (ISA)*, a repeal of which had been long since demanded (Abraham, 2006: 121; Soong, 2012: xiii, 29–35; Rahman, 2013: 37, 48).

It thus appears that fora like the UM one in March 2013 discussing the impact of students in politics are becoming more 'normal' against the background of more outspoken political discourse in the country, both inside and outside academia. When government representatives such as Deputy Higher Education Minister Datuk Saifuddin Abdullah are participating, student politics can become linked with wider concerns, such as government funding for universities and graduate employment prospects. In its article on the March 2013 event at UM, the writer for the *Star* newspaper was only slightly exaggerating when he pointed out that 'such a forum at a public university would be unthinkable [sic] just five years ago – the mere sight of unspoken students must surely be a sign of progress' ('Voices of Young Minds', *Star/StarEducate*, 17 March 2013: 3).

Indeed, meetings such as the 2013 forum stood in marked contrast to the comments of the Malaysian Council of Professors' Chairman, Professor Emeritus Datuk Dr Zakri Abdul Hamid, as reported a year before, when he advised students that they should 'concentrate on gaining knowledge and academic excellence, as these were their core duties' (*New Straits Times*, 16 April 2012: 23). Perhaps it was a measure of the speed and depth of the development of democratic discourse in Malaysia that not long before the event I witnessed in 2013, the main themes concerning the issue of student politics, as reported in the public media, had been efforts to 'instil' love for the country (*rukun negara*) in undergraduates (*New Straits Times*, 17 April 2012: 12) and the claim by one commentator that students who protested, for example, against the National Education Fund Corporation (PTPTN) of Malaysia, 'have way too much free time' ('Rebels Without a Cause', *New Straits Times*, 19 April 2012: 18).

One year after comments like these, it remained difficult to assess how much of the liberated rhetoric of 2013 was owing to the impending event of the thirteenth General Election in Malaysia. In this context, Kassim (2013: 119) opines that,

> so, yes, people, we have Malaysian students all around the world setting up political branches, like the *Student UMNO Clubs* in the UK. And it's perfectly legitimate to do so. Indeed, they are patronised by our politicians visiting these far-off places on their study-trips, I'm sure. But right here, at our doorstep, we refuse to allow our students that right to be politically-affiliated, that ability to be involved in political abilities such as campaigning, which is part and parcel of a democracy.

In addition to these issues, some Malaysian commentators on Higher Education – such as there are – have begun to furnish a wider setting, critically examining, impending changes in Higher Education in the country. Abraham (2006, 4–8, 18–24), for instance, has suggested analysing market-driven education and quality assurance in research in the context of Malaysia's needs for new technical, IT and vocational skills. The question over the degree to which courses ought to be taught in English is a constant backdrop to these debates, as is regional integration in Europe and Asia, especially the comparability of the ASEAN and EU models, legal frames and ambitions of integration, which remains a dominant theme of enquiry on the research agenda (Abraham, 2006: 89–92).

Teaching a regional integration module at the Asia–Europe Institute (4–15 April 2011 and 9–19 April 2012)

My initial 'Visiting Lecturer' (VL) assignment at the AEI in 2012 came about by nothing less than a 'lucky coincidence'. I came to teach in Malaysia through the kind mediation of a friend and colleague from South Korea, alongside whom I had been working a year before at the National Centre for Research on Europe (NCRE) at the University of Canterbury, Christchurch, New Zealand (see Chapter 8). My colleague contacted me in March 2011 to ask whether I might be able and willing to teach on an MA programme of the Asia–Europe Institute. As chance would have it, I found that I could be available for the two weeks of teaching required, and so I soon found myself on a Malaysia Airlines plane to Kuala Lumpur (KL).

I had been aware of the Asia–Europe Institute, mainly because of professional friends and colleagues, and through a small group of students I had actually taught while they temporarily participated in the Chulalongkorn University Master's Degree Programme in European Studies (MAEUS) in Bangkok a few years before. Preparing to leave for KL, I found that I could in fact remember that small group of Malaysian students – perhaps incorrectly – as having stood out in the crowd of Thai students on the course.

At the time, I recalled them as having been somewhat 'quiet' in class – one might say passive. It appeared to me that, somehow, they had struck me as modest and subdued, compared to the more extroverted, ebullient Thai students. This memory continued to colour my expectations and influenced my thinking as I landed in KL. In retrospect, I should, of course, not have trusted my memories of those Malaysian students, as I learned almost from the first minute I met my group of students in 2011. The students at UM were on an International MA Programme in Regional Integration (IMRI), one of several specialized Masters' Degree Programmes at the Institute. The course materials outline the IMRI MA route as follows:

> This *International Masters Programme in Regional Integration (IMRI)* examines the origins and consequences (for nation states as well as firms and citizens) of efforts and strategies to redraw boundaries of authority at the regional level in the context of intensified globalization. Using an interdisciplinary and comparative approach, the programme focuses on explanations of the intensity and type of authority shift to regional institutions across issues and across regions. It places particular emphasis on understanding the relationship between regional integration and processes of economic globalization, the development of new forms of governance, and the reconfiguration of the state.
>
> (AEI, IMRI Brochure, 2013)

Some of the other programmes on offer, especially the *International Master's in ASEAN Studies* (IMAS, see AEI, 2013), were in harmony with this brief. The academic themes of the AEI's overall teaching strategy had been developed as a follow-up from the 22nd *ASEAN University Network Board of Trustees* (AUN-BOT) meeting in Thailand, from 1–2 November 2007. Consequently, it translates the AEI programmatic aims into the broader historical, social and cultural contexts of Malaysia and ASEAN (cf. Saravanamuttu, 2010). The other MA routes at the AEI achieve the same for the study of the digital economies and technologies for successful regionalism and the role of SMEs in the framework of 'inter-regionalism'. Throughout this chapter, I will be placing a particular focus on the IMRI route, as I was most closely involved with it over the space of nearly five years.

It was apparent to me from class one on day one that the standard of English language capacity in evidence in the Malaysian students was high, as was their grasp of foundational ideas and concepts in international relations. It had to be:

all the participants of the course had undergone rigorous pre-admission screening; consequently, there was a genuine desire to learn and share knowledge about the EU with the lecturer – as well as the usual 'Asian' respect and appreciation for the efforts of the 'Professor Georg'.

And the Professor did find that he had to make an effort, both physically and mentally: the UM AEI IMRI programme was, without doubt, the most intensive 'European Studies in Asia' programme I had experienced until then. Forty-two contact hours over two weeks, which translated into seven hours of class time, Monday to Friday, in week one and a slightly more relaxed agenda in the second week. This was not 'European Studies Lite', by any stretch of the imagination. It was relaxed and reorganized at a later stage.

I went through a syllabus in those two weeks which I would normally take 12 weeks to do 'back home' – distributed, what is more, over two of my (then) 'home' modules, *The European Union* and *Crime and Justice in Europe*. I had taught both of these modules a few times before at the University of Central Lancashire, my 'home institution' until 2012. However, as I learnt very quickly indeed, preparing a seven-hour stretch is quite a different matter from the usual two-hour sessions at home. The only way to do this, without inducing fatigue or overload in either lecturer or student, was to make generous use of group work, case studies, simulation exercises and group discussions (See Appendix 13: *An EU module in Malaysia, 2012 and 2013: Multi-lateral Institutions and Asia–Europe Economic Development*).

And it worked. The group was very coherent and played the game beautifully. It seemed that, whatever I threw at them, they responded to in constructive, innovative ways; they seemed unfazed by anything. A ten-point 'Action Plan against Drugs' for the European Monitoring Centre for Drugs and Drug Addiction? We did it. A press release on the EU response to the crisis in Libya? It took longer but it produced constructive results – arguably more constructive than the real thing at the time. In the same vein, the students worked on new EU 'Anti-Terrorism Legislation', reformed the Committee of the Regions; they discovered some 'Mothers of Europe', rather than the usual 'Founding Fathers'; they debated policies on climate change – a pertinent issue in EU–Malaysia dialogue at the time; and they discussed – always constructively and at length – issues of 'identity', 'language', 'conflict' and 'ethnicity' in the European Union, always with close reference to ASEAN, and inspired by research events (for instance, on 'ethnicity') at the AEI (see: *AEI Post*, Vol. 3, June 2010: 18).

Towards the end of week one, these students had blown me away. There were no words to describe how exhausted I felt as I returned to my accommodation at night. But I also felt elated, appreciated and energized. In week two – following a short weekend trip to Singapore, during which I stocked up on some books – I deliberately accelerated the pace, intensified the theoretical aspects of the course (inter-regionalism, EU actor-ness, spill-over, social-constructivist approaches) and moved to book a guest speaker from the local EU Embassy in Kuala Lumpur. I had the freedom to do this, within the confines of the module template (module descriptor) for my course.

This turned out well, and my belated thanks go to Ms Eszter Nemesz, Press and PR Officer at the EU Delegation to Malaysia, for an inspiring overview of EU–Malaysia relations, delivered with aplomb and diplomacy on 13 April 2011, to a rapt audience of students. This is when I learned – we all learned – how significant 'green' issues were at the time in the Malaysia–EU partnership. I 'integrated' the guest talk into the course, and when the speaker had left, the students and I stayed on until after closing time to try and resolve the conundrum of the EU as an 'external actor' and 'global player'.

The day after, I delivered a guest lecture myself, to my colleagues at AEI and a somewhat 'captive' audience consisting of a group of students from all four current Masters' programmes at the Institute. I spoke about Higher Education cooperation between the EU and Asia. Most of the material I had used for this presentation was drawn from my 2011 book on *Enhancing Asia–Europe Relations through Educational Co-operation*, in which I had looked, among other things, at the content and the 'construction' of the academic discipline of European Studies in Asia (*AEI Post*,[37] Vol. 4, June 2011: 13).

What I feel my talk did show – in particular during the discussion that followed – was the significant degree to which issues of Higher Education and HE 'reform' in Asia and the EU were framed by the same issues of concern to both students and lecturers: 'massification', 'commodification' and 'commercialization' of HE, expectation of students towards the HE experience, the new teaching challenges entailed in the more widespread use of IT, to name only a few. It was interesting to see both students and their course leaders enter into an open exchange over the roles of academics, the future of universities or the way in which scholarly research can influence and benefit the students' daily learning experience, but is itself driven by new, and sometimes worrying, commercial agendas and forces.

The rest of week two at the AEI saw the end of my module and brought a number of student presentations, which were part of the assessment schedule of this module. In UK terms, many would say that five assessed items would, perhaps, be a case of too much of a good thing, but it has to be borne in mind that two of these items consisted of 'class attendance' and 'contributions to the class', and that the visiting Professor has the freedom of 'weighting' individual assessments as they see fit, within the confines of UM and AEI stipulations.

Working at the AEI as Senior Visiting Research Fellow (visiting only) (March to June 2013)

Talk about being thrown in at the deep end: during my first full working week at the AEI, and in the middle of preparing my module for April 2013, I had the opportunity to attend a guest lecture by the former Malaysian Prime Minister Tun Dr Mahatir Mohamad, who visited Universiti Malaya on 14 March 2013. The event, ambitiously entitled *On the Feasibility of a Two-Party System in Malaysia*, took place in *Perdana Siswa*, one of the university's larger lecture theatres.

The lecture which 'MM' started in *Bahasa Malaysia* (*Bahasa Melayu*) – but which he continued in English after being handed a brief note – was significant in two ways. First, it occurred a few weeks before Malaysia's thirteenth General Election in April 2013, and could be interpreted as serving the function to drum up support for the ruling coalition (*BN – Barisan Nasional*), led by the current Prime Minister, Dato'Seri Mohd Abdul Najib Tun Razak, son of independent Malaysia's second Premier (Tun Abdul Razak bin Hussein Al-Haj, 1922–1976) (Ooi Kee Beng, 2010).

Second, and perhaps more remarkably, the event unfolded in the presence of a large number of students, both domestic and international (and of visiting lecturers) from the university. The students, especially, were not shy in addressing the former PM. The question that stood out for me was that of a young student who went straight to the very jugular of Malaysian politics, namely the issue of a 'Malaysian Malaysia' and the relations between modern Malaysia's three 'races' which make up the population – citizens of Indian, Malay and Chinese origin. The student's query, which the former PM answered by avowing his identity as a 'Malaysian Malay', raised a number of questions about the current Malaysian Constitution, about government policies of 'special privileges for people of the Malay ethnicity (*Bumiputera*, i.e. 'sons of the soil'), and about Malaysian national identity.

Throughout the lecture, some cleavages in Malaysian politics became clearly evident and were often commented on – issues such as 'race', 'identity' and 'privilege' The issue was picked up in the *New Straits Times* the next day, through the prism of emphasizing the racial equality achievements of the present government.[39] The well-attended and thought-provoking address was an illustration of the kind of change Malaysia is going through in the year of the thirteenth General Election in Malaysia (5 May 2013), especially with regard to freedom of political debate and student participation in the nation's present and future political life.

Box 7.3 A brief 'snapshot' of the 2013 cohort: deepening knowledge and venturing onto new territory

The 2013 cohort differed little from previous ones in its geographical spread, and contained a more diverse range of student motivation for study. The spectrum of motives for taking up an EU course once again ranged widely. *Mr A*, like others in the group, had studied Political Science, Social Science and International Relations before and wished to deepen his knowledge of South East Asia's place in the world. He too aspired to becoming a diplomat or civil servant; an ambition that *Ms B* had already achieved. She possessed a TESOL background, like at least one other student on the course, and she now wanted to advance her knowledge and, in her own words, study *the mechanisms of how countries treat each other*.

Maybe because of the way the students had been screened, most students in the group seemed to share a love for reading and, naturally, were multi-lingual. This also applied to the only European student in the course, *Debora*, who was, however, now resident in Malaysia. She wanted to study Politics, Regional Development and the EU because she found traditional degrees in Europe, in her words, *too euro-centric*. She reflected about the opportunities inherent in studying the EU from a South East

Asian angle and decided she was most interested in what she called *models of regional integration*. Ms C had pursued Media Studies and Gender Studies in her undergraduate degree, and wished to acquire a wider, comparative view of the place of Malaysians, and Malaysian women, in the region and in the wider world.

Mrs D had achieved a BA in Journalism and found the visibility of the EU, as well as the volume of reporting about the EU, to be very low in Malaysia (Holland). She planned to become a local businesswoman in Kuala Lumpur. Mrs E was, perhaps, the most surprising participant in this group, in terms of previous experience, having pursued both a significant military career, and an undergraduate degree in Psychology. Her main interest in European Studies was *to connect the human side of international relations to the institutional side*. It was clear that she was interested in NGO and basic educational work, especially with refugees in neighbouring Thailand, and she had chosen to spend her one-month internship in a refugee camp in Mae Hong Son, a key centre for refugees from Burma/Myanmar. Mrs E came from a more traditional background in East Asia Studies and was keen to acquire a wider international framework for the development of her skills, which she was planning to make use of in the context of either a government job or future NGO work.

Ms F came from a background of studying Biological Sciences, Ecology and Biodiversity and genuinely appeared to want to learn something new, having found that work in laboratories was not for her. She had successfully applied for a full scholarship for the MA and envisaged a career as a lecturer – and a future writer of *motivational books*, as she put it. Mrs G, like some other students in the 2013 group, already worked for the Malaysian Government and the Ministry of Education as a government-paid primary school teacher. She intended a career move into the Foreign Ministry and was curious about *the parallels and similarities of ASEAN and the European Union.*

Mr H was a former Sociology student and wished to explore the political and inter-regional aspects of this subject a little further, once again with the ambition to join – or act as an advisor for – future Malaysian Governments. Ms I from KL was a singer and a performance-level professional ukulele player (there had been a professional musician in the 2012 cohort too; see above). She had studied English Language and Linguistics at undergraduate level and chose to pursue further studies in regional integration because, in her words, *a lot of people here do not realize how regional integration affects the people here*.

Taking advantage, perhaps, of the newly liberalized Malaysian laws regarding the political involvement of students (see above), she was looking for a challenge, aiming to find a cause, create awareness and become an activist – albeit of an as yet unspecified nature. I could see in her, and indeed in some of the other students, many of the skills and the potential for future work in a lobby group or interest representation – a subject that was to loom large in the two-week course.

I had many opportunities to think back to this public lecture from March to June 2013, during which time I worked at the Asia–Europe Institute – mainly on this present book – before I moved on to the university's Institute of Educational Leadership from 1 July 2013. Next to undertaking my research and finding out more about Higher Education and European Studies in Malaysia, perhaps the most significant aspect of my time at the AEI was that I had ample time to gather the opinions and gauge the attitudes of those who study subjects like European Studies and Regional Integration in Malaysia. In the following sections, I have, therefore, attempted to give some room to the student voice, especially of those on 'my' modules.

Leaders, learner voices and career choices: student views of European Studies in Malaysia

---

Box 7.4 The idea of 'student leadership' in Malaysian universities

Many of the students at the AEI displayed clear potential for leadership in their communities and on campus. In spite of significant restrictions on the political freedoms and activities of students in Malaysia (see Box 7.3), there is a surprisingly large volume of research, comprising both published literature and unpublished studies, surrounding the issue of undergraduate student leadership at the country's public and private universities. A good, and recent, example is the study by Jamaliah Abdul Hamid and Steven Eric Krauss (Hamid and Krauss, 2010) on *Motivating Our Undergraduates to Lead: Facing the Challenge.*

In this process-study, the authors start from the premise that the inculcation of 'leadership' and 'soft-skills' competencies in undergraduate students was one of the universities' top priorities since the move towards 'internationalization' from the late 1990s onwards. In distinction to many similar studies, Hamid and Krauss focus on areas which are relevant to students of European Studies in Malaysia, such as motivation levels and involvement in social change. Departing from position-based models of leadership, this study looks at factors like 'desire', 'readiness to lead', 'self-awareness' and 'perceptions of leadership ability', to draw inferences about various groups of undergraduate students. One of the study's findings is that (ibid.: 86): 'undergraduates from the Social Science cluster generally had significantly higher mean scores in their motivation to lead, leadership ability, self-knowledge and campus factors, in comparison to their peers in Applied Sciences and IT Computer clusters'.

Among the authors' recommendations was the idea of not only using the campus as an 'incubator' for leadership talent, but also to provide 'learning platforms' and opportunities for students to practise leadership skills. For me, studies such as this one connected very well with curriculum and class design, especially since I was then in transition from the Asia–Europe Institute to the Institute of Educational Leadership at the University of Malaya. The course plan, attached as Appendix 13 (*An EU module in Malaysia, 2012 and 2013: Multi-lateral Institutions and Asia–Europe Economic Development*), is one result of my interpretation of these studies, and an attempt to nurture the incipient leadership abilities of Malaysian and international students in the context of European Studies in Asia. In connection with my AEI teaching, this could, and did, easily happen, by means of the inclusion of 'leadership challenges' in the classroom, such as asking students to chair discussions, defend a position and engage in confrontational role-play and simulations.

Many students in the group had studied aspects of political science, social science and international relations, before taking up a (postgraduate) European Studies course to deepen their knowledge.

In both my capacities as a 'short-term' lecturer, and during my more prolonged stay as a 'Visiting Research Fellow' at the AEI, I had the opportunity to interview students about why they were there, what they wanted to know about the EU and what their future plans were. I also spoke to the centre's management about both history and future strategy for the AEI (see above). From the large number of student interviews I collected from 2011 to 2014, I have concentrated exclusively on the students' views in regard of three key issues:

- the participants' individual educational and professional backgrounds, before taking up postgraduate degree studies ('what have you done so far?');
- the students' reasons for choosing a postgraduate degree involving an element of European Studies ('why are you studying this subject?');
- the learners' future career ambitions and job strategies ('what are your future plans?').

I am offering here a shortened and edited transcript of selected answers, with the students' names altered, in order to protect their identities, in line with the Asia–Europe Institute's and the University of Malaya's own (research) ethics regulations. I have sought to include, in equal measure, answers from all four main sections of the Malay population as reflected in the enrolment on this MA programme (IMRI): students of Malay, Indian and Chinese origin, and international participants (exchange students). All students were interviewed while we were all together in class; no one was interviewed on their own.

One very noticeable trend in the individual responses and the class debates which inevitably ensued was that the students weighted their responses more or less heavily towards the third of my main questions, i.e. issues of future career plans and 'employability'. Many students already had work experience and career development behind them and wanted to broaden their interests. Almost all of them had 'leadership' potential (see above). A point that came up repeatedly was that the students also hoped, through the study of Europe, to benefit and 'serve' their country and become, in a way, 'better' (or, at least, 'better informed') Malaysians. There was also the strong wish to be able to learn more about how to 'deal' with Europeans, and to learn more about the major cultural differences.

All students agreed that the EU was all but invisible in Malaysia, but that it was sometimes – and very slowly – 'climbing up the ladder' or news-worthiness in direct proportion to the amount of 'bad news' happening in Europe, such as the Euro-zone crisis and EU immigration/visa policies. The activities of some of the new EU *Business Information Centres* (BICs) in Asia came in for considerable criticism throughout, on account of their perceived 'narrowness of purpose'. A concern uniting most students was the EU 'imitating' US policies and concentrating too much on development policy.

A majority of students also strongly expressed that their perceptions of subjects like ASEAN Studies, Regional Integration (IMRI, see: AEI, 2013) and European Studies (EUS) taught at the AEI were significantly shaped by the way they were taught by lecturers, both foreign and domestic, by the teaching methods and the amount of interactivity adopted, and the degree of interest in the students shown by the lecturers. As far as my own case was concerned, some students also commented on the fact that I lived and worked in more than one EU country (Germany and the UK); the students felt that this introduced a useful, comparative perspective, but also that they required more on current affairs and news from Europe.

As far as possible, I have attempted to keep the 'original student voice' and some Malay-language-inspired sentence structures and idiosyncratic constructions intact, even when there was some source-language interference, as well as 'anglicized' words of foreign (Malay, Indian and Chinese) origin. I have, however, edited answers for grammatical correctness, coherence and vocabulary. I have included answers from both the 2012 and 2013 cohorts on the AEI's IMRI postgraduate degree programmes, especially the *International Master's in Regional Integration (IMRI)*, which I was involved with.

Ms A, one of the participants in the 2012 IMRI group, began by stating:

> I have no previous employment experience. In school I studied Science, and when I did my first degree I did English. Right after that, I wanted to study Political Science because I am interested and I feel like I want to go into Public Relations in the future. English is a broad subject, but, career-wise, you can go to schools, you can go to magazines, you go to public relations, and I want something that can bring me outside – I have always wanted to travel. When I came to the UM Education Fair, I asked and they showed me the subjects I would learn. Then I 'googled' the subjects and got interested. I asked the previous batch [the student cohort of the previous year] about what they were doing now and I liked what I heard. So far I think there is more to European Studies. I don't expect to learn history, because for me this Master's course, I hope what I learn can really help me for my future career.

Mr B, a student with a significant professional background, added:

> I stay in Kuala Lumpur. I am 34 years old and already married. I have four kids. I have several years of technical experience in engineering. But I find that it is not very much suitable to my life. I need to find something to suit my interests. I will develop my career and transform myself; now my ambition is to become a diplomatic officer and join the government soon. I have already been assessed for this. This will have benefits for me. So I need to have the knowledge of the international regional organizations, in order to become a diplomat. The EU is a model for other regional organizations, such as ASEAN. That's why I came here.

Ms C, a very enthusiastic student, came from a surprising background:

> After my first degree, I lost my passion for architecture and I was looking around to diversity a bit to see what I am really passionate about. I came

across IMRI. What sparked me off was the regional dimension, rather than studying just technical things. I did some counselling with the office here, as to what the future career of this course and they said, for example, you can become a diplomat. This was a good foundation for me. I have no politics background, so this will give me some foundation. I would love to be in negotiations, to re-develop the world and to learn from other countries' and regions' policies.

Ms D, an international student from Mexico, was the only 'foreign' exchange student in the 2012 group. A 'global forum' had previously been launched between the AEI and the Embassy of Mexico in 2008 (AEI Annual Report, 2008: 9.2), and this student may have been one result of this. She was attracted to Malaysia since she could not find a suitable course at home:

I wanted to study more about the ASEAN region and Asian views of the world. First, after university, I was working in the Australian Embassy. I also wanted to be part of the diplomacy and worked there for six years. I realized we were too focused on the US. I was interested to look for other options and look at ways of studying an alternative view of the world, not through a North American lens. I was looking around for some time actually – then the University of Malaya gave me a scholarship, now I'm here.

Mr E, a Chinese participant, introduced himself as follows:

I am a graduate student, and I studied Linguistics and English at UM. I was hired as a Research Assistant for two years. During that time, I had a lot of opportunity to study local and national government policies in terms of educational policies, so I got an idea that after graduation I wanted to learn more about the world, not just Malaysia. I started looking for IR courses. UM was the first place I looked and I got a place, so I chose AEI to study regional integration in Europe. From talking to my former lecturers here, I saw the EU as a model kind of thing. I have two choices: after I graduate I can either go work in the Foreign Ministry or to work in the academic environment, do a PhD. I haven't really decided one hundred per cent yet.

Ms F, a Malaysian student, explained:

I live just ten minutes from here; I am from here. I came from a background of broadcasting. I majored in Mass Communication and specialized in Electronic Media and Broadcasting and did my internship in this local TV9 [a Malaysian TV News Channel]. I was attached to News and Current Affairs. This made me curious about the 'depth' of the news. But my training was more about technical aspects of media, and I decided to do the Master's in here because, I don't know, it allows me to compare different views and conspiracies in politics. I realized there was a lot I did not know about IR, because my training had focused on programming and technical matters. My dad is a diplomat in the Middle East, and I have lived there and in America as well. But I wanted to learn about Europe. When I was working in TV9 I was reading Reuters and getting the news from Associated Press; there's not much on EU as compared to others, the EU does not seem very visible. Sometimes, when you choose it for the producers – when you give the producers news about Europe – they don't find it that important, maybe for lack of interest of the public. Many people do not know, for example, what is the difference between EU and Euro-zone [pause]. So I wanted to know more, and my childhood was in Europe for ten years, but I don't have any memory of it.

Mr G, a student of Chinese extraction, added:

I am 30 years old. My first BA degree is in Innovation and Management and worked for three years as a political research assistant for three years in local politics. After that I was private secretary in the Malaysian Higher Education Ministry in Putrayaya [Malaysia's administrative capital, near Kuala Lumpur]. After three years I decided to go for Master's; my life planning is that I want to achieve a Master's degree before I am 33 and to get involved in political campaigning. I do political campaigning in my leisure time too.

Ms H, a very well-read student, said:

I am from Selangor state and I have a degree in International Business from UM. I always thought that IR was just more about economy and business. I was not really used to studying history, and much of what we studied was presented from the US point of view. After I graduated I worked at a bank, in the anti-fraud department, for about five months; and then I try this programme because I wanted to study a new thing and get away from business for the moment. I realized regional integration and different cultures are very important. We have to know the different cultures. Before, I just knew that EU was a strong power and economy player.

Mr I, an outgoing Indian student, elaborated:

I was born in Penang, the island part. I was brought up in KL. I started my education in a Christian missionary school and studied Political Science at UM. After graduation I worked in an American company for six months and then moved on to City Bank. I love reading and also travelling – in the northern part of Malaysia. The reason why I joined this Master's (IMRI), basically I love to do something connected to history and social science. Also, they (AEI) said you will learn in IMRI about the world and become multi-skilled, and I was interested. From my high school, I have an interest in Europe, ASEAN and Asia because I want to look beyond economics, at history and culture. All they talk about in high school is Euro football. I only know Europe because of the Euro currency, as well as the sports. And I learned a lot about Europe from Bollywood movies because, for example, they promote London a lot. So, I thought will I have the opportunity to learn more about the culture and history of the UK? Actually, my plan is to become a lecturer and I think I have to be very patient for this, yes?

Ms J, a mature student already in work, stated:

I am from the South: I am town planner by profession. I graduated from the University of Newcastle-upon-Tyne. I helped to plan a few places in Malaysia, like Langkawi, and I was involved in some of the documentation for some Malaysian town planning and action plans on a national level, and in the liberalization of our profession. I was to be in charge of the FTAs and all the negotiations and market intelligence.

Now, we are involved in the EU–Malaysia FTA, so it's only right that I go to understand this. I am here because town planning is a very wide subject, and there were things I did not learn during my degree studies. I want to fill the gaps in my learning to learn some new information about things that were not involved in my town planning studies. UM was not my first choice, I have actually applied to the World Trade Institute in Geneva because I was very much involved in the FTAs. In Malaysia, this AEI course [IMRI] is the nearest thing they have on regional integration. Some things that I expect from the course I have yet to get; there is nothing much on the FTAs and trade, for example. Frankly, I think this course should be called 'European Studies', instead of 'Regional Integration'.

In the 2012 group, Mr K was the oldest of the students, with significant working experience. He explained:

OK, actually my background is in marketing. I am also a government servant; so now I am taking study leave and I am from Sarawak [one of Malaysian states on the island of Borneo]. I am taking this course because it is actually closely related to my job, because I have worked on international matters for three years, with the International Division of the Ministry of Information, Communication and Culture.

I travel a lot, I met a lot of foreigners and I have moved, and lived also, in Europe, in Switzerland, Italy, the UK and France. I want to know more about especially Europe. I think a person, especially from Malaysia, who knows about other regions will be at an advantage in their work environment, since they see the world from different angle. One think interesting about Europe is that it is a single block and it is unique, in my view, as compared to other regions. That really attracts me. I like singing, and I am in a group with my siblings; we have just released an album.

Chapter conclusions

This chapter has offered a critical review of my teaching experience at the Asia–Europe Institute (AEI), as well as in other centres, at the University of Malaya in Kuala Lumpur, both in terms of initial, annual, short-term engagements to teach an MA module on Regional Integration (see Appendix 13: *An EU module in Malaysia, 2012 and 2013: Multi-lateral Institutions and Asia–Europe Economic Development*) and, subsequently, as a Senior Visiting Research Fellow and Visiting Professor at UM. In this chapter, I have found that teaching European Studies and Regional Integration in Malaysia is, more so than in other Asian contexts, dependent to a high degree on the political background of the country, on significant changes in its HE landscape ('internationalization', 'massification', 'commoditization') and on tight government control of public and private universities, and foreign branch campuses establishing themselves increasingly widely in Malaysia, especially in and around Kuala Lumpur.

The chapter offers the view that by far the most serious impediment to teaching and developing the discipline in Malaysia is the dead hand of the *Bumiputera* affirmative action programme, which affords preferential treatment, admission and quota to students of the Malay ethnicity, whilst driving gifted students of Chinese and Indian backgrounds to the increasing number of the more meritocratically oriented, private HE providers. In these constrained circumstances, the European Studies discipline can be held back by unnecessary bureaucratic hurdles, an over-inflated bureaucracy and problems with initiative and lateral thinking in departments. Having said that, the (mostly Malay) students I encountered over some years at Universiti Malaya were outstanding, in terms of their motivation; they showed a strong career propensity towards government and diplomatic service. Their 'Asian' ethos of self-improvement was stronger than those in other Asian countries such as Thailand (Wiessala, 2011).

The Asia–Europe Institute in Kuala Lumpur has a clearly articulated and convincing vision for Asia–Europe academic exchange and was, in late 2013, more involved in the priorities of the Asia–Europe Meeting (ASEM) Education Ministers Meeting (ASEMME), in relation to addressing the persisting imbalances in student mobility between Asia and Europe. In the focus on this task, the centre both ensured its own immediate future and made a mark on the area of curriculum development in European Studies in Asia, through positioning itself more strongly within ASEM, and by means of innovative new postgraduate provision, which has the potential of moving the EU Studies discipline forward in Asia as a whole.

Notes

1 UMNO (www.umno-online.my/) has 3.5 million members; in 2008, it lost its two-thirds majority in Parliament; the other two 'race-based' parties are the *Malaysian Chinese Association* (MCA, www.mca.org.my/en/) and the *Malaysian Indian Congress* (MIC, www.mic.org.my/).
2 See: www.keadilanrakyat.org/; other key opposition parties are the DAP (Democratic

Action Party, http://dapmalaysia.org/newenglish/) and the PAS (Pan-Malaysian Islamic Party [Parti Islam se Malaysia], www.pas.org.my/v2/).
3 An 'affirmative action', or 'positive discrimination', wealth-creation programme designed to improve the economic situation of Malays ('sons of the soil') within Malaysia's three constituent races (Malay–Chinese–Indian), by means of quota systems and special privileges.
4 The historical entity of the Sultanate of Sulu was conquered by Spain in September 1878.
5 Sabah abounds in natural gas reserves and has the third-largest oil reserves in Asia, after China and India.
6 See: 'King of the Past Reaching for Malaysia Oil Reserves': *Russia Today*, 19 March 2013: http://rt.com/op-edge/malaysia-sulu-sultan-security-462/.
7 The territories of North Borneo were a protectorate of the British North Borneo Company from 1888, until Japanese Occupation in 1941. From 1946 onwards, British North Borneo became the 'Crown Colony of North Borneo'.
8 Defined as 'carnal intercourse against the order of nature', punishable with imprisonment of up to 20 years, and possibly a whipping, under Section 377B of the Malaysian Penal Code (Marican, 2012: 2).
9 EU Council Resolution: www.consilium.europa.eu/uedocs/cms_data/docs/pressdata/en/cfsp/ACF5F.htm.
10 See: www.hrw.org/news/2012/01/09/malaysia-opposition-leader-anwar-ibrahim-acquitted.
11 Report at: www.ipu.org/hr-e/187/anwar.pdf.
12 See BBC: www.bbc.co.uk/news/world-asia-22610210.
13 The two constituent Malay words are *bumi* ('earth', 'land', 'soil') and *put(e)ra* ('son', 'prince'). The official definition of *Bumiputra* extends (arguably) to the Orang Asli (the aboriginal inhabitants of the Malay Peninsula) and (definitely) the ethnic minorities of Sabah and Sarawak, on Malaysian Borneo, which joined Malaysia in 1963.
14 See: BBC: *Is Malaysia University Entry a Level Playing Field?* (Jennifer Pak, 2 September 2013): www.bbc.co.uk/news/world-asia-23841888.
15 The University of Malaya (*Universiti Malaya, UM*) was the first public university to respond to the call for 'internationalization' and 'corporatization' in 1996.
16 This is the term generally applied to the crackdown on the workers' and anti-colonial movement in Malaya.
17 *Free Malaysia Today*: www.freemalaysiatoday.com/category/nation/2013/01/15/batang-kali-massacre-appeal-filed/.
18 See BBC News item, at: www.bbc.co.uk/news/world-19473258.
19 A full-text copy of this book can be found at: http://muse.jhu.edu/journals/journal_of_the_malaysian_branch_of_the_royal_asiatic_society/summary/v084/84.2.rivers.html; a summary of a related BBC Video, *In Cold Blood*, is at: http://batangkalimassacre.wordpress.com/bbc-video-in-cold-blood/.
20 Asia–Europe Institute, University of Malaya, 50603 Kuala Lumpur, Malaysia; Tel.: (+60)-3-7967-4645/6920; Fax: (+60) 3-7954-0599/6908; E-mail: asia_euro@um.edu.my.
21 Ethnic Malays make up 67.4 per cent of the 28.3 million citizens of Malaysia; 24.6 per cent of the population are of Chinese extraction, and Indians comprise around 7.1 per cent of the populace (Rahman, 2013: 89–101).
22 See: http://jpt.mohe.gov.my/ARKIB%20dan%20PENERBITAN/BERITA/MYEULINK/myeulinkflyer.pdf, and www.mohe.gov.my/portal/images/iklan/MYEULINK%20Brochure%20w%20MOHE%20Logo.pdf.
23 http://cordis.europa.eu/projects/rcn/78672_en.html
24 See also: *Institute of Graduate Studies*, Universiti Malaya: http://ips.um.edu.my/.
25 AEI Annual Reports, 2008–2012.
26 UM had approximately 20,000 undergraduate and 7,000 postgraduate students (as of

176 *Teaching Europe in Asia: case studies*

      2011). In 2008, there were just 700 international students; in 2012, this figure has quadrupled.
27 www.pmo.gov.my/dokumenattached/RMK/RMK10_Eds.pdf; the principal points of the plan are summarized at: www.themalaysianinsider.com/business/article/key-points-of-10th-malaysia-plan; see also: www.rsmi.com.my/WebLITE/Applications/productcatalog/uploaded/Docs/The%2010th%20Malaysia%20Plan%202.pdf.
28 See the *Straits Times Special* on the 10th Malaysia Plan (11 June 2010): it can be downloaded from: www.btimes.com.my/Current_News/BTIMES/Econ2007_pdf/10th%20Malaysia%20Plan%202011-2015.
29 Professors Dato Mat Amir Jaffar, MD Nasruddin, MD Akhir, Azmi Mat Akhir and Siti Rohaini Kassim.
30 The ASEAN Secretary-General 2013–2017 is H.E. Le Luong Minh, from Vietnam.
31 In 2013, my two colleagues as visiting Research Fellows at the AEI were Professor Fumitaka from Japan and Professor Karim from Bangladesh.
32 Next to AEI/UM, the co-hosts of this event were the *Higher Education Leadership Academy (AKEPT)*, the *Planning and Research Division of the Ministry of Higher Education* and *University of Malaysia, Kelantan Campus.*
33 See: COM (2006) 33 final.
34 It is tempting to think that this title is a deliberate allusion to Kishore Mabubani's book, *Can Asians Think?*
35 International MA in: *Regional Integration, SME Studies, ASEAN Studies* and *Information Management* (see: AEI, 2013).
36 Some of the other print and e-media controlled by the government are *Berita Harisan, Utusan Malaysia* and *TV3.*
37 ISSN 1985-2185.
38 *New Straits Times,* Friday 15 March 2013: 3 ('Dr M: All Races Enjoy Special Privileges').

8 The art of good *Feng Shui* in Brussels

Taking European Studies in Asia to the capital of Europe, 2002–2012

Background: the evolution of the EU Foreign Policy Seminar series and EIPA

This chapter, next to offering food for thought regarding adult teaching pedagogy and related experiences, is all about locations of knowledge transfer, points of view and perspectives. In what follows, I am placing in the centre of the analysis a training event which, for me, has always been about Asia and 'European Studies in Asia', but which nevertheless happened entirely in Europe; in the 'capital of Europe', in fact.

These were the regular EU Foreign Policy Seminars of the *European Institute for Public Administration (EIPA)*[1] *Directorate General for External Relations (DG RELEX)* and (now) the *European Union External Action Service (EEAS)*, on the subject of *External Perspectives on External Relations: Geopolitics and the EU* (henceforth: 'EIPA Seminars'). In terms of the activity profile of EIPA, the Seminars Programme is categorized under 'contracted activities' (see, for instance, EIPA Report 2010).[2] I made a number of regular contributions on EU–Asia relations over a period of some ten years, learning much about the real sources, practicalities, enabling conditions and inhibitory aspects of a 'European Studies in Asia' discipline on the way.

Here, far away from my normal 'playing field' of teaching the EU at universities in East or South East Asia, was the geographical and mental distance I believed I needed, in order to acquire a much more holistic perspective on teaching about the 'West' in the 'East'. Here too, I did not export 'European Studies' to 'Asia'; more often than not, *Asia* came to *Europe*, in the shape of experts, policy-makers, learners and practitioners, in order to discuss *Europe in Asia* – and much else besides. The EIPA *External Perspectives on External Relations: Geopolitics and the EU* Seminars were, of course, not exclusively about the EU and Asia. They covered EU foreign policy on a global scale (cf. Duke, 2012). However, countries and regions such as East and South East Asia, India, China and Indonesia, I feel it is true to say, acquired a progressively more significant space in the context of these training events, in line, perhaps, with wider geopolitical changes in the new 'Asian Century' – or should that be the 'New Great Game'?

178 *Teaching Europe in Asia: case studies*

This series of European Union foreign policy training interventions, targeted at EU officials and the EU *corps diplomatique*, was, until 2012, jointly organized by the then DG RELEX of the European Commission in Brussels and the EIPA[3] in Maastricht. From 2013 onwards, in the context of a reorganization of the programme, the European Commission, the EEAS and the College of Europe (CoE) in Brugge (Bruges)[4] began to play a somewhat more pronounced role in the general planning and organization of these events, and in the identification of expert speakers and contributors. The College of Europe also developed its own 'brand' of *EU Diplomacy Training*.[5] Notwithstanding this, the EIAS Seminars focusing on EU foreign policy, which I continue to be involved with at the time of writing this (August 2013), had always been run under the aegis of the European Institute for Public Administration (see below).

This EIPA training programme, like many of EIPA's other sector-specific seminars,[6] aims to reach EU civil servants and *fonctionnaires* from the EEAS, including officials, temporary and contract agents, as long as they work in external relations, both at headquarters and in delegations. The training is complementary to more specialized EU-internal initiatives, such as the *High Level Traineeship Programme in the Delegations of the European Union*, which was reorganized by a Joint Decision of the Commission and the High Representative of the European Union for Foreign Affairs and Security Policy in 2012.[7]

The EIPA training interventions are also open to staff from other institutions and to Member State officials. The increasing rates of recruitment of the latter to the European External Action Service, an emerging *esprit de corps*, and the close control the EEAS appears to exert over the recruitment process is a solid justification for the inclusion of this group in the EIPA Seminars. In scrutinizing the relevant recruitment processes and procedures, Murdoch *et al.* (2013: 22), for instance, are finding that:

> the European External Action Service has managed to establish a firm control over the recruitment process, which overall has been largely informed by Commission hiring rules and practices thus far. Consequently, this has also brought up new aspects with regard to the hiring procedures of diplomats, such as technical expertise and management skills that have not necessarily been at the core of diplomatic training and education.

Following the slogan of *Learning to Build Europe*, EIPA is a Europe-wide think-tank and research institution, affiliated to the University of Maastricht, aiming to increase public awareness of current European issues and to provide information and training to, amongst others, the staff of the European Union's institutions, such as the European Commission or the Council of Ministers. It is comparable – and competes – with other such bodies, such as the *European Institute for Asian Studies (EIAS)* and the *European Policy Centre (EPC)*, both in Brussels, and some others. In 2013, the priority ('focus') areas of EIPA (training) activity were:[8]

- European Decision-Making;
- European Public Management;
- European Policies;
- European Union Law;
- Regional and Euro-Med Activities.

The EIPA *External Perspectives on External Relations: Geopolitics and the EU* Seminars are aiming to deepen participants' knowledge of EU activities in the external relations area, under a number of priority areas – such as Development Policy, Common Foreign and Security Policy (CFSP), Asia Policy and European Neighbourhood Policy – which, naturally, shifted over time. Participants in these events are invited to consider a number of challenges facing the EU in an interactive manner with a number of speakers and trainers.

One of the further objectives of the seminar series from its inception was to select recognized experts in their respective fields, asking them to deliver a teaching intervention to a mixed audience, in terms of specific knowledge about Asia (and other regions and subjects), and to afford the delegates the necessary intellectual distance and 'thinking-space' to step back for a day or two from their respective daily routines, in order to be encouraged to look at a slightly broader picture and to 'compare and contrast' their own daily work with that of others and with over-arching, 'horizontal' concerns linking several EU regional policies towards Asia.

In terms of my contribution on EU–Asia relations, for example, there would be opportunities to look at the EU's main Country Strategy Papers and other policy blueprints connected to Asian regions, themes, countries and non-state actors; in addition to this, however, the assembled groups would also frequently be discussing cross-policy issues such as human rights, 'Asian values' and perceptions of the European Union across Asia, and among the Member States of relevant regional bodies and policy mechanisms, such as the Association of South East Asian Nations and the process of the Asia–Europe Meetings.

The seminars were initially designed to provide a learning and development environment, as well as a space for the exchange of experience and 'good practice' for European civil servants and officials working predominantly for the External Service of the Commission and now the European Union External Action Service. The participants, who routinely numbered around 30 per session, were drawn from EU delegations around the world – from nearly all the EU's embassies across Asia.

However, the circle of eligible participants was progressively widened to incorporate employees of Member State representations in Brussels, and staff from other EU bodies and international organizations. The delegates to the EIPA *External Perspectives on External Relations: Geopolitics and the EU* Seminars thus always reflected a very wide variety and experience, ranging from the relative 'newcomers' to the job, to the very senior, 'old foreign policy hands' and seasoned negotiators, including, on more than one occasion, a number of heads of delegation.

From around 2007 onwards, there was talk, among the organizers, of making some major changes, in order to better reflect the dynamic and changing nature of geopolitics. In terms of the Asia-part of the seminars, preliminary discussions yielded the idea of separating out the more 'general' aspects of EU–Asia relations, linking them to the overall, geopolitical themes of the teaching and offering them as one distinct type of seminar, emphasizing 'policy' and 'strategy'. This was to be complemented by a new range of sessions specifically dealing with key EU dialogue partners in Asia (India, China and Indonesia).

There was, for a time, also the proposal to offer (UK) 'Open University-style', intensive, weekend programmes on these topics. I felt privileged to have been repeatedly involved in developing these ideas, as far as Asia–EU relations were concerned, and to have been asked by the programme coordinator[9] to supply a number of initial drafts for future China and India content, in particular. The result of successive, prolonged discussions within both DG RELEX and EIPA was that, from 2011 onwards, this plan was duly implemented, offering me more opportunities to share knowledge about those three world regions in particular.

An integrated programme content with a broad remit

Throughout 2012,[10] the design of the overall programme and the content of the EIPA training sessions appeared premised on the assumption that EU–Asia relations are often perceived as being dominated by China, and that this perception does not do full justice to the more complex nature of the EU's relations with Asia, which are notable for their contrasts as well as linkages. As a consequence of this, from 2011, separate training events were organized to examine more closely the EU's relations with China, as well as with its main 'strategic partners' partners with whom the Union is holding annual summit meetings (for example, USA, Russia, India).

In thus 'homing in' on South East Asia and North East Asia, EIPA was showing a trend that closely paralleled the 'branching-out' phenomenon in the Commission's own Country Strategy Papers, Regional Policies for Asia, and Multi-Annual Indicative Programmes for the region, which had shown a tendency towards more 'specialization' since at least the 1990s. Key actors and EU dialogue partners from Asia were 'clustered' in the programme, to allow for separate considerations of EU policies and practices vis-à-vis:

- Afghanistan and Pakistan, India;
- Indonesia, South East Asia and the Association of South East Asian Nations;
- North Korea (DPRK) and South Korea (ROK);
- South East Asia and East Asia, Japan.

Whilst each of the cases offers its own challenges and opportunities, the programme structure was firmly 'held together' by a number of regionally relevant 'thematic strands', 'horizontal' issues, and by the consideration of significant common concerns shared by the EU and its Asian partners, for example, in the areas of security and terrorism, the rule of law and narcotics, trade and development, human rights, environment and climate change, the promotion of good governance and the people-to-people-dimensions, such as Higher Education and the contributions of think-tanks and NGOs. Overall, the sessions seemed to me to have been carefully planned so as to be 'connected' to the wider, geopolitical concerns examined in the more general, introductory parts of the training programme. Education was, indeed, a recurring feature of the programme; so much so that the topic of 'intellectual exchange' assumed a central position in my own contributions, for instance, on EU–Asia policies and EU interaction with Indonesia.

It was interesting to note that this kind of programme held together, as it were, foreign policies of the – still relatively new – EU External Action Service with a considerable scope and density, ranging from the Union's involvement in the Six-Party-Talks on the DPRK and the very incipient EU dialogues with South East Asian (ASEAN) partners such as Laos on the one hand, to the fully fledged and significantly institutionalized relationship with 'established' interlocutors, for example, in India and Japan.

As a 'trainer' on the programme, I felt that the ability of the training course to 'accommodate' such a multiplicity of broad perspectives from informal dialogue to free trade agreements and very high regulatory density, spoke very much of the logical coherence and the solidity of planning lying at the heart of this particular foreign policy training. It was, arguably, this aspect which not only appeared to appeal most to the participants but also set the EAS/EIPA Seminar apart from the many 'ad-hoc', low-impact offerings by a small number of self-styled 'training consultants, for whom Brussels seems to be such a bee hive.

A hint of adult pedagogy: assessing and meeting learner preferences

From their inception, the EIPA *External Perspectives on External Relations: Geopolitics and the EU* Seminars were very good examples of an international adult education activity at the intersection of European (Union) Studies, Politics and Adult Learning. The multi-faceted research agenda concerned with culture as the context for adult learning, and with what may be termed *culturally responsive teaching*, or *culturally pertinent adult education* (Guy, 1999), can, therefore, be usefully applied to them.[11] In this context, some research has been undertaken (Phuong-Mai *et al.*, 2005) but this is primarily focused on 'traditional' student cohorts, rather than adult pedagogy. Moreover, some existing work on education and *social cohesion* and *social inclusion* is further extending the scope to the area of teaching adult professionals. The *Life-Long Learning Programme* of the European Commission (of which both the *Jean Monnet* and the *ERASMUS* initiatives are branches) and the *Grundtvig* project yield important insights into the kind of research conducted by the EU, in teaching a range of adults across Europe.[12]

Furthermore, global initiatives, such as the EU's strategies on *Cooperation in Education and Training: EU–Australia, Canada, Japan, New Zealand, South Korea and the USA*,[13] as well as the *Action Jean Monnet*, are beginning to conceptually extend some of the European expertise and guidelines on teaching adults to Asia. The *European Association for the Education of Adults* is an important forum for ideas in this area.[14] However, much research still needs to be done in this area, in order to connect European Studies in Asia to Educational Sciences and Adult Pedagogy.

However, by far the most important 'skills asset' that I felt I could bring to the EIPA teaching experience in Brussels – next to my subject knowledge and experience of working in Asia – was a PTLLS qualification (Preparing to Teach in the Life Long Learning Sector), which I gained in the UK (Myerscough College, Lancashire),[15] as a part of my CPD training. In preparing and conducting my presentation for the EIPA Seminar, I drew on the PTLLS materials I had studied in respect of learner styles and preferences, and learner-centred teaching.

Against this background, I feel that I benefited greatly from attempting to put into practice various pedagogic models of how different people learn, such as Carole Dweck's *Theories of Motivation and Mind-sets* (1999), Smith and MacGregor's *Collaborative Learning* (1992), Bloom's *Taxonomy of Learning Domains in Action* (cognitive-affective-psychomotor),[16] Honey and Mumford's (1986a, 1986b) *Learning Styles* ('activist'–'theories'–'pragmatist'–'reflector'),[17] Kolb's (1984) *Learning Cycles* ('experience'–'observation'–'conceptualization'–'experimentation'), Gardner's (1983–2000) *Multiple Intelligences* (e.g.: 'logical', 'musical', 'kinaesthetic', 'inter-personal', etc.) and Bender's (2012) ideas about *Reciprocal, Co-constructed Teaching* and *Transactional Distance*. Since I often advocate the use of social-constructivist conceptual lenses in International Relations, Human Rights and European Studies (Wiessala, 2007, 2011), it seemed only a small leap from there to look at *constructivist theories in education*, with their foci on 'engagement' and 'group learning' (e.g. Vygotsky, 1978).

Many of my seminar participants displayed the archetypal characteristics of adult learners, such as experience, independence, life-long learning orientation and the 'need to know'; in regard of the latter, considerations of career development and career advancement were often at the forefront of the motivational bundle that motivated people to register for the EIPA Seminars, followed by those who were told to go. In this context, it was useful to be mindful of Bartlett's *Threshold Model*, which may be used to evaluate the origins of professional motivations, 'changing' professional identities and personal development plans.

I found that – since all seminar participants were professional adults – Bartlett's ideas of the three 'circles' of 'being', knowledge' and 'identity', overlapping and determining choices of career goals and learning motivations, could transfer easily from its original focus on teachers to the audience in these seminars. Bartlett's categories of 'professional knowledge', 'being a professional' and 'professional developmental actions' could match many of the seminar delegates' backgrounds, helping to explain why they were there, and hence, what sort of approach to the teaching of EU–Asia relations and European Studies in Asia they needed.

Last but not least – and bearing in mind that this is, in the end, not a book on adult pedagogy – some basic knowledge of 'organizational cultures' and structures is, in my view, an increasingly important prerequisite for instructors in these seminars. Against the background of the involvement of a growing number of actors in the preparation and dissemination of the EIPA Seminars, I found the work of Handy (2009) on role-, task- and person-aligned cultures extremely relevant when it came to assessing the background and resulting training needs of the participants. Knowing whether a delegation member or EU official came from a 'person-focused', group' or 'task-oriented' working environment was easy to find out in the 'interactive' parts of my 'Asia' sessions; it made a significant difference to my choice of instructional style. This is why it is important that trainers on this programme are sent the list of participants, as far in advance as is practicable, of the individual training sessions.

The geopolitical embedding of the training and the content of the 'Asia' section

The content of my section as reflected in the seminar programme, above, was the result of a development over several years, during which the dynamism of the presentation underwent two fundamental kinds of evolution. In the first few years of the training programme, the Asia section was offered as an overview presentation of some of the most significant themes, developments and policy strategies pertaining to EU–Asia relations. The move from this, more general, mode of presentation to a more specialized focus on South East Asia, China and Indonesia, as shown in the 2012 Seminar Programme (see above), may have been inspired by the research interests of some of the seminar organizers (e.g. Duke, 2012).

It constituted the first larger dynamism in the development of the sessions. The shift from a 'survey-style' kind of presentation to a much more 'harmonized' and structured content was reflected, from around 2011 onwards, in the practice increasingly adopted by all speakers on the programme, of aligning the content of their training interventions with an overall scheme, which, as far as I can remember, required speakers on individual topics/Asian countries to cover, at least, the following aspects in their presentations:

- the history of the EU's relations with the country/countries in question;
- the principal legal agreements between the EU and the country in question;
- political/economic/religious/cultural components of the country in question;
- the EU's key objectives in its relations with the country in question;
- the objectives of the country in question in its relations with the EU;
- the applicable horizontal elements;
- a summary of the key challenges/opportunities for the EU in its relations with the country in question.

The second, larger, development of the training sessions pertaining to the development of EU–Asia relations lay in the introduction, and subsequent expansion, of a constructivist counterpoint at the heart of my presentation. This means that, for the sake of comprehensiveness, I endeavoured to 'balance out' the naturally strong institutional and functional foci on 'Declaratory Diplomacy', 'Political Document-Drafting', 'Policy Blueprints', 'Country Strategy Papers' and Commission 'Asia-Strategies' of the session with excursions into the role of 'tropes', 'themes', 'images', 'identities' and 'ideas' in international relations in general, and in EU–Asia interaction in particular. Over time, these excursions became increasingly more frequent.

Seeing that this approach produced results, especially in terms of learner participation and interactivity, it became increasingly important for me to build into my teaching intervention a series of images and visual cues which at times reinforced the political messages discussed, and at other times seemed to contradict them. In this way, it was possible for me to bring a social-constructivist flavour to the heart of EU policy-making, to offer the groups food for thought and a different outlook on matters relating to this part of geopolitics.

Structure and content of the 'Asia session'

Introducing a social-constructivist perceptual lens on EU–Asia relations also fulfilled a significant pedagogical purpose in relation to teaching adults (see also above), in that it facilitated group-work, impromptu discussions, controversial debate, team spirit and role-play. In time, the inclusion of this approach not only began to address different learning preferences and styles (reflective, visual, kinaesthetic), but also deliberately disrupted instructor-focused presentation, modified speed of delivery and enhanced interactivity and engagement of the groups.

The visual materials and Asia–Europe 'iconography' which I used as *matières à reflexion* ('food for thought') for this presentation over a period of two to three years were always derived from two key sources: I would seek out a visual representation (artwork, caricature, photograph) of a current issue making the headlines of the day, or revert to the rich, overall pool of 'stereotypical' imagery which is so characteristic of Europe's and Asia's perceptions, stereotypes and mental images of one another.

Thus, some of the material I employed would show the drawing of a globe with a 'Made in China' tag on it; alternatively, I frequently reverted to the 'traditional' iconography of 'Chinese Dragons' and 'Indian Tigers' to make a point. Many of the images I used surrounded the area of human rights in Asia and Europe, and were meant to stimulate analysis of the failures and successes of the European Union's human rights promotion policies, in Asia and on a comparative level. One memorable image I remember now was that of a Chinese athlete, depicted on a blue-and-white Chinese Ming vase, attempting to out-run the confines of the vase. This image I offered for discussion at around the time of the Beijing Olympics.

The art of good Feng Shui *in Brussels* 185

Using both these images and textual information in as balanced and pedagogically effective manner as I was able to, I attempted to both offer food for thought for the 'reflectors' in the audience and encourage those who learned best by talking and interactivity. A typical structure for one of my presentations in the framework of this training programme incorporated, amongst others, the following sections, taken from an overview slide of mine in 2010, before the 'separating out' of the material on India and China into presentations of their own:

- EU–Asia Relations and the New Geopolitics;
- Theorizing EU–Asia Relations;
- Images of Globalization and EU–Asia Dialogue;
- Pause for Thought 1 (Imagery);
- The EU and China;
- The EU and India;
- Regional and Inter-regional Aspects of EU–Asia Cooperation;
- ASEAN and the EU–ASEAN Cooperation Framework;
- The Asia–Europe Meeting;
- Two 'Random-Choices' of EU Partners in Asia (Japan and Australia);
- Pause for Thought 2 (Vote, see below);
- Conclusions, FAQ and Discussion;
- Hints and Tips for Further Reading.

It may be seen from this that introducing such a broad range of EU policy areas with respect to 'Asia' was, at times, an ambitious and difficult task, which, I felt, could only be achieved through the liberal use of interactive breaks, modifications of delivery speed and variations in voice and body language, amongst other techniques. It was, perhaps, this idiosyncrasy of mine which led the EIPA Seminar Leader to characterize my teaching style as a form of *Feng Shui* – an observation I took as a compliment of course!

The two Pauses for Thought introduced at various, and sometimes moving, positions in my talk were designed to do just that: pause, stop and think. Whilst I invariably chose an image for the first of these pauses, in the second one, near the end of the presentation, I introduced the idea of an ad-hoc vote, asking the audience to decide which areas of EU–Asia cooperation ought to assume a central position in the future dialogue (see below). It may, perhaps, be seen in conclusion to this section that the sub-division of this schedule, from 2010 to 2012, into discrete sections on South Asia, South East Asia and North East Asia was a rather good idea.

In terms of the overall structure and the content, my 'EU–Asia' part of the session would, invariably, start with a three-fold 'embedding' of the subject matter. First, the presentation would seek to invite analysis of the rationale for 'EU–Asia policy' and for teaching 'Europe' in 'Asia', offering, for instance, a range of explanations revolving around enlarged constituencies and memberships in regional bodies in East and West, similar global challenges, regional diversification of functional cooperation and historical legacies, to name but a few, as starting points for the subsequent analysis.

I attempted to link the 'particular' to the 'general', emphasizing a number of *leitmotifs* which had been set at the beginning of the overall training programme, seeking to interpret them for the specific concerns of Asia–EU dialogue, and 'connecting' them, where possible, to the key concerns of other speakers on the programme in relation to other regions. Such recurrent themes as could be identified in this context remained relatively stable over the years; they frequently revolved around geopolitical concepts like 'The New Great Game', 'The Asian Century', 'Mismatched Expectations in Asia and the EU', the 'Clash of Civilizations' and 'Cooperation between Civilizations' paradigms, and geopolitical strategies relevant to Asian–EU partners. An example of the latter was the idea of 'multi-polarity' promulgated by, inter alia, successive Chinese governments.

Second, anchoring a presentation on EU–Asia relations in a social-constructivist frame of reference meant that, at this theory stage of the session, constructivism was introduced as a possible model to explain why so much of the contemporary EU–Asia dialogue rested on matters of 'identities', 'ideas' and 'perceptions'. Divergent perceptions of, for example, what should be taught within 'European Studies' syllabi in Asia, and different notions of what 'Asia' actually was and how it should be seen in the US and the EU played a part here, defining, as it were, political and pedagogic approaches ranging from 'strategic reassurance' to 'constructive engagement', in regard to states such as the People's Republic of China.

Third, I set the scene by offering for critical examination a selection of key reports and documents pertaining to *future scenarios* involving Asia–EU relations and European Studies in Asia, in order to encourage a debate surrounding the value and credibility of 'predictions' about both Asia and Europe in the future. Among the documents I introduced most frequently, and for the longest periods of time since their publication, were the following reports and documents. They make interesting reading, in connection with Europe's and Asia's relative positions of power and influence in the world of tomorrow:

- *The World in 2025 – Rising Asia and Socio-Ecological Transition* (European Commission, 2009);[18]
- *Europe 2020* (European Commission, COM (2010) 2020 final, of March 2010);[19] and
- *Project Europe 2030* (Reflection Group Report to the Council).[20]

This introductory task was made easier by the fact that there is hardly any other area of EU foreign policy analysis which benefits to a similar degree as do EU–Asia relations, from the dynamic presence of so many research institutes, think-tanks and professional organizations with an EU–Asia remit. These would not only be invaluable sources of up-to-date information; they would also often offer alternative agendas; perspectives and points of view on European Studies in Asia and EU–Asia relations which turned out to be very different from the 'official' and officially sanctioned policies, strategies and country reports of the EU institutions. Among the contributions made to my talks, I found the offerings of the *European Institute for Asian Studies (EIAS)*, the *International Institute for Asian Studies (IIAS)*, the *Nordic Institute for Asian Studies (NIAS)* and the academic networks of *ECAN (EU–China Academic Network)* and *ENCARI (European Network for Contemporary Academic Research on India)* to be invaluable (see 'Selected websites' at the end of this book).

Interactive elements: 'images' and 'votes'

In the subsequent section on the iconography and imagery in the process of globalization of EU–Asia relations, the training emphasis switched, for the first time in this presentation, from a 'text-based' to a 'pictorial' mode of delivery, relaxing the pace somewhat, seeking to give people time to think, and addressing different modes of learning which were always clearly evident within the groups.

This section began with a 'word-picture' derived from one or the other of the latest EU 'Asia-strategies' and visualized by means of using such software such as *Wordle* or *Tagxedo*.[21] I derived many such images, from the Asia-related examples of the 'Declaratory Diplomacy' of the Commission and the European External Action Service. One example I used was the EU's *Regional Programming for Asia – Strategy Document for 2007–2013*, which was very comprehensive and thus could be 'summarized' as an eloquent 'word-picture'.[22]

The images which followed this initial impetus were diverse visual representations of a number of different 'modalities' or 'modes' of East–West encounter. They ranged from the mythology of euro-centric foundational narratives (for instance, Princess *Europa* and mediaeval *mappae mundi* and *portolan charts*), and from the mutual influences through art and architecture, to the deeply entrenched, stereotypical representations of the 'colonial' aspects of this dialogue of civilizations, including the trope of Europeans 'going native' in Asia, in dress and habits. Other aspects covered in this section invited participants to investigate the scholarly encounter and the historical, cultural and ideological foundations of the emerging discipline of 'European Studies in Asia' (which was introduced by means of Shiba Kōkan's famous image; see Chapter 4).

This included a look at the role of the strategies of education, accommodation, 'inculturation' and adaptation, utilizing the examples of European imperialism and the Jesuit missionary enterprise in Japan, China and India (see Chapters 3 and 4). It seemed to me that a number of the participants were not always aware that six current EU Member States had contributed major – and on-going – colonial legacies in Asia and the Pacific (Britain, France, Germany, Spain, Portugal, Holland), and that many other current EU Member States (e.g. Denmark, Sweden) had made an impact on the trade patterns, sciences and societies of the East.

This first section of my EU–Asia training intervention culminated in a 'Pause for Thought' (*matières à reflexion*), inviting the group to speculate on the question of what 'lessons' the makers of the contemporary EU–Asia dialogue might conceivably learn from those earlier, visualized, historical encounters, and how educational, political, cultural and economic Asia–Europe relations of today may be indebted to the globalization of the ages of Zheng He, Marco Polo and Aurel Stein.

The subsequent group-analysis of these images, which I facilitated – but tried not to 'nudge' into any particular direction – paved the way for a more in-depth examination of specific, bilateral aspects of the contemporary Asia–Europe interaction. For some years of delivering this session, I prefaced this section by an overview of 'brakes' and 'accelerators', i.e. those aspects which 'enabled' a dynamic EU–Asia collaboration and those which I saw as 'inhibitory', slowing down collaboration rather than invigorating it.

This gave me opportunities to introduce matters such as the EU's experience in dealing with Asia, its institutional infrastructure facilitating dialogue with Asia, and its areas of previous work such as the 'Asian branch' of the Common Foreign and Security Policy (CFSP). On the 'debit' side of the balance-sheet, this was the point at which to introduce political asymmetries and EU preferences in respect of Asian regions and countries, human rights disparities, re-prioritization of EU foreign policy foci and the lack of consistency, as well as the plethora of competencies, layers and actors within the EU and EAS dealing with Asia. I abandoned the 'enabling' versus 'inhibiting' dichotomy at a later stage, distributing these points instead over some of the other sections in the course of the presentation.

On account of its status within the wider hierarchy of EU policy preferences vis-à-vis Asia, China–EU relations took pride of place in this part of the intervention. Here, I sought to stress a number of controversial issues, such as human rights and the 'sinification' of Tibet, sometimes in deliberately provocative counter-distinction to the directions of 'official' EU–China dialogue, which is often constrained, as it were, by the influence of business and the requirements of official diplomatic channels.

Attempting to lead the participants beyond the 'official' strategy papers and other pertinent communications of the Commission, and paying more heed to the pronouncements of the European Parliament on human rights in China and Chinese activities in Africa, for instance, helped to bring to the surface many open and frank debates amongst the groups, which, perhaps, would have been much more difficult in the participants' 'normal' working environments, but which were 'protected' during this seminar by the application of 'Chatham House Rules'.

As the seminars, and 'my' part in them, developed further, I realized that the 'critical distance' some group members developed towards the EU–Asia and China policies dreamt up in their own offices increased significantly. This part of the presentation finished with an assessment of EU–India relations, once again homed in on human rights, before moving on to the inter-regional and multilateral sections of the talk. On account of the many layers of inter-regional EU–Asia connections, I approached this part of the intervention through a range of short overviews, coupled with a few concrete case studies. In this way, I avoided lengthy 'lecture-style' presentation, and the participants were encouraged to remain critically involved and active. We covered a range of areas, in such diverse issues as development assistance, EU cooperation in Higher Education with Central Asia, climate change in EU–Pacific relations and, of course, the keystones of EU dialogue with the Association of South East Asian Nations (ASEAN) and the summitry of the Asia–Europe Meetings.

In the context of the last two relationships, and on account of their complexity, I made a point of placing a particular stress on the priority topics of *Higher Education* and *Models of Regional Integration*. For me, this had the added advantage of being able to introduce – and 'road-test' as it were – some of my own, more recent, research results and publication activities in this area. After the 'inter-regional' parts of the session, I would – if there was sufficient time – insert some changing, and 'random', topics in dependence on political developments and activities of the new EU External Action Service. In this way, I introduced, for example, short sections on EU–Japan relations, and on the EU's dialogue with Australia and New Zealand (see also Chapter 9). This part of the talk closed with a second period of deliberation during which the group was invited to comment.

The session closed with some advice in regard to finding more information, further reading and websites. During the more recent presentations, I closed with a final 'activity'; this was a vote, put to each group I encountered, asking individual participants on where the future priorities of EU–Asia relations should lie. The two main questions on the 'voting slip' were phrased like this:

Who, in your view, are the most important EU partners in the Asia-Pacific, now and in the future: ASEAN, ASEM or Others?

What is the most important issue in future EU–Asia dialogue?
- *Treaties and Institutions*
- *Doing Business*
- *Supporting Democracy and Human Rights*
- *Learning and Culture*

This was an interesting attitudinal research exercise since it sought to reveal the audience's 'informed attitudes' towards the desirable future directions of overall EU–Asia interaction. I deliberately restricted the choices to four possible key processes: institutional, ideational, normative and commercial. My hope was that this rather crude device would not only say something about what the participants – who were, in most cases, at the very heart of making EU–Asia policies – were drawing on, in terms of values and world views.

I also expected to gain some insight into whether or not participants' views might have shifted, or been enlarged, as a result of the training seminar. The results clearly showed that, although over time there were some minor variations to the overall picture that emerged from the (always anonymous) answers, there was always a very comfortable majority advocating that *Doing Business* ought to be the prime focus of future Asia–EU interaction. This may reflect, perhaps, the overwhelmingly neo-liberal ideological persuasion and the intense institutional–organizational ideological coaching many EU civil servants would have been experiencing.

Mission impossible: the role of evaluation and the impact of feedback

The regular, and extensive, feedback on the sessions came from a very wide range of EU professionals, both 'old EU hands' and novices to their jobs. As the EIPA *External Perspectives on External Relations: Geopolitics and the EU* Seminars went on, geographical distribution of the participants became wider, in the same measure as the seminars were 'opened up' to a wider circle of learners, such as representatives of EU Member State delegations in Brussels, civil servants from a broader range of EU institutions and embassies, and staff from the EU delegations (embassies) abroad. There were always a few participants from one or the other region in Asia, ranging from Central Asia and Turkey in the West to Japan and the Pacific in the East.

From the point of view of a presenter, the post-Lisbon establishment of the European External Action Service as the 'diplomatic arm' of the European Union, and of the post of High Representative of the Union for Foreign Affairs and Security Policy, in 2009 (Duke, 2008; Blockmans and Hillion, 2013), had two tangible effects on the training: first, it continued to significantly widen the circle of participants and their professional backgrounds and experiences; as a direct consequence of this, it, second, and considerably, changed the training dynamics of the programme, mainly by introducing a far greater emphasis on the geopolitics of Asia, and of the actors shaping it.

Feedback from the delegates was regular and thorough, since all participants in the programme were asked to evaluate each and every speaker immediately after the respective session, ensuring that impressions and learning outcomes stayed 'fresh' in the minds of the members of the groups. This was important because the seminar as a whole was very intensive, offering a wide array of presenters and subjects over just a few days, often with only short breaks in between sessions. The edited results of an individual teaching intervention would be sent to the presenter or facilitator of the talk a few weeks after its completion. Thus, over four to five years, a picture would build up, which provided speakers like me with substantive information in regard to just the 'right' structure, method and 'tone' of individual sessions.

By far the most frequent theme to emerge from those learner assessments – apart from the fact that there never seemed enough time dedicated to a particular subject – was the question of the right balance, and the 'weighting' between the more 'theoretical', and general, parts of a specific topic such as EU–Asia relations, and the more 'practical' and case study focused aspects of any such session.

It soon became clear to me that finding an 'ideal' distribution of emphases was akin to 'mission impossible', since all but one or two of the groups I encountered over the years consisted of an equal mixture of very experienced negotiators, policy-makers, senior managers and diplomats, and a number of 'beginners', barely out of their initial stages or work placements, and now in their first EU civil service post. What may have bored the former constituency to tears was just what the latter part of the groups would desperately want to work on – and vice versa.

Responding to this, and reacting to the comments on these divergences which found their way into the feedback questionnaires, was no easy task. However, appropriate group-work distribution involving both 'experienced' and 'younger' colleagues in the same groups could, of course, go a long way towards addressing this issue, as would case study and decision-making simulations, observant pairing-up of participants and role-play. In my experience, this made it vital for me to 'come into class' early, as it were – at least one or two sessions before my own was about to start – in order to observe the group and identify the different skills sets which were, inevitably, present at all times.

The many evaluations I received in the course of eight years would appear to contain much detailed evidence in favour of not just assuming that if one was a good 'European Studies' scholar, and a master of one's subject, one would also automatically be an efficient teacher of adult and professional learners. Getting the balance right, between 'lecturing' and 'facilitating', 'probing' and 'presenting', 'interactivity' and 'up-front-teaching' was, in my view, considerably helped by being aware of even just the most fundamental background information about underlying factors like personality types, learner preferences, group dynamics, time-management and other areas. The positive feedback from what was quickly dubbed, by my fellow presenters, the *customer satisfaction questionnaires* seemed at least to reward this attitude from my point of view. Feedback was organized into broad categories, akin to the module evaluation questionnaires circulating in many UK universities, and the respondents were invited to comment on the 'Lecture' and the 'Group Discussion' sessions *separately*, in terms of what they 'liked', and what 'could be improved'. Interestingly, they were also encouraged to evaluate the presenters' more general pedagogic abilities, delivery style and levels of interactivity, if any. The facilitators' routine was then ranked on a scale from 1 to 5:

1   *Very Poor*
2   *Poor*
3   *Average*
4   *Good*
5   *Excellent*

In addition to these more 'formal' processes, I often received – as did most other speakers, as far as I can tell – both praise and criticism from a wide range of group members themselves, who would inevitably come up to me after the session to share their thoughts about what I had just done. More than that, though, they invariably shared more: facets of their own work experience, contacts and networks, hints and tips on how to teach 'Europe' in Asia. For me, this was extremely valuable, since it showed me how certain aspects of EU–Asia relations – policy areas, initiatives, programmes – would, over time, 'shift' in and out of focus and up and down a ladder of preferences, which often reflected the changes in the official Asia policies of the Commission and the European External Action Service.

It is from those post-presentation glimpses into the minds and experiences of those who practised what I preached that I received the most valuable ideas and insights into which changes I would need to make to my European Studies (and EU Studies) curriculum in Asia, in order to stay relevant and abreast of the most recent developments germane to my field. The very 'randomness' of this process of who came to talk to me and who did not also ensured that I talked to EU civil servants, diplomats, representatives of Member State delegations and EU representations (in Asia) of all ranks, and from a broad scope of professional development; both the 'old Asia hands' and those who had just joined the service – and all in between – would be represented here. Here is where I was most constructively critiqued, and where the source of many new lectures and changes to existing modules originated, in my own, continually evolving but necessarily subjective version of the European Studies in Asia discipline.

Although I feel privileged to say that what I glimpsed from the feedback mechanisms, both formal and informal, led me to believe that there was a high level of overall satisfaction with both the content and the delivery of my Asia–EU presentation, I do remember one occasion at least when the participants asked me to include more analysis of the 'substance' and legal framework of the issues presented – in that case, the EU–China partnership, and on Chinese foreign policy towards Europe. This particular result showed me that it was time to, once again, 're-vamp' the China session, to make it more attractive and relevant to all who were in the session. Perhaps my presentation had, on this occasion, offered too much showy interactivity and focus on 'images' and 'stereotypes', and too little 'meat', i.e. concrete China content?

Connections with my general work

In terms of my other work, and in connection with my own publications and other scholarly activities, the EU Foreign Policy Seminars played a key part, over almost a decade, in the development of my research foci. Not only was my participation in this event concrete evidence that (some of) my work had some 'impact', and that it would, on occasions, reach, and maybe even to some degree influence, European decision-makers; my interventions in Brussels also provided me with numerous contacts across Asia, and with indirect exposure to decision-makers and leaders in Asia, since those who were trained in the seminar would often return to the region with information and impressions that, on more than one occasion, did influence their professional work.

A good opportunity of a connection to be made in this way presented itself when, during one of the earlier EIPA Seminars, two representatives from the EU delegation office in Bangkok were among the participants of the training programme. Since I was then also teaching, once a year for up to six weeks, on an MA Programme in European Studies, at the Interdisciplinary Centre for European Studies (CES) of Chulalongkorn University in Bangkok, this was an appropriate way to 'connect' my work on European Studies in Asia from both continents. Contact was duly made with the relevant EU delegation staff, one of whom had actually been a student on the Bangkok programme some years ago.

As a result of the EIPA EU Foreign Policy and Geopolitics Training Seminars in Brussels, therefore, European Studies curricula in Asia underwent some change and development, and the European Studies Centre at Chulalongkorn University became much more closely linked with the activities of the EU delegation, which, in this period, also covered Burma (Myanmar), Cambodia and Laos to some degree.

One quite tangible result of this process of cooperation and *rapprochement* was the subsequent organization of a number of events in Bangkok: thus, for example, I would in the years that followed always bring my Thai students, once or twice during their four-week course, to the EU delegation in *Kian Gwan House II* on *Thanon Witthayu* in Bangkok. The instruction the students received here from the helpful and knowledgeable staff was, arguably, far more useful and practical to them than some of my lectures.

In addition to this singular connection, the EIPA Seminar series afforded many other opportunities to disseminate – with prior permission of the organizers – relevant information about my research, and my new and on-going publications, especially two edited books on *EU–China* and *EU–Asia* with *Rodopi*, a key European publisher better known in continental Europe, perhaps, than in the UK. The feedback gathered from thus introducing my publications, in turn, informed and inspired my future writing.

Naturally, I found that I had to constantly adapt and develop the content and emphasis of my own presentation on EU–Asia relations; more than one of the groups I encountered also became, perhaps unwillingly, a sounding-board for new ideas, changed approaches and revised priorities. Many aspects in more than one of my most recent books, as far as they are investigating the educational and intellectual dimensions of EU–Asia exchange, are indebted to interventions, conversations and discussions which developed freely during the EIPA Seminars, either during the teaching sessions themselves or in the space between sessions. When I researched, for example, the Commission's declaratory and strategic policy papers on China and South East Asia, I found that I benefited enormously from the wealth of knowledge assembled in the seminar room; a wealth from which I drew both inspiration and concrete direction for my own writing.

Moreover, I routinely used my time in Brussels, before and after the seminar, in order to build on contacts made during the sessions. I paid regular visits to the European Institute for Asian Studies (EIAS),[23] and I visited and interviewed many Commission officials. Beyond that, however, I also chose to take in a relevant exhibition when there was one available. Over the years, there were many 'blockbuster' exhibitions which linked extremely well with both the thrust and the content of the EIPA Seminars, and connected with, for instance, the summitry of the Asia–Europe Meetings (ASEM). Pertinent examples include the shows *A Passage to Asia*, *Europalia China* and *Encompassing the Globe – Portugal and the World in the 16th and 17th Centuries* (see Chapter 5 for more details). More than once, my more or less impromptu visits, undertaken in order to take in some of these exhibitions, resulted in some urgent, last-minute changes to the 'visuals' of my talk, or even, occasionally, to its structure and content.

Lessons learned and the theory–practice nexus

Throughout the period of my involvement with the EIPA Seminars, one of the most illuminating experiences for me has been the wide range of competencies, experiences and views assembled in any one seminar group. I found that, more often than not, audiences were extremely demanding and required awareness of advanced skills in adult pedagogy and effective communication (see above), as well as diplomacy, tact and mediation between often extremely diverse negotiating positions and political views.

None of the latter reached the outside world, of course, since EIPA *External Perspectives on External Relations: Geopolitics and the EU* Seminars are conducted under 'Chatham House Rules'. Perhaps the most important lesson I learned from my participation in the seminar was due to the time constraints that existed with regard to the individual teaching interventions. Having just a maximum of two hours at one's disposal meant that enormous attention had to be paid to both content and presentation style, and that both these aspects had to be constantly refined, in response to the feedback received (see above).

And last, but certainly not least, I became a learner myself, of course. This meant mainly two things: first, I learned an inestimable amount of news, facts, interpretations and concepts from the many members of delegations, civil servants and international diplomats I encountered during my ten EIPA years. This was a learning experience which has enriched me, perhaps more than any textbook on EU external relations, diplomacy and human rights ever will. Second, I learned much from the presentations of other colleagues during those sessions in the two-day programme which did not deal with Asia.

One experience which stands out, for example, is that I often attended the presentations on the EU's relations with the Mediterranean and the Middle East. This was for the simple reason that it was scheduled just before my own talk, and I wanted to sneak in and 'gauge' the nature and interactivity of the audience in advance. Listening to my colleagues' interventions in other EU policy areas not only exposed me to different styles of instruction and interaction, it also enhanced my awareness of those issues, for example, that were common to the EU's relations with the Near East and the Far East. I learned a lot about EU foreign policy and the EEAS in this way. On more than one occasion, I took notes, picking up on matters revolving around 'values', 'human rights' and 'stereotypes', to name but a few, which I would then pick up on again at the beginning of my own talk, to establish coherence and to emphasize common strands and themes in EU policy. More often than not, it was not difficult to find those strands.

The future of the EIPA Seminars

At the time of writing this, in August 2013, the future of the EIPA *External Perspectives on External Relations: Geopolitics and the EU* Seminars had come to be seen in the context of the stronger involvement of a number of other players on the foreign and public policy training stage in Brussels. The markedly stronger involvement of the European External Action Service on the one hand and increased synergies with the work, for instance, of the College of Europe on the other hand were evidence of greater competition for this lucrative EU training market. More than that, however, these processes, by encompassing, almost by default, a greater number of experts, also directly impinged upon the further modelling of the European Studies discipline in Asia, as those institutions and think-tanks with a more pronounced oriental expertise have made their presence felt more visibly throughout the Brussels bureaucracy and NGO networks.

The European Institute for Asian Studies, for example, experienced a revival from 2010–2012, and new actors such as the *InBev Baillet Latour Chair in EU–China Relations* and *TOTAL Chair* at the College of Europe[24] re-developed the educational aspects of their work by contributing more to public discourse about Asia–Europe, by means of an occasional focus on (Higher) Education, soft-power and education-diplomacy, in its conferences and in the largely 'on-message' newsletter, the *EU–China Observer* (e.g. *EU–China Observer*, Vol. 2–2013: 30–33). The speculations on student exchanges with China in the pages of the *EU–China Observer* (Hong, 2013) did much to raise awareness for how 'European Studies' might have to change in both China and Europe. By early 2014, these changes were being felt by those who taught the discipline in the East.

As far as EIPA itself was concerned, the institution underwent successive, significant commercialization drives in and around 2011–2014, reflected most clearly in the job descriptions for a number of new positions at the senior level of the organization. Next to what might, arguably, be seen as further evidence for a 'commodification' and 'managerialization' of Higher Education and Training, however, there was also a significant widening of the scope of EIPA's training programmes, as well as the branching-out of the EIPA Seminars, from a mere 'survey' of Asia–EU areas of concern, to a much more regionally and thematically specialized training portfolio.

In summer 2013, preparations had already started for the next session in December, for which I was writing a presentation on EU–Indonesia relations. This in itself revealed the very real changes the programme had undergone, from a series of 'survey-lectures' to a 'hub-and-spokes' model of delivery. In this model, certain general, geopolitical, 'horizontal' concerns formed the connective strength of the hub, and the individual sessions on India, China, Japan,

Indonesia, Afghanistan and Pakistan, and so on, branched out from the centre to form the spokes. Although this model was a genuine reflection of the development of the Asia policies of the Commission and the EEAS on the whole, it could, naturally, not cover everything, and it was tied up with the demands of a fast-changing landscape in the EU civil service and the EEAS, and with the concomitant learning needs of EU staff.

In connection with the latter, I will finish this chapter by arguing that, aside from shaping the discipline of European (Union) Studies in Asia, the EIPA *External Perspectives on External Relations: Geopolitics and the EU* Seminars will make a very significant contribution in terms of the skills set required from current and future EU civil servants, officials and diplomats. EIPA, perhaps increasingly in conjunction with EU educational agents with a similar interest and brief, therefore has an important role to play, in terms of defining (and refining) the future CPD competency model of the EU institutions' employees, desk officers, officials and diplomats.

Stephan Keukeleire (2012) strongly emphasizes this point, in the context of what he calls the EU's 'structural diplomacy'. Defining 'structural diplomacy' (ibid.: 2) as 'a process of dialogue and negotiation with third countries aimed at sustainably influencing or shaping political, legal, economic, financial, social, security and/or other structures in target countries', he argues for a process of 'upgrading the position of "learning" and "dialogue" within the EU's diplomatic system and activities' (ibid.: 5). Keukeleire's recommendations and conclusions in terms of training transfer easily to EU–Asia relations and European Studies in Asia. They represent a suitable final word for this chapter (Keukeleire, 2012: 6, 7):

> this implies that the EU's diplomats and civil servants need to be able to rely not only on excellent generalists or specialists in specific policy fields (such as police reforms), but also on area specialists with a sound knowledge of the third country, long-term experience in these countries, and a solid network of contacts within these countries. What the EEAS and the EU delegations need are not just diplomats or civil servants specialized in the EU's policy towards the Balkans and Central Africa, but specialists in the Balkans and the DR Congo.
>
> [...] a major objective of the recruitment policy of the EEAS should be to attract top experts on China, Asia, the Arab world, Islam, etc. This is pertinent in order to further strengthen the expertise available to the EEAS and the EU Delegations as well as to overcome the often too EU-centric or Western ethnocentric perspective on non-European countries.

Chapter conclusions

To sum up, there were perhaps two main ways in which my participation, in the course of almost ten years, in the EIPA/EEAS EU Foreign Policy Seminars had a palpable impact on my teaching of European Studies in Asia. First, the experience of repeatedly leading a teaching intervention on EU–Asia relations in Brussels brought with it much constructive potential for interactions, both formal and informal, with policy-makers, as well as practitioners of EU–Asia relations, from the EU civil service and Member State delegations.

This, in addition to the more 'traditional' ways of staying abreast of developments, such as reading the relevant publications and policy papers, helped me considerably to keep my own teaching programme for European (Union) Studies in Asia 'fresh' and up-to-date. It bears re-emphasizing, in this context, that it was predominantly the post-session encounters with officials in the group which invariably yielded the most valuable insights into the progress of a certain policy area, for example. This affected module work in Asia directly.

Second, my own curriculum for the EU modules I have been privileged to plan and lead across Asia was changed and enriched by the significant networking potential inherent in the EIPA Seminars. A group member would thus lead to a new contact on the ground in Asia, for instance, and this contact would be able to provide vital information on bilateral relations between the EU and, say, Malaysia and Thailand, as well as offering, more often than not, a range of 'free' and up-to-the-minute teaching materials for my courses.

These, although never of the 'confidential' sort, were frequently not available elsewhere and would make valuable additions to a classroom exercise, role-play or simulation, since they were often taken from the 'real life', as it were, of those who worked in an EU delegation. Over the years, I have found that the lead contacts, and the follow-on meetings, originating in those Brussels seminars, contributed infinitely more to my module and lesson plans for European Studies courses in Asia than the many, lengthy, official, multi-layered 'validation' processes at local universities in Asia, and the responses to new HE teaching initiatives from Asian education ministries and governments.

In addition to these key influences, I found that a number of 'ancillary' activities which developed *on the occasion* – rather than as a direct consequence – of the EIPA Seminars provided me with the more 'rounded' picture I required, in order to expand the traditional European Studies in Asia syllabus. One example that comes to my mind, and is still on-going, is the *europalia* (China and India) art scene, including a range of attendant exhibitions in Belgium (see also Chapter 5 and 'Selected websites' at the end of the book).

What I experienced at cultural events like these convinced me that East–West dialogue processes like ASEM are right in having a 'cultural–educational' pillar, for it is the focus on the 'cultural software' of societies in both Europe and Asia which underlies – and sometimes re-directs – much of the official dialogue, and which is instrumental in realizing the vital processes of 'identity-building', 'localization of European Studies in Asia' and 'inter-cultural dialogue', which are being further analysed in the course of the later chapters of this book.

Notes

1. For some of the information in this section, I have relied on a letter kindly supplied to me, as a reference, by Professor Simon Duke of the European Institute for Public Administration (EIPA) in Maastricht on 31 March 2009, and on some additional information provided by Professor Duke in June 2013.
2. See: www.eipa.eu/files/annual_report/EIPA_Annual_ReportEN10.pdf.
3. The EIPA website is at: www.eipa.nl.
4. The College of Europe (CoE) website is at: www.coleurope.eu/.
5. CoE: EU Diplomacy Training Course: http://do.coleurope.eu/prof/EUDiplomacy/.
6. The EIPA 2013 catalogue is at: www.eipa.eu/files/Catalogue_2013web.pdf.
7. See: JOIN (2012) 17 final, Brussels, 12 June 2012: http://eeas.europa.eu/delegations/jed/docs/20120612_joint_decision_en.pdf; Implementation: DEC(2012) 009/2.
8. See the EIPA website: www.eipa.eu/en/pages/display/&tid=114.
9. Professor Simon Duke, European Policies Unit – Common Foreign and Security Policy, European Institute of Public Administration (EIPA), Maastricht (www.eipa.eu).
10. The exact content of these training programmes is subject to the copyright of the European Commission and European Union External Action Service; what follows here are my own recollections of an event in 2012.
11. Cf.: http://9020fall2003.jbthomas.com/AMSTUTZ1.pdf.
12. See: http://ec.europa.eu/education/lifelong-learning-programme/doc78_en.htm; Grundtvig: http://ec.europa.eu/dgs/education_culture/documents/publications/success-stories_en.pdf.
13. Factsheet: http://ec.europa.eu/education/external-relation-programmes/doc/factsheet_en.pdf.
14. See: www.eaea.org/index.php?k=7197&member=00874.
15. College (UCLan) website: www.myerscough.ac.uk/.
16. See, for instance: www.edpsycinteractive.org/topics/cognition/bloom.html.
17. I suggest that all potential participants in the EIPA Seminars are sent Honey and Mumford's Learning Style Questionnaire before the sessions, and are encouraged to share their 'scores' with others.
18. See: http://ec.europa.eu/research/social-sciences/pdf/the-world-in-2025-report_en.pdf.
19. See: http://eur-lex.europa.eu/LexUriServ/LexUriServ.do?uri=COM:2010:2020:FIN:EN:PDF.
20. See: www.consilium.europa.eu/uedocs/cmsUpload/en_web.pdf.
21. www.wordle.net/create and: www.tagxedo.com/.
22. http://eeas.europa.eu/asia/rsp/07_13_en.pdf.
23. EIAS website: www.eias.org.
24. See: www.coleurope.eu/website/study/eu-international-relations-and-diplomacy-studies/inbev-baillet-latour-chair-european.

9 'Between Vladivostok and Africa'[1]

Teaching and debating EU studies in New Zealand and Australia, 1999–2014[2]

Introduction: some background to European Studies in the Antipodes

The EU's general and educational relations with Australia and New Zealand (NZ, Aotearoa)[3] are well developed, in terms of a structural dialogue based on a widening perspective, by means of which both countries are now more engaged with more individual Member States, as well as with the EU institutions, than ever before, and are pursuing this engagement in more sector-specific areas than before. The evolution of Australia's and New Zealand's EU engagement from the time of the Commission's first recognition of the need for an official dialogue[4] shows a movement away from 'eclipsing', and single-issue, concerns, such as the Common Agricultural Policy (CAP) and the fallout from the UK's EU accession (1974), to broader dialogue, including, especially, Higher Education (Wiessala, 2004a; Murray and Zolin, 2012).

Membership in ASEM for both Australia[5] and New Zealand[6] (Kelly, 2010; Doidge, 2013) has, arguably, added another significant networking dimension to this.[7] In the face of varying political strategies of successive governments in Australasia, which seem to have alternatively appeared to prefer closer relations with either Asia or Europe (the 'Near-Abroad' or the 'Far-Abroad'), the discourse, academic and in the media, has at times vacillated between a historically informed (European) and an economic/migratory (Asian) identity perspective, up to and including the current Australian and New Zealand Governments of Kevin Rudd and John Gray (as of August 2013). For Australia, in 2012, the Labor Government released a White Paper entitled *Australia in the Asian Century*, which synchronized the country's priorities closer with Asia. As *Time* magazine pointed out in its issue of 19 August 2013:

> Other Governments – from that of Gough Whitlam, who in 1973 became the first Australian Prime Minister to visit China, to Bow Hawke, who inspired the formation of APEC [the Asia-Pacific Economic Cooperation forum], and Paul Keating, who furthered regional economic engagement – have edged the country closer to Asia.
>
> (*Time*, 19 August 2013: 20–21)

The fast-changing demographics of Australia, as well as the contemporary perceptions of the 'Rise of Asia', can be said to have accelerated this trend for Australia. Australian Foreign Minister Bob Carr's remarks for a 2012 anniversary publication commemorating 50 years of EU–Australia relations perfectly encapsulated the push-and-pull aspects of both 'EU' and 'Asian' engagement – as well as the 'compromise view', in regard to the Asia–Europe Meeting (ASEM):

> Although Australia is deeply embroiled in the Asian Century, for us Europe remains an integral partner in promoting the values of freedom and democracy. We are both committed to greater global integration, freer movement of people, goods, services and investment, and promotion of good governance and human rights. We have a common interest in Asia's continuing development and in being constructive partners. Our productive involvement in forums like the Asia–Europe Meeting shows our commitment to greater political and cultural dialogue with Asia.
> (EU Delegation to Australia, 2012, *Celebrating 50 Years: EU–Australia*: 8)

A high degree of 'Asian-ization' is evident too, in the foreign, cultural and economic politics of the Pacific country, in Aotearoa's self-perception and in the EU's recurring descriptions of New Zealand as 'Asian'. Notwithstanding New Zealand's Asian 'orient-ation', however, Kelly ([quoting McMillan] 2010: 213) has argued that there continue to be firm connections between the UK and New Zealand – the 'English Farm in the Pacific'. Perhaps this means that times have become more ambivalent for the EU seeking to develop closer ties with its Southwest Pacific partners. Overall, though, the emphasis of 'common values', and of Australia and NZ being broadly 'beneficial' for the process of EU integration, are recurring *leitmotivs* in the trilateral dialogue. The brochure *Celebrating 50 Years: EU–Australia* in 2012,[8] issued by the EU delegation to Australia, was not the first document, nor will it be the last, to drive home this point.

Arguably more importantly though than anniversaries, it is mainly perceptions (Kelly, 2010) and interests which continue to jointly engage Australia, New Zealand and the EU, for example, as regards development policy in the Pacific, product safety[9] and in connection with the *ASEAN Regional Forum (ARF)*. The 'timeline' of relations between Australia, NZ and the Union[10] also reveals that diplomatic interaction has become progressively more 'strategized', on the basis of general *Joint Declarations* (A1997; NZ1999 and 2007), *Partnership Frameworks* (A2008;[11] Murray and Zolin, 2012: 197–200), *Cooperation Agendas, Priorities* and *Action Plans* (A2003; NZ2004), *Mutual Recognition Agreements* (A2009), as well as a broadening range of bilateral agreements and treaties,[12] on topics ranging from consumer protection to wine, animal health, science and technology, and many more areas.[13]

In this context, (Higher) Education and Training have been described as 'more than meets the eye' (*EU Insight*: Delegation of the EU to Australia and New Zealand, December 2009). The area has become important to the EU's relationship with Australia and New Zealand and was the specific focus of *Joint Declarations on Cooperation in Education* (A2007) and *Partnership Agreements* (A).[14] Early educational 'pilot' projects led to an opening of *ERASMUS Mundus* to the Pacific from 2004. A 2008 Commission Report by the Directorate for Education and Culture on *EU Cooperation with US, Canada, Australia, Japan and New Zealand in Higher Education and Training*[15] showcased significant case studies of 'good practice' in both New Zealand and Australia, among them. More recent research has begun to look at the relationship between Australia and the EU or its Member States in a comparative, pedagogical perspective, looking, for example, at correlations and possible convergence between economic and education systems, approaches to capitalism and conceptions of the welfare state (Murray and Polesel, 2013).

Moreover, the European Studies discipline in connection with both New Zealand and Australia is benefiting – if anything, more so than in areas geographically 'closer' to Europe – from a lively academic discourse and a solid underlying body of research. These processes are conducted through the prisms of some (former and still existing) European Studies and European Union[16] Centres and University Consortia. For New Zealand, the *European Union Centres Network (EUCN)* unifies all eight NZ universities under one umbrella; it is the only such consortium in this region and is thematically connected to the *EU Studies Association (EUSA)* of New Zealand and to *EUSA Asia-Pacific*. In Australia, there are some stand-alone EU Studies Centres at the Australian National University (ANU), Monash and RMIT University Melbourne (see also 'Selected websites' for details).

These centres and consortia provide internationally known platforms to study and discuss the long-distance relationship between the EU and its partners in the Southwest Pacific, Australia and New Zealand, and to translate the political priorities of the EU into a modern HE teaching methodology, and a European Union Studies curriculum appropriate to the vast region in question. The creative academic work of these networks is frequently far ahead of the official priorities the EU and its representations want to see in the region. A *50th Anniversary Publication*, for example, of the EU delegation to Australia (Delegation of the European Union to Australia, 2012: 74) seemed as parochial in its conception of a key EU Studies curriculum as were many of the very early EU strategy papers on Asia, narrowing the European Studies programme down to just the following key priority areas:

- the role of the EU as a major economic and trade partner;
- EU as a political actor and its international relationships, in particular in the Asia-Pacific region;
- the integration process of the EU (e.g. single market, monetary union, economic and social cohesion);
- the policies of the EU (e.g. single market, competition, environment, climate change, energy and transport, security, education and science; and their relevance for Australian/New Zealand partners).

Some of the literature on the EU's relations with Australia and New Zealand is also pointing to important common concerns, such as the need for lecturers to 'ground' their teaching in students' pre-existing experiences and understandings of Australia's relations with Europe (Wellings, 2009: 26), to examine issues of the 'new bilateralism' and the 'perceptions' of the EU[17] in the region (Murray, 2003; Holland *et al.*, 2007) and to include the matter of HE reform, staff and student mobility as a reference point (for ASEM context, see Chapter 6). Some of these concerns have been addressed in the shape of individual projects, such as the *EU–Australia Tuning Pilot Project*,[18] and policy platforms like the *EU–Australia Education and Training Policy Dialogue*, which investigated 'international education' in 2012 and 'globalization' in 2013. Its 2014 focus will be on life-long learning.

Similarly, curriculum development and mobility projects in the context of the *EU–New Zealand Programme for Cooperation in Higher Education and Training*[19] have brought institutions of higher learning in both hemispheres much closer together, in a more focused way. Last but not least, the Union has founded an alumni organization entitled (completely appropriately) 'OCEANS' (*Organisation for Cooperation, Exchange and Networking among Students*). Its members engage in Europe–Asia-Pacific networking, and curriculum development, through its orientation towards 'modern and innovative approaches, methods and practices'. Aiming to contribute to the contemporary 'knowledge-society', OCEANS has begun to co-establish larger networks such as the *International Network of Innovators in Education*, with a conspicuously more 'engaged', social-responsibility-guided approach to the curriculum.[20]

The CERC in Melbourne and the School of Social and Political Sciences at the University of Melbourne (2000–2010)

The Contemporary Europe Research Centre (CERC), at the University of Melbourne, a (former) Jean Monnet European Centre of Excellence, was, arguably, one of the most dynamic European Studies intellectual hubs in the region and made a number of long-lasting contributions to the way 'Europe' and the 'EU' are still being taught in Australia – either as a sub-discipline' of Politics, or under its own steam. It did so mainly through the dissemination of ideas through its academic seminars, networks and conferences. From a (European) scholar's point of view, two undisputed highlights of CERC's work were its international conferences *Europe and Asia – Regions in Flux*, 6–7 December 2006, and *EU–Asia Relations: A Critical Review*, 27–28 March 2008 (CERC Newsletter, Vol. 9, No. 1, January–December 2006; CERC Newsletter, Vol. 12, No. 1, January–December 2008). I have included a brief overview of the main areas of activity of the (former) CERC as Appendix 14, at the end of this book (*The Contemporary Europe Research Centre (CERC) at the University of Melbourne*).

A Jean Monnet public lecture at the University of Melbourne, 2010

While the CERC ceased to exist from 2009, European Studies in Australia, and a lively debate of all matters European, did not. I feel privileged to have been a continuous part of these processes. On Friday 30 July 2010, from 6 to 7pm, for example, I had the great pleasure of delivering a Jean Monnet public lecture on the subject of *EU–Asia Relations and the EU Diplomatic Service in 2010/11: Priorities, Policies and the Doors of Perception*, at Theatre B of the Old Arts Building, University of Melbourne.[21]

In this presentation, I attempted to offer a critical analysis of the 'network of relations' between the European Union (EU), Australia and Asian countries, within a rapidly changing geopolitical context, and against the background of the plans for a new – and controversial – EU Diplomatic Service. Using examples, case studies and interactive materials, in the presentation I examined the origins, issues, levels, processes and actors involved in EU 'Asia-policies'. I focused on several key issues which, in my view, exerted both an 'accelerating' and a 'decelerating' influence on EU–Asia and EU–Australia policy. Together with the audience, I also investigated wider questions, such as the 'EU as an international relations actor', and the group seemed keen to examine EU 'strategies' towards selected Asian states and regions, for instance, ASEAN, Burma, Central Asia, China, India and, of course, Australia. The lecture proceeded by offering up for analysis some priority areas of the EU–Asia and EU–Australia dialogue, for example, human rights, development and education. I concluded by suggesting likely future developments in the emerging geopolitics of the twenty-first century, and in the evolution of the EU's, and Australia's, place in it.

Box 9.1 Structure of my Jean Monnet public lecture on 30 July 2010

1. The 'Crystal Ball': Facts and Predictions about Asia, from the EU
2. Asia–Europe Relations: from 'Myth' to 'History'
3. The Origins, Issues and Challenges of Asia–EU Relations
4. The 'Accelerators' and 'Inhibitors' of EU–Asia Dialogue
5. The Role of 'Perceptions' and 'Stereotypes'
6. The EU, China and India
7. Other Areas of EU–Asia Cooperation
8. The New EU External Action Service
9. 'Horizontal' Issues in EU–Asia Relations
10. Policy Categories and Future Trends
11. Geopolitics and EU–Asia Interaction
12. Conclusions and Reading Suggestions
13. Q & A

In addition to this guest lecture, I was asked to deliver a workshop, on Saturday 31 July 2010, to a class on a University of Melbourne Master's degree course on

204 *Teaching Europe in Asia: case studies*

The EU and Globalization. This intensive (weekend) workshop was attended by 25 MA (and some PhD) students. In the course of the few hours during which I met the very lively and well-prepared group of students, we discussed, following an 'introductory' lecture, a number of seminar questions, examples of which I have listed in Box 9.2.

Box 9.2 *The EU and Globalization*: selected seminar questions from an Australian course in European Studies

- How significant are the legacies of East–West exchanges in former ages for the contemporary EU–Asia relationship?
- Through which ways and channels have EU–Asia relations developed since the early 1990s?
- Which aspects of International Relations Theory/European Integration Theory can best 'unlock' EU–Asia relations?
- To what extent are EU–Asia relations dominated by trade?
- Are relations with Asia and the 'East' important for the way the EU sees itself?
- How significant are 'culture', 'intellectual exchange' and 'academic cooperation' in EU–Asia collaboration?
- How consistent is the EU as a human rights promoter in its foreign policies towards Asian countries, regions, think-tanks and associations?
- How are Asia–EU relations affected by debates about perceptions and values?
- What is the ASEM and why has the EU been keen to promote it?
- How do the EU and Asia develop dialogue on the ASEAN Regional Forum?
- To what extent is the EU encouraging regionalism in Asia?
- Are EU–China relations too dominant in the EU–Asia dialogue?

In connection with this workshop, and in subsequent discussions with the course leader at the School of Social and Political Sciences at the University of Melbourne, I was given the opportunity to learn how 'European Studies' and 'EU Studies' can be meaningfully distinguished (Wellings, 2009: 28) in Australia, to understand the ways in which issues of assessment of EU courses are handled, and to have sight of some of the topics which the students of this particular cohort were asked to address in their essays. Many of the essay topics reflected wider concerns for the 'European' roots of some of Australia's history, and for wider EU–Australia relations. The questions invited the students to work right at the forefront of the bilateral dialogue at the time. The course in question was *166–557 – Europe and Asia: Competing Hegemons*. I have reproduced a personal selection of some of what I thought were the most stimulating assessment titles in Box 9.3, acknowledging the kind permission of the course leader.

> **Box 9.3 Module 166–557 –** *Europe and Asia: Competing Hegemons* **(selected essay titles)**
>
> - To what extent is further cooperation between East Asia and the European Union, as regional actors, hampered by the European Union's current approach and policy to East Asia?
> - Should Asia emulate Europe? Or should it now be the other way round?
> - Why is there a perception among some East Asian actors and scholars that the EU constitutes a form of 'intrusive integration' (Acharya and Johnstone, 2007)?
> - One element which does not seem to have evolved greatly is the degree of mutual awareness between our two regions, with stereotypes on both sides still casting Europe as introspective and old-fashioned, and Asia as a distant and exotic continent, presenting more challenges than opportunities (EC, 2001, Asia Strategy). Discuss.
> - Both China and India are the EU's strategic partners. Why is the EU–India relationship lagging behind the EU–China relationship? Are there significant differences in the way the EU is developing its strategic relations with China and India?
> - 'Unlike the Americans, the EU does not see India as a counterweight to China in Asia.' Discuss.
> - The European Union is a model for regional cooperation among ASEAN member states, Japan, China and South Korea – a historical, political and social perspective.

The NCRE in Christchurch, New Zealand and my 2010 visit to the University of Canterbury

During my 2010 visit to the National Centre for Research on Europe (NCRE), I noticed that European Studies in New Zealand and its region had become networked and institutionally embedded in wider frameworks, such as the European Union Studies Association of New Zealand and its umbrella organization, the European Union Studies Association of the Asia-Pacific (EUSA-AP).

I became involved in teaching one of the key International Relations modules in the National Centre for Research on Europe: *EURO102: The European Union and Our Region*. In the space of about a month, I delivered four lectures-cum-seminars on the module, on 27 July and on 3, 10 and 17 August 2010. The overall plan, as it appeared in 2010, for this module is given in Table 9.1.

As my involvement with this module was happening just about as far removed from my 'usual' teaching environment (which was then UCLan – the University of Central Lancashire in Preston, UK), I sought to capture the 'success', or otherwise, of my attempts by means of a short module evaluation questionnaire (MEQ), modelled, in part, on similar forms then in use at UCLan. I was, of course, curious to see whether or not what I had learned and practised in Europe would be applicable in the Pacific. Box 9.4 shows a model of the questionnaire I used, showing the questions, and with the spaces and boxes for answers removed.

206 *Teaching Europe in Asia: case studies*

Table 9.1 NCRE module *EURO102: The European Union and Our Region*

1	13/7	Introduction	The EU as a global authority: trade, security, development and regionalism	Name removed
2	20/7	EU and NZ and Australia	EU–NZ	Name removed
3	27/7	EU and ASEAN	ASEAN and ASEM processes	Georg Wiessala
4	3/8	EU and ASEAN	EU and bilateral SE Asia relations	Georg Wiessala
5	10/8	EU and North Asia	EU–China	Georg Wiessala
6	17/8	EU and North Asia	EU–Japan	Georg Wiessala
Sem. break				
7	7/9	EU and NZ and Australia	EU–Australia	Name removed
8	14/9	EU and the Pacific	Historical relations until 2000	Name removed
9	21/9	EU and the Pacific	Economic partnership agreement 2008–	Name removed
10	28/9	EU perceptions in the Asia-Pacific	Media representations of the EU in our region	Name removed
11	5/10	EU perceptions in the Asia-Pacific	Asia-Pacific public opinion towards the EU	Name removed
12	12/10	Conclusion	Evaluating the EU impact on our region	Katharine Vadura

Box 9.4 A module evaluation questionnaire for an NCRE module (EURO102)

EVALUATION QUESTIONNAIRE – EURO102

Please can you take five minutes to give me your views (<u>anonymously</u>) on the <u>content</u> of the lectures/seminars, and on my teaching <u>style</u>, during the time that I have met with you (i.e. over the last 4 weeks). There is also room for your general comments. This is part of my staff-appraisal back home, under the headline of '<u>gathering teaching experience abroad</u>'.

- WHAT DID YOU LIKE IN THE CLASSES OF THE LAST FOUR WEEKS?
- WHAT DID YOU NOT LIKE?
- WHAT CHANGES WOULD YOU LIKE TO SEE IF I RAN THESE CLASSES AGAIN?
- HAVE YOU ANY GENERAL COMMENTS?

Thank you for your time and cooperation in compiling this questionnaire.
GW

During the same stay at the NCRE, I also taught two sessions on another NCRE module, *EURO101*, on *Discovering the EU*, and on some aspects of *EU Regional Policies*. Last, but certainly not least, I was asked to deliver one of the by now traditional *NCRE Friday Afternoon 'Round-Table' Seminars* on 13 August 2010, on the topic of 'Constructing New Silk Routes: the Role of Higher Education and Exchange in Asia–Europe Relations'. During this interactive event bringing together about 15 participants from the NCRE staff and student constituencies, I sought to inspire the group members to explore the role which education and Higher Education were playing in the relations between European and Asian countries.

The presentation began with a look at three short case studies from the wider educational and cultural history of Europe–Asia relations, to set the scene for the investigation which follows. These case studies started with a study of the international educational outlook of Nālandā University in India (from the fifth to the twelfth centuries; see Chapter 2), of the curriculum of the Jesuits in China (sixteenth and seventeenth centuries) and of the significance of the 'Dutch Learning' (*Rangaku*) movement for Japanese art in the Edo period (seventeenth and eighteenth centuries) – areas which, subsequently, informed the structure of this book (see Part I). Taking some personalities and examples of an 'early cultural and educational globalization' as a starting point, the workshop further explored the possible ways in which today's intellectual exchange between the European Union and its Asian partners can be conceptualized and placed into a theoretical framework.

The presentation included a look at those 'Asia-strategies' of the European Union which offered a focus on the role of Higher Education in the East–West exchange, specifically with Australia. In my intervention, I attempted to examine some pertinent examples of contemporary research regarding 'European' teaching experience in classrooms, and to investigate the development of the discipline of 'European Studies' and 'European Union Studies' in Asian and Australian universities, think-tanks and research institutes. The presentation closed by suggesting a few new criteria for the 'viability' and 'success' of the subject area of 'European Studies in Asia', and by drawing some preliminary conclusions about the role of 'European Studies' and 'Intellectual Exchange' as foreign policy tools in EU–Asia relations.

In the evening of the same day (13 August 2010), I had the pleasure of being able to attend a public lecture given by Helen Clark, a former Prime Minister of New Zealand, and, in 2010, administrator of the United Nations Development Programme, on the subject of *The Millennium Development Goals – the Next Five Years*, delivered on the occasion of the *2010 Cathedral Lecture* in (the now destroyed) Christchurch Cathedral. Little did the speaker know, when she referred to the earthquake in Haiti in 2010, that just a little over a year later, the beautiful cathedral chosen as the location for the lecture would be flattened by the 2011 Christchurch earthquake.

Helen Clark's public lecture[22] had a clear bearing on many international relations and European Union subjects which were taught at the NCRE in 2010.

Moreover, at least two of the more mature students on the NCRE EURO102 module, which I was then involved with, knew Ms Clarke personally and encouraged me to attend this public event, and to bring its main themes back into the class – which I did. It seemed to me unusual at the time that some students would have a personal acquaintance with the PM, but, apparently, it was not; New Zealand is a small country. From the point of view of 2013/2014, the development policy concerns evident throughout the former Prime Minister's speech were reflected in the areas of interest of (at least) one PhD student at the NCRE, who had begun to form his own development trust in aid of technology-assisted work with schools in a number of Pacific nations and in the context of the Pacific Islands Forum (PIF), their regional organization.

The NCRE in 2013

Three years after a busy 2010 visit, and two years after the devastating Christchurch earthquake of 2011, I returned to New Zealand, paying a visit to the National Centre for Research on Europe from 22 to 26 July 2013. The 2011 Christchurch earthquake had occurred between these two visits, and I found both the city of Christchurch and the University of Canterbury much changed this time. Since the university had lost about 80 buildings in total, the NCRE had been relocated to a purpose-built, but temporary building, in Kirkwood Village, on the University of Canterbury campus. This is where I was based this time, and where all my teaching and other activities took place.

The main reason for this return visit was the examination of one of the NCRE's PhD candidates, on Wednesday 24 July 2013. However, on Thursday 25 July, I also gave a three-hour lecture at the NCRE, on the subject of *Beyond the Secret Policemen's Ball: The European Union as a Human Rights Actor in the Asia-Pacific*. The presentation was in the context of an existing module at the NCRE (EURO318). I delivered the class in one of the (temporary) teaching buildings at NCRE (Kirkwood, KA04). However, around 15 students also joined the class, via video-conferencing (VC) link, from Victoria University in Wellington (VUW), on the North Island of New Zealand; VUW is part of the (seven-member) New Zealand *EU Centres Network*.[23]

I found this 'remote' set-up to be an interesting challenge, in terms of technology-assisted pedagogy. The delivery of what was, essentially, a traditional 'European Studies' class, with a human rights emphasis, was helped by the presence of a colleague at the other end, with whom I team-taught various sections of the class, such as 'mini-lectures', role-plays and simulations. The lecture was well-received and all students actively participated in it, in both centres. I found the technology mostly helpful, but there was a slight 'delay' in transmission, which tended to slow things down, and would have required more advance planning.

In 2013, as before, the NCRE was a very dynamic seat of international learning, and there were many additional events and activities organized during my stay. My lecture on 25 July, for example, was preceded by a short visit to the

NCRE, of Derek Vaughan, a Member of the European Parliament (MEP) from Wales, who gave a presentation about his work in the European Parliament, especially on the Budget Committee. In addition to this, I was interviewed myself, for the EUANZ.TV You Tube Channel of the NCRE.

Moreover, on Friday 26 July, I led a seminar on the subject of *Human Rights on the European Studies in Asia Curriculum*, also at the NCRE. This was an interactive, public event, and was attended by about 25 people, both staff and students. I conducted the seminar in the form of some human rights case studies, looking, in particular, at perceived learning styles of students from Asia, Australia and New Zealand, at linguistic issues connected with the formulation of human rights concepts in Asian languages and at the 'European Studies curriculum' proposals of the last meeting of the Asia–Europe Meeting Ministers of Education forum (ASEMME 4, in Kuala Lumpur, in May 2013). The group-work style suited this audience well, since there were many engaged postgraduate and mature students in this class, as well as interested members of the public (Kirkwood KA04).

In mid-July 2013, my most recent NCRE visit connected well with my new post as Visiting Professor at the Institute of Educational Leadership (IEL)[24] at the University of Malaya (see above). The NCRE was widely perceived as being in 'prime position', in regard to Higher Education leadership in the Asia-Pacific; a leader of international education and Asia–Europe exchange, and a flagship project of the University of Canterbury (UC) as a whole. Therefore, it made sense to put NCRE–IEL relations on a more 'official', institutional, footing, which was achieved through a *Memorandum of Understanding (MoU)* in August 2013. This envisaged future institutional contacts, staff and student exchanges and research collaboration, to mention only the major salient points. In 2013, the NCRE, and its Director, were also well connected with the Educational Leadership and Educational Policy-Making frameworks of the Asia–Europe Foundation (ASEF), the Asia–Europe Meeting's Education Ministers Meeting (ASEMME) and the European Union, which made the centre into a prime partner for IEL and for the Universiti Malaya.

Forming a second strand of potentially strong NCRE–IEL synergy, a number of PhD students on the postgraduate European Studies pathways of the NCRE in 2013 were working in areas which not only strengthened the European Studies discipline in New Zealand, but also helped to identify areas such as Development Aid and Educational Leadership as conceptual 'bridges' on the NCRE into South East Asia and Europe. One example was a mature PhD student, who had been associated with the NCRE for a significant time. He proved to be an emerging educational leading expert on Development Aid for the Pacific, and EU–ACP relations. Founder of the *EcoCARE Pacific Trust*, this PhD student was a good example of the kind of future leader the NCRE produced on a regular basis.

This student appeared to be a good example of a social entrepreneur: he was extraordinarily engaged in making his studies yield tangible results, by, for instance, working to initiate school and HE Leadership, Health and Educational IT programmes for some nations in the Pacific (e.g. Fiji and Tonga). This student's work was noteworthy because it opened up potential linkages between my (then) home institution in Malaysia (IEL, University of Malaya) and a large number of schools in these nations. This could help to open up opportunities to work with both the staff and the students of these schools, and to collaborate with the staff and postgraduates at both the IEL and the NCRE. There were also potential links directly into the relevant regional associations, the *Pacific Islands Forum (PIF)* and the *Australia-New Zealand Closer Economic Cooperation (ANZCEC)* framework. This was a fruitful opportunity to widen the circle of IEL clients across a vast area of countries, universities and schools in the Pacific.

The student voice from New Zealand, 2013

I had been privileged to have visited both Australia and New Zealand a number of times in the course of a decade, and I had never missed an opportunity to teach and to speak to the students I met, both informally and by means of semi-structured interviews (see Appendix 15: *Antipodean engagement: visiting, teaching and other activity in Australia and New Zealand*). My 2013 visit to the NCRE in New Zealand was no exception. After my public lecture on 25 July, I took the opportunity to interview briefly some of the postgraduate students on the European Studies programme of the NCRE. This proved to be an extremely valuable exercise in the context of this book. I asked the students questions which were very much along the lines of those I also posed to my Malaysian group in 2013, enquiring especially into their motivations for studying the EU in New Zealand, their experiences at the NCRE and their career ambitions.

I only met a small number of students on this occasion; of the three I spoke to, two were 'native' New Zealanders and one a 'naturalized' citizen, of Slovak origin. In spite of the small, and thus unrepresentative sample, the students' responses were revealing and betrayed a uniquely 'Kiwi' perspective and a specific outlook on the political world. The students' responses also clearly showed evidence of how teaching the subject of European Studies in New Zealand has been adapted to the needs of a country consisting of two large islands.

This means that the main centres of learning are often situated at considerable distances from one another, and where teaching 'on location', as it were, was challenging and prone to be disrupted by physical damage to buildings and equipment brought about by regular earthquake activity. It is not the main focus of this book to investigate the use of information and communication technology (ICT) in Higher Education pedagogy, but it was clear during my 2013 stay, as indeed before, that technology was increasingly being used to meet the unique needs of New Zealand students, and that it considerably widened learner interaction and awareness of the European Studies discipline across New Zealand.

One of the students had originally studied Political Science, was 'led' into European Studies through attendance at a conference and ended up choosing the subject. She started taking European Studies as a Minor, and continued to MA level, identifying the opportunities available for her research and the option of having an input in the selection of her own papers and supervisors as key reasons. In her view, this level of choice, across disciplinary boundaries (and New Zealand locations), the encouragement to participate in conferences and publication activity at an early stage, and the prospect of engaging with modern foreign languages was what was seen to set European Studies at NCRE apart from a 'standard' Political Science degree at UC.

All three students, like many others I interviewed elsewhere, agreed that the NCRE programme had a strong practical ('employability') dimension — none of them felt that this was a course of study that would result in them being stuck in 'ivory towers'. This theme of the programme appeared to be deliberately continued, throughout 2013, by means of the development of new, and distinctive, modules on such topics as 'European Fashion' (see below). The students also stated that, although it was not compulsory (any more) to take up a (European) language, a working knowledge of French, in particular, was seen as essential for this degree, especially in terms of access to materials and potential interviewees. In fact, the students opined that an interest in languages could also be a good gateway, or 'entry route', to a postgraduate degree in European Studies in New Zealand. Research for both NZ and Australia appears to bear out the assumption that languages can, indeed, serve a central function in European (and EU) Studies degree programmes (e.g. Wellings, 2009: 34).

Another NZ student interviewed on the day revealed a pattern that I had also noticed with Malaysian postgraduates at the Asia–Europe Institute (AEI, see above): she did a Science degree first, kept up her French training and discovered later that she was more interested in a Political Science subject for her Master's. European Studies at the NCRE met this student's needs well because she enjoyed comparative political analysis and was interested in how maps centred on New Zealand and the Pacific would inevitably shape a student's outlook on, and perceptions of, international relations, compared to, say, a fellow student from the EU who had grown up with a euro-centric conception of the world.

Other motivations for these students' choice of the European Studies discipline were less tangible, and ranged from what may perhaps best be described as 'romantic' notions of a 'traditional' Europe ('old' Europe) to a more concrete curiosity in the potential 'model-character' of the European Union form of integration for the Pacific, Australia and New Zealand. The students were aware, for instance, that this kind of study of comparative regional integration was a strong disciplinary focus of lecturers at Victoria University (Wellington) – a direct result, as far as I could tell, of the video-conferencing-based, multi-centred approach to teaching (see above), which brought together, in one EU lecture, students from New Zealand universities on both the North and the South Islands. All students I met were very curious about the European Union's relations with the 79 Asian, Caribbean and Pacific (ACP) group of countries.[25] This seemed likely to be a reflection, at least partly, of the strong research focus on EU development policy of the Director of the NCRE.

The variety of subjects available for study in the NCRE course portfolio, and especially a strong focus on human rights, was also repeatedly commented upon by the students I met. Once again, this is most likely due to the pronounced research interests and publications record of one member of staff at NCRE; however, a focus of this nature on human rights was also unique to the NCRE. This tallied with my own findings about the overall scarcity of critical and mature human rights content in European Studies throughout the Asia-Pacific, which had been one of my key points in the Roundtable Seminar on this subject (see above). It was good to see that in this way – as indeed in many others – the NCRE was continuing to strike out in new and innovative directions. One result of this seemed to be a certain 'shaping' effect of the NCRE postgraduate European Studies programme: I detected a clear correlation between individual staff preferences and academic interests, and the employability and future plans of the students; in this small group, for example, all three students showed a leaning towards an 'advocacy'-based international professional future.

The last student in this small group had chosen to undertake postgraduate study in European Studies in New Zealand because he was interested in issues of international student mobility at New Zealand universities – an area which connected well with many of the key concerns in this book, and with my own interests. He had spent time in Oxford and Prague before coming to New Zealand to learn English. Like the others in my small sample, he commented positively on the breadth of choice offered by the NCRE programme, focusing less on human rights this time, but on the opportunities to study matters of 'culture', 'history', 'social policy', and 'citizenship' in a comparative perspective, often by means of 'double-coded' modules across subjects like European Studies, Geography, History, Journalism and Diplomacy, and conceptually tied into an over-arching 'European Studies' theme.

A Malaysian student's outlook on the NCRE

An additional perspective on the NCRE programme in European Studies was provided through another channel: for some years now, significant numbers of Malaysian students on the Regional Integration Studies Master's Programme of the Asia–Europe Institute (AEI) at the University of Malaya (see Chapter 7) have travelled to New Zealand, in order to spend between four and six weeks of their AEI 'internship' at the NCRE. This provided an extremely interesting, cross-cultural perspective on the experiences of 'Asian' students of European Studies, especially as both teaching methods and the curricula in Malaysia and New Zealand were very different in terms of focus, student interaction and duration. The text in Box 9.5 is excerpted from the working diary of one of the students undertaking the Kuala Lumpur International Master's Degree in Regional Integration, whom I taught in Kuala Lumpur in April 2013, and who subsequently went to do her internship at the NCRE in New Zealand. It is an interesting document, on account of the way in which the student not only observes the daily routines in New Zealand, but also comments on working and learning styles of the 'Westerners' who work there. This sheds considerable light on the issue of 'perceptions' in East and West, which has been so central to a number of research projects – not least the NCRE's own *Europe in the Eyes of Asia* (see above) – but which, in as far as I can see, has never been applied to postgraduate students so far. I have but minimally edited the text that follows, in order to preserve the original flavour, freshness and power of the student voice.

Box 9.5 A Malaysian student's New Zealand diary

29 April

Today is the first day of my internship. I arrived at NCRE, which located at KD04, Kirkwood Village, University of Canterbury, at 10 AM. It took me 20 minutes' walk to NCRE from the place where I am staying for the next eight weeks while I am here. Upon my arrival, Yvonne Grosch (NCRE Administrator) greets me and I am introduced by her to all other staff here. She is a very nice and friendly person. She also briefs me about the rules and regulations and also shows me to the facilities in the surrounding area. Then, she takes me to the University Security Office in order for me to get my Visiting Academic Pass. She also informed me that Prof. Martin Holland (NCRE Director) is not here for this moment because he is attending a conference in Brussels and will be coming back in the next week and due to that I am not being assigned to any task yet. I have the break for the lunch hour from 12 PM to 2 PM. Then, I take tour inside the campus on my own and go back from work at 5 PM.

30 April

Today, I arrived at the office at 9 AM. I take the opportunity of not having any task to work on yet by starting with my project paper work. I search the books available at the library which related to my topic from the university library database and I find some. After lunch time, I go to the library and borrow some books. Then, I spend my time to read the books until I go back from work at 5 PM.

1–3 May

For the next three days, I normally get through the same routine. I arrived the office at 9 AM and go back from work at 5 PM. I am utilizing the time to do on-line searching for the materials for my project paper. I can access to the on-line journals and articles easily with the help of the university links to many database engines as my name is now registered as one of the staff of this university. This really helped me and I am so happy.

6–10 May

The rest of these five days, basically I am working on the same things. On Monday, Prof. Martin is coming back from Brussels and on the next day, I have been assigned by him to one special task to be completed throughout my time here as an intern to the NCRE. So, now I am dividing my time here for two things. First is to work on the task from Prof. Martin and the second one is to gather the information as much as I can for my project paper. Everything for these five days goes smoothly and like usual I will always come to work at 9 AM and go back at 5 PM.

13–17 May

All of my days of this week are spent for the task and the project paper. I used most of my time to read on articles and journals because I plan to start writing on my paper by next week because it is advised to send the chapter one and two to be checked by the supervisor by the end of this month. So, I get through the normal routine for the all five days, reach the office at 9 AM and go back home at 5 PM.

20 May–24 May

I have gone through my days similarly to the previous weeks. Coming to work at 9 AM and go back at 5 PM. Starting on Monday, I have started with the first chapter writing for my project paper. It really requires me to focus and I am almost done half of it when Friday comes. In between, I also spend my time for the task from Prof. Martin.

27 May–31 May

All of my days of this week are spent in writing my project paper. On Tuesday I have finished my chapter one and then I straight away start with the chapter two. On Friday evening, I emailed the first chapter to my supervisor but chapter two is not finished yet and I will complete it by the next week. Overall, again for this week I get through the almost same normal routine for the all five days, reach the office at 9 AM and go back home at 5 PM.

4 June–7 June

I start to work on Tuesday because yesterday (Monday – 3 June) was the public holiday due to the celebration of the Queen's birthday. Then the rest of these four days, basically I am working on the same things. I always come to work at 9 AM and go back eight hours later, normally at 5 PM. On Friday, I finish my chapter two and send it to my supervisor for checking. So, I will wait for the response from my supervisor before continuing to the next chapter.

10 June–14 June

I have gone through my days similarly to the previous weeks. Arrived in the office at 9 AM and go back at 5 PM; almost all of my time during these five days is spent on the task because I have to submit it next week.

17 June–21 June

For the last week of my internship, I feel a bit sad because I will go back home soon. Every day, I still go through the same daily basis where I reach the office at 9 AM and go back at 5 PM. I have submitted the task report to Prof Martin on Wednesday. Thursday is my last working day because the university is closed on Friday due to snow.

Every week, I attend either a Roundtable Public Seminar (Tuesday or Friday) or a class (Monday). The seminar is always presented by a special guest speaker on many topics which relate to the EU while the class is conducted by the NCRE lecturers. They are as follows:
[…]

Task basis

While I am here, I have been assigned by Prof. Martin to produce a handbook about, 'Study in Europe for New Zealanders'. I have to choose two countries and I chose the Netherlands and Spain. I have to get the latest information about the Higher Education system of each country, the scholarships offered, the tuition fees and living cost there and the contact information. So, I am supposed to contact the embassy of each country in New Zealand and do on-line searching about this topic. […]

Evaluation

This internship programme really gives me once in a lifetime experience. I have gotten through many unforgettable memories while I am here. Some are sweet while some are not so good. I believe that all the experiences which I gain from here can help me to prepare myself into the work life soon after I finish my study.

Strength and weaknesses

There are a few strengths and weaknesses which I have identified throughout my internship period. What I find to be a strength here, is that this place really gives me a chance of experiencing and observing how Western people work and conduct research. Every day I see people here communicate to each other in a very professional way which somehow these things are lacking in Asian countries. Everyone is focused on their work and they are not chatting or doing other things while they are working. I really hope that I can bring back this attitude to my home country and implement it.

   Besides, this place is a national Research Centre undertaking work in every academic year. Although I only being assigned with one task, but I still get the experience of how to handle a research professionally and how to get in touch with related agencies in order to collect data. The rest of my time is spent by observing the researchers here conducting their research projects. Furthermore, doing my internship here really help me with my project paper in order to collect data because I get the access to the library and the on-line database here. There are many materials like the books and the on-line journals which I needed and it really helps me. However, not all things are perfect here. I do notice a few weaknesses while I am here. Due to just a few workloads being assigned to me, I sometimes mistakenly used my time for another thing which is not really related to my work. One more thing which I notice is that no one is supervised me directly and I sometimes feel misguided.

Problems and challenges

I have faced a few problems and challenges while I am here which consists of internal and external problems. The internal problem is the office facilities. Due to the size of this Centre which is not so big whereas it is occupied by quite many people, I cannot get my own computer to do my work. I have to bring my own laptop to the office every day and sometimes I feel quite exhausted, because I have to walk about 20 minutes to reach the office. But, it is just a small problem and I have gotten used to it.

> Most of other problems and challenges here are the external one. The first one is about the weather. Christchurch in May to July is encountering winter season. The normal daily temperature is around 5 to 15° Celsius. While on rainy or cloudy day it may just reach up to a few degrees Celsius below zero. In my first few weeks here, I have to struggle myself to adjust my body to this new weather, and it requires a lot of determinations especially to face the cold weather in the early morning. The next challenges that I think is the currency here. I can say that all the things here really expensive because of the high standard of living and I have to be extra careful with my daily expenses so that I can survive until the end of my internship time here. The culture differences also one of them. I have to adapt myself with all the differences to live happily here.
> [...]
>
> *Conclusion*
>
> As a conclusion, I will say that my eight week internship at the NCRE was very meaningful to me. I gained a lot of experiences in the terms of work life because NCRE is a good place to gain the work experience for the research based working type. While overall, my time here in Christchurch really gives me a sweet memory because I learn many new things while I am here. I make a lot of new friends at the place where I work and I stay, and also through all the way. Different culture and atmosphere makes me more mature and open-minded in justifying something and I really enjoy my time here. I would like to suggest NCRE for the future students.

The future of the NCRE: curriculum development in the face of change

This widening focus of the NCRE, in terms of offering for postgraduate study a range of perspectives – economic, political and cultural – on Europe, continued unabated in 2013, in the face of massive change across the University of Canterbury as a whole. This was exemplified by the consultation surrounding a new course at the NCRE in 2013, entitled EURO202 *Europe – The Power of Fashion*. This new teaching initiative opened a new window on Europe from New Zealand. The relevant validation/consultation materials described this new part of the NCRE European Studies postgraduate learning experience as follows (Box 9.6).

This is a good example of an innovative and timely proposal for a new Social Science course on Europe, when much of the curriculum development in this area has gone 'stale' and is stuck in disciplinary 'silos'. The proposed new course also broke new ground, was unique, as far as I could see, and has significant potential to attract many new students to the subject and to raise postgraduate numbers – as well as raising the game for the University of Canterbury. The key idea of this course was well-timed, since it links in consciously with the themes of 'rebuilding', 'creativity' and 'contemporary societies', which have to be such dominant themes in the post-earthquake Higher Education landscape at UC and in NZ. The proposed course, from a domestic point of view, makes an

> **Box 9.6 EURO202:** *Europe – The Power of Fashion* (from: 'aims and objectives')
>
> The aim of the course 'Europe – The Power of Fashion' is to systemically consider an important aspect of the EU's identity – its 'soft' power. EU 'soft' power is defined as the 'ability to affect others to obtain the outcomes one wants through attraction rather than coercion or payment ... rest[ing] on its resource of culture, values and policies' (Ney, 2008: 94). Yet, currently, Europe and the European Union are involved in complex political and economic matters that rank among the most significant changes on the continent since World War II. The changing profile of the European Union societies serves to underline the necessity for a systematic analysis of integrating Europe and its 'hard' and 'soft' powers – inside the EU and outside it.
>
> This course will offer an opportunity for its students to systematically consider the phenomenon of the fashion in Europe as one possible answer to the questions 'What is Europe?', 'Where do its borders lie?' and 'Who is a European?'. The conceptual elements of the course cover the theory of individual, group and national identities formation; the debate over 'new' and 'old Europe'; divisions between 'East' and 'West' of the continent; cultural practices and history of Europe as expressed in texts and images of fashion; relations of Europe with the world and branding of Europe/EU as an element of its present-day cultural and public diplomacies.
>
> EU public diplomacy is of special interest in this course. Conceptualized within a theoretical model of 'new' public diplomacy – the transnational impact of all government or private activities 'from popular culture to fashion to sports to news to the Internet – that inevitably, if not purposefully, have an impact on foreign policy and national security as well as on trade, tourism and other national interests', this course will treat images and reputation as valuable commodities in international relations.
>
> Not only do they help to 'attract business', elicit respect and convey influence to foreign partners, but they hark back to the feeling of pride and identity among domestic audiences (van Hamm, 2008). With both state and non-state actors in the EU eager to be publicly present on the international stage, powerful images and good reputation become the key to secure visibility and frame positive responses in the world characterized by the deficit of attention – not information. This quest for images and reputation is challenging views of the 'traditional' diplomacy of the EU and its Member States, as a non-transparent, secretive and elitist activity, targeting top state-level actors. In contrast, changing global paradigms requires reflection on the 'soft' power contribution in international relations, and the course will focus on the power of fashion in understanding Europe and EU.

invaluable contribution to contemporary New Zealand identity, especially amongst younger people, students who may be tempted to leave the country and other Christchurch residents. It is exactly innovative, cutting-edge courses like this one which will demonstrate that it is well worth the home student constituency continuing to come to Canterbury to study.

In addition to this, an understanding of – and exchanging ideas with – international and European societies has never been more important than at the present time for New Zealand graduates, since it plays an important part in the course that New Zealand will choose to take in regard of accelerated globalization and international relations. In this regard, the course benefits, of course, from the internationally renowned work of the NCRE, which has, of course, made the name of the University of Canterbury much better known in the world for almost two decades now, through its former students, staff and impact on decision-makers globally. The proposed course – with its focus on cultural interactions and the conceptual lens of fashion – has a solid theoretical focus and an academic identity, which encourages critical debate. The new module seemed well-chosen, in terms of curriculum development at NCRE and UC. It will significantly aid in implementing the University of Canterbury's senior management team strategies for 'research', 'internationalization' and 'student recruitment', and will bring many new partners from Europe and elsewhere to the NCRE and to UC. This new offering also has the potential to attract significant numbers of research collaborations and industry links with the international fashion industry, and it will thus positively impact both on the international research rankings of the centre and the university, and on the development of the NCRE's and the university's partnerships with industry and other stakeholders. This course will place UC more firmly on the map of the international fashion world. I feel that, in regard to private–public partnerships in particular, and in connection with important issues such as student employability and work placements, the possibilities a course such as this one offers – to both a future student and UC – are almost endless. Perhaps more importantly, however, this proposal is of very high value in terms of the centre's and the university's reputation management. Its successful delivery will amply demonstrate to an international audience that the University of Canterbury is a young, creative and dynamic place to come and study, and the leading hub of innovative knowledge and research in the Southern Hemisphere. From the point of view of my home institution – the Institute of Educational Leadership at the University of Malaya in Kuala Lumpur – the proposed course also demonstrates high levels of awareness for leading educational change and a conscious effort on behalf of the NCRE and UC to produce an inter-culturally literate and internationally minded future workforce which will be of incalculable value for New Zealand's road ahead.

At the time of writing, the NCRE and its staff and students faced both exciting opportunities and severe challenges. The significant structural damage to university real estate and a subsequent steep decline in student numbers brought about by the 2011 Christchurch earthquake meant that the University of Canterbury undertook a 'restructuring exercise' from 2011 to 2013. The resulting proposal, *Change and Renewal: A Proposal for Strategic Development and Financial Sustainability*, of August 2013, while recognizing that 'a vibrant and sustainable College of Arts is of critical importance to the success of the University of Canterbury', and that 'the University's commitment to excellence in research' was embodied, inter alia, in the NCRE, UC introduced some considerable reductions in staffing, rationalized the number of degrees available in areas such as European and EU Studies, and merged the NCRE's *European Union Studies* degree with the *European Cultures and Languages* programme in the UC Department of European Languages and Cultures, whilst, nevertheless, leaving the NCRE intact as an independent research centre. It was thought that these changes would affect the NCRE's undergraduate (albeit not its postgraduate) teaching portfolio in European Studies to some degree from 2013 onwards.

Chapter conclusions

This chapter has combined an overview of some more recent developments in the teaching of European (Union) Studies in Australia and New Zealand with a critical evaluation of my own teaching experience in both countries, both in the form of short guest lectures and in relation to longer teaching engagements. It has found that the international relations perspectives of students in the region are different from Europe, shaped by their governments' Asian priorities and channelled through a number of old and new EU Studies centres and University Consortia in Australasia.

These centres, and the networks of EU Studies they are often linked to, have a significant function in developing the European Studies curriculum in Australia and New Zealand beyond the, often narrow, conceptions of the EU's own embassies and representations in this region. The chapter also highlighted a correlation between academic staff working at the centres, and the career aspirations and postgraduate ambitions of some of their students. The chapter has highlighted, in particular, the case study of the National Centre for Research on Europe (NCRE), at the University of Canterbury in Christchurch, New Zealand, which is engaged in an on-going, deliberate process of innovative curriculum-building in European Studies in Asia, in the face of significant change in both its embedding in its home institution and in its connections to the wider region.

The chapter has, last but not least, attempted to offer an insight into some of the reasons why students from Australia and New Zealand undertake degree-level study in European Studies in the first place, finding that motivations can be a mix of 'romantic' perceptions of 'Europe', linguistic and travel interests, and career planning. This has been juxtaposed with a review of the experience of a Malaysian student undergoing her internship in New Zealand, who was able to look at European Studies in the region from an outside perspective.

Notes

1 This revealing description of the 'European Studies' discipline, from the point of view of (a student in) Australia, has been – respectfully – borrowed from an equally revealing article by Ben Wellings (2009: 25–35).
2 My warm thanks go to Professor Martin Holland and Associate Professor Philomena Murray, for allowing me to use some NCRE and (former) CERC materials on EU Studies in this chapter, and for proofreading the chapter in August 2013.
3 See: Wiessala (2002b, 2004b).

220   *Teaching Europe in Asia: case studies*

4   See: COM (2001) 469.
5   See: www.dfat.gov.au/geo/asem/.
6   As neither an 'Asian' nor a 'European' member.
7   See also the *Special Report (Australia)* of the *Economist* (UK), of 28 May 2011 ('No Worries?').
8   See: http://eeas.europa.eu/delegations/australia/documents/more_info/eu-austfinal.pdf and http://eeas.europa.eu/delegations/australia/press_corner/newsletter/all-newsletters/369_en.htm.
9   See the 2012 EU–Australia collaboration on the 'Global Recalls Portal': http://europa.eu/rapid/press-release_MEMO-12-791_en.htm?locale=en.
10 http://eeas.europa.eu/delegations/new_zealand/eu_new_zealand/chronology_bilateral_relation/index_en.htm.
11 See: http://eeas.europa.eu/delegations/australia/documents/eu_australia/partnership_framework2009eu_en.pdf.
12 For Australia: http://ec.europa.eu/world/agreements/searchByCountryAndContinent.do?countryId=2131&countryName=Australia. For New Zealand: http://ec.europa.eu/world/agreements/searchByCountryAndContinent.do?countryId=2121&countryName=New%20Zealand.
13 See: European Commission, *Rapid Database*: SPEECH/07/434, on 'New Perspectives' in EU–NZ Relations (2007).
14 EU–Australia HE Collaboration: http://ec.europa.eu/education/eu-australia/australia_en.htm.
15 http://ec.europa.eu/education/external-relation-programmes/doc/goodpractices_en.pdf.
16 See: http://eeas.europa.eu/eu-centres/index_en.htm.
17 See: Wiessala (2010).
18 See: http://ec.europa.eu/education/eu-australia/doc/tuning_en.pdf; and: http://ec.europa.eu/education/eu-australia/doc/statement2010_en.pdf (2010 Joint Statement); http://ec.europa.eu/education/eu-australia/doc/statement2011_en.pdf (2011 Joint Statement) and http://ec.europa.eu/education/eu-australia/doc/statement2012_en.pdf (2012 Joint Statement).
19 See: http://ec.europa.eu/education/eu-new-zealand/doc/sele04.pdf.
20 See: www.oceans-network.eu/INIE; www.inie.eu/; and: www.inie.eu/conference/.
21 http://ces.anu.edu.au/events/jean-monnet-public-lecture.
22 See: www.undp.org/content/undp/en/home/presscenter/speeches/2010/08/13/helen-clrak-the-millennium-development-goals---the-next-five-years.html.
23 See: www.eucnetwork.org.nz/.
24 The wonderfully entitled *Institut Kepimpinan Pendidikan* in Bahasa Melayu.
25 www.acp.int/.

10 Overall conclusions

Priorities and pedagogies of the 'European Studies' discipline in Asia

In the preceding chapters of this book, I have attempted to offer a three-fold perspective on the academic discipline of 'European Studies in Asia', or 'European Union Studies in Asia'. This is still a very young discipline, which has largely grown out of the 'Area Studies' courses of an earlier time, whilst being integrated more strongly with the European Union's wider cultural and political priorities in Asia.

European Studies and European Studies in Asia, of this there can be little doubt, have also become instruments of foreign policy, 'soft', cultural diplomacy, and of the neo-liberal economic programme the EU so visibly subscribes to – whatever else this discipline may be. The 'branching-out' of the European Studies curriculum in Asia, over the last decade or so, has largely mirrored the development of the European Union's own economic, political and development-oriented 'Asia' policies towards thematic, sector-specific and regional specialization.

But there is more to it than that. Those chapters in this book which have delved into the historical and cultural background to the modern discipline of European Studies in Asia have sought to emphasize a number of significant aspects of what has been found to be a much wider, civilizational' dialogue of Asia and Europe. The meetings of Europe and Asia in education in earlier, but no less significant, periods of 'globalization' have thus produced a number of historical precedents for European Studies in Asia, many of them hitherto unrecognized.

These earlier encounters were conditioned by a range of themes, cross-cultural approaches and developments which, I argue, have produced lasting legacies and repercussions for those engaged in teaching European Studies in Asia today. In more than one of the preceding chapters, I have stressed, for example, that concepts such as 'seats (and seeds) of learning', religious tolerance and syncretism, didactic use of art and culture, and the pedagogic techniques of 'inculturation, adaptation and accommodation' have, at various times and in different guises, been among the cornerstones of the 'learning dimension' of the Asia–Europe dialogue. This I see as a direct consequence of Europe meeting Asia in China, Siam, Japan and elsewhere.

I have further offered the suggestion that the artistic–cultural inter-penetration of Asian and European societies and cultures represents, sadly, a much-neglected aspect of the syllabus in the contemporary study of Europe and Asia, and that teachers, lecturers and Professors should make much more use, in Asian lecture theatres, of the resources and insights to be mined from this rich seam of inter- and cross-cultural East–West encounter.

The chapters on the Portuguese and the Jesuits in Asia, on the Dutch in Japan and the European and Chinese travellers on the Silk Road have pointed to another aspect of the contemporary European Studies in Asia scene which, in my view, is in need of revival: this is the idea of wider 'visions' and intellectually curious 'personalities' and 'leaders' who have driven forward into unchartered territory the process of Asian and Europe learning from (and with) one another for many centuries.

I am, therefore, contending that, in the construction of the modern academic subject of European Studies, progress continues to depend on such visionary leaders. I have found that, among those who are 'leading' in this field today, the most successful initiatives and ideas for a European Studies curriculum come from those who lead through the open-source method of creating integrative, inspirational, interactive epistemic and learning communities in Europe and Asia.

In examining some key contemporary actors in this area, next to open-source leadership and visionary curriculum-thinking, this study has found three key aspects of teaching Europe in Asia to be of overwhelming relevance: the concept of 'localization', in the sense in which it has recently been applied to inter-civilizational dialogue, i.e. 'selective' learning about Europe in Asia, according to a dialectic of local preferences; a logic of appropriateness; and regional relevance. In this context, the recent work, in related contexts, by Acharya (2013) and others adapts seamlessly to the Europe–Asia context. I have found also that a social-constructivist approach to European Studies in Asia, with its focus on ideational structures constituting the work of modern institutions, remains the most persuasive theoretical grounding for the further development of the European Studies in Asia discipline.

In the middle-section chapters of this book, I have attempted to show that useful 'ideas' and 'values', to continue the process of mutual 'constitution' amongst the institutions of learning in East and West, do not exclusively emanate from the European Commission's and the EU's 'policy papers', 'Country Strategy Papers' and related documents of declaratory diplomacy – important as those, no doubt, are.

The analysis of the 'contemporary players' section in this book has found that there is a plethora of 'knowledge-multipliers' and think-tanks that are constantly engaged in contributing to the edifice of European Studies in Asia, as providers of resources, fora for discussion and intellectual repositories. The main reason that these – under-represented – actors are so valuable for the European Studies lecturer in Asia is that they are natural 'hubs', enabling those very processes by means of which European Studies curriculum development becomes a communal, 'co-constructed' activity, involving both learners and teachers, instead of a merely politically driven, top-down process maintained by the EU's embassies and cultural institutes in Asia. Thinking about what exactly European Studies in Asia is – and what it should be – therefore, becomes a more open, 'democratic' activity, using the creative 'cloud-thinking' of many diverse participants.

In addition to this, I have also sought to argue in the preceding pages that there are other, largely 'neglected' resources and aspects of European Studies in Asia that deserve to be moved to a much more 'central' position in the subject's pedagogical arsenal. My principle example has been the use of art, and the investigation of how the subjects of 'International Relations', 'Asia–Europe Relations' and 'European Studies in Asia' are represented in public 'blockbuster' exhibitions, as well as in many smaller displays, shows and gallery-spaces across Asia and Europe.

I am claiming in the pages of this book that a closer look at this 'pictorial' aspect of East–West exchange is long overdue, and that it has been surprising to see that this has not so far found entry into the mainstream curriculum in European Studies in Asia – especially as so many of these exhibitions and representations were organized to coincide with significant 'political' developments in Asia–Europe (or Asia–EU) relations, such as the Asia–Europe Meetings and the 'celebrations' of anniversaries of relations between Asian countries and EU Member States. Extending European Studies in Asia into this, more visual, field can also begin to determine future research agendas – for example, by complementing the work that has already been undertaken in respect to how Europe and Asia 'perceive' one another through media-reports and similar agenda-setting phenomena (e.g. Holland *et al.*, 2007).

Last, but by no means least, I have continued in this book what I started in my last one (Wiessala, 2011): the inclusion of three chapters on my own experience with the teaching of European Studies in Asia has still been a relatively new intellectual undertaking, but I have found that it was more than worth it when coming to think about what the multi-layered, 'interdisciplinary discipline' of European Studies in Asia actually is, and how it unfolds 'on the ground', or 'in the field' if you like. I have been very lucky in benefiting from teaching experience, mostly towards young adults and some mature learners, across (South East) Asia, and in New Zealand and Australia.

I have encountered vastly different conditions framing the 'how' and the 'why', and the nuts and bolts of teaching European Studies in Asia. In some of the places in which I have taught and otherwise worked, the discipline was strongly linked to a small cluster of motives for bringing 'Europe' to Asia; most of them had to do with enabling people in the host society to make contact and do business with, and travel to, Europe and the EU. In many cases, the European Studies teaching agenda was, thus, no more than a European *Union* Studies programme. In an equal number of examples, it had become more than that, on account of visionary centres and personalities, as well as pedagogically gifted Professors and lecturers. In some countries in which European Studies is being taught with a strong emphasis on human rights and civil liberties, this is not really needed; in other countries where it is badly needed, the human rights flavour has been forfeited on the altar of business.

The chapters on contemporary layers and players and on teaching experience are also intended to provide a reflection of socio-political conditions and limitations framing the planning, 'validation' and delivery of European Studies courses in Asia. On more than one occasion, I have found that, with the best will in the world, it was not possible to get messages across political and cultural divides, and it was tricky to live up to the image of an academic ambassador for the EU in Asia.

Some of what I experienced has made me think about the possible need for the EU to link its educational exchange and cooperation funding initiatives much more strongly and coherently with human rights concerns, on the one hand, and with the teaching agenda for European Studies in Asia on the other hand. In at least one case, I have encountered a deep conflict between desirable teaching content in the discipline and quite unjustifiable, systemic educational discrimination in the host country, which clearly runs counter to everything the EU's policies on education and human rights stand for.

Beyond these concerns, however, what I have taken from the teaching of Europe in Asia, and from the many interviews countless students of European Studies, in Asia, were generous enough to give me time for, is that by far the most neglected sources of inspiration for curriculum development in this area, and the most valuable resources pertaining to how the subject should develop, are the learners themselves. I have, therefore, in this book repeatedly tried to stress those examples, processes, teaching experiences and publications which have been premised on the assumption of a more learner-centred approach to European Studies in Asia, and on the powerful idea of instructors and students 'co-constructing' the timetable and the curriculum.

I find that this has tallied with some of the findings concerning the role of 'non-traditional' institutions and associations in building European Studies curricula (see above). It also links strongly with the work going on in those centres, training frameworks and institutions which I have afforded a particular emphasis to in this book – for example, the National Centre for Research on Europe in New Zealand and the European Institute for Public Administration in Europe. It has, of course, been very attractive, and intellectually stimulating, to compare such geographically distant seats of learning, and I have found that geographical distance is dead, the tyranny thereof is vanquished and air-miles do not equate, anywhere I looked, with mental detachment to Europe and Asia.

I wish to conclude these conclusions by gathering up the threads of one more theme I have attempted to pepper the pages of this book with in a number of places: one cannot really research the teaching of the theory and practice of a discipline like European Studies in Asia without constant reminders of the many wider changes in the international Higher Education landscape. In collecting the material for this book, and in interviewing staff and students at many universities across the globe, I could not help but notice that some of these universities were 'branch campuses' of European (US or Australian) mother institutions in Asia. This was just one development of many which throws into stark relief the 'globalized' nature of our discipline. Such pedagogic challenges, as there are inherent in such seemingly unstoppable phenomena like 'internationalization', 'commoditization', 'managerialization' and a host of other '-izations', will need of course to be progressively built into any future European Studies in Asia curriculum. That goes without question.

As I hope the chapters of this book have amply demonstrated, however, it has also been one of my strong concerns also to introduce a number of question-marks in connection with this, and in relation to the European Studies in Asia discipline. Working, for the same book, on such diverse topics as the ancient University of Nālandā, the conclusion of an *EU Joint Declaration on Higher Education with Central Asia* and teaching 'Europe and Asia' to the EU *corps diplomatique*, the public in New Zealand and the ambitious generation of enthusiastic postgraduate students of Malaysia, I feel I have encountered the best and the worst of 'Europe' and 'European Higher Education' in Asia. The best, as in a much stronger disciplinary focus on how European models can inspire ASEAN, how ASEF can facilitate much-needed inter-faith dialogue and how the European Commission can be an educational force for good in the Asian region.

On the other hand, it seems to me that many universities in Australasia are just a little too eager to replicate the worst mistakes and excesses currently committed in the UK, the US, Australia and, to a somewhat lesser degree, in Continental Europe. I have attempted to include such a relatively wide spectrum as regards the teaching of 'Europe' in Asia in this book, just because so many perspectives in international Higher Education are now so very narrow, in their foci on (Higher) education as a 'tradeable product', their emphasis on vacuous notions of 'employability' and 'excellence' and their obsession with meaningless rankings and league tables. I contend, nevertheless, that all these are present now in Asia, and are very definitely here to stay – sometimes with a four or five-year 'jet lag' when compared to Europe.

I would like to close by taking inspiration from the Buddha in exhorting his followers to always see for themselves whether or not his doctrine was suitable for them and for their communities, and to always endeavour to strike a middle way, the path between extremes, in humankind's search for learning, advancement and enlightenment. It is with sincere gratitude to my students and to my colleagues in East and West that I dedicate this book to them and offer for further debate what I have been finding.

Georg Wiessala
29 October 2013

Appendices

Appendix 1 The European revelation of Asia and the odyssey of the Orient: selected Portuguese writings on the East

In the Portuguese network of writings on Asia in this period, there are many gems. The *Universal History of China* by **Álvaro Semedo** (1586–1658), the first Portuguese Jesuit Procurator-General in China, represents a link between the Jesuit letter-reports and some larger 'Asian' publication projects. Semedo's book is unique: its author was the first European to describe the preparation and benefits of tea as a beverage, creating a Portuguese account with global ramifications which are still felt today. The *Suma Oriental* (*Sum of the Orient*, 1512–1516) by **Tomé Pires**, a Lisbon apothecary and ambassador for the Portuguese Crown to the Ming Court, is a key account of plants, markets and politics in maritime Asia (Villier, 1998: 120–121; Gordon, 2008: 157–175). The volume was kept secret in the *Casa da Índia* and was not published until 1550, and then only with Italian help. Notwithstanding this, this text is distinctive because of its information on South East Asia and on the lands, people and products of the time (Lach and Van Kley, 1994, Vol. I, Book 1: 339; Laven, 2011: 10). Pires, although not an enlightened thinker on matters of race or religion, had an advanced understanding of the international relations of his time, although, notably, not of local history, regional loyalties and family rivalries (Gordon, 2008: 165). 'Whoever is lord of Malacca', wrote Pires in 1516, 'has his hand at the throat of Venice' (Garnier, 2004, 68). Alfonso de Albuquerque took Malacca in 1511 the remnants of the Lusitanian fortress *A Formosa* are still a tourist draw of modern Malacca (not far from Kuala Lumpur in Malaysia).

The memoir-cum-travelogue *Peregrinaçao* (formerly spelled *Peregrinaçam*, 1614) of the prosperous merchant **Fernão Mendes Pinto** furnished Europeans with an 'amalgam of truth and fiction' (Foss and Lach, 1991: 171). His book has sometimes been called the 'Odyssey of the Orient' (Howgego, 2009: 92). In it, Pinto reports with matchless detail on the many realms then largely unknown in Europe, such as Burma, Siam and parts of South East Asia. Although, as Smithies (1997: 72) argues, Siam 'may not have been central to Mendes Pinto's wanderings in the East' he wrote about Ayutthaya, the Siamese capital (the *Venice of* *the East*, in his words). It was home to a sizeable Portuguese settlement, including a Portuguese gun foundry, and the Portuguese cemetery there can still be visited. Villiers (1998: 120) claims that Pinto's work is the only sixteenth-century secular travel book about Asia, in either Portuguese or Spanish, which contains information on countries such as Siam. Moreover, Newitt (2009: 77) argues that it was Mendes Pinto who first 'used the device' – which was to be copied by Enlightenment writers like Montesquieu in his *Persian Letters* (*Lettres Persanes*) – of using 'fictional Eastern characters to voice the most bitter criticisms of the conduct of his countrymen' (see also Lee, 1991a: 171). Mendes Pinto also unveiled Japan to Europe, introducing, in 1549, a Japanese refugee to Francis Xavier, who, 'with Pinto's support, went on to found the first Christian mission in Japan' (Howgego, 2009: 92). No other Iberian text on Asia enjoyed comparable dissemination (Foss and Lach, 1991: 170; Lach and Van Kley, 1994, Vol. II, Book 1: 65–66; Vol. 3, Book. 1: 324–325).

Damião de Góis (1502–1574) has already been described as the main chronicler and propagandist of Portuguese colonialism. He was a passionate Erasmus scholar, poet and musician, as well as an occasional diplomat for João III of Portugal. He wrote extensively about the East, and his text on India, *Commentarii rerum gestarum in India 1538 citra Gangem* (1539), was praised by his contemporaries because it did not perpetuate the 'fantasies about the East perpetrated upon an unsuspecting public by the fabricators of Antiquity' (Lach and Van Kley, 1994, Vol. II, Book 2: 22). He was, however, also one of the high-profile cases under scrutiny from the Portuguese Inquisition (Newitt, 2009: 119). The chronicler **João de Barros** worked from home, as it were, within the confines of the *Casa da Índia* in Lisbon. His extensive collections and writings on the geography, cartography and ethnography of numerous Asian regions were used for, and edited in, his main work, *Décadas da Asia* (*Decades of Asia*, 1539–1615; Lach and Van Kley, 1994, Vol. II, Book 1: 10; Villiers, 1998: 120–121). His work includes early descriptions of the Ayutthaya kingdom and Siam, whose extent he described as *participa de dois mares* ('having a share of both seas', i.e. the Bat of Bengal in the West and the South China Sea to the East) (Chapter 1). Newitt (2009: 76) describes the *Décadas* as 'not just a chronicle of warlike deeds but a vast compendium, an encyclopaedia almost, of the knowledge the Portuguese had acquired'. On the Chinese, de Barros claimed that 'in this pagan people there are all the things which Greeks and Romans are praised for'. Sentiments like this one gave rise to a certain degree of relativism in European thought vis-à-vis China (Demel, 1991: 49). Last but not least, **Duarte Barbosa**, a secretary to the Portuguese factory in the Indian port of Cannanore from around 1500 to 1517, authored his key text on Asia in 1518. His *Livro em que da relação do que viu e ouviou no Oriente* (unsurprisingly knows as *The Book*) was considered to be a key authority on Portuguese India and Siam for centuries. However, not unlike the text by Tomé Pires, it was long kept under lock and key (Lach and Van Kley, 1994, Vol. I, Book 1: 170, 226). It was only published from the mid-sixteenth century onwards.

Appendix 2 P. Adam Schall Germanus, I. Ordinis Mandarinus

I have previously considered the German Jesuit Johann Adam Schall von Bell, SJ (T'ang Jo-wang, Tang Ruowang 1592–1666) – a son of Cologne – as a 'symbolic' figure in China–Europe relations (Wiessala, 2011: 35). However, as a missionary, mathematician and astronomer, Schall, who left for the East in 1618, can also stand for European pedagogies in Asia and for West–East knowledge transfer in general, including the ambiguous inter-dependencies of learning and politics. Schall volunteered for the East, and he achieved fame in the Asian missionary field for a number of reasons. He has become, arguably, one of the key Jesuit icons of all time.

The figure of Schall can also be a key to understanding that knowledge – in this case, astronomical knowledge – is often politicized (Laven, 2011: 130). There can be little doubt that Schall was a committed and effective teacher, perhaps a precursor of European Studies pedagogy in Asia today, in a number of ways: first, he integrated his own training, most notably by employing and expanding the Jesuit *modus Parisiensis*, betraying a strong pedagogic preference for teaching through debate, disputation and competition in the unique Jesuit mode, which he often employed vis-à-vis his colleagues of other faiths (Wright, 2005: 51) – perhaps this would be called 'research-informed teaching' today. Second, Schall had 'transferable' skills and embodied Jesuit opportunism.

Clements (2005: 94) cites a good example:

> rumour had it in Beijing that Christianity was a 'lucky charm' in the (palace-) household, and that those concubines who accepted Schall's alien God had enjoyed greater success in the imperial bedchamber. It was not exactly what the Pope had in mind when he sent missionaries to the Far East, but the Jesuits were a pragmatic order, and would try anything to get their message across, even if the message lost a little in translation.

Third, Schall also made use of what, in today's parlance, would be called 'interactive' and 'blended' learning, integrating into the Jesuit classroom religious art, iconography, imagery and narrative, and regaling his disciples with stories about Galileo's telescope. This anecdotal style reveals that Schall tried to impress by Western science, carrying with it the political and religious assumptions and subtexts of the day, in terms of conversion and European pre-eminence. Fourth, Schall used his strong personality-derived and persuasive skills, even with courtiers close to the Emperor, as Clements' anecdote shows.

In terms of tangible career achievements, Schall managed to refine the Chinese calendar, based on exactly those new ideas of heliocentricity and astronomy which had enabled European Jesuits to contribute to the Gregorian calendar reforms 'at home' and, at long last, to 'fix' the date for Easter in the year 1582. Moreover, in 1626, Schall published his book *Yuanjing shuo (On the Telescope*), introducing the instrument to China. Although he is said to have stopped short of discussing heliocentricity (Wright, 2005: 195), his cartographic work was groundbreaking. By reforming the Chinese imperial calendar and by predicting solar eclipses in 1629 and 1644, he 'clinched his position' (Ross, 1994: 169).

At the same time, his actions helped to consolidate the legitimacy of the Qing Emperor. In his book on the history of the Jesuits in China (*Historica Narratio de Initio et Progressu Missionis Societatis Jesu apud Chinenses*, 1665), he explicitly defended his use of science for the cause of religious orthodoxy (Brockey, 2007: 154). He became a *Mandarin of the 1st Order*. He is often depicted, in full regalia, astronomical instruments in hand, world map behind him, in Jesuit artworks and book illustrations (Reed and Demattè, 2007: 15, 17; BWB, 2009: 10, 43). Eventually, and reluctantly, Schall became the head of the Chinese Bureau of Astro-Calendrical Sciences (*Qintianjian zheng*) in 1646. Clements (2005: 146) points out the irony in this; an irony that would not have been lost on Schall himself: 'he was talked into this by his fellow Jesuits, and found himself, at the age of sixty, becoming the chief vizier of China's heathen religion'.

More controversially, Father Schall also offered his knowledge of military designs and artillery to the Ministry of War. Obeying an imperial decree, he built a cannon foundry in Beijing, redesigned the city's fortifications and fought battles with the Dutch and Portuguese in Macao and Beijing (Wills, 2011a: 135). Waley-Cohen (2000: 119) shows that military hardware designs by Schall and his successors were used in China until the Opium Wars in the nineteenth century. His military know-how protected Schall's position at a time of dynamic, dynastic transition from the Ming to the Qing. But his activities made him enemies among his indigenous, neo-Confucian colleagues like Yang Guangxian (1597–1669), Schall's arch-nemesis (Ross, 1994: 156, 172–173; Hsia, 1998: 190; Wiessala, 2011: 35–36; Witek, 2011: 139). His detractors' machinations put Schall and others on trial for treason in 1665. His death sentence was commuted as a consequence of an earthquake and conflagration, interpreted as ill omens by some – and saving Schall's skin. Schall remained in China for almost 50 years and passed on in 1666.

The final word on him comes from a modern perspective: Joachim Kurtz draws, from Schall's biography, some wider inferences about knowledge:

> Knowledge is never a mere commodity. Perspectives on its meaning, value, uses, and capacities undergo frequent shifts and are almost always contested. In its diverse forms – discursive and embodied, practical and esoteric, open and secret – knowledge can become an object of desire, indifference, or revulsion. As such, it is appropriated, exploited, domesticated, molded, ignored, or rejected by concrete agents acting in specific circumstances; at the same time, it is inevitably embedded in larger structures of power, habitus, and convention that it helps to legitimate, stabilize, or subvert.

And Kurtz concludes:

> When knowledge is set in motion, the intricacies of its formation and reconfiguration are thrown into particularly sharp relief. Knowledge travels in multiple ways. Most conspicuously, it is transported and shared, voluntarily or involuntarily, by traders, migrants, missionaries, itinerant scholars, pilgrims, professionals, and other individuals or groups that cross boundaries of language and culture; it also moves as encoded in texts, attached to objects, or embodied in social and cultural practices. In some instances, it enters the trading zones and borderlands in which people and ideas meet in decontextualized fragments, in others it is presented as (part of) an integrated system. In either case, it becomes a site of multilayered and extended negotiations that affect both the contexts of its arrival and departure in unexpected, and often, unintended ways.
> (Source: www.asia-europe.uni-heidelberg.de/de/lehre/summerschool/archive/ss10/concept.html)

More reading suggestions on Schall: Saraiva and Jami (2008), Wiessala (2011: 36).

Appendix 3 The *sankin kôtai* system; stability, balance and constraint

Measures like the *koku* survey were followed, from around 1635–1639, by the perfecting of a 'rural-elite buddy-system'[1] of centralized feudalism, which had originally been developed in the *Sengoku* ('Warring States') period. Tokugawa Ieyasu decreed an alternate-attendance (*sankin kôtai*) system, which required the up to 300 regional commanders (*daimyō*) tied to him by bonds of fealty, to commute, with their entire retinues, between their fiefdom homes and the capital every other year.[2] *Daimyō* were organized into 'even' and 'odd' years, in order not to 'empty' regions of their lords. Limited exceptions to the dual residency rule applied to lords with vital duties at home, such as coastal defence or jurisdiction (Hiroshi, 2006: 70–73). The *daimyō* families remained in Edo permanently, as quasi-hostages to the government (Gordon, 2003: 14).

The implementation of this system has been interpreted as a 'civilizing' force. It temporarily separated regional retainers from their power-bases, enforced loyalty and mobility, placed heavy financial burdens on local lords, discouraged major dissent and drained *daimyō* wealth. This produced a new, urbanized Edo populace which was more than 60 per cent male (Nishiyama, 1997: 37, 41), enabling the conditions for the 'night-less city' of the *Yoshiwara* entertainment district, by which so much of the art of the period was broadly inspired. Moreover, the *sankin kôtai* structure contributed to the diffusion of a 'common', 'upper-class' Edo culture, national consciousness and introduction of 'foreign' ideas, via *rangaku*, into most of the Japanese provinces, by means of the amount of travel it necessitated. The herbalist, playwright and *rōnin* (masterless *samurai*)

Hiraga Gennai (1729–1780), for example, when in Edo, encountered people from the Akita domain (Masanobu, 1978: Chs 5 and 8; Plutschow, 2006: 126; Roberts, 2009: 67), who invited him back home to teach them how to paint in oil in the 'Western' style. Among them were Satake Shozan (1748–1785), the Lord of Akita, and Ōtsuki Gentaku (1757–1827).

This exchange gave birth to an entire sub-genre of Dutch painting – Akita Ranga (秋田蘭画). The system connected Edo to the rest of Japan through highways, which became channels of infrastructure, inspirations for the art of the period, locales for travelling artists, byways of national tourism and pilgrimage, and conduits for the dissemination of popular culture. Nishiyama (1997: 113, 228–250) finds more than 100 types of traditional performing artists among the travellers of this time. The most important route was the *Tōkaidō* ('Eastern Sea Road'), dotted with inns and post towns, and linking the government in Edo with Kyoto, seat of the imperial house. The arrangement worked both ways, conveying many local and regional produce, and ideas, into the urban centres. The *sankin kôtai* system may thus be seen as a kind of glue, connecting the entire country. Hobson (2004: 90) has claimed that the strategy mirrored the one adopted by European rulers, executing their own programmes of centralization.

More detail at: www.nakasendoway.com/?page_id=144; www.pbs.org/empires/japan/resources_4.html; the *Samurai Archive* series of podcasts has an idiosyncratic contribution at: http://samuraipodcast.com/ep58-an-introduction-to-sankin-kotai.

Appendix 4 The class system and the politics of art in Edo period popular culture

The four-tier Tokugawa social pyramid (Dunn, 1972) was based on birth, on group dynamics and on individuals' 'value' to society. The top-tier *samurai* were followed by the *peasants*, who acted as essential food suppliers to the former. In third place came the *artisans*. Near the bottom rung – in stark contrast to Europe at the same time – were the urban bourgeoisie; the merchants, who, with the artisans, were known as *chōnin* ('townspeople'). Merchants were not seen as providing 'productive labour'. Outcasts (*eta*, lit.: 'filth') were the untouchables.

In *The Politics of Art in Edo Culture*, Katsuya Hirano argues that art, popular entertainment, parody and theatre (*kabuki*, see: Bullen *et al.*, 2009: 24–32) was seen by the Tokugawa *bakufu* as 'immoral', antithetical to the virtues of economic thrift and a kind of urban disease which mocked, destabilized and disrespected the established social order and needed to be prevented, at all cost, from spreading to the countryside and from 'vulgarizing' established culture and religion. It has been argued that, in officially constructed Tokugawa ideology, the strong philosophical emphasis on learning meant predominantly cultivating one's mind and understanding one's place in society. Leisure, pleasure and play, by contrast, were seen as endangering the 'eternal' Confucian values of 'loyalty', 'propriety', 'hierarchy' and 'virtuousness', and official government policy did all it could to contain the hybridization, or inter-mingling, of 'high' and 'low' culture, city entertainments and countryside.

The Tokugawa regime's anxieties seem to have extended to painting, and Hirano employs the term 'dialogical imagination' to contend that many social actors and artists of this period used prevailing discourses about learning, the class system and art, in order to engage in contestations with the regime and its official state authority of separating 'high' and 'low' cultural spheres. The *Rangaku* movement[3] fits into this context of new forms of discourse over the values of knowledge and the culture of the ruling class. It also chimes with the emerging erosion of status hierarchies, the transgression of social boundaries and the commingling of people of various backgrounds, through the vehicle of a new 'hybrid culture' and 'imported' art in this Japanese period of emerging heterogeneous, dynamic values (see also: Lee, 1983: 188–189; Bullen *et al.*, 2009).

Download: www.international.ucla.edu/asia/podcasts/article.asp?parentid=93558 (podcast of a seminar on this topic at UCLA Asia Institute).

Appendix 5 Chinese Zhu Xi thought and its influence on Japanese intellectuals of the Edo period

Zhu Xi, whose prolific writings were well known to Western philosophers, such as Leibnitz, commented on the set of ethical values embodied in the Confucian classics, especially the *Four Books* and *Five Classics* (Nosco, 1997: 23; Huang, 1999: 139–140)[4] Zhu Xi framed his ontology in terms of 'reason' (*ri*), 'vital force' (*qi*) and the triad of a 'supreme ultimate' (or: 'heaven', 'principle', *li*), 'earth' and 'humankind' (Ellwood, 2008: 159).

His educational philosophy stressed tenets such as hierarchy, moral rectitude, 'practical learning', 'self-cultivation', 'personal virtue', 'motivation' and the 'investigation of things' (*ge wu*), an approach some have compared to the method of scientific enquiry of Francis Bacon (1561–1626; Huang, 1999: 137–138, 141; Tillman, 1982: 143–152; Bellah, 1985: 76; Xinzhong, 2000: 133; De Bary *et al.*, 2006: 98). Memorably, Tillman (1982: 152) characterizes Zhu Xi in a way that ought to act as a stark warning to today's decision-makers and curriculum planners: 'Standards or ideals built upon a preoccupation with results, advantages and utility would only pervert the moral sensitivity of later generations and destroy the foundation of real accomplishment.' Nosco (1997: 6) suggests that:

> the joy of the Chu His [*sic*] mode of thought was that it was both scholarly and spiritual; while it emphasised the quasi-scientific examination of the external world, it nonetheless provided for the development of the individual mind, recognising the spiritual dimensions of such development.

De Bary (1998: 17, 20; Twiss, 1998, 41–42) finds the keynote of Zhu thought in the concept of 'dedicated service of the Confucian noble man, totally at the service of the public good, and defiant of all despots', and the idea of 'individual perfectibility' and 'self-cultivation of the leadership elite'; and Ellwood (2008: 159) condenses:

> acceptance of one's role – parents over children, husband over wife, older brother over younger brother; one's social rank and one's duties as a subject of the state, with mutual obligations all around – is simply like accepting gravity. To reject them is to go against nature, which can only bring dire consequences.

It was through both Chinese philosophers like Chu Hsi and Wang Yang Ming (1472–1525), and Japanese scholars such as Hayashi Razan (1583–1657) and Kaibara Ekken (alt.: 'Ekiken', 1630–1714), that *shushigaku* ('Zhu Xi Learning') grew into an official moral 'code of the shōgunate' (Xinzhong, 2000: 129; Goodman, 2000: 165; Ellwood, 2008: 160). Waley-Cohen (2000: 58) suggests that this 'Japanized' neo-Confucian value-philosophy was, at times, more metaphysical than Confucianism: it 'laid particular emphasis on moral strength, the pursuit of self-cultivation through education and study, and on public-spirited activism'.

De Bary *et al.* (2006: 97) assert that the writings of Kaibara Ekken, in particular, are a call to more active engagement in socio-political affairs, informed by empirical-rationalist enquiry. Plutschow (2006: 34) cites Ekken's core belief that 'knowledge should be made useful to the public and should improve life' – i.e. by its practical application, rather than theoretical sophistication (see also: Bellah, 1985: 17).

Moreover, Xinzhong (2000: 132) claims that the 'practical dimensions of Confucianism were emphasised in Tokugawa Japan, at the expense of its more philosophical deliberations'. Indeed, the utilitarian ethic of 'end-results' and the questions of 'good government' and 'political ethics' have framed much of the debate about Zhu Xi (e.g. Tillman, 1982: 133–142). As a compromise, De Bary *et al.* (2006, 40) recommend that 'there is in Zhu Xi a kind of positivism that affirms the reality of things and the validity of objective study'. Some analysts find, however, that Tokugawa governments did not, in fact, promote a single orthodoxy, blending instead the teachings of Japanese Confucianism into a more 'instrumentalist ideology' (Collcutt, 1993: 131).

Appendix 6 Samurai William

The ship decorated with wood-carvings by Dutch humanist Desiderius Erasmus (1466–1536) was famously piloted by the Englishman William Adams (1564–1620), the 'first known Englishman to see Japan' (Ellwood, 2008: 157). Adams was born in Gillingham, Kent. When young, he had been apprenticed to one Nicholas Diggins of Limehouse on the Thames, so that he may learn the arts of shipbuilding and navigation (Farrington, 2002: 42). He initially participated in early Dutch expeditions to the Arctic, in order to explore the fabled *North East Passage*. In terms of his connections with Japan, Adams's colourful life story has been famously fictionalized in James Clavell's *Shōgun* (1975).

The key threads of his biography were taken up more recently in Giles Milton's novel *Samurai William* (Milton, 2002). Sentenced to death at first, Adams later became a trusted foreign policy adviser to Tokugawa Ieyasu. He was later made a *daimyō*, and allocated a fief, 'on which lived eighty to ninety husbandmen', something, as Adams himself observed, never been granted to any foreigner (Lach and Van Kley, 1994, Vol. III, Book 4: 1850; van der Cruysse, 2002a: 55–56). Japanese trade with the West continued to exist, to a significant degree, on account of Adams's solid and fruitful relationship with Tokugawa Ieyasu. Adams was also one of the first Europeans to 'go native', taking a Japanese wife. He described his journey and life in Japan in his two sets of letters – one, private, sent to his wife and one, official, in the collection to the English East India Company.

His writings, however, have so far not been seen as a rich resource on Tokugawa Japan, and analysts such as Lach have generally found that they contain 'disappointingly little about Japan and the Japanese' (Lach and Van Kley, 1994, Vol. III, Book 1: 558).In Japan, Adams was also known as 'Miura Anjin', or 'Anjin Sama' ('Mr Pilot'). William Adams's fortunes continue to exert a powerful influence on the European imagination, as the theatre bill for a 2013 show at Sadler's Wells in London shows (www.independent.co.uk/arts-entertainment/theatre-dance/reviews/anjin-the-shogun-and-the-english-samurai-sadlers-wells-london-8481737.html). Many facets of the life of Adams, as interpreted in both works of art and various biographies, show striking parallels with the experiences of the Cologne-born Jesuit Johannes Adam Schall von Bell in China (Wiessala, 2011: 35–36; see Chapter 3).

Appendix 7 Watanabe Kazan, the 'frog in the well' and the 'risky' business of *Rangaku*

Shíba Kōkan's contact with Watanabe Kazan (1793–1841) is believed to have been of a very formative nature for him. Kazan, an impoverished *samurai* and avid collector of Dutch books, was the chief retainer in the small fief of Tawara (in modern Aichi prefecture) and a *bunjin* – an amateur scholar-painter, portraitist and draughtsman (Lee, 1983: 166–168). His life story stands out because he was made to suffer for his interests in *rangaku*. Guth (1996: 124) points out that his association with Shíba Kōkan and a group of like-minded intellectuals dedicated to Western learning conflicted with the shōgun's politics and personal grievances of the day and led to his arrest in 1839, his incarceration for sedition and his eventual ritual suicide. This, one consequence of *bansha no goku*: the increasing, systematic, suppression of the *rangakusha* by the government. Goodman (2000: 205), Lee (1983: 200) and Plutschow (2006: 284) are united in concluding that it was the Kazan affair which helped to place those Japanese Dutch scholars, who were disaffected by the increasingly isolationist foreign policies of the shōgunate, under stricter surveillance; many of their voices were stifled and cut off.

Amongst the written output on the West by Watanabe Kazan, his works *Gekizetsuwakumon* ('Dialogues with Foreigners'), *Shinkiron* ('Restraint in

Critical Times') and *Seiyo Jijosho* ('Conditions of the West') are notable, on account of his perspicacious commentary of the international relations of the day, and as regards Japan's place in the world. Keene (2006: 2) finds that Kazan:

> wrote harshly about run-of-the-mill Confucian scholars, who – shutting their eyes to Japan's position in the world – refused to admit that anything could be learned from the West. He declared, 'Only the Confucian scholars have a conscience, but they are of shallow aspirations and choose the small, not the great.' He likened them to the frog in the well who knows nothing of the ocean.

Keene (2006: 135) points out that Kazan deployed the expression 'seia' ('the frog in the well') repeatedly, in order to characterize the Japanese.

Goodman (2000: 210) argues that one of the hallmarks of this group of *rangakusha* was their preference for a Japanese foreign policy which combined diplomatic negotiation, intensive study and adaptation, lest Japan be overwhelmed by foreign states knocking at the Japanese door. As far as Kazan is concerned, his immediate impact was limited. Keene (2006: 232) concludes that, 'only in retrospect did Kazan's advocacy of opening Japan to the knowledge of the world acquire importance; he came to be seen as a martyr to this cause'.

Guth makes a related point when she argues that Kazan and his group rejected the artistic orthodoxies of the day, turning instead to *rangaku* and other alternatives, not on stylistic but on social grounds, 'as part of a rational quest for historical and empirical knowledge that might contribute to national political and social reform'; and Plutschow (2006: 283–284) calls Kazan 'a pragmatist, more interested in solving the immediate problems of his country', who advocated the 'adoption of western "know-how" in order to solve Japan's problems'. This pragmatism can be said to have been representative of the overall views of many of the scholar-artists and intellectuals of the time towards Europe (see also Appendix 9: *Dutch, Germans and Swedes in Tokugawa Japan*).

Appendix 8 Intellectual exchange: original works and translations by prominent *Rangaku* scholars, and some examples of Western texts available to them

Arai Hakuseki (1657–1725): *Sairanigen* ('Collection of Strange Things', 1708); *Seiyo kibun* ('Report on the Occident', 1713).
Hiraga Gennai: *Butsurui hinchoku/hinshitsu* ('Classification of Plants and Minerals', 1763); *Hyakko jijutsu* ('Translation of Schouwtoneel der Natuur', above, 1763).
Sugita Genpaku: *Kaitai shinsho* ('New Book on Anatomy', 1774); *Rangaku kotōhajijme* (*Rangaku jishi*; 'Origins of Rangaku', or: 'The Dawn of Western Science in Japan', 1815) (Ranzaburō, 1964: 269–270; Goodman, 2000: 83–84; Horiushi, 2003: 150, 165ff.; Keene, 2006: 30).
Ōtsuki Gentaku: *Rangaku kaitai* ('A Ladder to Dutch Learning', 'First Steps in

Dutch', 1788); *Ransetsu benwaku* ('Clarification of Misunderstandings in Theories of the Dutch', 1799).

Satake Shozan: *Gahōkōryō (*'Summary of the Laws of Drawing'*)*; *Gazu [Gato] rikai* ('On the Understanding of Painting and Drawing').

Shíba Kōkan: *Sayū Ryodan* ('Story of a Western Journey', 1794); *Sayū Nikki* ('Diary of a Western Journey', 1815); *Seiyōga Dan [Seijō Gwadan]* ('Discussion of Western Painting', 1799); *Seiyōga Hō* ('Principles of Western Painting'); *Kōkan kōkaidi* ('Record of Kōkan's Regrets' [or: Repentances], 1799); *Oranda tensetsu* (1796); *Oranda tsūhaku* (1805/1808); *Kepler Tenmon Zukai, Kopperu temmon zukai* (1808) (the latter are rare astronomical writings; Boxer, 1968: 57; 112; Masanobu, 1978: 74) (source: Johnson, 2005, esp. Chapters 2 and 4; see also: www.ndl.go.jp/nichiran/e/list.html).

Caspar Bartholin: *Ontleedkundige Tafelen*; *Anatomicae Institutiones Corporis Humani* (Goodman, 2000: 84).

Volcher Coiter: *Externarum et internarum principalium humani corporis partium tabulae.*

Rembertus Dodonaeus: *Cruyd-Boek/Cruijdeboek* ('A New History of Plants', 1554) (Michel, 2007: 289)

Jan Jonston (Johannis Jonstonus): *Naeuwkeurige Beschryving van de Natuur der Vier-voetige Dieren, Vogelen, Kronkel-Dieren, Slangen en Draken* ('Natural History of Quadrupeds').

Johannes Adam Kulmus: *OntleedkundigeTafelen/Anatomische Tabellen/Tafel Anatomia* (1725) (Ranzaburō, 1964: 266)

Govard (Govert) Bidloo: *Ontleeding des Menschelyken Lichaams/Anatomia Humani Corporis* ('Human Anatomy', 1685).

Gerard de Lairesse: *Het Groot Schilderboek* ('The Great Book of Painting/Painters' Book', 1707).

Jan Luyken: *Spiegel van het menselykbedryf* ('Mirror of Human Trades', 1694).

Joseph Moxon: *Practical Perspective*, or: *Perspective Made Easie* (1690).

Ambroise Paré: *De Chirurgieende Opera van alle de Wercken* (1649).

Noël-Antoine Pluche: *Schouwtoneel der Natuur, of Samenspraaken over de bysonderheden der natuurlyke historie* ('Spectacle of Nature, or Discourses on the Curiosities of Natural History', 1736).

Jan Swammerdam: *Historia Insectorum Generalis* ('General History of Insects', published 1682, in French).

Andreas Vesalius: *De Humani Corporis Fabrica* (1543).

Juan de Valverde de Amusco: *Vivae imagines partium corporis humani aeries formis expressae.*

Francis Willughby: *De Historia Piscium* ('The Study of Fish').

(Further examples in: Ranzaburō, 1964: 266–267 [medicine] and Johnson, 2005: Chapter 4 [some other areas])

Appendix 9 Dutch, Germans and Swedes in Tokugawa Japan

There are significant testimonies contributed by non-Dutch travellers and residents. Arguably the best-known source is the book *The History of Japan*, authored by German physician **Engelbert Kaempfer** (1651–1716), who worked on Deshima from 1690 onwards (Ranzaburō, 1964: 262–263; Keene, 2006: 18). Kaempfer's diary entries for the court journeys in 1691 and 1692 contain illustrations such as 'Dutch Audience with the Shōgun' (De Bary *et al.*, 2006: 292–295). Kaempfer is dismissive of the 'innumerable other monkey tricks' the Dutch were required – both by Japanese protocol and the shōgun's whims – to perform (Boxer, 1968: 128). Whatever 'antics' the Dutch may have been asked to execute, however, they would not have missed the political sub-text the hofreis was designed to underscore: the consolidation of a patron–client relationship along the same lines as the shōgun maintained with the other (approximately 250) daimyō (Goodman, 2000: 30).

The opperhoofd Jan Cock Blomhoff (1779–1853, at Deshima from 1817–1823) undertook embassies to Edo in 1818 and 1822, keeping a meticulous, 'official', diary, and also maintaining regular correspondence with his wife in Holland. Together with Engelbert Kaempfer's account, his writings are among the most interesting contemporary accounts we have of this journey. Kaempfer's book was published in English in 1727, by Sir Hans Sloane, the founder of the British Museum (BM). According to the BM's own displays (in 2013), Kaempfer's book became a first, systematic source of information about Japan in the Europe of the time. It is still widely used as a key text on Tokugawa Japan. Kaempfer's accounts of the annual court journey are among the liveliest descriptions of Japan of this time (De Bary *et al.*, 2006: 292–295).

In addition to Kaempfer's *History*, there were the writings of Swedish botanist **Carl Pieter Thunberg** (1743–1828), who stayed from 1775 (Boxer, 1968: 51; Keene, 2006: 19–20) and the (seven-volume) collection *Nippon – Archiv zur Beschreibung von Japan und dessen Neben- und Schutzländern*, by **Philipp Franz von Siebold** (1796–1866).[5] Although of German extraction, von Siebold was the Dutch Factory's medical officer from 1823 to 1829. Keene (1969: 126) sees his stay as pivotal to 'a brief new period of relations' between the Japanese and the Dutch; it ended with his expulsion in 1629.

Von Siebold was known to have exchanged maps and books with Japanese contacts – not always a risk-free endeavour, given the stringent Japanese laws of the time (Keene, 1969: 150–155). He is seen by some as having initiated medical education in Japan (Ranzaburō, 1964: 271). Von Siebold also befriended local artists, such as Kawahara (or Kawara) Keiga (1786–1860). As artist-in-residence on Deshima, Keiga, with the encouragement of von Siebold, produced paintings like *Court Procession, Portrait of the Opperhoofd Jan Cock Blomhoff and his Family* and *Dutchman and Servant*, in what is a European style (see: British Museum JA 1881.12–10.02758; Boxer, 1968: 103).

Appendix 10 The writing on the wall: foreigners and Europeans (*falang*) in Thai art

The foreign presence in Ayutthaya and the kingdom's relations with Western powers are strongly reflected in Thai sources such as the *Phraratcha Phongsawadan* ('The Annals of Ayut'ia', 'Royal Chronicles'), and – often in a strikingly lively manner – in the Thai art of the time. Many temple murals depict the Dutch, French or Portuguese as soldiers, merchants and visitors; and not just in what is known as the Ayutthaya-style of Thai art.[6] Peleggi (2013: 61) points out that Thai images of strangers were 'iconic', representing 'types', rather than individuals; types, moreover, who were shown with a range of standard iconographic traits. Moreover, Ringis (1990: 14) explores the Thai mural painting tradition of painting Europeans with a 'didactic' purpose: as part of the 'Demon Army' that assails the meditating Buddha-to-be, just prior to His Enlightenment. European *falang* (foreigners) were depicted as the 'Other' of the Thai 'native' version of (Theravada) Buddhism. In some murals, Europeans are seen to wear a curious *mélange* of European outfits and Buddhist attire. There is a tendency to depict Europeans in costumes of the past. For Peleggi (2013: 65), this 'archaizing exoticism' points to the fact that Ayutthaya art was 'naturalizing' and 'neutralizing' the foreigners, by integrating them into Thai cosmology as 'a benign rather than maleficent presence'. Ringis (1990: 100) links the representation of Europeans in old-fashioned clothes to the practice first adopted by the European Jesuits, to dress as Buddhist priests, in order to indicate status. This did not work in Siam, and not very well elsewhere either (see Chapter 3). Elsewhere, the most engaging examples of Europeans in Thai Buddhist art are the works of the Thai nineteenth-century painter Khrua In Khong. In Bangkok, murals depicting *falang* can be found in *Wat Phra Chetuphon* (*Wat Pho*). In *Wat Suwannaram*,[7] an unfortunate foreigner (in a Dutch hat) is still fighting. A range of foreign faces are found on the walls of the *Buddhaisawan* chapel (Van Beek and Tettoni, 1999: 38, 214–215; Garnier, 2004: 181, 185), while Chinese and Europeans populate *Wat Chong Nonsi* in Bangkok. On the lacquered panels of the scriptorium of *Suan Pakkad Palace*, a golden Thai interpretation of French troops in the uniforms of the age of Louis XIV stands out[8] (Leksukhum, 2000: 36–37, 64–65, 70, 93; Garnier, 2004: 185, also: 187–188). Other examples are in Bangkok's *Wat Bang Yi Khan* in Ayutthaya, Petchaburi, and in many other places throughout Thailand (cf: Ringis, 1990: 18; Peleggi, 2013: 57ff.).

Appendix 11 Contemporary European accounts of the Kingdom of Ayutthaya and related modern publications (see also the overall bibliography of this book)

Gervaise, Nicholas (1688) *Histoire Naturelle et Politique du Royaume de Siam*, Paris: Claude Barbin (cf: Trakulhun, 1997).
Hutchinson, E.W. (1940) *Adventurers in Siam in the Seventeenth Century*. London: Royal Asiatic Society. Repr. (1985) Bangkok: DO Books.

Jacques Hergoualc'h, Michel (1987) *Etude Historique et Critique du Livre de Simon de La Loubere 'Du Royaume de Siam'* (Paris, 1691). Paris: Editions Recherche sur les Civilisations.
La Loubère, Simon de (1691) *Du Royaume de Siam*, 2 vols. Paris: J.-B. Coignard (cf: Trakulhun, 1997).
La Loubère, Simon de (1693) *A New Historical Relation of the Kingdom of Siam*. London: T. Horne. Repr. (1969) as *The Kingdom of Siam*, Kuala Lumpur: Oxford University Press, and (1986) Bangkok: White Lotus.
Morden, Robert (1680) *Geography Rectified*. London: repr. for Robert Morden and Thomas Cockerill.
Placide, Reverend Père (1696). *Carte du Royaume de Siam et les Pays Circonvoisins*. Paris: Duval.
Schouten, Joost (1638) *Notitie van de Situatie, Regeeringe, Macht, Religie, Costumuyen, Traffijquen ende andere Remercquable Saecken des Coninghrijks Siam.* The Hague.
Tachard, Guy (1686) *Voyage de Siam des Peres Jesuites envoyes par le Roi aux Indes eta laChine*. Paris: Seneuze et Horthemels.
Tachard, Guy (1688) *A Relation of the Voyage to Siam [...]*. London: A. Churchil. Repr. (1981) Bangkok: White Orchid.
Vliet, Jeremias Van (1910) 'Beschrijving van het Koningrijk Siam' ('Description of the Kingdom of Siam'), *Journal of the Siam Society*, 7: 1–105.
Vliet, Jeremias Van (1975) *The Short History of the Kings of Siam*, ed. David K. Wyatt. Bangkok: The Siam Society.
Winichakul, Thongchai (1994) *Siam Mapped: A History of the Geo-body of a Nation*. Honolulu: University of Hawai'i Press.
(Sources: Smithies, 1995: 78; see also: Smithies, 1993: 129, for many further examples)

Appendix 12 A selection of exhibitions and museum displays on Europe–Asia relations

Asia in the Eyes of Europe: Sixteenth through Eighteenth Centuries, Department of Special Collections, the University of Chicago Library, 23 January–1 May, 1991. www.lib.uchicago.edu/e/su/southasia/lach.html

Red-haired Barbarians: The Dutch and Other Foreigners in Nagasaki and Yokohama, 1800–1865, International Institute of Social History, Amsterdam, The Netherlands. www.iisg.nl/exhibitions/japaneseprints/

Shiba Kokan hyakkaji (*Shiba Kokan – A Versatile Life*), Machida City International Woodblock Art Museum and the Kobe City Museum, 1996. www.worldcat.org/title/shiba-kokan-hyakka-jiten-oite-machida-shiritsu-kokusai-hanga-bijutsukan-1996-nen-8-gatsu-10-nichi-9-gatsu-23-nichi-oite-kobe-shiritsu-hakubutsukan-1996-nen-11-gatsu-2-nichi-12-gatsu-23-nichi/oclc/36698444

Tsingtao – A Chapter of German Colonial History in China. 1897–1914, German Historical Museum, Berlin, 27 March–23 June 1998. www.dhm.de/ausstellungen/tsingtau/tsingtau_e.html

Japanse Verwondering: Shiba Kōkan 1747–1818: Kunstenaar in de ban van het Westen (*Japanese Amazement: Artist under the Spell of the West*), Amsterdam Historisch Museum (now: Amsterdam Museum), 2000. www.amsterdammuseum.nl/

Rangaku – Western Sciences in Japan during the Edo Period, Arithmeum, Bonn, 22 June–16 July 2000. www.arithmeum.uni-bonn.de/en/events/33

Trading Places – The East India Company and Asia 1600–1835, British Library, London, 24 May–15 September 2002. www.bl.uk/onlinegallery/features/trading/world1.html; www.bl.uk/onlinegallery/features/trading/home.html

The Silk Road – Trade, Travel, War and Faith, British Library, London, from 7 May 2003. www.bl.uk/onlinegallery/features/silkroad/main.html (temporarily unavailable in December 2013)

Encounters – The Meeting of Asia and Europe 1500–1800, Victoria and Albert Museum, London, 23 September–5 December 2004 (International Conference: 12–13 November 2004). www.vam.ac.uk/page/t/trade-with-asia-1500-1800/

Mirror of the World – Books and Ideas, State Library of Victoria, Melbourne, Victoria, Australia. www.slv.vic.gov.au

The Portuguese and the Orient: Siam, China and Japan (1840–1940), Biblioteca Nacional (National Library of Portugal), Lisbon, 4 November 2004–6 January 2005. http://purl.pt/711/1/about-exibiton.html

Encompassing the Globe – Portugal and the World in the 16th and 17th Centuries (Autour du Globe: Le Portugal Dans Le Monde aux XVIe et XVIIe Siècles), Palais des Beaux Arts ('Bozar'), Brussels, 26 October 2007–3 February 2008. www.bozar.be/activity.php?id=7340&lng=en (see: Levenson, 1997)

On the Nālandā Trail – Buddhism in India, China and South East Asia, Asian Civilizations Museum (ACM), Singapore, 2 November 2007–23 March 2008. www.acm.org.sg/exhibitions/eventdetail.asp?eventID=186; www.asianartnewspaper.com/article/nalanda-trail

Heaven on Earth – Missionaries and the Mathematical Arts in 17th Century Beijing, Museum of the History of Science, Oxford, 24 May–7 September 2008. www.mhs.ox.ac.uk

China on Paper: European and Chinese Works from the Late Sixteenth to the Early Nineteenth Century; Getty Center, J. Paul Getty Museum, Los Angeles, 6 November 2007–10 February 2008. www.getty.edu/art/exhibitions/china_paper/

Gandhara – The Buddhist Heritage of Pakistan: Legends, Monasteries, and Paradise, 21 November 2008–15 March 2009 at the Art and Exhibition Hall, Bonn, and 9 April–10 August 2009 at the Martin Gropius Bau, Berlin, Germany. http://artdaily.com/news/27303/Gandhara---The-Buddhist-Heritage-of-Pakistan---Legends--Monasteries--and-Paradise#.UsP6rKOGlok

Holland and Japan – 400 Years of Trade (*400 Jaar Handel*), Rijksmuseum, Amsterdam, 11 January–25 May 2009. www.codart.nl/exhibitions/details/1918/

Westerse Reizigers in China: De Ontdekking van het Rijk van het Midden – Voyageurs Occidentaux En Chine: La Découverte de l'Empire du Milieu (Western Travellers in China: Discovering the Middle Kingdom), 28 October 2009–10 January 2010 (europalia.china). www.wittockiana.org; http://arabelgica.be/en/node/144;www.europalia.be/archives/china/spip.php?rubrique1&lang=en [archival only]

Son of Heaven (Fils du Ciel – Zoon van de Hemel) – Bozar, Brussels, 10 October 2009–24 January 2010 (europalia.china). www.bozar.be/activity.php?id=9132 (see: De Coster, 2009)

Pleasure and Play in Edo Japan, Canterbury Museum, Christchurch, New Zealand, 5 December 2009–28 February 2010

A Passage to Asia, BOZAR, Brussels, 25 June–10 October 2012 (Bullen et al., 2009). www.bozar.be/activity.php?id=9135&lng=en; www.asem8.be/event/exhibition-passage-asia

Namban Commissions – The Portuguese in Modern Age Japan; Museu do Oriente; Avenida de Brasília, Doca de Alcântara (Norte), Lisbon, Portugal, 17 December 2010–31 May 2011. www.museudooriente.pt/; http://asianartnewspaper.com/article/namban-commissions-portuguese-modern-age-japan

Speaking to the Future Series: Information and Media in the Edo Period, Tokyo National Museum, Room 16, Honkan, 3 August–5 September 2010. www.tnm.jp/modules/r_free_page/index.php?id=685&lang=en

500 Years of Thai-Portuguese Relations, Museum Siam, Bangkok, 2012. www.coconutsbangkok.com/features/museum-siam-exhibition-illuminates-500-year-relationship-between-thailand-and-portugal/

Encomendas 'Namban' – Os Portugueses No Japão Da Idade Moderna ('Namban' Commissions – The Portuguese in Modern Age Japan), Museu Fundação Oriente, Avenida de Brasília, Doca de Alcântara (Norte), Lisbon, Portugal, 17 December 2010–31 May 2011. www.museudooriente.pt

The Buddhist Heritage of Pakistan: Art of Gandhara, Asia Society Museum, New York, 9 August–30 October 2011. http://asiasociety.org/new-york/exhibitions/buddhist-heritage-pakistan-art-gandhara; http://sites.asiasociety.org/gandhara/

The Renaissance in Astronomy – Books, Globes and Instruments of the 16th Century, Museum of the History of Science, Oxford and Royal Astronomical Society, 11 May–9 September 2012. www.mhs.ox.ac.uk/exhibits/the-renaissance-in-astronomy/

Travelling the Silk Road: Ancient Pathway to the Modern World, National Museum of Australia, Canberra, 31 March–29 July 2012. www.nma.gov.au/exhibitions/travelling_the_silk_road/home

Mughal India: Art, Culture and Empire, British Library (PACCAR Gallery), London, 9 November 2012–2 April 2013. www.bl.uk/whatson/exhibitions/prevexhib/mughalindia

Empires of Faith, Research Project, British Museum and University of Oxford, British Museum, 2013. www.britishmuseum.org/research/research_projects/all_current_projects/empires_of_faith.aspx

Buddhism along the Silk Road, 5th to 8th Century, Metropolitan Museum of Art, New York, 2 June 2012–10 February 2013. www.metmuseum.org/exhibitions/listings/2012/buddhism

Sulla Via della Seta. Antichi Sentieri tra Oriente e Occidente (On the Silk Road – Ancient Pathways between East and West), Palazzo delle Esposizioni, Rome, 27 October 2012–10 March 2013. http://english.palazzoesposizioni.it/categorie/exhibition-018

Dunhuang – Buddhist Art at the Gateway of the Silk Route, China Institute, New York, 19 April–21 July 2013. www.chinainstitute.org/gallery/exhibitions/traveling-exhibitions/

Appendix 13 An EU module in Malaysia, 2012 and 2013: *Multi-lateral Institutions and Asia–Europe Economic Development*

Module Code: IMRI – QXGB6106
Module Title: Multi-lateral Institutions and Asia–Europe Economic Development
Module Tutor: Prof. Georg Wiessala – Visiting Senior Research Fellow, Asia–Europe
Dates and Times: 08–21 April 2013
Class Structure: Lectures – Workshops – Seminars
Location: ASEAN Room (Ground Floor AEI)

Week 1 (Building Blocks of Regional Integration)
Monday, 08 April 2013 (Inaugural Session: 10:00–12:00 and 14:00–16:30)
Principles, Theories and Discourses in Regionalism and Regional Economics.
Introduction (Lecturer-Structure-Learning-Assessment-Resources): HOW YOU CAN GET THE BEST OUT OF THIS COURSE.
What is Regional Integration? What is Europe? What is EU? (Activities, Policies, Myth, Continent, Idea, Ideal, Theories, People, 'Brand').
Elements of EU-style Integration (Pillar-System, Gradualism, Supranationalism, Intergovernmentalism, Subsidiarity...).
Theories of Regional Integration in Asia and Europe.
WORKSHOP
EU Symbols and the EU 'Brand' (How to sell regional economic and political integration to a sceptical public); design a 'logo' for EU/ASEAN and 'sell' it to us.
SEMINAR/PRESENTATION(S): Please sign up for your presentation topic(s) today!

Tuesday, 09 April 2013 (10:00–12:00 and 14:00–16:30)
Regional Integration Treaty Frameworks and EU Enlargement.
The EU Treaties: key themes, ideas and challenges compared to ASEAN; the idea of a 'concert'.

Enlargement and its Narratives: The political ideologies of 'Solidarity', 'Loyalty', 'Legitimacy' and 'Historical Duty' in regional integration.
LIBRARY WORK TO SELECT BOOK FOR REVIEW (hand-in date for Book Review is Friday, 19 April 2013).
WORKSHOP
(1) Should the EU accept Turkey as a Member? (Press release/discussion paper by the group); group debates (chaired)
(2) Has the EU reached a 'terminal capacity' as a regional body?
SEMINAR/PRESENTATION(S):
What are the Key Issues in Comparing Regional Economic and Political Integration in ASEAN and the EU?
TODAY'S PRESENTERS ARE:

Wednesday, 10 April 2013 (10:00–12:00 and 14:00–16:30)
Inter-Regionalism and EU Institutions including EU Court System and Human Rights.
EU Institutions (Overview and Key Challenges in 2012).
The European Court System (ECJ and ECHR) and their dual roles; the 'integration-friendly-jurisdiction' of the ECJ.
Human Rights in Europe and Asia.
WORKSHOP
(1) How can voter turnout for European Parliament Elections be increased? (Promotion/design of a brochure and a website; other activities)
(2) Mock case in the European Court of Human Rights: wearing religious symbols at British Airways (moot).
(3) Write the programme and agenda (themes) for an Amnesty International HR conference in KL in 2014: which topics should be debated and why?
SEMINAR/PRESENTATIONS:
Which candidate countries will join the EU next, and why?
TODAY'S PRESENTERS ARE:

Thursday, 11 April 2013 (10:00–12:00 and 14:00–16:30)
EU–Asia and EU–ASEAN Relations – Economic and Educational Cooperation.
A SWOT-Analysis of the Relations between the European Union (EU), ASEAN and other Asian Countries.
Education in inter-regional relations; culture and the 'learning-dimension' in regional integration (Learning FROM and WITH one another).
WORKSHOP
The role of perceptions and stereotypes in Asia–Europe inter-regional cooperation (individual and group work); Studying in Asia and Europe (comparison).
SEMINAR/PRESENTATION(S)
(1) Introduce, and discuss, a (recent) case decided by the European Court of Justice (ECJ) or the European Court of Human Rights.
(2) How are the EU and the ECHR protecting and promoting national and regional economies? How are they safeguarding Human Rights, including Women's Rights?

(3) How is ASEAN approaching the same issues? Please compare the two approaches.
TODAY'S PRESENTERS ARE:

Friday, 12 April 2013 (10:00–13:00 only)
Economic and Re-Distributive Regionalism – Enhanced Multilateralism or a Third Level of Governance?
Cohesion and Loyalty: Regional Policies and Regional Funding in the EU: the 'hollowing-out' of the nation-state, or the future of Europe?
Regional Identity in Asia: The Asia–Europe Foundation (ASEF) and Asia–Europe Meetings (ASEM): construction of a regional identity?
WORKSHOP
'Closer Regionalism is the Future – Nationalism Means War!' (Debating Competition, 20 minutes' time).
SEMINAR/PRESENTATION(S)
Introduce and Analyse Examples of International Regional Integration other than the EU and ASEAN (e.g. in the Middle East, Australia and New Zealand, North or South America, and elsewhere).
TODAY'S PRESENTERS ARE:

Week 2 (Consequences of Regional Integration)
Monday, 15 April 2013 (10:00–12:00 and 14:00–16:30)
Fighting Organized Crime, Drugs and Terrorism in Regional Associations.
The Key Catalysts for Regional Integration in Asia and Europe and the Potential for the Abuse of Freedoms.
The Fight against Drugs and Organized Crime in Asia and Europe and the Challenge to Regional Integration.
International Terrorism ('old' and 'new' terrorism; changing parameters of terrorism; motives for terrorism; EU and ASEAN strategies and approaches to counter-terrorism).
WORKSHOP
(1) An Issue Relating to Terrorism (Podcast: Advanced Group Listening and Note-taking Exercise).
(2) Policy-Design: A New Anti-Drugs Approach in EU/ASEAN (Written exercise: *10-Point Anti-Drugs Plan* for EMCDDA).
(3) Policy-Design: ASEAN 2020 Anti-Terrorism Strategy (Written Exercise: 10-Point Anti-Terrorism Plan for ASEAN Summit).
SEMINAR/PRESENTATION(S): Compare the work of the European Union Committee of the Regions to the work of ASEAN in the areas of Education, Crime and the Environment.
TODAY'S PRESENTERS ARE:

Tuesday, 16 April 2013 (10:00–12:00 and 14:00–16:30)
Foreign Policy, Diplomacy and External Relations.
The EU and ASEAN on the International Stage.

The New EU External Action Service (EAS).
EU and Malaysia.
WORKSHOP
A Negotiation in the Council: Advancing Democracy in Burma (two Sub-Groups Negotiation Exercise and Presenting to the Group).
SEMINAR/PRESENTATION(S)
(1) Evaluate the Work of EUROPOL and the EMCDDA in the Fight against Drugs.
(2) How Can Regional Associations best Fight International Terrorism?
(3) How can ASEAN and the EU best Cooperate in the fight against Organized Crime, Cyber-Crime and Cyber-Terrorism?
TODAY'S PRESENTERS ARE:

Wednesday, 17 April 2013 (10:00–12:00 and 14:00–16:30)
Exercising Influence: Lobbying, Economic and Other Interests and Interest-Representation in Regional Associations.
Lobbying and Lobbying Skills – What Skills Do You Need to Influence the EU?
Economic and Other Group Interests in Regional Associations and their Organization.
WORKSHOP: Simulation-Exercise: Lobbying Meetings/Simulation Exercise/ Role-Play: 'Lobbyist versus Parliamentarian'; Preparation of a Programme for an International Conference in KL in 2014.
SEMINAR/PRESENTATIONS
(1) Are the EU and ASEAN visible and effective foreign policy agents? Illustrate your answer with at least two examples of your choice (e.g. Development Policy, Military Intervention, Educational and Trade Policies etc.).
(2) Will the EUEAS make the EU more successful?
TODAY'S PRESENTERS ARE:

Thursday, 18 April 2013 (10:00–12:00 and 14:00–16:30)
Protecting Cultural Diversity, Languages and Multiple Identities.
Regional Integration and National Identities.
Languages, Language-Policies and Minority-Cultures.
Translation and Interpretation: Costly Luxury or Cultural Identity?
WORKSHOP: (1) Is there a common 'European' ('EU') Identity? Should there be one? (Moot Debate Exercise: 'Pros and Cons') – (2) Is there an 'ASEAN Identity', and an 'Asian Way' of Doing Things? If so – what does it consist of?
SEMINAR/PRESENTATION(S): How does the EU protect Minority Languages, and how does this affect EU–ASEAN Relations?
TODAY'S PRESENTERS ARE:

Friday, 19 April 2013 (Valedictory Session: 10:00–13:00)
Focus on Personal Skills, Your Learning Styles and Future Career Development.
Simulations and Role-Plays regarding personal skills: chairing meetings, defusing conflict and diplomacy, being assertive.

Recognizing people's different learning styles and how to work with people.
Final Plenary-Discussion, Feedback/Production of Video or Press Release/Podcast (please bring your cameras).
LAST HAND-IN DATE FOR YOUR BOOK REVIEW.

Appendix 14 The Contemporary Europe Research Centre (CERC) at the University of Melbourne

The work of the CERC was framed by the wider professional body of the period, the *Contemporary European Studies Association of Australia (CESAA)*.[9] Both the CERC conferences mentioned in Chapter 9, and to which I enjoyed the great privilege of contributing scholarly papers (on *Human Rights* and on *EU–Asia Relations*), can be said, perhaps, to have marked a transition in, or widening of, the disciplinary remit of the CERC, from an initial concern with Australia's evolving political and economic relations with the European Union, to a broader perspective, embracing EU–Asia relations as a whole, examining Australia–EU dialogue as a 'hinge' for international relations, and looking increasingly at areas of commonality in the foreign policies of the EU and Australia.

Beyond conferences, the *CERC Working Papers* series, to which I made a contribution on *Human Rights in EU–Asia Relations* (Wiessala, 2007), reached an above-average level of awareness in Europe, by means of attracting many well-known 'names' in the European Union Studies field, especially in the UK, and by thus making a significant contribution to the development of the European (Union) Studies curriculum 'Down Under'.

In this context, the CERC published the e-book *Europe: New Voices, New Perspectives* in 2007,[10] as a result of a series of postgraduate conferences, which had helped to bring the centre's postgraduate students right to the heart of developing their own learning agendas. This became evident in the particularly 'Australian' focus of looking at topics such as citizens, refugees, minorities and identities. To some degree, European Studies in Australia, therefore, took on a flavour which mirrored domestic political preoccupations and concerns, and sought to compare them to the European Union. 'European Studies' in Australia, it has been said, begins at home.

Unfortunately, the CERC closed at the end of 2009 and left an inheritance of European Studies courses at individual Australian universities (Sydney, Melbourne, ANU, Monash, RMIT[11]), none of which, however, as far as can be seen in 2013, is concerned with the critical investigation of a European Studies curriculum in Australia to the same degree as was CERC. The ANU Contemporary Europe Learning Community (CELC) appears to have been the only attempt to involve the student community, in Canberra and beyond, in European (Union) Studies curriculum development.

There is, perhaps, no better retrospective endorsement of its work than that contained in the words of its Director, Professor Philomena Murray, in the final, two-part *CERC Bulletin* (No. 21/2009), its official newsletter. I feel that they deserve to be quoted here more fully – with due respect to the CERC's excellent international work over the years, and with gratitude for the research support and inspiration received by this author.

It is with regret that I inform the recipients of the *CERC Bulletin* that CERC, the only Jean Monnet Centre of Excellence in Australia, will be closed at the end of 2009. There are many good experiences to reflect on and these will feature in CERC's last Annual Newsletter, which will be sent out with the CERC Bulletin before the end of the year. Over twenty years, CERC has provided both the physical and virtual hubs of the largest network of scholars, government officials and the public interested in Europe in Australia. We have held very successful public seminar series, international conferences and produced excellent research publications and our Working Papers Series[...].

[...] We have had extensive relations with government, the EU and the media, important community outreach and excellent knowledge transfer activities. For many years, CERC has been an important destination in Australia for visiting scholars and officials from Europe and we have welcomed visiting scholars and postgraduate scholars. CERC established an excellent reputation in providing research support, training and networks to a broad range of scholars across many disciplines including political science, history, education, economics, law, cultural studies and languages. Over the last twenty years, the University, the Australian and international scholarly community and thousands of students, the public and community and specialized groups and business have benefited from CERC's a situation of which we can be proud. It has been a great privilege for all of us at CERC to work with so many committed people. It has been an honor to serve.

Appendix 15 Antipodean engagement: visiting, teaching and other activity in Australia and New Zealand

AUSTRALIA: Universities of Sydney and Melbourne, and Contemporary Europe Research Centre (CEERC), University of Melbourne

2006

Conference Paper: *Human Rights in the Foreign Policy Arsenal of the EU in Asia*; International Conference: *Europe and Asia – Regions in Flux*, 6–7 December 2006, Contemporary Europe Research Centre (Jean Monnet European Centre of Excellence), The University of Melbourne, Melbourne, Victoria, Australia.

2008

Conference Paper: *Engaging with the Other East: A Critical Analysis of the Current State of the European Union's 'Asia-Policy'*; International Conference: *EU–Asia Relations: A Critical Review*, 27–28 March 2008, Contemporary Europe Research Centre (Jean Monnet European Centre of Excellence), The University of Melbourne, Melbourne, Victoria, Australia.

248   *Appendices*

2010 (29–31 July)
Lecturing: *Australian Foreign Policy* (POLS3024, two lectures).
Public Lecture: *EU–Asia Relations and the New European Diplomatic Service* – Annual Jean Monnet Public Lecture, University of Melbourne and Australian National University, Faculty of Arts, Friday 30 July 2010.

NEW ZEALAND (*Aotearoa*) and National Centre for Research on Europe (NCRE)
1999
Conference Paper: *ASEM-metries in the EU–Asia Dialogue and the 'Asian Values' Discourse – New Perspectives for a New Millennium: Local, National, Regional and Global* – Joint Conference of the Third Wellington Conference on World Affairs, the European Studies Association of New Zealand and The New Zealand Political Studies Association; Victoria University, Wellington, New Zealand.

2007
Examining a PhD Thesis: *Abridging the Tyranny of Distance: EU and NZ Security Cultures in the Asia-Pacific Region.*

2010 (July to August)
Lecturing: *The EU and our Region* (EURO102, four lectures).
Lecturing: *EU Regional Policies.*

2013 (22–26 July)
Lecturing: *The EU and Human Rights* (Lecture: EURO318).
Examining a PhD Thesis: *Constructivism and EU–Australia Relations* (PhD Viva, 24 July).
Interviews: *Studying the EU in NZ* (Student Interviews, 25 July).
Public Lecture: *Human Rights on the 'European Studies in Asia' Curriculum* (Roundtable Seminar: 26 July)

Notes

1. See: www.artsales.com/ARTistory/Xavier/James_I.htm.
2. See *Samurai Archive* podcasts (7 January 2013): http://samuraipodcast.com/ep58-an-introduction-to-sankin-kotai.
3. See informative text on *Rangaku* at: www.hokusaionline.co.uk/code/foreign.html.
4. The 'Four Books' of Confucianism are: *The Great Learning, The Doctrine of the Mean, The Analects* and *The Book of Mengzi*. The 'Five Classics' are: *The Book of History, The Book of Odes, The Book of Changes, The Book of Rites* and *The Spring and Autumn Annals*.
5. A brief biographical sketch, with a cameo-portrait, is at: www.botanischestaatssammlung.de/collectors/siebold.html.
6. See also: www.aseanworldheritage.com/2011/10/ayutthaya-art.html.
7. *Wat Suwanaram*: www.thailandsworld.com/en/bangkok/bangkok-temples/wat-suwannaram/index.cfm; www.pbase.com/chounws3/mural_painting_in_bangkok_temples.
8. *Suan Pakkad Palace Museum*: www.suanpakkad.com/.

9 See: http://cesaa.org.au/.
10 Available at: http://diasporic.org/wp-content/uploads/2010/09/New_voices_full.pdf.
11 RMIT organized an event in 2012, celebrating *Europe and Australia in Conversation: 50 Years of EU–Australia Relations (1962–2012)*, http://mams.rmit.edu.au/o9nphl-hiuq1c.pdf. See also the website of the EU Delegation to Australia: http://eeas.europa.eu/delegations/australia/index_en.htm, and the Anniversary. Booklet: http://eeas.europa.eu/delegations/australia/documents/more_info/eu-austfinal.pdf.

Selected websites

400th Anniversary of Japanese–British Relations (1613–2013): http://japan400.com/
Academia Sinica Europaea (@ China–Europe International Business School, CEIBS): www.ceibs.edu/ase/ASE.htm
Academic Cooperation Association (ACA): www.aca-secretariat.be
Academy for Cultural Diplomacy (Germany): www.culturaldiplomacy.org/academy/index.php?en_conferences_nbiw
Amsterdams Historisch Museum (AHM, now: Amsterdam Museum): www.amsterdammuseum.nl/en
APEC Studies Centre Consortium: www.apec.org/Groups/Other-Groups/APEC-Study-Centres-Consortium.aspx
Art of the Silk Road: http://depts.washington.edu/silkroad/exhibit/index.shtml
ASEAN – Association of Southeast Asian Nations: www.aseansec.org (see also the following ASEAN sub-websites)
ASEAN + 3 Summit: www.asean.org/asean/external-relations/asean-3
ASEAN Education Ministers Meeting (ASED): www.asean.org/communities/asean-socio-cultural-community/category/asean-education-ministers-meeting-ased
ASEAN–European Union University Network Programme: http://globalhighered.files.wordpress.com/2010/02/aunp.pdf
ASEAN Regional Forum (ARF): www.aseanregionalforum.org/
ASEAN University Network (AUN): www.aunsec.org/
Ashmolean Museum of Art and Archaeology, Oxford, UK: (www.ashmolean.org/)
Asia and Europe in a Global Context (Heidelberg): www.asia-europe.uni-heidelberg.de/en/students/summerschool.html
Asia–Europe Classroom Network (Asia–Europe Foundation): www.aec.asef.org/
Asia–Europe Foundation (ASEF): www.asef.org/ (see also the following ASEF sub-websites)
Asia–Europe Foundation Classroom Network (ASEF ClassNet) (formerly known as the Asia–Europe Classroom Network (AEC-NET) http://asef.org/index.php/projects/programmes/516-asef_classroom_network-(asef_classnet)
Asia–Europe Foundation Database on Education Exchange Programmes (DEEP-ASEF): http://deep.asef.org/
Asia–Europe Foundation University Library: www.asef.org/index.php/projects/programmes/522-asef-university
Asia–Europe Institute, University of Malaya: http://aei.um.edu.my/
Asia Europe Journal (ASEF): http://aej.asef.org/

Asia–Europe Meeting (ASEM, 'ASEM Info-Board'): www.aseminfoboard.org/ (see also the following ASEM sub-websites)
Asia–Europe Meeting Education Hub (ASEM): http://asemlllhub.org/
Asia–Europe Meeting Education Ministers Meeting (ASEMME): www.aseminfoboard.org/2011-12-22-05-57-34.html
Asia–Europe Meeting Education Secretariat: www.asem-education-secretariat.org/en/12183/
Asia–Europe Meeting Rectors' Conferences (ASEM RC): www.asef.org/index.php/projects/programmes/529-ARC
Asia–Europe Museum Network (ASEMUS): http://asemus.museum/
Asia–Europe Museum Network Virtual Collection of Masterpieces: http://masterpieces.asemus.museum/default.aspx and http://asemus.museum/project/virtual-collection-of-masterpieces-vcm/
Asia For Educators: http://afe.easia.columbia.edu/tps/1750.htm
Asia House (UK): http://asiahouse.org/
Asia Link (European Studies Curriculum) Projects (2002–2005): http://ec.europa.eu/europeaid/where/asia/regional-cooperation/higher-education/documents/asia_link_2002-05_en.pdf
Asia Link Programme: http://ec.europa.eu/europeaid/where/asia/regional-cooperation/higher-education/index_en.htm
Asia-Net Finland: www.asianet.fi/asianet/etusivu.html
Asia-Pacific Association of International Education (APAIE): www.apaie.org
Asia-Pacific Centre of Education for International Understanding (APCEIU): www.unescoapceiu.org/en
Asia-Pacific Centre, University of New England, NSW, Australia: www.une.edu.au/asiacentre/
Asia-Pacific Journal of European Union Studies (New Zealand): www.europe.canterbury.ac.nz/publications/journal.shtml
Asia-Pacific Quality Network: www.apqn.org/
Asia-Portal: www.asiaportal.info/
Asia Regional Integration Centre: http://aric.adb.org/
Asia Society (Museum), New York: http://asiasociety.org/arts/asia-society-museum
Asia Times (on-line): www.atimes.com/
Asian Art Museum (Muzium Seni Asia), Universiti Malaya, Kuala Lumpur, Malaysia: www.museum.um.edu.my/
Asian Civilizations Museum (ACM), Singapore: www.acm.org.sg/home/home.asp
Asian Development Bank (ADB) Institute: www.adbi.org/
Asian University (Bangkok, Thailand): www.asianust.ac.th
Asian University Network (AUN): www.aun-sec.org/
Association for Central Asian Civilizations and Silk Road Studies (ACANSRS): www.acansrs.org/
Association of Jesuit Universities and Colleges in Asia-Pacific: www.ajcu-eao.org/
Association of Pacific Rim Universities (APRU): http://apru.org/
Association of Southeast Asian Institutions of Higher Learning (ASAIHL): www.seameo.org/asaihl
Association of Universities of Asia and the Pacific (AUAP): http://auap.sut.ac.th
Aurel Stein: http://stein.mtak.hu/index-en.html
Australian Education International: https://aei.gov.au/Pages/default.aspx
Australian Government: Department of Education: http://education.gov.au/

252 Selected websites

Australian Government: Department of Employment: http://employment.gov.au/
Australian National University Centre for European Studies (ANUCES): http://ces.anu.edu.au/
Auswärtiges Amt (German Foreign Office): www.auswaertiges-amt.de/EN/Startseite_node.html
Ayutthaya Historical Research: www.ayutthaya-history.com/index.html
Baltic Research Centre for East Asian Studies (AsiaRes): http://asiares.lv/
Bath EU–China Network: www.realisingtransitionpathways.org.uk/eri/research/becan/
Brisbane Initiative/Communiqué: https://www.aei.gov.au/About-AEI/Policy/Pages/Brisbane Communiqu%C3%A9.aspx
British Library: www.bl.uk
British Museum, London: Japanese Galleries (2013): www.britishmuseum.org; www.britishmuseum.org/about_us/news_and_press/press_releases/2006/japanese_galleries_reopen.aspx
Brussels Institute for Contemporary China Studies: www.vub.ac.be/biccs/site/
Buddhist Pilgrims (Victoria and Albert Museum): www.vam.ac.uk/content/articles/b/buddhist-pilgrims/
Bulletin of Portuguese/Japanese Studies: http://cham.fcsh.unl.pt/pages/eng/publicacoes_bpjs_eng.htm
Central Asia Research and Education Network (CAREN) http://ec.europa.eu/europeaid/where/asia/regional-cooperation-central-asia/education-and-research/caren_en.htm
Centre for European Policy Studies (CEPS): www.ceps.eu/
Centre for the Law of EU External Relations (CLEER): www.asser.nl/default.aspx?site_id=1&level1=13693&level2=14560&level3=14569
Centre for the Study of International Governance (Loughborough University): www.lboro.ac.uk/research/csig/
China and Europe 1500–2000: What is Modern? http://afe.easia.columbia.edu/chinawh/index.html
China: EU-Policy Paper (MFA): www.fmprc.gov.cn/eng/topics/ceupp/t27708.htm
China-Europe International Business School: www.ceibs.edu/bmt/
China IPR (SME Helpdesk): www.china-iprhelpdesk.eu/
China Radio International (CRI): http://english.cri.cn/
Chinese History Podcasts: http://chinahistorypodcast.com/
Chinese Rites Controversy: www.fordham.edu/halsall/mod/1715chineserites.asp
Chronicle of Higher Education (US): http://chronicle.com/section/Home/5/
Chronology of Japanese History: www.shikokuhenrotrail.com/japanhistory.html
Chulalongkorn University, Bangkok, Centre for European Studies (CES): www.ces.in.th/main/
Chulalongkorn University, Bangkok: MA (Programme) in European Studies: www.maeus.grad.chula.ac.th/newweb/
Clark Centre for Japanese Art and Culture: www.ccjac.org/
College of Europe (Bruges/Brugge): www.coleurope.be
College of Europe, EU–China Observer: www.coleurop.be/template.asp?pagename= EUCO
Connected Histories, Shared Future (ASEF Travelling Exhibition, in 2012, on the occasion of ASEF's fifteenth anniversary): http://asef.org/index.php/projects/themes/education/2489-towards-a-shared-future-travelling-exhibition
Contemporary Europe Research Centre (CEERC [*now defunct*]), University of Melbourne: https://archive-it.org/collections/1148?fc=meta_Publisher%3AContemporary+Europe+Research+Centre%2C+Faculty+of+Arts%2C+University+of+Melbourne

Selected websites 253

Contemporary European Studies Association of Australia (CESAA): http://cesaa.org.au/

Council of the European Union: EU–Asia Relations: www.consilium.europa.eu/showPage.aspx?id=399&lang=en

Crossroads: A Journal of Nagasaki History and Culture: www.uwosh.edu/home_pages/faculty_staff/earns/home.html

Culture 360 – Connecting Asia and Europe through Arts and Culture: http://culture360.org/

Dag(h)registers (Official Diaries) of the Dutch in Japan: www.hendrick-hamel.hennysavenije.pe.kr/Dutch/bijlagene.htm

Dejima: The Island Comes Back to Life: www1.city.nagasaki.nagasaki.jp/dejima/en/index.html

Dejima Island: A Stepping Stone Between Civilisations (Gilbert): http://worldhistoryconnected.press.illinois.edu/3.3/gilbert.html

Delegation of the European Union to Australia: http://eeas.europa.eu/delegations/australia/index_en.htm

Delegation of the European Union to Central Asia: http://delkaz.ec.europa.eu/joomla/

Delegation of the European Union to China: www.delchn.ec.europa.eu/

Delegation of the European Union to Nepal: www.delnpl.ec.europa.eu/

Delegation of the European Union to New Zealand: http://eeas.europa.eu/delegations/new_zealand/

Delegation of the European Union to Pakistan: www.delpak.ec.europa.eu/

Delegation of the European Union to Singapore: http://eeas.europa.eu/delegations/singapore/index_en.htm

Delegation of the European Union to Sri Lanka and the Maldives: www.dellka.ec.europa.eu/

Delegation of the European Union to the Philippines: www.delphl.ec.europa.eu/

Delegation of the European Union to Thailand: http://eeas.europa.eu/delegations/thailand/index_en.htm

Deutsche Gesellschaft für Asienkunde: www.asienkunde.de/index.php?file=71.html&folder=zeitschrift_asien/archiv

Development Cooperation (EC-China): http://ec.europa.eu/europeaid/where/asia/country-cooperation/china/china_en.htm

Diplomatic System of the EU (DSEU) Network, Loughborough University: http://dseu.lboro.ac.uk/

Directory of 'European Studies' Programmes in Asia: www.asef.org/index.php/projects/programmes/548-european-studies-in-asia-(esia)

Dutch (and Portuguese) Colonial History in Southeast Asia: http://17thcenturysiam.blogspot.com/2009/11/q.html

Dutch–Japanese Relations: http://japan.nlembassy.org/you-and-netherlands/dutch-japanese-relations.html

East India Company: Reading List: www.bl.uk/onlinegallery/features/trading/booksgifts1.html

Economist (UK): 'Asia-View': www.economist.com/asiaview

Edo Period Art (Metropolitan Museum, New York): www.metmuseum.org/toah/hd/edop/hd_edop.htm

Edo Period in Japanese History (Victoria and Albert Museum): www.vam.ac.uk/content/articles/t/the-edo-period-in-japanese-history/

Education Services Australia: www.esa.edu.au/

ENCARI (European Network for Contemporary Academic Research on India): www.casaasia.es/pdf/10290765832PM1193680712283.pdf

ERASMUS Mundus: http://eacea.ec.europa.eu/erasmus_mundus/index_en.htm

ERASMUS Mundus Projects Relating to Asia: http://eacea.ec.europa.eu/erasmus_mundus/results_compendia/documents/projects/action_3_promotion_projects/regional/a3fiche_asia.pdf

ERASMUS Mundus Student and Alumni Association: www.em-a.eu/en/home.html

ERASMUS Mundus Student and Alumni Association/Chinese Chapter: www.em-a.eu/en/about-ema/regional-chapters/chinese-chapter.html

EU4Asia Programme (2009–2011): www.euforasia.eu/

EU–China Business Association: www.eucba.org/

EU Network of European Studies Centres in Asia (EU-NESCA, 2006–2008): Research Dialogue: http://ec.europa.eu/research/social-sciences/pdf/group_5/eu_nesca_en.pdf and http://ec.europa.eu/research/social-sciences/projects/184_en.html

EU–New Zealand Programme (Ghent University): www.ugent.be/en/teaching/internationalisation/programmes/eunz.htm

EurActiv.com: www.euractiv.com/en

Eurasian Silk Road Universities Consortium: http://esruc.atauni.edu.tr/

Euro-Chinese Centre for Research and Development (ECCRD): www.eucba.org/members/ECC.html

Europalia (International Arts Festival, Belgium): www.europalia.be/?lang=fr

Europalia China: www.europalia.be/archives/china/spip.php?rubrique1&lang=en

Europalia India (2013/2014): www.europalia.eu/en/home/home_82.html

EuropeAid: Education and Science in Asia (Commission): http://ec.europa.eu/europeaid/where/asia/regional-cooperation/higher-education/index_en.htm

European Association for International Education (EAIE): www.eaie.org/home/about-EAIE/our-partners.html

European Association for South East Asian Studies (EuroSEAS): www.euroseas.org/platform/en

European Association for the Education of Adults (EAEA): www.eaea.org/index.php?k=7197&member=00874

European Association of Institutions in Higher Education (EURASHE): http://eurashe.eu/about/experts/

European Commission: Directorate-General for Education and Culture: http://ec.europa.eu/dgs/education_culture/index_en.htm

European Council on Foreign Relations (Asia-Section): http://ecfr.eu/content/programmes/C11/

European Higher Education Area (EHEA): www.ehea.info/

European Institute for Asian Studies (Brussels): www.eias.org

European Navigator Database: www.ena.lu/

European Network for Contemporary Academic Research on India (ENCARI, defunct, slides only): www.powershow.com/view/141200-NGRhN/European_Network_for_Contemporary_Academic_Research_on_India_ENCARI_powerpoint_ppt_presentation

European Policy Centre (EPC): www.epc.eu/

European Policy Centre: EU–Asia Dialogue: www.epc.eu/prog_forum.php?forum_id=14&prog_id=3

European Studies in Asia (ESiA) Network: www.asef.org/index.php/projects/programmes/548-european-studies-in-asia-(esia)

European Studies Programme, Ateneo de Manila University (The Philippines): http://socsci.ateneo.edu/module.php?LM=programs.detail&id=1204132336495

Selected websites 255

European Union and Asia (European Union External Action Service, EEAS): http://eeas.europa.eu/asia/index_en.htm
European Union and China (European Union External Action Service, EEAS): http://eeas.europa.eu/china/
European Union Asia Centre (EU): www.eu-asiacentre.eu/
European Union Asia Higher Education Platform (EAHEP): www.eahep.org/eahep-project/about-the-project.html (archival) and www.eahep.org/web/
European Union Central Asia Monitoring Project (EUCAM): www.eucentralasia.eu/
European Union Centres Network (New Zealand): www.eucnetwork.org.nz/
European Union China Academic Network (ECAN): www.ec-an.eu/
European Union China Information Society Project: http://ec.europa.eu/europeaid/documents/case-studies/china_information-society_en.pdf
European Union China Newsletter: www.delchn.ec.europa.eu/newsletters/200904/index.html
European Union China Youth Policy Dialogue: http://euchinayouth.eu/
European Union for Asia (Image Gallery): www.google.co.uk/search?q=European+Union+4+Asia:&tbm=isch&tbo=u&source=univ&sa=X&ei=WQPEUuGCK6mM7AaXmIGoBQ&ved=0CHAQsAQ&biw=1152&bih=603
European Union in the Eyes of Asia Project (Overview): www.asef.org/index.php/projects/themes/education/1123-eu-through-the-eyes-of-asia
European Union Institute in Japan, Kansai (EUIJ): http://euij-kansai.jp/
European Union Least Developed Countries Network: www.eu-ldc.org/
European Union Observer ('EU Observer'): http://euobserver.com/
European Union Observer (Special China Business Section): http://euobserver.com/884
European Union Studies Association (EUSA): www.eustudies.org/
European Union Studies Association Asia-Pacific (EUS-AP): www.eusaap.org.nz/
European Union Studies Association of Japan: www.eusa-japan.org/index-e.html
European Union Studies Association of Korea: www.keusa.or.kr/html/e_activity.htm
European Union Studies Association of New Zealand (EUSA-NZ): www.eucnetwork.org.nz/12/index.php/home/2-uncategorised/122-eusanz-welcome
European Union Studies Institute (EUSI, Tokyo, Japan): http://eusi.jp/content_en/ (see also: www.euij-tc.org/index.html)
European University Association (EUA): www.eua.be/Home.aspx
European University Institute (EUI, Florence): www.eui.eu/Home.aspx
Europe China Research and Advice Network (ECRAN): www.euecran.eu/
Europe's Trading Centuries (Trading Eurasia, 1600–1830): www2.warwick.ac.uk/fac/arts/history/ghcc/eac/
Europe's World: www.europesworld.org/
Euro Politics: www.europolitics.info/external-policies/asia-hopes-new-eu-heads-will-facilitate-bilateral-relations-art255262-44.html
Eurostat: http://epp.eurostat.ec.europa.eu/portal/page/portal/eurostat/home/
EURYDICE Network: http://eacea.ec.europa.eu/education/eurydice/index_en.php
Expert on Europe (UACES): www.expertoneurope.com/Home
Finnish University Network for Asian Studies: www.asianet.fi/asianet/english/
Foreign Policy Research Centre (EU–India Paper) (New Delhi): www.fprc.in/fprc_journal.php
Friends of Dunhuang: www.friendsofdunhuang.org/eternal-dunhuang.php?lang=en
From Silk to Oil (Book, China Institute, New York, 'China 360 online'): www.china-360online.org/learning-materials-and-resources/curriculum-guides/from-silk-to-oil/

256 *Selected websites*

Fudan University Centre for European Studies: www.cesfd.org.cn/index_en.html
Fujiland Exhibit: 'The Dutch in Dejima': http://fujiland-mag.blogspot.co.uk/2010/10/exhibition-dutch-in-dejima.html
Fundação Oriente (Study Centre and Museum, Lisbon): www.museudooriente.pt/
Geschiedenis van Japan (Japanese History – *Rangaku*) (in Dutch): http://mediawiki.arts.kuleuven.be/geschiedenisjapan/index.php/Rangaku_(%E8%98%AD%E5%AD%A6)
Global Ethics Network (see Carnegie Council): www.globalethicsnetwork.org/
Global Institute for Asian Regional Integration (Waseda University): http://waseda-giari.jp/
Government of Tibet in Exile: www.tibet.com/
Graduate School of East Asian Studies (Free University Berlin): www.geas.fu-berlin.de/index.html
Heilbrunn Timeline of Art History (Metropolitan Museum of Art, New York): www.metmuseum.org/toah/
Hokusai Online (Edo Period and *Rangaku*): www.hokusaionline.co.uk/index.html
Holland and Japan (400 Years of Trade): www.codart.nl/exhibitions/details/1918/
How Rome Went to China: www.loc.gov/exhibits/vatican/romechin.html#mamtjic
Human Rights Watch Asia: www.hrw.org/asia
Human Rights Without Frontiers (HRWF): www.hrwf.net/
In-Bev Baillet Latour Chair in EU–China Relations (College of Europe): https://www.coleurope.eu/website/study/eu-international-relations-and-diplomacy-studies/inbev-baillet-latour-chair-european
Institut of European Studies of Macau: www.ieem.org.mo/
Institute for Cultural Diplomacy (Germany): www.culturaldiplomacy.org/index.php?en
Institute of Educational Leadership (*Institut Kepimpinan Pendidikan*), University of Malaya, Kuala Lumpur, Malaysia: http://iel.um.edu.my/
Institute of International Education (IIE): www.iie.org/
Institute of Southeast Asian Studies (ISEAS – Singapore): www.iseas.edu.sg/
Institutito do Oriente (Orient Institute, Technical University, Lisbon): www.iscsp.utl.pt/index.php?option=com_content&view=article&id=116&Itemid=425
International Association of Universities (IAU): www.iau-aiu.net/
International Campaign for Tibet: www.savetibet.org/
International Council for Open and Distance Education: www.icde.org
International Dunhuang Project: 'The Silk Road On-Line': http://idp.bl.uk/ (includes free newsletter: *IDP News*)
International Education Association of Australia (IEAA): www.ieaa.org.au/
International Institute for Asian Studies (IIAS, The Hague): www.iias.nl/
International Institute of Social History (IISH, Amsterdam): www.iisg.nl/index.php
Islamic Arts Museum, Kuala Lumpur, Malaysia: www.iamm.org.my/
Japan and the West: Artistic Cross-Fertilization: www.loc.gov/exhibits/ukiyo-e/japan.html
Japanese Manuscripts: www.bl.uk/reshelp/findhelplang/japanese/japanesesection/japanmanuscripts/japanmanuscripts.html
Japanese Prints: The Dutch: www.iisg.nl/exhibitions/japaneseprints/dutch.html
Japan–Netherlands Exchange in the Edo Period: www.ndl.go.jp/nichiran/e/index.html
Japan–Netherlands Relationship: 400 Years (Paulus Swaen Gallery): www.swaen.com/japanNED.php
Japan–Netherlands Society: www.j-nls.org/about-us2.html
Japan Society in the UK: www.japansociety.org.uk/about/

Jesuits in China: www.ibiblio.org/expo/vatican.exhibit/exhibit/i-rome_to_china/Jesuits_in_China.html
Kobe City Museum: www.city.kobe.lg.jp/culture/culture/institution/museum/pdf/kcm_e_guide.pdf
Linking European and Asian Networks in the Field of Environmental Sciences (LEANES): www.environmentportal.eu/content/leanes.html
Ministry of Education, New Zealand (Māori: Te Tāhuhu o te Mātauranga): www.minedu.govt.nz/
Ministry of (Higher) Education, Malaysia: www.mohe.gov.my/portal/en/
Monash University European and EU Centre (MEEUC): http://artsonline.monash.edu.au/europecentre/
Muzium Seni Asia (Asian Arts Museum, University of Malaya, UM): www.museum.um.edu.my/
Nālandā International University: www.nalandauniv.edu.in/
Nālandā-Sriwijaya Centre (Institute of South East Asian Studies, Singapore): http://nsc.iseas.edu.sg/index.htm
National Centre for Research on Europe (NCRE), University of Canterbury, Christchurch (New Zealand): www.europe.canterbury.ac.nz/
National Museum of Malaysia (Muzium Negara), Kuala Lumpur: www.muziumnegara.gov.my/main/
Nederlands Economisch-Historisch Archief (NEHA): www.neha.nl/
Netherlands Mission, Japan: http://japan.nlembassy.org/you-and-netherlands/dutch-japanese-relations.html
Network for Education and Academic Rights (Wikipedia entry): http://en.wikipedia.org/wiki/Network_for_Education_and_Academic_Rights
Network for South East Asian Studies: http://cseas.net/en/index.html
Network of European Studies Centres in Asia (NESCA) (Presentation): http://ec.europa.eu/research/social-sciences/pdf/group_5/eu_nesca_en.pdf
New Zealand–Europe Business Council: www.nzebc.org.nz/
Nordic Institute for Asian Studies (NIAS): http://nias.ku.dk/
On-Line Museum: Resources on Asian Art: http://afemuseums.easia.columbia.edu/cgi-bin/museums/search.cgi/topic?topic_id=170
Organisation for Cooperation, Exchange and Networking among Students (European Commission): www.oceans-network.eu/
Policy Innovations (Carnegie Council, US): www.policyinnovations.org/index.html
Portuguese Presence in Asia, Museo Fundação: www.museudooriente.pt/1524/portuguese-presence-in-asia.htm
Rangaku (Famous Scholars): www.museumstuff.com/learn/topics/Rangaku::sub::Famous_Rangaku_Scholars
Rangaku (You Tube): www.youtube.com/watch?v=9Ns4n5AEFRA
Red-Haired Barbarians (Exhibition): www.iisg.nl/exhibitions/japaneseprints/index.html
Regional EU–ASEAN Dialogue Instrument (REDI – Education): http://readi.asean.org/activities/education
RMIT University European Union Centre: www.rmit.edu.au/eucentre
Sacred Texts (on-line gallery): www.bl.uk/onlinegallery/sacredtexts/index.html
Samurai Archives (Japan History Podcasts): http://samuraipodcast.com
Samurai Archives (Shíba Kōkan): http://wiki.samurai-archives.com/index.php?title=Shiba_Kokan
School of African and Oriental Studies, London: www.soas.ac.uk

258 Selected websites

School of African and Oriental Studies, Centre of South East Asian Studies: www.soas.ac.uk/cseas/
Science and Technology Programme in China: www.euchinastf.eu/
SEAMEO (South East Asian Ministers of Education Organization): www.seameo.org/
SEAMEO Open Learning Centre (SEAMOLEC): www.seamolec.org/
SEAMEO Regional Centre for Higher Education and Regional Development (SEAMEO-RIHED): www.rihed.seameo.org/
Seventeenth Century Siam (A Writer's Guide): http://17thcenturysiam.blogspot.co.uk/
Shiba Kōkan (Samurai Archives – Samurai Wiki): http://wiki.samurai-archives.com/index.php?title=Shiba_Kokan
Siam Society (Bangkok, Thailand): www.siam.org
SIL International: www.sil.org/
Silk Road: www.ess.uci.edu/~oliver/silk3.html
Silk Road (Asia for Educators: Special Topic): http://afe.easia.columbia.edu/special/silk_road.htm
Silk Road Bibliography: http://hua.umf.maine.edu/China/silk.html
Silk Road Chronology: www.silk-road.com/artl/chrono.shtml
Silk Road Digital: http://dsr.nii.ac.jp/
Silk Road Foundation: www.silroadfoundation.org/toc/index.html
Silk Road Foundation (Korea-Central Asia): www.silkroad-foundation.org/
Silk Road Journal (Silk Road Foundation): www.silkroadfoundation.org/toc/newsletter.html
Silk Road Links (Kenyon College): www2.kenyon.edu/Depts/Religion/Fac/Adler/Asia201/links201.htm
Silk Road Music Project (Yo Yo Ma): www.silkroadproject.org/
Silk Road Project (Harvard University): www.silkroadproject.org/Programs/TheSilkRoadProjectatHarvard/tabid/158/Default.aspx
Silk Road Religions: http://depts.washington.edu/silkroad/exhibit/religion/religion.html
Silk Road Society: www.travelthesilkroad.org/content/view/15/29/
Silk Roads in History (Materials for an e-History): http://faculty.washington.edu/dwaugh/srehist.html
Singapore EU Centre: www.eucentre.sg/
Singapore Institute of International Affairs (SIIA): www.siiaonline.org
Social Transformation and Educational Prosperity (STEP): http://steporg.tripod.com/
South East Asia – EU Net (SEA-EU-Net): www.sea-eu.net/
South East Asia Education Network (SEA-EU Net): http://seaedu.net/
Southeast Asia–Europe Higher Education and Research Forum (ASEM 8, 2010): www.asem8.be/event/south-east-asia-europe-higher-education-and-research-forum
South East Asian Educational Leadership Conference (2012): http://go2fresnostate.com/seaconference/
South East Asian School Principals Forum (SEASPF): www.seaspf.org/
TEMPUS: http://ec.europa.eu/tempus
Tertiary Education Commission New Zealand: www.tec.govt.nz/
Thai–Europe Net: http://news.thaieurope.net/
The Spice Trail, British Library: www.bl.uk/onlinegallery/onlineex/spicetrail/index.html
Trans-Eurasia Information Network (TEIN): www.tein3.net/
Understanding China (Commercial Training Website): www.understandingchina.eu/
UNESCO: www.unesco.org
UNESCO Bangkok (e-Library): www.unescobkk.org/resources/e-library/

Selected websites 259

UNESCO's Asia and the Pacific Education for All (EFA) website: www.unescobkk.org/education/efa

United Nations Economic and Social Commission for Asia and the Pacific: www.unescap.org/

Universitas 21: www.universitas21.com/

University Association for Contemporary European Studies (UACES, London): www.uaces.org

University Mobility in Asia and the Pacific (Australia): www.umap.org/

University of Canterbury (UC), Christchurch (New Zealand): www.canterbury.ac.nz/

University World News (Global Edition): www.universityworldnews.com/staticpages/index.php?page=he_events

Victoria University (Wellington, New Zealand): www.victoria.ac.nz/home

Virtual East Asia Library (German): http://ead.staatsbibliothek-berlin.de/index.html

Working Group for an ASEAN Human Rights Mechanism: www.aseanhrmech.org/

World Bank (Education): www.worldbank.org/education

Xinhua News Agency (Xinhua Net English): www.xinhuanet.com/english/

Zürich University: ('Asia–Europe Research-Priority-Focus 2009'): www.asienundeuropa.uzh.ch/index_en.html

Bibliography

Abraham, C. (2006) *Speaking Out: Insights into Contemporary Malaysian Issues* (Kuala Lumpur: Utusan Publications; www.upnd.com.my).

Acharya, A. (2013) *Civilizations in Embrace: The Spread of Ideas and the Transformation of Power* (Singapore: Institute of Southeast Asian Studies, ISEAS).

Acharya, A. and Buzan, B. (2010) *Non-Western International Relations Theory* (London: Routledge).

Allen, C. (2003) *The Buddha and the Sahibs: The Men Who Discovered India's Lost Religion* (London: John Murray).

Allen, C. (2012) *Ashoka: The Search for India's Lost Emperor* (London: Little, Brown).

Amsterdams Historisch Museum (AHM, now: Amsterdam Museum) (2000) *Japanse Verwondering – Shiba Kokan 1747–1818: Kunstenaar in de ban van het Westen* (*Bijschriften*) (Brochures: Amsterdam: AHM) (see also: Parthesius and Schiermeier, below).

Anderson, B. (1990) *Language and Power: Exploring Global Cultures in Indonesia* (Ithaca: Cornell University Press).

Apfelthaler, G., Hansen, K., Siow-Heng, O. and Tapachai, N. (2006) *Intercultural Communication Competencies in Higher Education and Management*, Proceedings of the International Conference on Intercultural Communication Competencies, 6–7 October 2005 (Singapore: Marshall Cavendish Academic).

Archibugi, D. and Coco, A. (2005) 'Is Europe Becoming the Most Dynamic Knowledge Economy in the World?', in: *Journal of Common Market Studies*, 43(3): 433–459.

Asia–Europe Institute (AEI), University of Malaya: *AEI Post* (ISSN 1985–2185).

Asia–Europe Institute (AEI), University of Malaya: *AEI Post, Volume 1 (September 2007)*.

Asia–Europe Institute (AEI), University of Malaya: *AEI Post, Volume 2 (June 2009)*.

Asia–Europe Institute (AEI), University of Malaya: *AEI Post, Volume 3 (June 2010)*.

Asia–Europe Institute (AEI), University of Malaya: *AEI Post, Volume 4 (June 2011)*.

Asia–Europe Institute (AEI), University of Malaya (*Brochures*, 2007–2013).

Asia–Europe Institute (AEI), University of Malaya: *Building Ties beyond Boundaries*.

Asia–Europe Institute (AEI), University of Malaya: *Graduate Study at AEI*.

Asia–Europe Institute (AEI), University of Malaya: *International Masters in ASEAN Studies (IMAS)*.

Asia–Europe Institute (AEI), University of Malaya: *International Masters in Information Management (IMIM)*.

Asia–Europe Institute (AEI), University of Malaya: *International Masters in Regional Integration (IMRI)*.

Asia–Europe Institute (AEI), University of Malaya: *International Masters in Small-and-Medium Enterprises (IMSME)*.

Bibliography 261

Asia–Europe Institute (AEI), University of Malaya: *International Masters Programmes and PhD Programme.*

Asia–Europe Institute (AEI), University of Malaya: *PhD Programme, Asia–Europe Institute.*

Asia–Europe Institute (AEI), University of Malaya (*Annual Reports*, 2007–2012).

Asian Civilizations Museum (ACM, eds.: Ham, S. and Wolody, S., plus contributors) (2003, 2nd reprint, 2006) *The Asian Civilizations Museum A–Z Guide* (Singapore: ACM).

Asian Civilizations Museum (ACM)/Krishnan, Gauri Parimoo (2008, 3rd reprint 2010) *On the Nālandā Trail: Buddhism in India, China and Southeast Asia* (Singapore: Asian Civilizations Museum, ACM) (published in conjunction with the exhibition *On the Nālandā Trail*, 1 November 2007–23 March 2008) (ISBN-13:978-981-059-569-2).

Askew, M. (2002) *Bangkok – Place, Practice and Representation* (London: Routledge).

Bailey, Gauvin Alexander (2001) *Art on the Jesuit Missions in Asia and Latin America, 1542–1773* (Toronto: University of Toronto Press).

Baker, C. (2011) 'Markets and Production in the City of Ayutthaya before 1767; Translation and Analysis of Part of the *Description of Ayutthaya*', in: *Journal of the Siam Society*, 99: 38–66.

Bell, David (2004) *Ukiyo-E Explained* (Global Oriental: Folkestone/Kent).

Bellah, R. (1985) *Tokugawa Religion – The Cultural Roots of Modern Japan* (New York: The Free Press/Macmillan/Collier).

Bender, T. (2012) *Discussion-Based Online Teaching to Enhance Student Learning – Theory, Practice and Assessment* (Sterling, Virginia: Stylus Publishing, LLC).

Bernades de Carvalho, R. (2011) *La Présence Portugaise à Ayutthaya (Siam) aux XVIe et XVIIe Siècles* (Lisbon: Instituto do Oriente).

Bibliotheca Wittockiana Brussels (BWB) (2009) *Western Travellers in China: Discovering the Middle Kingdom* (Brussels: Bibliotheca Wittockiana).

Blockmans, S. and Hillion, C. (eds, 2013) *EEAS 2.0 – A Legal Commentary on Council Decision 2010/427/EU Establishing the Organisation and Functioning of the European External Action Service* (Maastricht: EIPA): http://publications.eipa.eu/en/details/&tid=1846.

Borschberg, P. (2002) 'The Seizure of the Santo António at Pattani: VOC Freebooting, the Estado da Índia, Peninsular Politics, 1602–1609', in: *Journal of the Siam Society*, 90: 59–72.

Boxer, C.R. (1968) *Jan Compagnie in Japan, 1600–1817. An Essay on the Cultural, Artistic and Scientific Influence Exercised by the Hollanders in Japan from the Seventeenth to the Nineteenth Centuries* (London, New York, Tokyo: Oxford University Press, 'Oxford in Asia' Historical Reprints).

Boxer, C.R. (1969) *The Portuguese Seaborne Empire 1415–1825* (London: Hutchinson).

BOZAR (From: 'Beaux Arts': Centre for Fine Arts, Brussels)/Jan van Alphen *et al.* (2010) *Passage to Asia: 25 Centuries of Exchange between Asia and Europe* (Brussels: BOZAR).

Breazeale, K. (ed., 1999) *From Japan to Arabia: Ayutthaya's Maritime Relations with Asia* (Bangkok: The Foundation for the Promotion of Social Sciences and Humanities Textbooks Project).

Breazeale, K. (2006) 'Whirligig of Diplomacy: A Tale of Thai-Portuguese Relations, 1613–1619', in: *Journal of the Siam Society*, 94: 51–110.

Brockey, L.M. (2007) *Journey to the East – The Jesuit Mission to China, 1579–1724* (Cambridge, Mass.: The Belknap Press of Harvard University Press).

262 Bibliography

Brotton, Jerry (2002) *Renaissance Bazaar – From the Silk Road to Michelangelo* (Oxford: OUP).
Brotton, Jerry (2012) *A History of the World in Twelve Maps* (London: Allen Lane/Penguin).
Brown, C. (2009) *Ashmolean: Britain's First Museum* (Oxford: Ashmolean Museum).
Bullen, R., Bell, D., Lummis, G. and Payne, R. (2009) *Pleasure and Play in Edo Japan* (Christchurch, New Zealand: Canterbury Museum and University of Canterbury).
Burke, Peter (2000) *A Social History of Knowledge: Part 1: From Gutenberg to Diderot* (Cambridge: Polity Press).
Camões, Luíz Vaz de, *The Lusíads*, translation of Landeg White, 1997 (Oxford: OUP, Oxford World Classics); translation of William C. Atkinson, 1952 (London: Penguin).
Chartsuwan, C. (2004) 'Asia-Europe Foundation: Multilateral Efforts to Enhance Artistic and Cultural Co-operation between Asia and Europe', in: Fisher, R. (ed.) *Developing New Instruments to Meet Cultural Policy Challenges* (Report of an Asia–Europe Seminar on Cultural Policy, Bangkok, Thailand, 24–27 June 2004) (Bangkok: Centre for European Studies, Chulalongkorn University): 174–181.
Chirathivat, S. and Lassen P.H. (eds, 1999) *European Studies in Asia* (Bangkok: Interdisciplinary Centre for European Studies at Chulalongkorn University).
Chong, A. (2010) 'Southeast Asia: Theory between Modernization and Tradition', in: Acharya, A. and Buzan, B. (eds) *Non-Western International Relations Theory* (London: Routledge): 117–147.
Christiansen, T., Jørgensen, K.E. and Wiener, A. (2001) *The Social Construction of Europe* (London: Sage).
Clark, Timothy (2011) *Hokusai's Great Wave* (London: The British Museum Press).
Clarke, J.J. (1997) *Oriental Enlightenment* (New York: Routledge).
Clements, J. (2005) *Coxinga and the Fall of the Ming Dynasty* (Stroud, Gloucestershire: Sutton Publishing).
Collcutt, M. (1993) 'The Legacy of Confucianism in Japan', in: Rozman, G. (ed.) *The East Asian Region – Confucian Heritage and its Modern Adaptation* (Princeton, NJ: Princeton University Press): 111–154.
Collini, S. (2012) *What Are Universities For?* (London: Penguin).
Cotterell, Arthur (2010) *Western Power in Asia: Its Slow Rise and Swift Fall, 1415–1999* (Singapore: John Wiley & Sons, Asia).
Cronin, Vincent (1961) *The Wise Man from the West* (London and Glasgow: Fontana Books).
Curtin, Philip D. (2000) *The World and the West – The European Challenge and the Overseas Response in the Age of Empire* (Cambridge: CUP).
D'Ávila Lourido, R. (1996) 'European Trade Between Macao and Siam, From Its Beginnings to 1663', in: *Journal of the Siam Society (JSS)*, 84(2): 75–101.
Da Silva Tavares, C.C. (2004) *Jesuítas e Inquisidoresem Goa* (Lisboa: Roma Editora).
Dalrymple, W. (2004) 'Personal Encounters: Europeans in South Asia', in: Jackson, Anna and Jaffer, Amin (eds) *Encounters. The Meeting of Asia and Europe, 1500–1800* (London: V&A Publications): 156–169.
Davies, Norman (1996) *Europe: A History* (Oxford: OUP).
De Bary, Wm. Theodore and Tu, Weiming (eds, 1998) *Confucianism and Human Rights* (New York: Columbia University Press).
De Bary, W.M.T, Gluck, C. and Tiedemann, A.E. (eds, 2006) *Sources of Japanese Tradition, Volume Two, 1600–2000 (Abridged) – Part One: 1600–1868* (New York: Columbia University Press).

De Coster, Anne (2009) *Western Travellers in China: Discovering the Middle Kingdom* (Brussels: BibliothecaWittockiana).
De Prado, C. (2007) *Global Multi-Level Governance: European and East Asian Leadership* (Tokyo: United Nations University Press).
De Prado, C. (2009) 'Comparing European and East Asian Experiences in Higher Education Regionalism', in: *Global Institute for Asian Regional Integration*, GIARI Working Paper, Vol. 2008-E-23, 31 January (*Waseda University Global COE Program*).
Deem, R., Ka Ho Mok and Lucas, L. (2008) 'Transforming Higher Education in Whose Image? Exploring the Concept of the "World-Class" University in Europe and Asia', in: *Higher Education Policy*, 21/2008: 83–97.
Delegation of the European Union to Australia (2012) *Celebrating 50 Years: EU–Australia* (Yarralumla, ACT: EU Delegation).
Demel, W. (1991) 'China in the Political Thought of Western and Central Europe, 1570–1750', in: Lee, T.H.C. (ed.) *China and Europe – Images and Influences in Sixteenth to Eighteenth Centuries* (Hong Kong: The Chinese Library/University Press): 45–98.
Der Spiegel No. 5/2009: *Geschichte: Die Geburt der Moderne* (Hamburg: Spiegel-Verlag).
Dhivarat Na Pombejra (2011) 'Conflict and Commerce in the Gulf of Siam, c. 1629–1642: Using Dutch Documents to "De-centre" Ayutthayan History', in: Grabowsky, V. (ed.) *Southeast Asian Historiography: Unravelling the Myths* (Essays in Honour of Barend Jan Terwiel) (Bangkok: River Books): 142–161.
Disney, Anthony R. (2009) *A History of Portugal and the Portuguese Empire from Beginnings to 1807 – Volume 2: The Portuguese Empire* (Cambridge: CUP).
Doidge, M. (2013) 'New Zealand and the Asia–Europe Meeting', in: *Asia Europe Journal*, 11: 147–162.
Doniger, Wendy (2010) *The Hindus – An Alternative History* (Oxford: OUP).
Duke, S. (2008) 'The European Commission Inside and Out: Administering EU Foreign Policy After Lisbon – The case of the EEAS', Working Paper 2008/W/01 (Maastricht: European Institute for Public Administration).
Duke, S. (2012) 'The Euro-Crisis, the Other Crisis and the Need for Global Thinking', in: *EIPASCOPE* 2/2012 (Maastricht: European Institute for Public Administration).
Dunn, Charles J. (1972) *Everyday Life in Traditional Japan* (Tokyo: Tuttle Publishing).
Dweck, C.S. (1999) *Self Theories: Their Role in Motivation, Personality, and Development* (Hove: Psychology Press, Taylor and Francis Group).
Edwards, R. and Usher, R. (2008) *Globalisation and Pedagogy: Space, Place and Identity* (London: Routledge).
Effert, F.R. (ed.), with Forrer, M. (2000) *The Court Journey to the Shōgun of Japan – From a Private Account by Jan Cock Blomhoff* (Leiden: Hotei Publishing).
Elisseeff, V. (2000) *The Silk Roads, Highways of Culture and Commerce* (Oxford: Berghahn, in conjunction with UNESCO Publishing).
Ellwood, R. (2008) *Introducing Japanese Religion* (New York/London: Routledge).
Elman, B.A. (2008) *A Cultural History of Modern Science in China* (Cambridge, Mass. and London: Harvard University Press).
Elverskog, (2013) *Buddhism and Islam on the Silk Road* (Philadelphia: University of Pennsylvania Press).
Enoch, Luca and Di Vincenco, Maurizio (2007) *Rangaku (Tome 1) La Cité sans Nuit* (Paris: Les HumanoïdesAssociés).
European Commission/ERASMUS-Mundus Programme White Paper (2010) *Strategies*

to Strengthen Collaboration in Higher Education between Europe and South East Asia (ACCESS-Survey: Academic Cooperation Europe South East Asia Support).

Farrington, A. (with: The British Library, 2002) *Trading Places: The East India Company and Asia, 1600–1834* (London: The British Library).

Febvre, Lucien and Martin, Henri-Jean (2010) *The Coming of the Book: The Impact of Printing, 1450–1800* (London: Verso).

Fisher, R.E. (1993) *Buddhist Art and Architecture* (London: Thames & Hudson).

Foss, T.N. and Lach, D.F. (1991) 'Images of Asia and Asians in European Fiction, 1500–1800', in: Lee, T.H.C. (ed.) *China and Europe – Images and Influences in Sixteenth to Eighteenth Centuries* (Hong Kong: The Chinese Library/University Press): 165–188.

Freeman, C. (2011) *Holy Bones, Holy Dust: How Relics Shaped the History of Medieval Europe* (New Haven, CT: Yale University Press).

French, Calvin L. (1974) *Shiba Kokan – Artist, Innovator and Pioneer in the Westernization of Japan* (New York and Tokyo: Weatherhill).

Frey, M. (2011) 'Eurasian Interactions: Siam and the Dutch East India Company during the Seventeenth Century', in: Grabowsky, V. (ed.) *Southeast Asian Historiography: Unravelling the Myths* (Essays in Honour of Barend Jan Terwiel) (Bangkok: River Books): 162–177.

Fritze, Ronald H. (2002) *New Worlds – The Great Voyages of Discovery 1400–1600* (Stroud, Gloucestershire: Sutton Publishing).

Gadman, L. and Cooper, C. (2009) *Open Source Leadership* (London: Palgrave Macmillan).

Gardner, H. (1983) *Frames of Mind: The Theory of Multiple Intelligences* (New York: Basic).

Garnier, D. (2004) *Ayutthaya – Venice of the East* (Bangkok: River Books).

Gelber, H.G. (2007) *The Dragon and the Foreign Devils – China and the World, 1100 BC to the Present* (London: Bloomsbury).

Ghosh, A. (1939) *A Guide to Nālandā* (Delhi: Archaeological Survey of India).

Gomez, E.T. and Saravanamuttu, J. (2013) *The New Economic Policy in Malaysia – Affirmative Action, Ethnic Inequalities and Social Justice* (Singapore: NUS Press/ISEAS).

Goodman, Grant K. (2000) *Japan and the Dutch 1600–1853* (London: RoutledgeCurzon).

Goodman, Grant K. (2006) 'Dutch Learning', in: De Bary, W.M.T, Gluck, C. and Tiedemann, A.E. (eds) *Sources of Japanese Tradition, Volume Two, 1600–2000 (Abridged) – Part One: 1600–1868* (New York: Columbia University Press): 289–313.

Gordon, Andrew (2003) *A Modern History of Japan from Tokugawa Times to the Present* (Oxford: OUP).

Gordon, Stewart (2008) *When Asia was the World* (New Haven and London: Yale University Press).

Goto-Jones, Christopher (2009) *Modern Japan – A Very Short Introduction* (Oxford: Oxford University Press).

Gregory, John S. (2003) *The West and China Since 1500* (London: Palgrave).

Guth, Christine (1996) *Art of Edo Japan* (London: Yale University Press).

Guy, T.C. (1999) 'Culturally Relevant Adult Education: Key Themes and Common Purposes', in: Guy, T.C. (ed.) *New Directions for Adult and Continuing Education*, 1999(82): 93–98.

Hall, D.G.E. (1981) *A History of South-East Asia* (London: Palgrave/Macmillan).

Hall, John Whitney and McClain, James L. (eds) (1991) *The Cambridge History of Japan: Volume 4: Early Modern Japan* (Cambridge: CUP).
Hall, K.R. (2011) *A History of Early Southeast Asia: Maritime Trade and Societal Development, 100–1500* (Plymouth: Rowman & Littlefield Publishers Inc.).
Hamid, J.A. and Krauss, S.E. (eds, 2010) *Motivating our Undergraduates to Lead: Facing the Challenge* (Serdang: Universiti Putra Malaysia Press).
Handy, C. (2009) *The Gods of Management – The Changing Work of Organisations* (London: Souvenir Press).
Hansen, Valerie (2012) *The Silk Road – A New History* (Oxford: OUP).
Harvey, Peter (1990) *An Introduction to Buddhism* (Cambridge: CUP).
Hastings, M. (1971) *Jesuit Child* (Newton Abbot: Michael Joseph Ltd/Readers Union).
Hiroshi, M. (2006) *Escape from Impasse: The Decision to Open Japan* (Tokyo: International House of Japan).
Hobson, John M. (2004) *The Eastern Origins of Western Civilisation* (Cambridge: CUP).
Holland, M., Ryan, P., Nowak, A. and Chaban, N. (eds, 2007) *The EU through the Eyes of Asia* (Singapore-Warsaw: ASEF).
Holland, M., Chaban, N. and Ryan, R. (eds, 2010) *The EU through the Eyes of Asia, Volume II: New Cases, New Findings* (Singapore: World Scientific).
Honey, P. and Mumford, A. (1986a) *The Manual of Learning Styles* (Oxford: Peter Honey Associates).
Honey, P. and Mumford, A. (1986b) *Learning Styles Questionnaire* (Oxford: Peter Honey Publications Ltd.).
Hong, Yan (2013) 'Attracting Chinese Students to the European Union: An Effective People-to-People Strategy?', in: *EU–Asia Observer*, 3: 7–12 (Bruges: College of Europe).
Horiushi, A. (2003) 'When Science Develops outside State Patronage: Dutch Studies in Japan at the Turn of the 19th Century', in: *Early Science and Medicine*, 8(2): 148–172.
Howgego, R. (2009) *The Book of Exploration* (London: Weidenfeld & Nicolson).
Hsia, F.C. (2009) *Sojourners in a Strange Land – Jesuits and Their Scientific Missions in Late Imperial China* (Chicago, IL: University of Chicago Press).
Hsia, R. Po-Chia (1998) *The World of Catholic Renewal, 1540–1770* (Cambridge: CUP).
Huang, Siu-chi (1999) *Essentials of Neo-Confucianism: Eight Major Philosophers of the Song and Ming Periods* (Westport/Connecticut, London: Greenwood Press).
Huffman, James L. (2010) *Japan in World History* (Oxford: OUP).
Ibrahim, Z. (2013) 'The New Economic Policy and the Identity Question of the Indigenous Peoples of Sabah and Sarawak', in: Gomez, E.T. and Saravanamuttu, J. (eds) *The New Economic Policy in Malaysia – Affirmative Action, Ethnic Inequalities and Social Justice* (Singapore: NUS Press/ISEAS): 293–313.
Instituto de Estudos Europeus de Macau (IEEM) (2001) *European Studies in Asia* (Macao: IEEM and European Commission).
Ishii, Y. (1971) 'Seventeenth Century Japanese Documents about Siam', in: *Journal of the Siam Society (JSS)*, 59(2): 161–173.
Iwamoto, Y. (2007) 'Yamada Nagamasa and his Relations with Siam', in: *Journal of the Siam Society*, 95: 73–84.
Jackson, A. (2004) 'East meets West', in: *BBC History Magazine* (October): 20–22.
Jackson, A. and Jaffer, A. (2004) *Encounters. The Meeting of Asia and Europe, 1500–1800* (London: V&A Publications).
James, R. and Mok, K. (eds, 2005) *Globalization and Higher Education in East Asia* (Singapore: Marshall Cavendish Academic, Contemporary Issues in Education).

Jansen, Marius B. (2000) *The Making of Modern Japan* (Cambridge, Mass.: The Belknap Press of Harvard University Press).

Jarves, J.J. (1984) *A Glimpse at the Art of Japan* (Rutland, Vermont and Tokyo: Tuttle).

Johnson, Hiroko (2005) *Western Influences on Japanese Art – The Akita Ranga School and Foreign Books* (Amsterdam: Hotei Publishing).

Kaempfer, Engelbert (1999) *Kaempfer's Japan – Tokugawa Culture Observed* (edited, translated and annotated by Beatrice M. Bodart-Bailey) (Honolulu: University of Hawai'i Press).

Kamei-Dyche, A.T. (2011) 'The History of Books and Print Culture in Japan – The State of the Discipline', in: *Book History*, 14: 270–304: http://muse.jhu.edu/journals/book_history/v014/14.kamei-dyche.pdf.

Kao, M. (1991) 'European Influences in Chinese Art, Sixteenth to Eighteenth Centuries', in: Lee, T.H.C. (ed.) *China and Europe – Images and Influences in Sixteenth to Eighteenth Centuries* (Hong Kong: The Chinese Library/University Press): 251–303.

Kassim, A. (2013) 'Public Universities: Development and Internationalization', in: Tham Siew Yean (ed.) *Internationalizing Higher Education in Malaysia* (Singapore: Institute of Southeast Asian Studies, ISEAS): 41–65.

Keene, Donald (1969) *The Japanese Discovery of Europe* (Stanford, Calif.: Stanford University Press).

Keene, Donald (2006) *The Frog in the Well – Portraits of Japan by Watanabe Kazan, 1793–1841* (New York: Columbia University Press).

Kelly, K. (2001) *The Extraordinary Museums of Southeast Asia* (New York: Harry N. Abrams, Inc.).

Kelly, S. (2010) 'Clutching at the Apron Strings? New Zealand's Relationship with the EU and the Possible Consequences for ASEM', in: *Asia Europe Journal* (2010): 211–226.

Keukeleire, S. (2012) *EU Foreign Policy and the Challenges of Structural Diplomacy: Comprehensiveness, Coordination, Alignment and Learning*; Diplomatic System of the EU (DSEU) Network; DSEU Policy Paper 12, February: http://dseu.lboro.ac.uk/Documents/Policy_Papers/DSEU_Policy_Paper12.pdf.

Khoo Joo Ee (1991) *Kendi – Pouring Vessels in the University of Malaya Collection* (Singapore, Oxford and New York: Oxford University Press).

Kiechle, Stefan S.J. (2009) *Die Jesuiten* (Herder: Freiburg).

King, James (2010) *Beyond the Great Wave: The Japanese Landscape Print, 1727–1960* (New York: Peter Lang Publishing).

King, V. (ed., 1995) *Explorers of South-East Asia – Six Lives* (Kuala Lumpur: OUP).

Kolb, D.A. (1984) *Experiential Learning: Experience as the Source of Learning and Development* (Englewood Cliffs, NJ: Prentice Hall).

Lach, Donald F. and Van Kley, Edwin J. (1994–1998) *Asia in the Making of Europe.*

Lach, Donald F. and Van Kley, Edwin J. *Volume I: The Century of Discovery* Book 1 (Chicago: University of Chicago Press).

Lach, Donald F. and Van Kley, Edwin J. *Volume I: The Century of Discovery* Book 2 (Chicago: University of Chicago Press).

Lach, Donald F. and Van Kley, Edwin J. *Volume II: A Century of Wonder* Book 1 (Chicago: University of Chicago Press).

Lach, Donald F. and Van Kley, Edwin J. *Volume II: A Century of Wonder* Book 2 (Chicago: University of Chicago Press).

Lach, Donald F. and Van Kley, Edwin J. *Volume II: A Century of Wonder* Book 3 (Chicago: University of Chicago Press).

Lach, Donald F. and Van Kley, Edwin J. *Volume III: A Century of Advance* Book 1 (Chicago: University of Chicago Press).
Lach, Donald F. and Van Kley, Edwin J. *Volume III: A Century of Advance* Book 2 (Chicago: University of Chicago Press).
Lach, Donald F. and Van Kley, Edwin J. *Volume III: A Century of Advance* Book 3 (Chicago: University of Chicago Press).
Lach, Donald F. and Van Kley, Edwin J. *Volume III: A Century of Advance* Book 4 (Chicago: University of Chicago Press).
Lackner, M. (1991) 'Jesuit Figurism', in: Lee, T.H.C. (ed.) *China and Europe – Images and Influences in Sixteenth to Eighteenth Centuries* (Hong Kong: The Chinese Library/ University Press): 129–148.
Laven, M. (2011) *Mission to China – Matteo Ricci and the Jesuit Encounter with the East* (London: Faber & Faber).
Lawson, S. (2006) *Culture and Context in World Politics* (London: Palgrave/Macmillan).
Lee, H.G. (2013) 'Racial Citizenship and Higher Education in Malaysia', in: Gomez, E.T. and Saravanamuttu, J. (eds) *The New Economic Policy in Malaysia – Affirmative Action, Ethnic Inequalities and Social Justice* (Singapore: NUS Press/ISEAS): 235–261.
Lee, S.E. (1983) *Reflections of Reality in Japanese Art* (Cleveland, Ohio: Indiana University Press and Cleveland Museum of Art).
Lee, T.H.C. (1991a) *China and Europe – Images and Influences in Sixteenth to Eighteenth Centuries* (Hong Kong: The Chinese Library/University Press).
Lee, T.H.C. (1991b) 'Christianity and Chinese Intellectuals: From the Chinese Point of View', in: Lee, T.H.C. (ed.) *China and Europe – Images and Influences in Sixteenth to Eighteenth Centuries* (Hong Kong: The Chinese Library/University Press): 1–27.
Leidy, D.P. (2008) *The Art of Buddhism* (London: Shambhala).
Leksukhum, S. (with Mermet, G., 2000) *Temples of Gold – Seven Centuries of Thai Buddhist Paintings* (Bangkok: River Books).
Letta, C.G.M. (2003) *EA-EU Partnerships – the Future Dynamics of the East Asia–European Union Relationships* (Seoul: Sejong Institute).
Levenson, Jay A. (1997) *Encompassing the Globe: Portugal and the World in the 16th and 17th Century* (Washington, DC: Smithsonian Institution Press).
Lottes, G. (1991) 'China in European Political Thought, 1750–1850', in: Lee, T.H.C. (ed.) *China and Europe – Images and Influences in Sixteenth to Eighteenth Centuries* (Hong Kong: The Chinese Library/University Press): 65–98.
Lowenstein, T. (2006) *Treasures of the Buddha – The Glories of Sacred Asia* (London: Duncan Baird Publishers).
Macfarlane, Alan (2008) *Japan through the Looking Glass* (London: Profile Books).
Macfarlane, B. (2012) *Intellectual Leadership in Higher Education* (Research into Higher Education Series; London: Routledge).
MacGregor, Neil (2010) *A History of the World in 100 Objects* (London: Allen Lane).
Mahbubani, K. (2008) *The New Asian Hemisphere: The Irresistible Shift of Global Power to the East* (New York: Public Affairs Publishers).
Maillard, Christine (2008) *L'Inde vue d'Europe; Histoire d'une Rencontre (1750–1950)* (Paris: Albin Michel).
Marican, P. (2012) *Charade of Justice – Anwar's Third Trial* (Petaling Jaya: Gerakbudaya Enterprise; www.gerakbudaya.com).
Marks, A. (2010) *Japanese Woodblock Prints: Artists, Publishers and Masterworks 1680–1900* (Tokyo: Tuttle Publishing).

Masanobu, Hosono (1978) *Nagasaki Prints and Early Copperplates* (translated and adapted by Lloyd R. Craighill; Tokyo: Kodansha International Ltd. and Shibundo).

McBurnie, G. and Ziguras, C. (2001) 'The Regulation of Transnational Higher Education in Southeast Asia: Case Studies of Hong Kong, Malaysia and Australia', in: *Higher Education*, 42/2001: 85–105.

McNeely, I.F. and Wolverton, L. (2009) *Reinventing Knowledge – From Alexandria to the Internet* (New York and London: W.W. Norton & Company).

Meissner, W. (2002) 'Cultural Relations between China and the Member States of the European Union'; in: *The China Quarterly*, 2002: 181–203.

Michel, W. (2007) 'Medicine and Allied Sciences in the Cultural Exchange between Japan and Europe in the 17th Century', in: Ölschleger, H.-D. (ed.) *Theories and Methods in Japanese Studies: Current State and Future Developments – Papers in Honour of Josef Kreiner* (Göttingen: Vandenhoeck & Ruprecht Unipress): 285–302: https://qir.kyushu-u.ac.jp/dspace/handle/2324/14227; http://wolfgangmichel.web.fc2.com/publ/books/32/032index.htm.

Millward, James A. (2007) *Eurasian Crossroads – A History of Xinjiang* (London: Hurst & Company).

Millward, James A. (2013) *The Silk Road: A Very Short Introduction* (Oxford: OUP).

Milton, Giles (2002) *Samurai William – The Adventurer Who Unlocked Japan* (London: Hodder & Stoughton).

Mitchell, D. (1980) *The Jesuits – A History* (London: Macdonald Futura Publishers).

Mitchell, D. (2010) *The Thousand Autumns of Jacob De Zoet* (London: Hodder and Stoughton/Sceptre).

Moran, J.F. (1993) *The Japanese and the Jesuits – Alessandro Valignano in Sixteenth-Century Japan* (London: Routledge).

Morgan, J. and Walters, C. (2012) *Journeys on the Silk Road* (Guilford, Conn.: Lyons Press): www.journeysonthesilkroad.com/index.html.

Morgan, L. (2012) *The Buddhas of Bamiyan* (London: Profile Books).

Mormando, F. and Thomas, J.G. (eds, 2006) *Anniversary Exhibition of Early Printed Works From the Jesuitana Collection of the John J. Burns Library, Boston College* (Chestnut Hill, Mass.: The Jesuit Institute of Boston College).

Mullett, M.A. (1999) *The Catholic Reformation* (London: Routledge).

Murdoch, Z., Trondal, J. and Gänzle, S. (2013) *Making the Grade, Keeping the Gate: The Recruitment of Member-State Diplomats to the European External Action Service (EEAS)*; Diplomatic Service of the EU (DSEU) Network; DSEU Policy Paper No. 13, February: http://dseu.lboro.ac.uk/Documents/Policy_Papers/DSEU_Policy_Paper13.pdf.

Murphy, C. (2013) *God's Jury – The Inquisition and the Making of the Modern World* (London: Penguin).

Murray, P. (2003) 'An Asia Pacific Response to the European Union: Australian elite Perceptions', in: *Asia Europe Journal* 1/2003: 1–17.

Murray, P. and Polesel, J. (2013) 'A Comparative Exploration of Learning Pathways and Transition Systems in Denmark and Australia', in: *European Journal of Education*, 48(3): 233–246.

Murray, P. and Zolin, M.B. (2012) 'Australia and the European Union: Conflict, Competition or Engagement in Agricultural and Agri-Food Trade?', in: *Australian Journal of International Affairs*, 66(2): 186–205.

Nain, Z. (2013) *Rhetoric and Realities: Critical Reflections on Malaysian Politics, Culture and Education* (Petaling Jaya: Strategic Information and Research Development Centre).

Newitt, Malyn (2009) *Portugal in European and World History* (London: Reaktion Books).
Niemann, U. (2001) 'The Dynamics of People-to-People Exchanges between Asia and Europe', in: *Chulalongkorn University Journal of European Studies*, 9(2): 28–34.
Nishiyama, Matsunosuke (1997) *Edo Culture: Daily Life and Diversions in Urban Japan, 1600-1868* (Honolulu: University of Hawai'i Press).
Norell, M., Leidy, D.P. and Ross, L. (2011) *Travelling the Silk Road: Ancient Pathway to the Modern World* (New York: The American Museum of Natural History).
Nosco, P. (ed., 1997) *Confucianism and Tokugawa Culture* (Honolulu: University of Hawai'i Press).
Ooi Kee Beng (2010) *Between UMNO and a Hard Place* (Singapore: Institute for Southeast Asian Studies, ISEAS).
Open University (OU) (2010) *Exploring History: Seven Ages of Britain* (Milton Keynes: Open University/BBC SUP015737): www.open.edu/openlearn/history-the-arts/history/heritage/seven-ages-britain-quest.
Osborne, M. (1997) *Southeast Asia – An Introductory History* (7th ed., St Leonards, NSW, Australia: Allen & Unwin).
Pace, M. (2007) 'The Construction of EU Normative Power', in: *Journal of Common Market Studies*, 45(5): 1041–1064.
Pagden, Anthony (2008) *Worlds at War* (Oxford: OUP).
Pang, N.S-K. (2006) *Globalisation, Educational Research, Change and Reform* (Hong Kong: The Chinese University Press).
Parthesius, Robert and Schiermeier, Kris (with a contribution by Yasumasa Oka) (2000) *Japanse Verwondering: Shiba Kōkan 1747–1818, Kunstenaar in de ban van het Westen (Japanese Amazement: Shiba Kōkan 1747–1818, Artist under the Spell of the West)* (Amsterdam: Amsterdams Historisch Museum (AHM); Kobe: Kobe City Museum).
Patail A.-G. (2013) *Putting to Rest the Claim to Sabah by the Self-Proclaimed Sultanate of Sulu* (Kuala Lumpur/Putrajaya: Institut Terjemahan and Buku Malaysia Berhad/ Razak School of Government; www.rsog.com.my).
Patry Leidy, D. (2008) *The Art of Buddhism – An Introduction to its History and Meaning* (Boston and London: Shambhala).
Pearson, M.N. (1987) *The Portuguese in India (The New Cambridge History of India, Vol. I, Book 1)* (Cambridge: CUP).
Peleggi, M. (2013) 'The Turbaned and the Hatted: Figures of Alterity in Early Modern Thai Visual Culture', in: Eisenbeiß, A. And Saurma-Jeltsch, L.E. (eds) *Images of Otherness in Medieval and Early Modern Times: Exclusion, Inclusion and Assimilation* (Berlin and Munich: Deutscher Kunstverlag): 57–69.
Peterson, W.J. (2011) 'Learning from Heaven: The Introduction of Christianity and Other Western Ideas into Late Ming China', in: Wills, J.E. (Jr.) (ed.) *China and Maritime Europe 1500–1800: Trade, Settlement, Diplomacy and Missions* (Cambridge: CUP): 78–134.
Phuong-Mai, N., Terlouw, C. and Pilot, A. (2005) 'Cooperative Learning vs Confucian Heritage: Culture's Collectivism: Confrontation to Reveal Some Cultural Conflicts and Mismatch' [sic], in: *Asia Europe Journal*, 3(2005): 403–419.
Pina, I. (2001) 'The Jesuit Mission in Japan and in China: Two Distinct Realities. Cultural Adaptation and the Assimilation of Natives', in: *Bulletin of Portuguese/Japanese Studies*, 2 (June 2001) (Lisbon: Universidade Nova de Lisboa): 59–76: http://cham.fcsh.unl.pt/pages/eng/publicacoes_bpjs_eng.htm.
Plutschow, Herbert (2006) *A Reader in Edo Period Travel* (Folkestone, Kent: Global Oriental Press).

Quigley, J. (2005) 'Integrating Culture into the Asia–Europe Relationship', in: *EurAsia Bulletin*, 9(5) and (6): 1–2.
Quigley, J. (2006) 'The Coming Generation: Education and EU–Asia co-operation', in: *EurAsia Bulletin*, 10(9) and (10) (Brussels: European Institute for Asian Studies, EIAS).
Rahman, A.R.A. (2013) *Electoral Reforms – Facts and Fallacies* (Petaling Jaya, Selangor: MPH Publishing Sdn. Bhd.).
Ranzaburō, Ōtori (1964) 'The Acceptance of Western Medicine in Japan', in: *Monumenta Nipponica*, 19(3/4): 254–274.
Reed, M. and Demattè, P. (2007) *China on Paper: European and Chinese Works from the Late Sixteenth to the early Nineteenth Century* (Los Angeles: Getty Research Institute).
Reiterer, M. (2004) 'The Role of Education and Culture in Contemporary International Relations: A Challenge for the Asia Europe Meeting', in: *Asia Europe Journal*, 2: 365–371.
Reynolds, C.J. (2006) *Seditious Histories: Contesting Thai and Southeast Asian Pasts* (Seattle and London: University of Washington Press, in association with Singapore University Press).
Ringis, R. (1990) *Thai Temples and Temple Murals* (Kuala Lumpur: OUP).
Ringmar, Erik (2007) *Why Europe was First: Social Change and Economic Growth in Europe and East Asia, 1500–2050* (London, New York, Delhi: Anthem Press).
Roberts, L. (2009) 'Orienting Natural Knowledge – The Complex Career of Hiraga Gennai', in: *Endeavour*, 33(2): 65–69; http://ac.els-cdn.com/S0160932709000313/1-s2.0-S0160932709000313-main.pdf?_tid=961aa926-c0fd-11e2-b4db-00000aacb361&acdnat=1369020795_deb7a2dfdb1d029ac542315e7aa16fc6.
Ross, A.C. (1994) *A Vision Betrayed – The Jesuits in Japan and China, 1542–1742* (Maryknoll, New York: Orbis Books).
Ruangsilp, Bhawan (2009) 'Dutch Interaction with Siamese Law and the City Rules of Ayutthaya in the Seventeenth and Eighteenth Centuries', in: Masashi, Haneda (ed.) *Asian Port Cities 1600–1800: Local and Foreign Interactions* (Singapore and Tokyo: NUS Press and Kyoto University Press): 139–161.
Russell-Wood, A.J.R. (1998) *The Portuguese Empire 1415–1808* (Baltimore and London: The Johns Hopkins University Press).
Saipradist, A. and Staiff, R. (2007) 'Crossing the Cultural Divide: Western Visitors and Interpretation at Ayutthaya World Heritage Site, Thailand', in: *Journal of Heritage Tourism (JHT)*, 2(3): 211–224; www.tandfonline.com/doi/pdf/10.2167/jht061.0.
Sankalia, H.D. (1972) *The University of Nālandā* (Delhi: Oriental Publishers).
Sansom (1963) *A History of Japan* (Stanford, Calif.: Stanford University Press).
Saraiva, José Hermano (24th ed., 2007) *História Concisa de Portugal* (Mem Martins: Publicações Europa-América).
Saraiva, Luís and Jami, Catherine (eds, 2008) *The Jesuits, the Padroado and East Asian Science, (1552–1773)* (History of Mathematical Sciences: Portugal and East Asia III) (River Edge, NJ: World Scientific).
Saravanamuttu, J. (2010) *Malaysia's Foreign Policy: The First Fifty Years* (Singapore: Institute for Southeast Asian Studies, ISEAS).
Screech, Timon (1996) *The Western Scientific Gaze and Popular Imagery in Later Edo Japan – The Lens within the Heart* (Cambridge: CUP).
Screech, Timon (2004) 'Europe in Asia: The Impact of Western Art and Technology in Japan', in: Jackson, Anna and Jaffer, Amin (eds) *Encounters – The Meeting of Asia and Europe 1500–1800* (London: V&A Publications): 310–323.

Seabra, L. (2004) *A Embaixada ao Sião de Pero Vaz de Siqueira* (1684–1686) (Macau: Instituto Português do Oriente and Fundação Oriente).
Sen, Amulyachandra (1954) *Rajagriha and Nalanda* (Calcutta: Indian Publicity Society).
Severy, M. and Stanfield, J.L. (1992) 'Portugal's Sea Road to the East', in: *National Geographic*, 6, 182/5 (November 1992): 54–92.
Shagdar, B. (2000) 'The Mongol Empire in the Thirteenth and Fourteenth Centuries: East-West Relations', in: Elisseeff, V. (ed.) *The Silk Roads, Highways of Culture and Commerce* (Oxford: Berghahn, in conjunction with UNESCO Publishing): 127–144.
Shiori, Ito (2009) 'Western and Chinese Influences on Japanese Paintings in the Eighteenth Century', in: Masashi, Haneda (ed.) *Asian Port Cities 1600–1800. Local and Foreign Cultural Interactions* (Singapore and Tokyo: NUS Press and Kyoto University Press): 63–87.
Shirahara Y. (ed., 2008) *Japan Envisions the West – 16th-19th Century Japanese Art from Kobe City Museum* (Seattle and London: University of Washington Press).
Sjursen, H. (2003) 'Understanding the Common Foreign and Security Policy: Analytical Building Blocks', in Knodt, M. and Princen, S. (eds) *Understanding the European Union's External Relations* (London: Routledge): 35–53.
Smith, B.L. and MacGregor, J.T. (1992) 'What Is Collaborative Learning?', in: Goodsell, A., Maher, M., Tinto, V., Leigh-Smith, B. and MacGregor, J. (eds) *Collaborative Learning: A Sourcebook for Higher Education* (*National Center on Postsecondary Teaching, Learning, and Assessment* (Philadelphia: Pennsylvania State University).
Smith, R.L. (2010) 'Nomads and the Chinese: The Making of the Silk Road in Asia', in: van Alphen, Jan *et al.* (2010) *Passage to Asia: 25 Centuries of Exchange between Asia and Europe* (Brussels: BOZAR): 71–91.
Smithies, M. (1993) 'Jacques de Bourges (ca. 1630–1714) and Siam', in: *Journal of the Siam Society*, 81: 113–129.
Smithies, M. (1994) 'A Stormy Relationship: Phaulkon and Forbin, 1685–1687', in: *Journal of the Siam Society*, 82: 147–154.
Smithies, M. (1995) 'Seventeenth Century Siam: Its Extent and Urban Centres According to Dutch and French Observers', in: *Journal of the Siam Society*, 83: 62–78.
Smithies, M. (1997) 'The Siam of Mendez Pinto's Travels'; in: *Journal of the Siam Society*, 85, Parts 1 and 2 (1997): 59–73.
Smithies, M. (2003) 'Eclipses in Siam, 1685 and 1688, and Their Representation', in: *Journal of the Siam Society*, 91: 189–204.
Smithies, M. (2011) *500 Years of Thai–Portuguese Relations* (Festschrift: Bangkok: Siam Society).
Smithies, M. and Dhivarat na Pombejra (2002) 'Instructions Given to the Siamese Envoys Sent to Portugal, 1684', in: *Journal of the Siam Society*, 90: 125–135.
Soong, K.K. (2012) *The End of Barisan Nasional? Malaysian Political Issues* (Petaling Jaya: SUARAM Kommunikasi; www.suaram.net).
Sørensen, H.H. (2000) 'Perspectives on Buddhism in Dunhuang during the Tang and Five Dynasties Period', in: Elisseeff, V. (ed.) *The Silk Roads, Highways of Culture and Commerce* (Oxford: Berghahn, in conjunction with UNESCO Publishing): 27–48.
Steenbrink, J. and Jansen H. (transl., 2006) *Dutch Colonialism and Indonesian Islam. Contacts and Conflicts 1596–1950* (Amsterdam/New York: Rodopi).
Sternstein, L. (1965) '"Krung Kao" – The Old Capital of Ayutthaya', in: *Journal of the Siam Society*, 1(1): 83–121.
Stewart, B. (1979) *A Guide to Japanese Prints and Their Subject Matter* (New York: Dover Publications).

Stokhof, W. (1999) 'Bringing the Communities Together: What More Can Be Done?', in: Stokhof, W. and Van der Velde, P. (eds) *ASEM: The Asia–Europe Meeting: A Window of Opportunity* (Leiden/Amsterdam: International Institute for Asian Studies, IIAS): 35–46.

Stokhof, W., Van der Velde, P. and Yeo, L-H. (2004) *The Eurasian Space: Far More Than Two Continents* (Singapore and Leiden: Institute of Southeast Asian Studies and International Institute for Asian Studies).

Stoneman, R. (2008) *Alexander the Great – A Life in Legend* (New Haven and London: Yale University Press).

Subrahmanyam, S. (1993) *The Portuguese Empire in Asia, 1500–1700: A Political and Economic History* (London and New York: Longman).

Subrahmanyam, S. (2004) 'When the World Discovered Portugal', in: *V&A Magazine*, Autumn 2004: 34–42.

Tadjbakhsh, S. (2010) 'International Relations Theory and the Islamic World View', in: Acharya, A. and Buzan, B. (eds) *Non-Western International Relations Theory* (London: Routledge): 174–196.

Tanaka, H. (1995) *A History of Japanese Art* (Akita: Akita International University Press).

Tankha, Brij and Thampi, Madhavi (2005) *Narratives of Asia from India, Japan and China* (Calcutta: Sampark Publishing).

Ten Brummelhuis, H. (2011) 'Knowledge and Interest in Cornelis van Nijenroode's Early Dutch Treatise on Siam, 1691', in: Grabowsky, V. (ed.) *Southeast Asian Historiography: Unravelling the Myths* (Essays in Honour of Barend Jan Terwiel) (Bangkok: River Books): 196–207.

Tham Siew Yean (2013) *Internationalizing Higher Education in Malaysia* (Singapore: Institute of Southeast Asian Studies, ISEAS).

Tillman, H.C. (1982) *Utilitarian Confucianism: Ch'en Liang's Challenge to Chu Hsi* (Cambridge, Mass.: Council on East Asian Studies of Harvard University).

Trakulhun, S. (1997) 'The View from the Outside – Nicolas Gervaise, Simon de la Loubère and the Perception of 17th Century Siamese Government and Society', in: *Journal of the Siam Society*, 85: 75–84.

Trakulhun, S. (2011) 'Suspicious Friends: Siamese Warfare and the Portuguese (c. 1540–1700)', in: Grabowsky, V. (ed.) *Southeast Asian Historiography: Unravelling the Myths* (Essays in Honour of Barend Jan Terwiel) (Bangkok: River Books): 178–195.

Twiss, S.B. (1998) 'A Constructive Framework for Discussing Confucianism and Human Rights', in: De Bary, Wm. Theodore and Tu, Weiming (eds) *Confucianism and Human Rights* (New York: Columbia University Press): 27–53.

University of Malaya Centre for Civilizational Dialogue (UMCCD/Pusat Dialog Peradaban Universiti Malaya, PDPUM) Bulletin (2013) No. 23, January to April 2013.

Van Alphen, Jan (2010) 'The Roots and Influence of "Hellenism" in Asia at the Beginning of the Common Era', in: BOZAR (Centre for Fine Arts, Brussels)/Jan van Alphen *et al.* (various contributors) *Passage to Asia: 25 Centuries of Exchange Between Asia and Europe* (Brussels: BOZAR): 93–105.

Van Beek, S. and Tettoni, I.L. (1999) *The Arts of Thailand* (Hong Kong: Periplus).

Van der Cruysse, D. (2002a) *Siam and the West, 1500–1700* (Chiang Mai: Silkworm Books).

Van der Cruysse, D. (2002b) *Le Noble Désir der Courir le Monde – Voyager en Asie au VIIe Siècle* (Paris: Fayard).

Van der Geest, W. (2006) 'Shaping Factors of EU–East Asia Relations', in: *Asia Europe Journal*, 4(2): 131–149.
Van der Kraan, A. (2000) 'The Dutch in Siam: Jeremias van Vliet and the 1636 Incident at Ayuttaya', in: *UNEAC Asia Papers No. 3* (Armidale, NSW, Australia: University of New England Asia Centre): 1–10.
Vanichviroon, Kunakorn (2004) 'Imagining Ayutthaya: A Recent Transformation in the Thai Collective Identity of the Past' (unpublished MA Dissertation, Department of History, National University of Singapore, NUS), available at: http://scholarbank.nus.edu.sg/termsofuse;jsessionid=3CEC00C2363E2766AB4AF28A6E93068B.
Villiers, J. (1998) 'Portuguese and Spanish Sources for the History of Ayutthaya in the Sixteenth Century', in: *Journal of the Siam Society*, 86: 119–130.
Vygotsky, L.S. (1978) *Mind in Society: The Development of Higher Psychological Processes* (Cambridge, Mass.: Harvard University Press).
Waley-Cohen, J. (2000) *The Sextants of Beijing – Global Currents in Chinese History* (New York and London: W.W. Norton & Company).
Ward, I. and Miraflor, N. (2009) *Slaughter and Deception at Bantang Kali* (Kuala Lumpur: Media Masters Publications).
Welch, A. (2013) *Higher Education in South East Asia* (London: Routledge).
Wellings, B. (2009) 'Between Vladivostok and Africa: Teaching European Studies in Australia', in: *Australia and New Zealand Journal of European Studies* (ANZJES), 1(1): 25–35.
Whitfield, S. (2004) *The Silk Road: Trade, Travel, War and Faith* (London: British Library).
Wiessala, G. (2002a) *The European Union and Asian Countries* (London: Sheffield Academic Press/UACES).
Wiessala, G. (2002b) 'Reading the "Software" of Asian Society'; in: *European Voice* (*Education Supplement*) 6–12 June 2002: 17–18 (cross-referenced in: *European Access* 2002, No. 4, August 2002, page 204, section 18.15, reference number 2479); www.europeanvoice.com/article/imported/reading-the-software-of-asian-society/44967.aspx.
Wiessala, G. (2004a) 'New Approaches to the Antipodes – Some Themes in EU Relations with Australia and New Zealand', in: *Asia-Pacific Journal of EU Studies*, 2(1), June 2004: 63–82.
Wiessala, G. (2004b) 'Beyond Approaching the Antipodes – European Studies in Australasia and the Pacific', in: *European Voice* (*Education Supplement*), February 2004: 5.
Wiessala, G. (2006) *Re-orienting the Fundamentals: Human Rights and New Connections in EU-Asia Relations* (Aldershot, Hampshire: Ashgate).
Wiessala, G. (2007) 'Catalysts and Inhibitors: The Role and Meaning of Human Rights in EU–Asia Relations', in: Contemporary Europe Research Centre (CERC), the University of Melbourne, Working Papers, No. 1/2007 (Melbourne: CERC).
Wiessala, G. (2010) 'Review of *The EU through the Eyes of Asia, Volume II (New Cases, New Findings)*, by Chaban, N., Holland, M., Ryan, P. (eds) (2009) (Singapore: World Scientific)', in: *Asia Europe Journal*, 8: 257–261, and for the ASEM 8 Summit (Brussels, October 2010); www.springerlink.com/content/1610-2932/.
Wiessala, G. (2011) *Enhancing Asia–Europe Co-operation through Educational Exchange* (London: Routledge).
Wills, J.E. (Jr.) (ed., 2011) *China and Maritime Europe 1500–1800: Trade, Settlement, Diplomacy and Missions* (Cambridge: CUP).
Winichakul, T. (1994) *Siam Mapped: A History of the Geo-Body of a Nation* (Honolulu: University of Hawai'i Press).

Winichakul, T. (2011) 'Siam's Colonial Conditions and the Birth of Thai History', in: Grabowsky, V. (ed.) *Southeast Asian Historiography: Unravelling the Myths* (Essays in Honour of Barend Jan Terwiel) (Bangkok: River Books): 20–41.

Witek, J.W. (S.J.) (2011) 'Catholic Missions and the Expansion of Christianity', in: Wills, J.E. (Jr.) (ed.) *China and Maritime Europe 1500–1800: Trade, Settlement, Diplomacy and Missions* (Cambridge: CUP): 135–182.

Wood, Frances (2003) *The Silk Road: Two Thousand Years in the Heart of Asia* (London: The British Library).

Wood, Frances (2009) *The Lure of China – Writers from Marco Polo to J.G. Ballard* (New Haven and London: Yale University Press).

Wriggins, S.H. (2004) *The Silk Road Journey with Xuanzang* (Boulder, Colorado: Westview Press).

Wright, J. (2004) *God's Soldiers: Adventure, Politics, Intrigue and Power; A History of the Jesuits* (New York: Doubleday).

Wright, J. (2005) *The Jesuits – Missions, Myths and Histories* (London: Harper Perennial).

Xinru, Liu (2010) *The Silk Road in World History* (Oxford: OUP).

Xinzhong, Yao (2000) *An Introduction to Confucianism* (Cambridge: CUP).

Yamada, C.F. (1976) *Dialogue in Art – Japan and the West* (Tokyo: Kodansha International Ltd.).

Yaqing Qin (2010) 'Why is There No Chinese International Relations Theory?' in: Acharya, A. and Buzan, B. (eds) *Non-Western International Relations Theory* (London: Routledge): 26–50.

Yavaprabhas, S. (2007) 'Quality Assurance in Sub-regional Contexts: Europe, Asia-Pacific and Southeast Asia', in: *SEAMEO Education Agenda*, 2, November 2007: 16–18.

Yoko, M. (2009) 'The Legal Position of Foreigners in Nagasaki during the Edo Period', in: Masahi, Haneda (ed.) *Asian Port Cities 1600–1800; Local and Foreign Interactions* (Singapore: NUS Press): 24–42.

Yoko, N. (1999) 'Ayutthaya and Japan: Embassies and Trade in the Seventeenth Century', in: Breazeale, K. (ed.) *From Japan to Arabia: Ayutthaya's Maritime Relations with Asia* (Bangkok: The Foundation for the Promotion of Social Sciences and Humanities Textbooks Project): 89–103.

Yoshiteru, I. and Bytheway, S.-J. (2011) 'Japan's Official Relations with "Shamuro" (Siam), 1599–1745: As Revealed in the Diplomatic Records of the Tokugawa Shogunate', in: *Journal of the Siam Society*, 99: 81–104.

Zhou, H. (2004) 'EU Social Policy Studies in China', IN: *Asia Europe Journal* 2/2004: 415–427.

Secondary sources

Akutagawa Ryūnosuke (2006) *Rashōmon and Seventeen Other Stories* (translated by J. Rubin; introduced by Haruki Murakami) (London: Penguin).

Attwater, R. (1963) *Adam Schall: A Jesuit at the Court of China, 1592–1666* (Milwaukee: The Bruce Publishing Company).

Bailey, Gauvin Alexander (2010) 'Religious Encounters: Christianity in Asia', in: Jackson, Anna and Jaffer, Amin (eds) *Encounters – The Meeting of Asia and Europe 1500–1800* (London: V&A Publications): 102–125.

Baker, J.S. (2000, repr. 2003) *Japanese Art* (London: Thames & Hudson).

Beckwith, C.I. (2011) *Empires of the Silk Road: A History of Central Eurasia from the Bronze Age to the Present* (Princeton and Oxford: Princeton University Press).

Boxer, C.R. (2010) *The Affair of the Madre de Deus – A Chapter in the History of the Portuguese in Japan* (London: Routledge).

Brotton, Jerry (2012) *Renaissance – A Very Short Introduction* (Oxford: OUP).

Byron, Robert (1937, republished 1992 and 2007) *The Road to Oxiana* (London: Penguin).

Chu, Lunghsing (2008) 'The Meeting of China, Japan and Holland: Dutchmen in Japanese Prints during the Edo Period', Design History Society Annual Conference 2008, University College Falmouth, UK; available at: http://npm.academia.edu/Lunghsing-CHU/Papers/866033/The_Meeting_of_China_Japan_and_Holland_Dutchmen_in_Japanese_Prints_during_the_Edo_Period.

Day, S. (2010) 'The Spread of Great Asian Religions until the First Millennium CE', in: BOZAR (Centre for Fine Arts, Brussels)/Jan van Alphen *et al.* (various contributors) *Passage to Asia: 25 Centuries of Exchange between Asia and Europe* (Brussels: BOZAR): 123–147.

Edmond, Martin (2009) *Zone of the Marvellous – In Search of the Antipodes* (Auckland: Auckland University Press).

Foltz, Richard (2010) *Religions of the Silk Road* (2nd ed., London: Palgrave-Macmillan).

Forêt, P. and Kaplony, A. (2008) *The Journey of Maps and Images on the Silk Road* (Brill's Inner Asian Library) (Boston, Mass.: Brill Academic Publishers).

Franz, Uli (2000) *Im Schatten des Himmels* (*In the Shadow of Heaven*) (München: dtv).

Gilbert, Marc Jason (n.d.) 'Deshima Island: A Stepping Stone between Civilisations', available at: *World History Connected*, http://worldhistoryconnected.press.illinois.edu/3.3/gilbert.html.

Goodman, Grant K. (2012) *Japan: The Dutch Experience* (London: Bloomsbury Academic Collections).

Grabowsky, V. (ed., 2011) *Southeast Asian Historiography: Unravelling the Myths* (Essays in Honour of Barend Jan Terwiel) (Bangkok: River Books).

Hamblyn, R. (2009) *Terra – Tales of the Earth* (London: Picador).

Headrick, Daniel R. (2009) *Technology – A World History* (Oxford: OUP).

Huo, An (2010) *Lettres à Matteo Ricci* (Montrouge: Bayard).

Jami, Catherine (eds, 2008) *The Jesuits, the Padroado and East Asian Science, (1552–1773)* (History of Mathematical Sciences: Portugal and East Asia III) (River Edge, NJ: World Scientific): 187–205.

Jones, W. (2010) 'European Union Soft Power: Cultural Diplomacy and Higher Education in Southeast Asia', in: *Silpakorn University International Journal*, 9–10; 2009–2010: 41–70.

Kelly, S. (2012) 'Great Expectations? Perspectives from the EU Asia-Pacific Diplomatic Community on the EEAS', in: *EU External Affairs Review* (Prague: Association for International Affairs): 18–33.

Keown, Damien (2005) *Buddhist Ethics – A Very Short Introduction* (Oxford: OUP).

Knodt, M. and Princen, S. (2003) *Understanding the European Union's External Relations* (London: Routledge).

Lambourne, L. (2005) *Japonisme – Cultural Crossings between Japan and the West* (London: Phaidon).

Masashi, Haneda (2009) *Asian Port Cities 1600–1800. Local and Foreign Cultural Interactions* (Singapore and Tokyo: NUS Press and Kyoto University Press).

McGettigan, A. (2013) *The Great University Gamble – Money, Markets and the Future of Higher Education* (London: Pluto Press).

Meech, J. and Oliver, J. (2008) *Designed for Pleasure: The World of Edo Japan in Prints and Paintings, 1680–1860* (Seattle and London: University of Washington Press) (published on the occasion of the exhibition *Designed for Pleasure, The World of Edo Japan in Prints and Paintings, 1680–1860*, organised by Asia Society and Japanese Art Society of America).

Merriman, J. (1996) *A History of Modern Europe (Vol. 1: From the Renaissance to the Age of Napoleon)* (New York and London: W.W. Norton & Company).

Milton, Giles (1999) *Nathaniel's Nutmeg* (London: Hodder & Stoughton).

Murase, M. (2000) Bridge of Dreams – The Mary Griggs Burke Collection of Japanese Art (New York: Metropolitan Museum of Art).

Nishimura-Morse, Anne (2007) Drama and Desire – Japanese Paintings from the Floating World, 1690–1850 (Boston: MFA Publications).

Ocampo, A.R., Mendes Pinto, M.H. and Dias, M.J. (2010) 'Europeans and Christianity', in: BOZAR (Centre for Fine Arts, Brussels), Jan van Alphen et al. (various contributors) Passage to Asia: 25 Centuries of Exchange Between Asia and Europe (Brussels: BOZAR): 167–181.

Okakura, K. (2007) The Ideals of the East – With Special Reference to the Art of Japan (Berkeley/California: Stone Bridge Press) (also consulted: 1970 edition [Tokyo: Tuttle, 5th printing, 1985]).

Rawson, P. (1967, reprinted 1990) The Art of Southeast Asia (London: Thames & Hudson).

Rozman, G. (ed., 1993) The East Asian Region – Confucian Heritage and its Modern Adaptation (Princeton, NJ: Princeton University Press).

Scharfe, H. (2002) Education in Ancient India (Leiden: Brill Academic Publishers).

Schlombs, Adele (2007) Hiroshige 1797–1858 (London: Taschen).

Screech, Timon (2000) The Shogun's Painted Culture (London: Reaktion Books).

Singer, R.T. (ed., 1998) Edo – Art in Japan 1615–1868 (Washington: National Gallery of Art).

Smithies, M. (2004) 'Four Unpublished Letters from Desfarges, Beauchamp and Vollant, Survivors of the Siege of Bangkok in 1688', in: Journal of the Siam Society, 92: 65–104.

Spence, J.D. (1985) The Memory Palace of Matteo Ricci (London: Penguin).

Sullivan, Michael (1973) The Meeting of Eastern and Western Art – From the 16th Century to the Present (London: Thames & Hudson).

Sutin, Lawrence (2006) All is Change – The Two-Thousand-Year Journey of Buddhism to the West (London: Little Brown and Company).

Thornton, Lynne (1983) The Orientalists: Painter-Travellers: 1828–1908 (Paris: ACR).

Tokyo Metropolitan Foundation for History and Culture (TMFHC) (1998) The Edo-Tokyo Museum (Tokyo: TMFHC); www.edo-tokyo-museum.or.jp/english/.

Van de Walle, W.F. and Kazubiko Kasaya (eds, 2002) Dodonaeus in Japan: Translation and the Scientific Mind in the Tokugawa Period (Leuven: Leuven University Press).

Vaporis, C.N. (2009) Tour of Duty: Samurai, Military Service in Edo, and the Culture of Early Modern Japan (Honolulu: University of Hawai'i Press).

Whitfield, S. (1999) Life Along the Silk Road (London: John Murray).

Wilson, Charles (1946) Holland & Britain (London: Collins).

Wright, A.A. (1959) Buddhism in Chinese History (Stanford, Calif.: Stanford University Press).

Xiaoqi, Shi and Yenhu, Tsui/Information Office of Xinjiang Uygur Autonomous Region of China (2005) Footprints of Foreign Explorers on the Silk Road (Beijing: China Intercontinental Press).

Aural landscapes: some of the music with an Asia–Europe theme referred to in this book

Amiot, Joseph-Marie: *Mass of the Jesuits in Beijing.*
Borodin: *In the Steppes of Central Asia.*
Glennie, Evelyn: *Fantasy on Japanese* Woodprints [*sic*] op. 211.
Hesperion XXI: *Francisco Xavier*, and *Hispania and Japan* (Jordi Savall).
Hovhaness, Alan (1911–2000) *Meditation on Ukiyo-e.*
Saint Saëns, Camille: *La Princesse Jaune.*

Index

Achaemenid Empire 20
Acharya, A. 2–3, 12
Acharya Śīlabhadra 36
Adams, William 80, 233–4
adult teaching pedagogy 177
Afghanistan 19, 24, 180, 196
Africa 7, 20, 42, 86, 114, 188
Akbar, Emperor of India 48, 55
Akita Ranga School 75–6
Albuquerque 53, 83, 226
Alexander of Macedon ('the Great') 2, 21–2, 27–9, 45, 101
Alexander Romance (Stoneman) 2
Alexander VI, Pope 43
Allen, C. 25
The Ambassadors (Holbein) 7
Amiot, Jean-Joseph-Marie 57, 106
Amsterdam 47, 73, 103, 107
Anderson, B. 3, 11
Antwerp 7, 47
Anwar Ibrahim 147–9
Aochababa (Green Tea Hag) 75
Apología (Valignano) 47
Aquaviva, Claudio 55
Arai Hakuseki 72, 79
ASEAN University Network (AUN) 133–6
ASEAN–EU University Network Programme 124
Asia, reasons for movement of Europeans into 5–6
Asia–Europe Foundation (ASEF) 117, 126, 127–9, 130, 138, 159, 209, 244
Asia–Europe Institute (AEI): academic self-image 155; and ASEM/ASEMME 131–2; brief 'snapshot' of the 2013 cohort 166–7; 'glocal' perspective 157–60; government policy compliance 154; key areas of research 156;
operating location 154; PhD students enrolled 156; proposed re-purposing of European Studies curriculum 132; reasons for uniqueness of International Master's Programme 158; regional integration module teaching experience 162–5; research ethos and academic identity 155–6; Senior Visiting Research Fellow experience 165–6; student body composition trends 155–6; student leadership potential 168; and the UM Museum of Asian Art 113
Asia Link 124, 126
Asia–Europe Meeting (ASEM) 9, 101, 127–36, 157, 179, 189, 194, 199–200, 204, 244
Asian Financial Crisis 128, 148–9
Askew, M. 88
Aśoka, Emperor of India 22, 28
astronomy 6, 36, 61, 74, 80, 86, 228
Aurel Stein, Marc 25, 28, 30, 108, 188
Australia and New Zealand: activities 247–8; ASEM membership 199; 'Asianization' 200; background to European Studies in 199–202; CERC in Melbourne 202; Christchurch earthquake 137, 207–8, 218; *EU and Globalization* workshop 204; *Europe – The Power of Fashion* course 217; *Europe and Asia: Competing Hegemons* module 205; future of the NCRE 216–19; Jean Monnet public lecture 203; the NCRE in Christchurch 205–10; student voices from New Zealand 210–16
Ayutthaya 80–91, 114, 117–18, 238–9

balanced mobility 131–2
Bamiyan Buddhas 24, 32

Barbosa, Duarte 83, 227
Bartlett's *Threshold Model* 182
Bender, T. 182
Bhawan Ruangsilp 85
Black Death 17
block-printing, Chinese invention 8
botany 6, 49, 73–4
Bourges, Jacques de 83, 85
Boxer, C.R. 52, 58, 65, 78
'Britain's My Lai' 153
Brockey, L.M. 52, 61
Brotton, J. 7, 43
Bruce, R. 90
Buchanan, Francis 36
Buddhist Art and Architecture (Fisher) 27
Buddhists/Buddhism 2, 21–4, 27–9, 31–2, 34–5, 37, 72, 88–9, 102, 112
Burke, P. 3, 9, 23, 32, 104
Burma 32, 90, 203, 226
Burnaby, Richard 89
Buzan, B. 12

Cabral, Francisco 55
Caron, François 78
Carreira da Índia 45, 53
Castanheda, Fernão Lopes de 49
Castiglione, Giuseppe 46
censorship: of 'Asian' knowledge 42; Jesuit reliance 53
Central Asia 6, 18–21, 24–6, 29, 31, 108, 124, 189, 203
Chandragupta 22
Charles V, Holy Roman Emperor 44
Chartsuwan, C. 128
Chaumont, Alexandre de 87
Chikyū Zu (map of the world) 104
China: early indifference towards the West 20; invention of block-printing 8–9; respect for the written word in 23; rites controversy 57–8, 65; Roman embassy to 20; Von Richthofen's awe at the prospect of surveying 18
China Illustrata (Kircher) 60
Chong, A. 13
Christchurch earthquake 137, 207–8, 218
Christianity 31, 41, 47, 57–60, 65, 70, 102, 228
Christiansen, T. 11
Church, M. 99, 108
Clark, H. 207
Clarke, J.J. 32, 51, 58
Clements, J. 228
climate change 164, 181, 189, 201
Cock Blomhoff, Jan 78

Columbus, Christopher 26
Confucius/Confucianism 13, 23, 58–9, 62, 65, 71, 79, 121
Constantine, Emperor of Rome 59
Contemporary Europe Research Centre (CERC), University of Melbourne 246–7
Cooper, C. 124
Council of Trent 44
Couto, Diogo do 84
Cunningham, Alexander 36
curriculum development 124, 128–9, 133, 137, 202, 216, 218
Cyrus 20

Dalrymple, William 110
Darius 20
Davies, N. 9
de Góis, Bento 26–7
de Góis, Damião 45, 227
de la Loubère, Simon 84–5, 87
De missione legatorum Iaponensium (Valignano) 47
de Nobili, Roberto 9, 50–1
De Prado, C. 120
declaratory diplomacy 121, 187
Demattè, P. 57, 59
Descartes, R. 79
Di Vincenzo, M. 1
Diamond Sutra 109
diplomacy 5, 11, 40, 43, 56, 84, 86, 89, 111, 116, 165, 194, 212, 245
Disney, A.R. 44, 65
Dunhuang Caves 102
Dutch capitalism 3
Dutch East India Company (VOC) 73, 78, 85, 112
Dweck, C.S. 182

East India Company 40, 89, 107
Eastern thought, supposed discovery of 2
EIPA Seminars: and Bartlett's *Threshold Model* 182–3; Chatham House Rules 188, 194; documents introduced 186; eligible participants 178, 179; as examples of international adult education activity 181–3; feedback and evaluation 190–2; function and aims 179; future of 195–6; geopolitical embedding and 'Asia' section content 183–4; interactive elements 187–90; pauses for thought 185, 187–8; planning and organization 178; research impact 192–4; scope 177;

EIPA Seminars *continued*
  structure and content 184, 187; teaching style 185; theory–practice nexus 194–5; voting questions 189
Elisseeff, V. 17
Elman, B.A. 61
Enlightenment 60
Enoch, L. 1
ERASMUS Mundus 124, 126–7, 130, 201
Euclid 59
Europe: the early print industry 7–9; rise of maritime trade 21
Europe 2020 Strategy 120
European Commission (the Commission) 120–6, 128, 132, 134, 137, 158, 178–81, 184, 187–8, 192–3, 196, 199, 201
European Institute for Public Administration (EIPA) 177–81, 190, 194–6; and evolution of the seminar series 177–80 (*see also* EIPA Seminars); function and activities 178–9; integrated programme content 180–1; training programme aims 178
exhibitions: *Asian Civilizations Museum, Singapore* 111–12; *Ayutthaya Historical Studies Centre, Thailand* 117–18; blockbuster exhibitions 98–107; *Crossing Cultures, Crossing Time* (Ashmolean Museum) 110–11; *Empires of Faith* (British Museum research project) 116; *Encompassing the Globe* (BOZAR) 107, 109; *Encounters* (V&A) 98–100; *Heaven on Earth* 105; *Japanese amazement: Shíba Kōkan* (Amsterdam Museum) 98, 103–4; *Japanese Galleries* (British Museum) 115–16; *Mughal India* (British Library) 107, 109–10; on-line museums and interactive installations 117; *A Passage to Asia* (BOZAR) 98, 100–2, 194; permanent displays, research projects and key publications 110–18; a selection of museum displays and 239–42; *The Silk Road* (British library) 107–9; smaller exhibitions 107–10; *Technocrats with art sense* (Asian Art Museum, Kuala Lumpur) 112, 114; *Trading Places* (British library) 107–8; *Tsingtao* (German Historical Museum, Berlin) 106–7; *Western Travellers in China* (International Arts Festival) 98, 104–6

Farrington, A. 18, 55, 90, 108, 110
Faxian 24, 36

Fisher, R.E. 25, 27, 29
Fitch, Ralph 90–1
Four Freedoms 19
Framework Programme for Research and Innovation 120
François-Timoléon, Abbé de Choisy 87
free trade 43
Freeman, C. 46
French, C.L. 63, 79
Frey, M. 82–3
Fur Road 18
fūsetsugaki (International Relations Digest) 78

Gadman, L. 124
Gaijin (read-haired barbarians) 73
Gandhara Buddha 27–9
Gardner, H. 182
Garnier, D. 81, 83
Gazu Saiyudan (Shíba Kōkan) 77
Gelber, H.G. 19, 62
Genghis Khan 25, 43, 101
Gervaise, Nicolas 84
Ghosh, A. 34
globalization 11, 17, 20, 40, 99, 121, 126, 154, 156–7, 187–8, 202, 204
Goodman, G.K. 73, 79
Gramscian hegemony of Western models 12–13
The Great Wave (Hokusai) 69
Gregory, J.S. 60
Gregory XV, Pope 47
Grotius, Hugo 43, 86
Guth, C. 72, 77
Güyüg Khan 25

Hakluyt, R. 90
Hall, D.G.E. 89
Hall, K. R. 37, 81
Hamid, J.A. 168
Han dynasty 19
Han Wudi 19, 23
Handy, C. 183
Hansen, V. 18
Hellenization 2, 29
Henry the Navigator, Infante of Portugal 49
Hesse-Wartegg, Ernst von 106
Higher Education regionalism 120
Hindus/Hinduism 2, 21, 27, 44, 47, 50–1, 54–5, 81
Hiraga Gennai 75
Histoire Universelle de la Chine (Semedo) 106

Historia del principio y progresso de la Compañia de Jésus en las Indias Orientales (Valignano) 47
Historiarum Sui Temporis (Jovius) 8
Hobson, J.M. 8, 47
Hokusai 1, 69
Holbein, Hans 7
Honda Toshiaki 75, 79
Honey, P. 182
Horizon 2020 120
Howgego, R. 26
Hsia 45, 65
Hsia, F.C. 45
Hsia, R.P.-C. 60
human rights 13, 22, 121, 123–4, 128, 137, 148, 153, 179, 181, 184, 188–9, 194, 200, 203, 208–9, 211–12, 243, 246–8
Husain, M.F. 113

Ieyasu, Tokugawa 69–70
Il Milione (Marco Polo) 26
Indonesia 3
Innocent IV, Pope 25
Inquisition, Holy 44–6, 49
intercultural education, Nālandā University and its modern legacies 33–7
Islam/Muslims 3, 12, 21, 31–2, 37, 44–5, 51, 54, 83, 102, 150, 196

Jade Road 18
Jahangir, Emperor of India 55, 109
Jansen, M.B. 73–4, 80
Japan: European discovery 62–3; Ming prohibition of Chinese trading with 56; *Shimabara* (Christian) revolt 5; Valignano lands 47; *see also* Tokugawa Japan
Japonisme 102
Jesuit Order: Chinese mission 55–62; Chinese rites controversy 57–8, 65; Church/Crown discrepancies 54; conversion approach 50–2, 60; educational reputation 52–3; employment of science and astronomy 61; foundation 43; headquarters 44; Higher Education monopoly 52; humanist education 52; Indian mission 53–5; inter-cultural approach 50–1; Japanese mission 62–4; missionaries' racism and ignorance 54; multi-cultural teaching approach 54; operation and aims 44; printing press 54; *ratio studiorum* 49, 52–3; resistance encountered by 64–5; 'special relationship' with Portuguese colonial bureaucracy 44; written contributions (*récits épistolaires*) 45–8
Jesuits 9, 27, 40–1, 44–6, 48, 86–7, 102, 105, 107, 228
João II, King of Portugal 49
João III, King of Portugal 46
John of Monte Corvino 26
Johnson, H. 76
Jovius, Paulus 8

Kaempfer, Engelbert 84
Kaibara Ekken 73
Kakiemon 115
Kassim, A. 153, 162
Katsushika Hokusai 69, 103
Kazan, Watanabe 234–5
Keene, D. 78–80
Kelly, K. 200
Kennedy, M. 99
Keukeleire, S. 196
Kircher, Athanasius 48, 60, 106
knowledge-multipliers, and intellectual networks 125
knowledge transfer 3, 6, 20, 40, 42–3, 55, 62, 73, 79, 89, 104, 109, 123, 177
Kōkan, Shíba 1, 63, 69, 72–4, 74–7, 78–80, 98, 100, 103–4, 187
Kolb, D.A. 182
Kosa Pan 86
Krauss, S.E. 168
Kublai Khan 26

Lach, D.F. 8, 18, 20, 26–7, 42, 46–8, 51, 53–4, 90
Laven, M. 45, 53
Lee, H.G. 61, 150–1
The Legend of the Silk Princess 29–31
Leidy, D.P. 29
Leo X, Pope 42
Lettres Chinoises et Indiennes (Voltaire) 61
Li Zhizao 60
Linné, C. von (Linnaeus) 79
Lottes, G. 60
Louis XIV of France 87
Lowenstein, T. 31
Loyola, Ignatius 46, 50, 63
The Lure of China (Wood) 105
Lutheranism 48

Macao 47, 52, 56–7, 59, 63, 81
MacGregor, J.T. 182
MacGregor, N. 18, 29–30, 69

Mahatir Mohamad 148, 150, 157, 161, 165
Maillard, C. 47, 50, 55
Malacca 3, 47, 53, 82–3, 90, 113–15, 226; Straits of 3, 21, 84
Malaysia: Asia–Europe Institute 154; *Batang Kali* incident 153–4; *Bumiputera* preference-code 147, 150–2; contemporary political dilemma 148; emergence of 'European' studies in 153; EU module 242–6; key factors influencing contemporary Higher Education in 149; March 2008 General Election 147–8; political students and student politics 161–2; race riots 150; 'sodomy' trials 148–9; student views of European Studies in 168–73
manga 1
Manuel I, King of Portugal 56
mappae mundi 49, 62, 187
Marcellinus, Ammianus 18
mare clausum (closed sea) 43
Masanobu, Hosono 5, 72
mathematics 36, 51, 61, 137
Mauryan Dynasty 22
McNeely, I.F. 45, 48, 60
medicine 6, 36, 73–4
Mémoires concernant l'histoire, les sciences, les arts, les moers, les usages &c. des Chinois, par les missionaires de Pékin (Amiot) 57
Mendes Pinto, Fernão 64, 83, 226–7
Millward, J.A. 19–20, 22
missionary enterprise, Portuguese designation 44
Mitchell, D. 46, 48, 51, 54, 63, 74
Moran, J.F. 23, 25, 28, 54
Mormando, F. 60
Mortier, Pierre 104
Motivating Our Undergraduates to Lead: Facing the Challenge (Hamid/Krauss) 168
Mumford, A. 182
Murdoch, Z. 178
Murphy, C. 46
Muslims/Islam 3, 12, 21, 31–2, 37, 44–5, 51, 54, 83, 102, 150, 196

Nagasaki 64, 73–4, 77, 104, 115
Najib Razak 166
Nālandā Mahavihara 6
Nālandā *stupa* 22
Nālandā University: admissions policy 36; destruction and restoration 37; excavations 36; international outlook 37; and its modern legacies 33–7; location 35; the 'Oxford of Buddhist India' 35; tri-partite curriculum 35–6
Narai, King of Siam 85–7, 90
National Centre for Research on Europe (NCRE) 136–9, 162, 205, 207–13, 216, 218–19, 248
natural philosophy 61
Needham, J. 20
A New Partnership with South East Asia (COM) 122
New Zealand (*see also* Australia and New Zealand) 125, 135–9, 160, 162, 182, 199–201, 205, 207–8, 210–13, 215–16, 218, 248
Newitt, M. 43, 227

Ochterlony, David 110
Oda Nobunaga 69
Odano Naotake 75–6, 100
Odoric of Pordenone 26
Ogyū Sorai 73
Orientalists/Orientalism 2, 21–2, 36, 45
Ōtsuki Gentaku 75
Ottoman Empire 12

padroão system (royal patronage) 40, 42–4, 46, 49, 51, 54, 60
Pagden, A. 25–6, 59
Paul III, Pope 44, 46
Pax Mongolica 20
Pax Romana 20
Pearson, M.N. 54
pedagogic models 182
Peleggi, M. 81, 84
Pereira, Tomé 59
Persian Letters (Montesquieu) 227
Petrie, Flinders 108
Phaulkon, Constantine 9, 87, 89–90
Phetracha, King of Siam 87
Philip II of Spain 43
Philippines 3, 65
Pian Del Carpini, Giovanni da 25
Pina, I. 63
Pires, Tomé 9, 56, 83, 226
Pius XII, Pope 58
Plutschow, H. 79
Polo, Maffeo 26
Polo, Marco 21, 26, 90, 101, 105, 188
Polo, Niccolò 26
Portuguese Empire: conquest methods 43; emergence of *Estado da Índia* 43; global maritime diplomacy 43; information control and censorship 49; legal

constructs of maritime sovereignty 43; maritime technology 42; relationship with the papacy 42; religious loyalty principle 44
Portuguese Jesuit missions: educational context 43–5; overview 40–1; *see also* Jesuit Order
Prester John 21, 45
Preußisch Blau (Berliner Blau) 69
printing press 7–8, 54–5, 64, 71, 76

racism, of Jesuit missionaries 54
Raffles, Stamford 112
Rahman, A.R.A. 148, 154
Rama IV (Mongkut), King of Siam 88
Rama V (Chulalongkorn), King of Siam 80, 88
Rangaku – La Cité Sans Nuit (Enoch/Di Vincenzo/Rouger) 1
rangaku (Western learning) 1, 64, 72–3, 74–7, 79, 98, 100, 103, 207, 232, 234–5
Record of the Buddhist Religion as Practiced in India and the Malay Archipelago (Yijing) 24
Reed, M. 57, 59
religious exchange, the role of 21–2
religious syncretism 22–3
Republic of Letters 45–6, 61
Rethinking Education 120
Ribadenaira, Marcelo de 83
Ricci, Matteo 27, 53, 57–60, 62
Rig Veda 27
Ringmar, E. 8, 44
Roberts, L. 80
Roe, Thomas 109
The Role of the Universities in the Europe of Knowledge (COM) 121–2
Roman Empire 20, 27, 59
Rome 7, 18, 29, 44, 46–8, 51, 64
Rouger, J.-J. 1
Ruebroek, Willem Van 105
Ruggieri, Michele 46, 53, 57–8
Russell-Wood, A.J.R. 43, 50, 61

Saifuddin Abdullah 161
Saipradist, A. 89
Saiyū Nikki (Shíba Kōkan) 77
Saiyū Ryodan (Shíba Kōkan) 77
Sankalia, H.D. 34
sankin kôtai system 70
sankokusekaikan (three-country view) 70
Santa Catarina incident 43
Satake Shozan 75–6
Savall, Jordi 18

A Scene with European Figures (*Sanvala*) 109–10
Schall, Adam 9, 58–9, 228–30
Schliemann, Heinrich 108
Schouten, Joost 84
scientific evangelization, Jesuit method 56
Screech, T. 62
secularism 3
Seleucid Empire 22
Semedo, Álvaro 106, 226
Sen, Amartya 34
Sen, Amulyachandra 34
Sequeira, Balthasar 83
Shimabara revolt, Japan 5
Shumparō Hikki (Shíba Kōkan) 77
Siam: arrival of first Europeans 89; and the 'burden of Higher Education' 83–4; early European–Asian encounters 81–3; early relations with Portugal 83
Siamese–European interaction 87, 91
Siberia 18
silk, etymological roots 18
Silk Road: alternative route 20; Asia-Europe knowledge transfer catalysts 31–3; Chinese perspective 18; concept analysis 17; earliest Western travellers 25–7; early Asian scholars 23; geopolitical enabling conditions 19–23; global research projects 23; impact of European maritime trade 21; learning and syncretism in art and culture 27–31; maintenance issues 19; and Mongol rule 20; most significant early Chinese travellers 24–5; strategic debate 17; term analysis 18; and the value of books and writings 23
Sima Qian 18–19
Sir David Ochterlony in Indian Dress and Smoking a Hookah and Watching a Nautch in his House in Delhi 110
Sjursen, H. 11
Slaughter and Deception at Batang Kali (Ward/Miraflor) 154
Smith, B.L. 19, 24, 182
Smithies, M. 86, 226
Sō Shiseki 75
Soame, William 87
social cohesion 121–2, 181, 201
social inclusion 181
social media 50, 124, 148
Société des Missions Etrangères 85
soft power 120–1
Sørensen, H.H. 31
South China Sea 21, 115

South East Asian Ministers of Education Organization (SEAMEO) 125, 131, 133–6
spice race 45
Staiff, R. 89
Straits of Malacca 3, 21, 84
student-centred learning 9
Subrahmanyam, S. 56, 99
Sugita Genpaku 100, 104
'Sultanate of Sulu' 148
Summaria (Valignano) 47
Suzuki Harunobu 76
Suzuki Shōsan 73
syncretism 27, 33, 65, 102

Tachard, Guy 87
Tadjbakhsh, S. 12–13
A Tale of the Floating World (Asai Ryōi) 71–2
Tamerlane 20
Tang Dynasty 18
Tankha, B. 70
Thai art, foreigners and Europeans in 238
Thailand 80, 88, 117, 136, 163
Tham Yong 154
Thampi, M. 70
Thomas, Antoine 89
Thomas, J.G. 60
Thongchai Winichakul 87–8
The Thousand Autumns of Jacob de Zoet (Mitchell) 74
three Unifiers 69
Thunberg, C.P. 79
Tibet 18, 27, 37, 188
Timurid Empire 20
Titsingh, Isaac 78
Tokugawa Japan: artistic activity 70–1; class system and the politics of art 231–2; Confucian culture 70, 72–3; derivation of state ideology 71; Dutch, Germans and Swedes in 237; exchange and international relations with Europe in Siam 80–1; importance of travel as mode of exchange 77–80; intellectual life 71–4; literacy rates 71; religion and politics 72; *sankin kôtai* system 70, 230–1; *sankokusekaikan* (three-country view) 70; Shíba Kōkan and the *Rangaku* Movement 74–7; Zhu Xi thought and its influence on Japanese intellectuals 232–3
Tordesillas treaty 43, 49
tourism 17, 89, 156, 217

Toyotomi Hideyoshi 69
Trakulhun, S. 84
traveller-explorers 42
Travelling the Silk Road (Norrell *et al.*) 17
Travels of Sir John Mandeville 45
Trigault, Nicolas 27, 46
True Meaning of the Lord of Heaven (Ricci) 59

Valignano, Alessandro 46–7, 50–1, 54, 56, 63–4
van Alphen, J. 29
Van Kley, E.J. 8, 26–7, 47–8, 51, 53–4, 90
van Nijenroode, Cornelis 84
Van Rompuy, Herman 100
Van Ruebroek, Willem 26
van Vliet, Jeremias 84
Vanichviroon, Kunakorn 118
Vaz De Camões, Luiz 45, 54, 83
Vaz de Siqueira, Pero 86
Venice 26, 48
Verbiest, Ferdinand 58, 61, 105
Villiers, J. 227
Voltaire 61
von Richthofen, Ferdinand 18, 106, 108

Waley-Cohen, J. 56
Walters, C. 23, 25, 28
Watanabe Kazan 234
Welch, A. 149, 152
Wills, J.E 56, 61
Witek, J.W. 58
Wolverton, L. 45, 48, 60
Wood, F. 60–1, 105
Wriggins, S.H. 25, 34
Wright, J. 44, 56, 61, 64–5

Xavier, Francis 46, 54, 58–9, 63, 227
Xiongnu tribe 24
Xu Guangqi 60
Xuanzang 24–5, 30, 36, 100

Yang Tingyun 60
Yaqing Qin 13
Yeh-lü Ch'u-ts'ai 25
Yijing 24
Yoko, M. 85
Yu, A. 25
Yuezhi tribe 24

Zakri Abdul Hamid 161
Zhang Qian 19, 23–4
Zhu Xi 71